Armada from Athens

By the Same Author

Armada from Athens

PETER GREEN

GARDEN CITY, NEW YORK
DOUBLEDAY & COMPANY, INC.
1970

ACKNOWLEDGMENTS

All translations from Thucydides are taken
from Rex Warner's version, published in the
Penguin Classics. Where I have quoted from
Plutarch's *Lives*, I have used Ian Scott-Kilvert's
translation, also published as a Penguin Classic,
under the title *The Rise and Fall of Athens*. Cita-
tions from Diodorus Siculus are in the Loeb version by C. H. Oldfather. The quotation from
Euripides' *Hecuba* on p. 348 is in the version by
William Arrowsmith, published in the Chicago
Complete Greek Tragedies series, edited by David
Grene and Richmond Lattimore, © 1958 University of Chicago. The quotations from Euripides'
Electra on p. 101 and p. 244 are in the version
by Emily Townsend Vermeule, published in the
same series, World Copyright 1959 by University
of Chicago. Grateful acknowledgment is made
to the publishers above for their permission to
reprint this material.

Crossroads of World History Series

For Joan and Peter Throckmorton
terrestris marinis

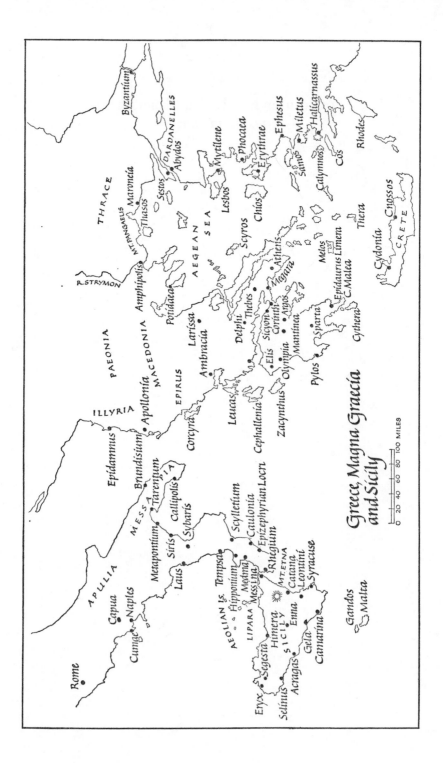

Greece, Magna Graecia and Sicily

0 20 40 60 80 100 MILES

CONTENTS

ACKNOWLEDGMENTS   iv
INTRODUCTION   ix
    I: Prelude to a War   1
    II: Wheat, Timber, Gold   11
    III: The Grand Design   37
    IV: Cleon and the West   57
    V: The Phoney Peace   77
    VI: An Embassy from Segesta   95
    VII: Herms and Mysteries   115
    VIII: The Armada Sails   129
    IX: Nicias Takes the Offensive   147
    X: The Heights of Epipolae   167
    XI: Walls and Counter-walls   191
    XII: Enter Gylippus   209
    XIII: A Dispatch to the Assembly   231
    XIV: The Capture of Plemmyrium   249
    XV: A Naval Reverse   265
    XVI: Demosthenes' Night Attack   281
    XVII: Death by Water   297
    XVIII: The Last Retreat   315
    XIX: The End of the Road   333
APPENDIX I: Distribution-figures for Attic Red-Figure
Pottery Overseas in the Fifth Century B.C.   357
APPENDIX II: Population and Grain-consumption
Figures in Fifth Century Athens   359
APPENDIX III: Sicilian Cities: Production and
Consumption in the Fifth Century B.C.   360
SELECT BIBLIOGRAPHY I: Ancient Sources   361
SELECT BIBLIOGRAPHY II: Modern Literature   365
GENERAL INDEX   381

INTRODUCTION

In the preface to his admirable handbook on Greek epigraphy, Mr. A. G. Woodhead observes: "When the writer of such a book as this first puts his pen to paper, or sets his first blank sheet in the typewriter, he is not at the beginning of his labours but approaching their end." At a less specialised level, I can say as much for the present study. All the real work—several years of reading, travel, synthesis, and interpretation—was complete when I began writing. The problems confronting me I had solved, at least to my own satisfaction. Now all that remained was to set down my conclusions.

Sometimes—especially in an academic publication—the historian will re-create his entire process of discovery, step by step, with full documentation. But since the proportionate relation of narrative and conclusions to exegesis is, roughly, that between the parts of an iceberg above and below water, such studies tend to reach a quite inordinate length. (Compare the size of Volumes I and II of Tarn's *Alexander the Great*.) They also make very heavy going for the non-specialist. I originally intended to write such a book, and indeed began it. But merely to tell the story of the Sicilian Expedition, without comment of any sort, would fill a sizable volume; and the present series is, in any case, designed for the intelligent general public.

This must be my excuse, to classical historians in particular, for having reduced documentation to a bare minimum throughout the present work. I have, I hope, made partial amends by printing a very full bibliography. In fact a considerable amount of original research has gone into the book (frequency of footnotes is not always an accurate guide to the amount of background work done), but there has seldom been room to demonstrate at length how my various conclusions were reached. A university-based historian will, in the ordinary way of things, prepare the way for his full-scale study with numerous specialist articles in the learned journals. The free-lance author and journalist has no leisure to do so. I therefore find myself somewhat in the position of the White Queen, who, you will remember, bandaged her finger first and pricked it afterwards. Nothing would please me better than to write a companion volume analysing my various researches—e.g. on population levels and the production and consumption of wheat in Attica and Sicily, or the topography of the Syracusan campaign, or the economic significance of red-figure pottery distribution figures. But without the support of some research institute this is likely to remain an unfulfilled ambition.

I only emphasise the point to counter a possible assumption that where I do not "show my workings" I have no firm grounds for the views I express, particularly when these happen to be controversial. For example, I agree with Mr. H. B. Mattingly in dating the Segesta Treaty inscription [IG i² 19/20] to 418–417, possibly as a renewal from 427. Behind a somewhat bare statement to this effect in my text lies a fortnight of close work on the treaty stone itself in the Epigraphical Section of the National Museum in Athens, together with an exhaustive survey of all available literature on the subject, and many hours of discussion with various scholars. Nor should my view be taken as implying that I agree with Mr. Mattingly's other attempts to down-date fifth-century inscriptions.

Similarly with the conclusions I have reached on the citizen and slave population of Attica and various Sicilian cities during the period covered by my book, and the linked problem of their wheat production and imports. This analysis occupied me for several months, and resulted in a bulky file of some two hundred pages. To explain and document my views on these topics would require an appendix perhaps one fifth as long as the present narrative text. I therefore, with some hesitation, decided to omit it altogether.

My statistics for Attic pottery distribution during the fifth century are largely based on the provenience indexes in Sir John Beazley's *Attic Red-Figure Vase-Painters*. Any supplementary information I have collected does nothing to modify the general pattern which can be extracted from that magisterial compilation. The reader should note, however, that I share the doubts expressed by Mr. Mattingly and others concerning fifth-century ceramic chronology.

Much of the dating of red-figure ware (R.F.), especially before 430, seems about a couple of decades too high; it produces an odd discrepancy of twenty years ± between R.F. and B.F. ware in identical deposits of the 480s. Perhaps it is optimistic to hope for closer accuracy in dating than twenty-five ± years in either direction. But a slight revision of the traditional chronology makes for considerable improvement in historical sense. The tentative figures I have arrived at for R.F. chronology (allowing a ± overlap of at least a decade) are as follows: Early, 520–490; Late Archaic, 490–460; Early Classical, 460–430; Classical, 430–410; Late Fifth Century, 410–390; Fourth Century, after 390.

Another field in which I have diverged fairly widely from generally accepted views is that of Sicilian topography. Here it is a good deal easier to document one's conclusions briefly, and wherever possible I have done so. In every instance I am relying on a detailed personal study of the terrain (sometimes augmented by the valuable conclusions of Leake and Pais), whether the topic of discussion is Epipolae, or the Great Harbour, or the final retreat to the Assinarus. Here at least I feel I can echo E. A. Freeman's claim: "I believe I may say with perfect truth that a diligent comparison of the site and the record, sometimes alone, sometimes with instructive companions, has enabled me to bring to light some facts, some views of facts, which have not been thought of by earlier scholars."

Like Freeman, too, I was—and remain—somewhat intimidated by the gigantic shadow of Thucydides, who in the present story must necessarily loom over the modern writer from first page to last, sometimes with a decidedly inhibiting effect. No one could hope to match the power and tragic sublimity of the two books—VI and VII—which he devotes to the Sicilian Expedition, and I have not attempted to do so. Much of the narrative, towards the end especially, can, by the very nature of the evidence, be little more than a paraphrase of the Thucydidean account, fleshed out with some topographical digressions and the occasional vivid detail from Plutarch or Diodorus.

Yet I believe that there is room for a new study of Athens' disastrous venture in the West. The last full-scale account in English, that by Freeman, was published as long ago as 1892, and since then the study of ancient history has advanced a very long way. New evidence, mostly archaeological and numismatic, has accumulated. The techniques for evaluating and interpreting our sources have been much refined. The economic approach to historical evidence—particularly illuminating when applied to fifth-century Athenian foreign policy—is no longer regarded as a suspect device employed only by Marxists. This is fortunate, since Athens' desperate search for adequate sources of grain and timber turns out to be perhaps the most significant single factor in her relations with the West.

Thucydides hints at this economic pattern, but in a curiously oblique and tangential way. Ancient writers (with one or two exceptions) tended to ignore economic motivation—which is not to say that they were ignorant of economics. The gaitered bishop who sits in the morning-room of a London club on Saturday afternoon checking his investments against the ticker-tape can still, with perfect sincerity and propriety, mount the pulpit on Sunday morning and preach a sermon on the virtues of poverty, thrift, and self-abnegation. This is a recognisable fact of human nature, and one with suggestive implications for the historian.

It is very hard to shake off one's preconceptions when approaching a subject of this magnitude. The inherited kudos of Thucydides, the splendour and tragedy of Periclean imperialism push one almost irresistibly along the high road of traditional eulogy and biassed platitude. (One scholar I talked to said: "Whenever I re-read Book VII of Thucydides I keep hoping it'll go the other way this time." I know just how he felt.) I can only say that I have tested all available evidence by the most stringent criteria I could devise; but human nature is frail, and I would not claim to be more immune to unconscious prejudice than the next man.

But equally I have tried not to be uncritical of my sources, in particular of Thucydides. This historian is seldom to be caught in errors of fact. Significant omissions are his forte (which may be why, unlike Herodotus, he never reveals his sources), and he gives himself away most—as Sir Alfred Zimmern saw so clearly—by his implied moral attitudes. The Thucydidean cult of power and success is not one which I personally happen to find attractive; nor, to be honest, is Pericles' cold intellectual paternalism. This, perhaps, has helped me to avoid some of the more obvious pitfalls in my chosen subject—though I am sure it will have exposed me to others, of which I am still unaware.

The story of the ill-fated Athenian expedition to Sicily has engaged my mind more or less continuously during the past four years, and at intervals for many more before that. My interest in it was first aroused during the dark days of 1940, when Book VII of Thucydides (which we were then studying at school) struck me as a good deal more relevant to the contemporary crisis than most classical texts I had seen hitherto. About the same time—an act for which I can never be sufficiently grateful—my friend and contemporary Mr. J. H. G. Woollcombe introduced me to Francis Cornford's *Thucydides Mythistoricus*, a remarkable pioneering work which (I am glad to note) is not quite so out of fashion with classical historians nowadays as it used to be.

My main object in writing the present book, then, has been to fill a gap. To the best of my knowledge this is the only full-scale modern account of the Sicilian Expedition in the English language: surprisingly, because the catastrophic defeat of Athens' forces by Syracuse marked the end of an era. It was the final failure of Pericles' experiment in democratic imperialism. If Athens had succeeded in her Western venture, the history of Greece, perhaps of all Europe, might have been very different. My secondary aim, more personal but I hope of equal general interest, has been to solve a number of problems which have long puzzled me about the campaign itself and its complex antecedents. I have done my best to tell the story in the way Ranke would have wished, "as it really happened," knowing that such an aspiration can never be more than imperfectly realised. But I have also, at every stage of my researches, borne in mind that it is at least as important to ask the question *why?* as *how?*

The period which I have spent researching and writing this book must count among the most satisfying of my entire life: in particular, two never to be forgotten weeks when, after long months of patient drudgery, the pattern of events suddenly clarified, and what had been mere accumulated facts coalesced into a logical, cohesive structure with a life of its own. Nor shall I readily forget a cloudless Sicilian December—"midwinter spring is its own season"—spent walking from river to river down the coast beyond Syracuse, exploring age-old tracks over the plateau of Monte Climiti, or re-enacting (with an ordnance survey map to supplement Thucydides) each successive stage in that last terrible march to the Assinarus.

A great number of people have, in diverse ways, given me most generous assistance during the gestation and writing of this book. The readiness of professional scholars to make the inquirer free of their expert knowledge has been a constant pleasure and inspiration. My deep and grateful thanks go to all those who have lent me rare books, sent me off-prints of their articles, written (most often in detail and at length) in answer to my queries, or discussed aspects of the Sicilian Expedition with me during visits to Athens: Prof. A. Andrewes, Sir John D. Beazley, Prof. Donald Bradeen, Mr. P. A. Brunt, Prof. J. L. Caskey, Prof. K. J. Dover, Prof. Sterling Dow, Prof. C. W. J. Eliot, Mr. M. I. Finley, Mr. D. M. Lewis, Prof. M. F. McGregor, Mr. H. B. Mattingly, Mr. Russell Meiggs, Prof. Arnaldo Momigliano, Mr. T. J. Quinn, Prof. A. D. Trendall, Prof. H. D. Westlake, and Mr. A. G. Woodhead. Professor Bradeen and Professor McGregor have also read my typescript and made many valuable corrections and suggestions. I must, however, emphasise that final responsibility for all opinions and statements expressed in the text rests with me alone.

The greater part of the research for this study was carried out in the pleasant and hospitable libraries of the American School of Classical Studies and the British School of Archaeology in Athens. To the Directors of both these institutions, and also to Mrs. Philippides and Mrs. Rabnett, who dealt so patiently with my many queries, I extend my warmest thanks for the excellent facilities which they accorded me. I also received much kindness and co-operation from Prof. Doro Levi of the Italian Archaeological Institute in Athens, and from the Librarians of the French School of Archaeology and the German Archaeological Institute. At Syracuse itself I benefited more than I can say from the wise counsel and unrivalled local expertise of Prof. Bernabò Brea. I am also much indebted to Miss Gabrielle Hosien for providing me with a translation of P. Karyškovsky's long and important article, in Russian, on "Olbia and the Athenian Sea-League," and to Miss Angela Parsons for locating and photostatting rare articles in London on my behalf.

Many other friends have helped me, in a number of ways, to make this book a less indifferent achievement than it might otherwise have been. Without some, indeed, it might never have seen the light of day at all. Among them I am particularly grateful to Miss Anne Carter, Mrs. C. W. J. Eliot, Mr. William Golding, Mr. Frederic Raphael, and Miss Caroline Stallworth. My wife has, as always, been a tower of strength and sensible advice—not always sensibly taken—throughout. What I owe to the never failing support, encouragement, and expert advice of my old friends Joan and Peter Throckmorton goes far beyond anything I can well express here; the affectionate dedication of this book is no more than a minimal return for many hours of pleasure and enlightenment spent in their company.

There is one name which I hold in very special regard. It was Donald Friede who gratified one of my lifelong ambitions by commissioning me to write about Athens and Syracuse, and my only real sadness, now my task is complete, is that he is no longer here to read what I have written. I knew of him as a legendary editor; I found him to be that indeed, and a fine and generous friend as well. Donald was unique; just how unique, I only realise in retrospect. I owe him a very great deal, and I miss him more than I can say. The world seems a smaller and duller place without him. *Requiescat.*

Peter Green

Athens.

CHAPTER I: *Prelude to a War*

On a fine summer morning, at the beginning of July 415 B.C., the whole population of Athens was up and abroad by dawn. Citizens, slaves, resident aliens, even casual foreign visitors: old and young, men, women, and children, they made their way in a vast straggling procession down the five-mile stretch of the Long Walls to the great fortified port of Piraeus. Excitement and expectation were in the air, and a certain amount of hysteria as well. It was two and a half months since the Assembly, after a dramatic and memorable debate, had voted to send a major expeditionary force to Sicily. The ostensible reason was an appeal for military aid from Athens' small and remote ally Segesta, in the north-west corner of the island. But the real object of the expedition—as everyone knew, and as the three joint commanders had agreed the previous night in secret session with the Council—was to conquer the island, subjugate the cities of Syracuse and Selinus, and add the rest to the already lengthy roll of Athens' contributory "subject-allies."

For weeks now the arsenals and dockyards had been loud with hammering and planing, as shipwrights worked to meet an ever-narrowing deadline. Masts and rigging must be fitted, rations checked and stored. Since this was a prestige expedition, to which all citizens were urged to contribute as lavishly as they could, craftsmen of every sort found themselves in constant demand. The war party's propaganda had proved highly effective. Each individual soldier was determined to prove himself worthy of so splendid an imperial undertaking, to outshine his neighbour in wealth and magnificence of equipment. So armourers and goldsmiths sat up late emblazoning rich shields, or gilding figureheads—most often of Pallas Athena, the city's guardian deity—to ride above the beak of each swift trireme. The streets and porticoes echoed with rumours and counter-rumours. Equipment piled up on the docks, stevedores were worked off their feet, and the ships' chandlers, eager for profit, kept longer and longer hours. Wealthy trierarchs—citizens delegated to equip triremes at their own expense—personally supervised the work being carried out for them. The noise and heat and urgency made tempers even shorter than usual. Quarrels flared up out of nothing. From time to time someone got a black eye. The Piraeus whores did a roaring trade.

But now, at last, all was ready, and the hysterical tension that had built up in Athens during the past weeks would soon find release. The crowds hurried on in the slanting morning sunlight, saying little, their minds suddenly filled with the imminent reality of departure. Some women were already weeping. There can have been few who did not have husband, father, son, brother, or lover among the complement of the departing armada, and the scarcely less vast merchant fleet of speculators and camp-followers which was sailing with it, in pursuit of profitable booty or trade agreements. But at this point it was the danger of the venture which lay uppermost in everyone's mind. Its potential glories and rewards were, for a little, forgotten.

Some things, however, it was hard to forget: above all, the unpropitious omens which had dogged those weeks of preparation. The crucial debate in the Assembly had been held on the very day that the women of Athens were mourning the death of the god Adonis, so that at least one speaker had been rendered almost inaudible by that dreadful wailing from the rooftops, the slow tattoo of the funeral drums. There had been a disturbing crop of oracles and portents, all prophesying disaster for the expedition. But no incident had been more startling, or more catastrophic in its immediate consequences, than the mysterious mutilation of those pillar-busts of Hermes which stood at the street corners or outside houses all over Athens. Hermes was, among other things, the god of travellers—and who could tell how many of those responsible for the outrage were about to sail for Sicily? The Council had talked darkly of a plot to bring down the democracy. There had been indiscriminate arrests, rewards for information, something very close to a reign of terror.

Yet when the crowd at last reached the harbour-basin of Zea—the modern Pacha Limani, south-east across a high neck of land from the main commercial port—their doubts and fears were soon stilled by the splendour of the scene before them. The basin is 1,225 yards in circumference, cut from the solid rock: it can have changed very little since the year of the Sicilian Expedition. It possessed hauling slips for 196 triremes, and on that July morning at least a hundred of them were occupied. As the last latecomers struggled for a good view of the proceedings, a trumpet sounded, long and clear, and the deep hum of conversation slowly dwindled away. All was still now except for the slap and knock of water against stone, the shuffle of feet, and then, sharp in the stillness, the herald's voice intoning the ritual prayer for a calm voyage and safe landfall.

Round the harbour basin, in vessel after vessel, sunlight glinted from richly chased gold and silver goblets, censers, and mixing-bowls. On this memorable occasion, as a token of unity, the prayers and libations were to be offered by the whole fleet together, rather than—as was the normal practice—by each vessel individually; and not by captains and generals alone, but by the whole complement of hoplites, sailors, and marines. The vast throng of spectators on the quayside joined in the responses with them, their voices meeting and cross-echoing over the horseshoe-shaped harbour, among the nodding masts and gilded beaks of the triremes. In old, time-honoured ritual phrases they paid due honour to the gods, and begged them to grant this venture—on which the future of Athens' greatness hung—their support and favour. The whole ceremony was charged with deep emotion.

Many eyes turned to the three commanders of the expedition: Nicias, Alcibiades, and Lamachus. Standing there on the afterdecks of their flagships, resplendent in scarlet and gold, the morning sunlight glinting from the libation cups they held aloft, they must have looked very impressive. Yet two of the three, Nicias and Alcibiades, detested one another fundamentally. To make matters worse, about the only thing they had in common was a certain condescending contempt for their colleague Lamachus. It was all very well for the Assembly to accord these joint commanders "absolute authority both at home and abroad for the planning and conduct of the campaign": before that authority could be exercised in the field there had to be unity of purpose behind it, and unity of purpose was precisely what this ill-assorted trio lacked. Indeed, they offered about as striking an instance of ineffectual democratic compromise as anyone could hope for.

Nicias, son of Niceratus, was over sixty years old in 415, and suffering from a painful disease of the kidneys, probably nephritis, which numbers among its side-effects chronic lassitude and an inability to make decisions. He was a wealthy man, with large investments in slave labour at the Laurium mines. On the other hand, he did not belong to one of Athens' leading aristocratic families. Nervous, vain, stand-offish, dilatory, and superstitious to a degree, he had nevertheless scored a remarkable series of minor successes as a field commander. His enemies explained this achievement by the suggestion that Nicias "did his best to evade any difficult or lengthy enterprise; whenever he served as general he played for safety." His riches (since he was lacking in political charm) he laid out in a series of public entertainments and dedicatory offerings. He had been the architect of peace between Athens and Sparta in 421, after a decade of inconclusive fighting—the so-called Archidamian War—during which Athens had twice suffered the ravages of the plague. As a political moderate, a middle-of-the-roader who clung to Pericles' obsolete war-policy of containment and consolidation —though by now it had become something more akin to isolationism—he could hardly help regarding the whole Sicilian venture as the rashest sort of irresponsible folly.

But there is one other curious fact about Nicias, which has received less attention than it surely deserves. He held the position of resident *proxenos* in Athens for Syracuse. (The functions of a proxenos were more or less those performed today by a consul and a commercial counsellor—except that the proxenos was a national of the country in which he resided, not of that whose representative he was.) He cannot possibly have acted in this capacity unless he had very close connections— whether commercial, political, or personal—with leading citizens of Syracuse. His speeches in the Assembly display a hardheaded grasp of Sicilian affairs, and it is hard to believe that the first time he actually set foot in the island was when he invaded it. What probably took him to Sicily in the first place was his large-scale interest in slave labour. Sicilian slave-dealers were a by-word as early as Homer's day.

So one reason for Nicias' appointment to the tripartite command may well have been his special knowledge of Syracusan affairs and the men who were conducting them. Indeed, it is by no means impossible that he hoped to gain all Athens hoped for by collusion with the democratic party in Syracuse, rather than on the field of battle, and that his gingerly strategy was a case of deliberate procrastination while a deal was being hammered out, rather than mere dilatory incompetence, heightened by disease. In a century when siege warfare had got little further than the principle of starvation by blockade, cities seldom fell without some discreet fifth-column work behind the walls, and a group of traitors (from the opposition party) willing to open those impregnable gates by night. Here, by no means for the only time during the story of the Sicilian Expedition, we sense more going on behind the scenes than our historical sources tell us directly.

There could hardly have been a more obvious contrast to Nicias than his fellow-commander Lamachus, son of Xenophanes. Aristophanes refers to him, sarcastically, as "heroic Lamachus": the repetitive Homeric epithet is no compliment. In several of the comedies he figures as a windy, officious braggart-soldier, a kind of military bugaboo with his Gorgon shield and huge helmet plumes. What we hear of him during the Archidamian War is not particularly to his credit; he seems to have had an unfortunate knack of getting himself involved in one military fiasco after another—a boon to the comic poets.

What is more, despite his vaunted military prowess, he does not seem to have been averse to wangling profitable appointments on embassies. His main motive, however, as Aristophanes makes clear, was not so much cowardice as the nagging demands of poverty. Ambassadorial duties carried a salary of three drachmas per day, and Lamachus' indigence was notorious. What little patrimony he had he seems to have squandered as a young man. Whenever he went on campaign as a general he submitted a small expense account, at the end of the year, for boots and cloak. If he, like other senior military commanders, was only paid so long as he remained on active service, it is not hard to see how he acquired his reputation as a fire-eater.

At the time of the Sicilian Expedition, Lamachus (although, like Nicias, now over sixty years old) was generally regarded as "quite as much of a firebrand in military matters as Alcibiades and equally adventurous in battle"—a verdict which events were to confirm only too well. But his lack of means was a formidable disadvantage. Twice Plutarch emphasises that it reduced him— despite his age and titular equality—to an inferior position vis-à-vis Nicias. Lamachus, it is clear, had no real political influence, much less a well-knit "club" of backers such as both Nicias and Alcibiades could command. Thus despite all his vigour and enthusiasm, he laboured under a fatal handicap as their fellow-general.

The third commander was a very different character: if not ultimately more complex than Nicias and Lamachus, at least more of an enigma both to his contemporaries and to posterity. To begin with, he was over twenty years younger than either of his colleagues. Personal magnetism and raffishly aristocratic good looks were allied in him with an insolent if stylish exhibitionism, which delighted the *jeunesse dorée* but infuriated almost everyone else. He had unbounded charm (which time and again saved him from the consequences of his worst excesses), a weakness for tortuous backstairs diplomacy, and a streak of quite murderous egotism which, when he failed to get his own way, was liable to leave its mark on public affairs—and seldom for the better.

This was the famous, or infamous, Alcibiades: Pericles' ward and the intimate of Socrates, allied by his Alcmaeonid blood to many of the noblest names in Athenian history, an ambitious bloodstock-fancier whose chariots (including a friend's team entered—without permission—as his own) had won first, second, and fourth places at the previous year's Olympic Games; whose financial embarrassment and reckless expenditure were the talk of Athens; and who had been the Sicilian Expedition's most vigorous and imaginative champion, both in and out of the Assembly. Lamachus was not the only commander determined to redeem his insolvency by a profitable overseas campaign.

In June 415 Alcibiades was thirty-eight years old: a little too old, perhaps, to persist in the role of *enfant terrible*. (The celebratory dinner party recorded in Plato's *Symposium* is set only just over a year earlier, in the February of 416.) Even on the solemn occasion of the fleet's departure he could not resist the dandified gesture, the touch of insouciant self-advertisement. That tall, elegant figure, with the Alcmaeonid profile—blown a little by good living, if we may trust his portraits—and the unfashionably long fair hair, would have caught the eye in any company. Golden libation cup raised high in his right hand, he stood now facing the expectant crowd ashore, many of whom had come, first and foremost, to catch a glimpse of their wayward young general in his hour of triumph. A long trailing purple cloak was wrapped round his shoulders; his gilded shield displayed no ancestral quarterings, but instead, the device of Eros armed with a thunderbolt. Observant spectators noticed that the afterdeck of his trireme had been cut away at one point, and a corded hammock slung across it: not for him the manly rigours of a blanket on the hard boards. Any criticisms of his scarcely excessive self-indulgence he could turn aside by pointing out that he was, in fact, carrying out the Assembly's decree: had it not been laid down that the vessels sailing on the expedition were to be "as well and finely equipped as possible"?

It says much for Alcibiades' hypnotic charm that he was elected to the High Command at all, since well before the fleet sailed he had got himself at odds with every major political group in Athens. He had snubbed the right-wing activists when they made secret overtures to him, with the result that they now feared him as a potential radical leader or future tyrant. The radicals hated him for getting their leader Hyperbolus sent into political exile (in peculiarly ludicrous and humiliating circumstances) and then adding insult to injury by blandly taking over Hyperbolus' Western policy as though it were his own. The old aristocratic families could not forgive him for—as they saw it—betraying his birthright and the code of obligations his blood entailed on him. Finally, moderates such as Nicias regarded him as the embodiment of insane imperialist expansionism.

On top of all this, Alcibiades had recently been formally charged with having held blasphemous parodies of the Eleusinian Mysteries in his private house. Despite his urgent request for an immediate trial, the case had been postponed until his return from Sicily. He thus found himself in the ridiculous and humiliating position of exercising supreme command over some 28,000 men while, to all intents and purposes, a prisoner bailed out on his own recognisances and awaiting trial. Whatever the outcome of the expedition, however much booty he brought back to stall his creditors, there would still be that reckoning to face when he returned to Athens. Nor, it was clear, would a change of government (which in effect, as the democracy was constituted, meant a coup d'état) be of the slightest benefit to him, whether it brought in the oligarchs or the city radicals. For Alcibiades the *apertura a sinistra* offered no more—perhaps less—than the *apertura a dèstra*. As a political opportunist who had fished both ponds for his own benefit, he could hardly be in any doubt as regards the lengths his enemies would go to in his absence to secure a conviction against him: rigged evidence was likely to be the least of his troubles.

A more disastrous combination of leaders for so crucial and hazardous an expedition it would be hard to imagine. There were reasons, of a sort, behind the Assembly's choice: they illustrate the peculiar dangers which beset any direct-assembly democracy—above all, the temptation to satisfy all factions at the cost of translating policy into action. "The people,"

Plutarch writes, "considered that Nicias's experience made him all the more essential to the enterprise, and that his caution would provide a most valuable safeguard against Alcibiades' daring and Lamachus's forthrightness." But this kind of compromise High Command was hardly calculated to produce coherent strategy, much less display vigorous and united enthusiasm in the field. The one safe prediction anyone could have made about these three men, surely, was that they were certain to disagree, fundamentally, over almost every crucial decision in the campaign before them—a truth which emerged with painful clarity when they held their first council of war, and which subsequent events did nothing to modify.

Lamachus, as we have seen, was handicapped at the conference table by his poverty. Thus the one member of the High Command who displayed any knowledge of aggressive strategy, and who realised that Athens' only hope was to strike hard and fast at Syracuse itself, while the enemy was still unprepared, found his opinions overruled from start to finish. Nicias had been against the whole expedition *ab initio*, and held his position under protest. He was also a very sick man. Alcibiades, for all his elaborate display of unconcern, had been forced to sail with serious—possibly capital—charges of blasphemy and iconoclasm hanging over his head. He and Nicias, moreover, were bitter personal enemies.

So any Sicilian or Corinthian agent who observed the fleet's departure, and reported on it, would not necessarily do so in panic-stricken terms. Quite apart from a chronic lack of cohesion in its High Command, this expedition, for all the tub-thumping propaganda it elicited, was considerably smaller than many which Athens had launched in the past. Only 134 triremes, as against 250 or more half a century before at Salamis; a mere 1,500 Athenian hoplites, compared with the 9,000 "men of Marathon"—and since then, in any case, the hoplite's morale and discipline had slumped disastrously. Did Nicias, if no one else, really intend to fight on land at all? Of the total complement, only just over half was supplied by Athens: the remainder consisted of contingents from the subject-allies. And all those official exhortations to private citizens to spend lavishly on equipment: was the Athenian government, one wonders, trying to mount this expedition on the cheap?

But in the thrill of the fleet's departure, his mind bemused— as so often at Assembly time—with fervid patriotic emotionalism, the average citizen would scarcely have entertained such cynical and defeatist notions. He would forget everything except the scene before him—the glitter and pageantry, the proud display of power, the golden dream of the West at last becoming tangible as this stately massed armada set forth.

When the last notes of the paean had died away, the triremes were slowly warped out of harbour, one by one, and the crowd broke into frenzied cheering. Offshore a steady breeze, precursor of August's fierce Etesian winds—the modern *meltemi* —ruffled the blue waters of the Saronic Gulf. The terrible brazen beaks and fresh-painted figureheads dipped and rose; the canvas of those great square-rigged sails flapped and bellied as the squadrons backed water in the swell and deployed into openline formation. At last they were all in position, a hundred and more of them: the trumpet rang out, with its shrill derisive note, the water creamed under the thrust of the oars, willing hands hauled at the stays, and Athens' expeditionary fleet plunged forward, ship racing ship till they were hull-down beyond Aegina—the tiny island Pericles had called "the eyesore of the Piraeus," the formidable sea power whose commercial supremacy Athens had smashed half a century before. It was a dramatic and memorable departure. But one man at least remained impervious to the spirit of high adventure which it embodied. Nicias sat hunched over the stern of his flagship, a tired, ill old man wrapped in the scarlet cloak of generalhood, a conscript commander, gazing back, back, with hopeless resignation through the morning haze to that distant, dwindling pinnacle of rock, the glittering fretted marble which embodied one man's vision of Athens' eternal glory.

This was by no means the first expedition to set forth against Sicily. Indeed, the pattern of events which it reveals recalls an almost identical episode which took place a thousand years earlier. Shortly before 1400 B.C. King Minos of Crete launched a naval force against the island. By now the Minoan dynasty was either in the last stages of over-civilised decadence, and dependent on Achaean mercenaries to maintain its power; or else, as some think, an Achaean warrior-prince had already usurped the throne of Cnossos. If this was so, his position was far from secure. There was fierce and increasing economic competition between Crete and the Mycenean mainland. Over-population was already becoming a dangerous problem, not surprisingly: Crete enjoys a healthy climate, and the lack of fortifications on the island reveal a civilisation untroubled by warfare. During the fifteenth century colonisation had begun, perhaps as one way of reducing the number of mouths to feed, and from the Linear B tablets it would appear that some form of rationing was in force.

The expedition against Sicily—or more specifically against the Minoan colony known as Sicania, near Acragas—had been occasioned, we are told, by a revolt of the colonists, led by their king, Cocalus, against the mother-city. Cocalus was assisted by a refugee from Cnossos itself, Minos' engineer-artist Daedalus. Daedalus taught the Sicanians how to fortify their city, Camicus, with huge defensive walls, like those still visible today at Mycenae and Tiryns. As a result the attacking force was unable to capture Camicus, and settled down to besiege it. The siege lasted five years, and eventually Minos himself was killed by Cocalus. At this the Cretans gave up, raised the siege, and sailed away. While they were circumnavigating the Iapygian promontory on the heel of Italy, their fleet was driven ashore

by a great storm. They now abandoned any attempt to return
to Crete, and founded a new city in Italy, called Hyria. The
loss of Minos, together with his entire expeditionary force, so
weakened Cnossos that, when a serious earthquake hit the
island, the Mycenaean barons from mainland Greece had no
difficulty in storming and capturing Crete's unwalled capital.
The proud Minoan civilisation went down in flames, never to
recover. From now on there are no more Egyptian tomb frescoes
of gift-bearing "Keftiu" (as the Cretans were known there);
instead, the pottery which appears at sites such as Tell-el-
Amarna is mainland Mycenaean.

Until quite recent times this whole episode was dismissed as
myth. But the archaeologist's spade, as so often, has confirmed
what scholars refused to believe. A Minoan necropolis has been
found at Sant'Angelo Musaro, close to Acragas (Agrigento) in
Sicily. Even more striking is Diodorus Siculus' description of
King Minos' burial-place there as "a tomb of two storeys: in the
part which was underground they placed the bones, and in that
which lay open to gaze they made a shrine of Aphrodite [the
Cretan mother-goddess?]." As Sir Arthur Evans realised, this
odd structure was exactly parallelled by the so-called "Temple
Tomb" at Cnossos—*which neither Diodorus nor his source
Philistus could possibly have seen or known about from direct
observation or even from hearsay.* So the myth, it would seem, is
based on a solid foundation of fact. This is extraordinary
enough; yet far more extraordinary, to my mind—and never, to
my knowledge, remarked on by historians—is the fact that
Minos' doomed venture to Sicily so uncannily foreshadows, in
almost every detail, that other, more famous expedition which
forms the subject of this book. Most historical coincidences
turn out, on examination, to be anything but accidental. As we
shall see, the circumstances responsible for Cnossos' downfall
were almost precisely those which resulted in the breaking of
that other great imperial thalassocracy, Athens. The point is
at least worth bearing in mind.

To understand the complex forces which brought about
Athens' great expedition to Sicily in 415 B.C., we must look

back over a century in time, and explore regions of the ancient world which might seem, at first sight, to have little connection with those dramatic events so memorably described by Thucydides. The trail leads us from Egypt to South Russia, from the Po Valley to the Orontes. Coin hoards and pottery sherds, soil erosion and deforestation, colonisation, trade monopolies and the market availability of gold—all these, and many other factors, contribute to the final picture. It is not quite so nobly tragic or symmetrical a picture as Thucydides paints it, in the memorable sixth and seventh books of his *History*. Nor, indeed, is it exclusively dominated by political passions, abstract concepts such as hubris and imperial necessity, or the unpredictable workings of man's tragic destiny and overreaching will. Men like Thucydides, who were consciously hammering out the foundations of modern rationalism, could hardly help overstating their claim for the omnicompetence of human reason. "Man is the measure of all things," Protagoras declared with characteristic self-assurance. To him and his contemporaries, living in the creative ferment of the Periclean Age, watching the great temples rise on the Acropolis, hearing Anaxagoras—perhaps more ironically than he knew—proclaim the supremacy of Mind, it must have seemed a self-evident truth.

Yet Protagoras might well have qualified his aphorism with the caveat "of all things—except of his material environment." That rider is not universally valid; but it was true of fifth-century Greece to a striking degree, and may partly explain the Greek passion for relating all concrete phenomena to some generalised abstract concept. Ideas are not, in the last resort, bound by climatic conditions; philosophers may with impunity thumb their noses at geography. But politicians and statesmen cannot afford such a luxury. There are some problems which cannot be solved by taking thought, where the individual will is helpless to shape events.

Without a Pericles, an Alcibiades, even a Nicias, the course of history, it is true, might have been changed—but only within certain well-defined limits. Economic reformers such as Solon and Peisistratus, in the previous century, had transformed the future of Athens more radically than any conventional politician could hope to do. Yet even they were forced to adapt themselves to the peculiar conditions which Attica's position, geography, and material resources—or lack of them—imposed. History is predetermined, to a greater extent than we sometimes care to admit, by the accidents of climate and environment. There can be few countries of which this is truer than Greece.

In relation to its size, Greece possesses one of the longest and most heavily indented coastlines in Europe: nearly two thousand miles for an area of only just over 31,000 square miles. The sea is never far away. A series of rugged mountain ranges both isolates the Balkan peninsula from Europe, and divides Greece itself into a series of self-contained cantons. Today rather less than one fifth of the whole peninsular land-mass is cultivable, and in antiquity the percentage may have been even less. A disproportionate amount of even this limited acreage is swallowed up by three fertile plains, in Messenia, Boeotia, and Thessaly. Other areas were renowned for their fertility, yet lacked the wide acres necessary to produce wheat on an economic scale. It is doubtful whether they grew enough to support their own populations: certainly not in the fifth century B.C., when almost all the Greek states, great and small alike, were forced to import wheat and barley from abroad to supplement their own resources. From Solon's time and even earlier, Greek landowners—Athenians in particular—had tended to put more and more of their land aside for vineyards and olive groves. With wine and oil they could pay for the grain they imported, and use the thin Greek soil to its best advantage.

Probably before the Persian Wars, Greece had largely switched from subsistence to commercial farming. The political effects of this change-over were incalculable. Above all, it left the mainland states dangerously vulnerable to economic blackmail from abroad. Any country that depends on an external source for essential raw materials must, whatever the cost, *secure those materials at source*. Failure to do so will inevitably produce a condition of helpless subservience to the supplying market. In the fifth century most of the Greek states knew this only too well. Their history reflects a constant struggle, not only to break into such markets, but also to monopolise them, against cut-throat competition—which by no means drew the line at force—from their neighbours and rivals. Wheat affected the existence of every man, woman, and child in the Aegean, and was therefore a strategic supply *in excelsis*: the staff of life indeed, a phrase which—granted the economic conditions of the time—is no mere Biblical hyperbole but the most literal of truths. Man may not live by bread alone; but assuredly he cannot live without it. As we map in the great wheat markets of the ancient world, and trace their connection with the (sometimes baffling) military history related by Thucydides and our other literary sources, we begin to perceive the motives that drove Athens to invade the glamorous El Dorado that was Sicily.

Grain was not the only commodity of which Greece stood in short supply. Before the middle of the fifth century her timber was almost all being imported. The combined depredations of goats, charcoal-burners, and invading armies, plus the annual requirements of a large sea-going fleet, ate up the forests far faster than it took young saplings to reach maturity. The fleet that defeated Xerxes at Salamis (480) was built from trees felled in Illyria and south Italy. By Plato's day—the early part of the fourth century—Attica was already a bare, unwooded region. With deforestation came progressive soil erosion. Once the trees were gone, heavy seasonal rains washed away the thin topsoil, exposing those bare limestone bones which form so large a proportion of the land-mass as we know it today—and reducing yet further the small percentage of arable land. Only in one or two fertile lowland plains—especially those of Messenia, Thessaly, and Boeotia—could large-scale stock breeding or arable farming be carried on. Most of the cantons remained at bare subsistence level, and with any significant rise in population soon reached a point where they were largely dependent on imports.

Nor was the position much better as regards basic mineral ores. Much fifth-century military history makes a good deal more sense when we realise that Greece possessed no copper deposits at all, and only two major concentrations of iron ore—both of which lay in Spartan territory. Laconian iron and steel were famous in antiquity. At this time the iron-fields of Boeotia had not yet been discovered. Athens' only source of iron within the empire was the little island of Cythnos—a fact which explains its surprisingly high tribute assessment. Presumably a large percentage of these dues were payable in unworked ore.

But Athens, at least after 484–483, had one enormous advantage over her neighbours: a plentiful and apparently inexhaustible supply of silver, which did much to rectify her otherwise disadvantageous balance of trade. Without the rich mines at Laurium, in south-east Attica, Athenian history might have been transformed beyond recognition. Laurium silver paid for the fleet which saved Greek freedom during the Persian Wars. Laurium silver, minted into the "Attic owls" (tetradrachms) which formed an international currency, financed Athens' long and ruinous war against Sparta. Laurium silver—apart from fine pottery clay and marble—was the only valuable raw material which Athens possessed in abundance.

Without this accidental bonanza, Athens' economic position during the fifth century would have been nothing short of disastrous. At the most liberal estimate, Attica did not possess much over 85,000 acres of arable land. To make matters worse, the soil was so poor that wheat accounted for no more than one tenth of the total yield, the remainder being barley. Even in a year of dearth, with fallow land reduced to a minimum, it is unlikely that more than 65,000 acres were under cultivation at any one time. From an inscription at Eleusis we can calculate total home production for the year 329 B.C. (which is unlikely to have differed substantially from the yield a century earlier). The figures obtained are 28,000 *medimni*[1] of wheat, and 340,-

[1] The *medimnus* was about a bushel and a half.

350 medimni of barley. This works out at an average of slightly under six medimni per acre, which—with primitive methods of cropping and fertilisation—is about what we might expect if all available land was under the plough.

Nearly all historians accept a figure between six and eight medimni as the amount of grain required per annum by the average Athenian. "Grain" here means, in effect, wheat, since barley was eaten only under protest, as a poor substitute. Slaves may have been fed on barley, but even so, a large proportion of this would have to be imported. With an average fifth-century slave population of 100,000, and allowing an annual ration of only five medimni, Athens still needed at least 800,000 medimni of barley to feed both her slaves and her livestock. In 329, as we have seen, the barley crop was less than half that figure. If we deduct 85,000 medimni for next season's sowing, the total is only about 255,000—which leaves a balance of 545,000 to be imported. At the time of the Persian Wars slaves formed no more than one fifth of the population (the proportion subsequently rose). The total population in 480, the year of Salamis, was about 285,000, of which the slaves accounted for some 54,000. Grain requirements, then, on average, were 1,655,000 medimni of wheat, and (at the lower rate, as before, with animal fodder included) at least 570,000 medimni of barley. It is possible, though unlikely, that Athens at this period could still grow enough barley, at home and on Euboea, to supply her own domestic needs. But the position over wheat was quite another matter. Even if we double the figure for 329, and assume a wheat harvest of, say, 50,000 medimni, this still represents no more than *one thirtieth* of Athens' annual consumption. Somewhere, somehow, another 1,605,000 medimni had to be found.

The problem was not new; it had begun to manifest itself a century earlier. Solon's legislation (?594) banned the export of any commodity except oil, and put severe restrictions on immigrants. But to export oil meant planting new olive groves, which in turn reduced the acreage available for cereals. So by the time of the Persian Wars, with specialist farming now widespread, we find an immense discrepancy between the amount of wheat *grown* in Attica and the total quantity *consumed*. Between 479 and 454, moreover, this gap widened rapidly. In twenty-five years—for the last six of which Athens controlled the great wheat granary of Egypt—the overall population of Attica almost doubled, from an estimated 286,000 to something in the region of 474,000. This increase took place despite continual war-casualties (which weighed most heavily on the hoplite class) and emigration schemes designed to siphon off proletarian troublemakers. By the 450s a combination of accelerated birth rate and over-liberal immigration had produced a population of crisis dimensions, which it was imperative to thin out by every possible means, from overseas settlements to restrictions on citizenship.

If the total population of citizens and resident aliens, or metics, was about 350,000, then the wheat required to support them would be 2,100,000 medimni.[2] The amount of barley needed for slaves and animals would be nearly 900,000 medimni, an increase of close on half a million. When we come to 431, we find that—for whatever reason—the total population has dropped by about 10,000. Energetic measures had been taken to check further expansion and deal with the crisis; but Athens was very far from out of the wood yet. Retrenchment at home had to be matched by the acquisition of large, dependable markets abroad. Where were they to be found? This problem was a major determinant of Athenian foreign policy throughout the fifth century—a period during which Athens' grain supply was always hazardous, often inadequate, and a standing item on the Assembly's agenda. It is small wonder that Socrates (as Xenophon tells us in his *Memorabilia*) should have regarded the maintenance of the country's grain supply —together with Athens' revenues, expenses, mines, and military installations—as the prime concern of any would-be statesman.

Timber was almost as scarce as grain, and no less vital to

[2] This, curiously, is the exact amount which Leucon, who ruled over the Crimean Bosporus in the first half of the fourth century B.C., sent to Athens c.360, during a year of famine.

Athens' survival. The city's imperial authority depended very largely on maintaining a large and efficient fleet. During the Peloponnesian War (431–404) Periclean strategy called for a standing navy of at least three hundred triremes, probably more. This entailed a minimum of sixty new keels being laid down annually; the number might be as high as a hundred. Such estimates presuppose an immense supply of high-grade timber. In order to maintain such an elaborate building programme, Athens was forced to import virtually all her timber during the second half of the fifth century, and large quantities of fir, pine, and cedar from the time of the Persian Wars.

For fifth-century Athens, then, foreign markets—especially those dealing in grain and timber—were of paramount importance. The nearest, though not the largest, lay in Thrace and Macedonia. Macedonian fir-trees made ideal masts and oars. Wheat grew abundantly in the Paeonian hinterland. But the most valuable product of this region was undoubtedly metal ore, in particular gold and silver. The mining district lay between Crenides, Mt. Pangaeus, and the river Strymon; it also included the off-shore island of Thasos. Another area which could export timber in large quantities was the southern Black Sea littoral. The vast forests of Pontus were prolific in oak, beech, and fir—three of the most essential trees for ship-building. Pontus also exported naval stores such as charcoal, pitch, and resin. Its two ports, Sinope and Amisus, handled the crude iron mined by the Chalybes of the interior—a tribe whose very name had, by the fifth century, become a poetic synonym for iron and steel. One other product vital to the Greek economy was available, in unlimited quantities, throughout the Black Sea region: salt or pickled fish.

But by far the most attractive—if the least reliable—market in these parts lay further north, beyond the misty shores of the Crimea, where barbarous chieftains reigned in splendour over the great wheatfields of south Russia and the Ukraine. Potentially, this was the best grain market for the ancient world. But the voyage was notoriously difficult, the overhead expenses astronomical, and the corn-barons sublimely indifferent to contracts. They had a marked preference for being paid in gold, and the only potential buyer with gold and to spare was the Great King of Persia. The last thing the south Russian market could be called was reliable—yet for a power operating on such a gross grain-deficit as Athens, reliability was the prime essential. The same drawbacks applied to the Phoenician coast, which could supply both Syrian wheat and timber from the great Lebanon ranges. The voyage, again, was both long and hazardous. Homecoming merchantmen were liable to be intercepted by Carian or Lycian freebooters, anxious to scoop up the copper ingots which so many traders took aboard before leaving Cyprus.

Egypt was always one of the most prolific wheat-producing areas in the Mediterranean basin—a fact which induced both Persia and Rome to annex it as an imperial granary. Westward along the North African coast from Egypt lay Cyrene, another spectacular "fertile crescent." It is no accident that the epithet Pindar chose for it was "wheat-bearing." Herodotus tells us —and his evidence is confirmed by modern observation[3]—that Cyrene enjoyed no less than three separate harvest seasons— one on the coast, one in the interior, and a third up in the highlands—so that the country enjoyed "a continuous autumn of eight months on end."

There remain to be considered the Western Mediterranean, in particular Illyria, the Po Valley, Etruria, Magna Graecia, Sicily, and Spain. Illyria—an area roughly equivalent to modern Yugoslavia—not only possessed fine forests and silver mines, but was also of great strategic and commercial importance. Epidamnus, on the coast, formed the terminus of the great trans-Hellenic overland trade-route to the Dardanelles and Byzantium—a route better known, in Roman times, as the Via

---

[3] Before the Second World War Italian agronomists had begun to see spectacular returns on their wide-ranging reclamation schemes for Cyrenaica: in the Barca region, about 1935, a good year's crop yielded 300,000–400,000 quintals, or something like 900,000 bushels (=600,000 medimni).

Egnatia. There was also Corcyra (Corfu), which looked both east and west and in a sense north too: this small island, with its powerful navy, dominated not only the Straits of Otranto and the approaches to the Via Egnatia, but also the Adriatic. Greek contacts with the rich wheatfields of the Po Valley go back as far as the early 600s. The bitter fighting in north-west Greece during the Peloponnesian War, the persistent raids and high-pressure diplomacy which preceded hostilities—all make much more sense when we realise just what was at stake there. So does the wealth enjoyed by Epidamnus and Corcyra alike from the beginning of the fifth century.

Middle Italy and Etruria had two vital raw commodities hard to come by in Greece: iron and copper. The rich iron-workings of Elba were famous throughout antiquity. A hundred miles south of Etruria lay Campania, for the most part an unbroken plain of rich volcanic soil, stretching from the Apennines to the sea. It produced superb wine, oil, and—above all—grain of every description. There were fine firs, beeches, and silver pines to be had in Latium, while Liguria, Strabo says, produced ample timber "suitable for shipbuilding, with trees so large that the diameter of their boles is sometimes found to be eight feet." Calabria and Apulia were famous for their wheat in Roman times; the great Bruttian forest, in the toe of Italy, was one of the few large-scale sources of pitch for caulking seams.

But for sheer variety and abundance of resources, the richest market by far was Sicily. Ever since Homer's day the island had been heavily wooded, especially in the north-east, where the Nebrodes Mountains still preserve part of the gigantic forest that once stretched from Mt. Etna to Acragas (Agrigento), from Himera eastward to the Straits of Messina. Furthermore, the island possessed a tradition of technical skill in addition to raw materials: shipbuilding was always an important Sicilian industry. Any Greek in a position to obtain Sicilian timber could build triremes on the spot, and sail them home free.

Sicily was famous for her luxury exports, food above all. Dairy produce—cheese in particular, since it was relatively nonperishable, and could therefore be exported without difficulty —is mentioned again and again. A flourishing dairy industry also implies, *a fortiori*, extensive cattle farming. During our period the Syracusans thought nothing of sacrificing 450 bulls annually to Zeus the Saviour, and Sicilian smothered beef was popular enough to figure in Attic comedy. Sicilian horses won prize after prize at the various Panhellenic Games: those great stud-farms must have tempted any rival city with a shortage of cavalry. Sicilian hogs enjoyed an international reputation as early as the sixth century. Fresh and sea fish of every variety—bass, crayfish, lamprey, lobster, mullet, eels, and above all tunny —were to be had in abundance. As the seas teemed with fish, so the forests and uplands abounded in game. Thyme-scented Sicilian honey rivalled the best that Attica could produce. Sicilian chefs were highly trained and fetched top prices in the slave market.

But Sicily's most important product, and that on which her fabulous wealth ultimately depended, was high-quality wheat. The island's amazing fertility is referred to again and again. At Catana the worship of Demeter went back to immemorial antiquity. Acragas, Gela, Leontini, Selinus—all derived vast revenues from their land by exporting grain abroad. In Alexander's day mainland Greece rated the wheat of Selinus highest; the giant temples which still survive suggest that the Selinuntines were wealthy enough a century or so earlier. Already in 535 the coinage of Zancle (Messina) bore a "bird's-eye view of granaries," which suggests a flourishing export trade. This glittering El Dorado had, nevertheless, one disadvantage, seldom emphasised, which must have caused endless frustration in mainland Greece. Each Sicilian city had to meet its own domestic requirements before it could export a surplus. There has been a consistent tendency to underestimate both the arable acreage and the overall productivity of Greek Sicily; but even after the figures have been adjusted, it is clear that a poor harvest could quite easily cancel out the year's export quota altogether.

Only Catana, Leontini, and Selinus could be sure of having a margin even when the yield was below average. Gela would just

about break even. But the most surprising and significant results are those in respect of Syracuse. With only about 40,000
acres of arable land available for any given harvest, Syracuse
could count at most on a return of 840,000 medimni per year,
and this might well be halved. The lowest estimate of Syracuse's
population is 400,000. At the standard ration of six medimni
a head, this would call for 2,400,000 medimni annually. In
consequence, the *minimum* deficiency in any given year would
be *nearly one and a half million*. In other words, however we
manipulate the figures, the remarkable fact remains that Syracuse and Athens appear to have shared a very similar economic
predicament. If this is true, it explains a good many hitherto
baffling problems: above all, the motives behind Syracuse's own
expanding imperial ambitions. No wonder that she cast covetous eyes on Catana and Leontini, her northern neighbours,
when between them they controlled the most fertile plain in
Sicily; no wonder that when Athens decided to back Leontini,
the Syracusans saw it as a direct threat to their own advance-
ment.

On the other hand, though each individual export surplus
may have fluctuated, total production on the island—gross
rather than net—was enormous. The latest modern estimate (an
ultra-conservative one) is 6,335,333 medimni of wheat per
annum, and 1,685,000 medimni of barley. The contrast between
Sicily's overall resources, and that percentage of them available
—at a price—for the overseas export market was too striking to
need emphasis. So was the immense power that would accrue
to Sicily under a strong central government. Her mighty fleets
would break the Carthaginian monopoly of trade with Spain
and the Western Mediterranean. Silver, iron-ore, wheat, wax,
pitch, ochre, copper from south-east Portugal, gold from
Iberia and the Río Tinto—all these would flow, inexhaustibly,
into Greek hands. Whoever ruled Sicily could become the master of an empire such as no Hellenic state had yet aspired to.
Here was a weapon with which to match the Great King, to pay
for mercenaries, to stabilise even the most shaky economy. What

ambitious and desperate statesman could ignore so rewarding
a prospect, whatever the hazards involved?

The more one studies fifth-century Greek history, in particular the long rivalry between Athens and Sparta which culmi-
nated (as we shall see) in the Sicilian Expedition, the more
clear it becomes that the real key to their actions lies in the
brute fact that there were simply not enough raw materials—
grain and timber in particular—available for general consumption. Athens' determination to destroy the Peloponnesian
League was prompted, in part at least, by fear of its competition
in vital markets; hubris alone simply will not do as an explanation. The Peloponnesian War, so memorably narrated by
Thucydides, was not a "commercial war" in our modern sense:
no Greek state was concerned to promote the interests of its
merchant-producers. But neither was it the purely imperial or
militaristic scheme of conquest which too many people still
regard it as today. Quite apart from the basic handicap imposed
by environment, no Greek state possessed enough skill or foresight to develop its own output beyond a mere subsistence
level. Most available colonisation areas had been swallowed up.
A good deal of Greek history in the Periclean Age can be seen
as a horrific game of economic musical chairs, with nation
fighting nation to lay hands on the bare necessities of life.

It would be hard to guess this from our primary written
sources. All ancient writers—Thucydides perhaps less than most
—virtually ignored the economic element as an operative factor
in history. Reading these sources is an oddly frustrating business, because we constantly glimpse significant patterns or actions which are never explicitly stated or given adequate weight.
Thucydides, as several scholars have made clear, was perfectly
well aware of economic realities; he simply did not regard them
as relevant to those universal laws of history he was attempting
to isolate. When, as so often, he gives away information of this
sort, it is almost always in a casual parenthesis.

But the larger pattern of events can also be revealing. Every
single major source of supply, from Phoenicia to Sicily, from

Egypt to the Crimea, was also, at one time or other in the fifth century, the object of very close attention (either military or diplomatic) on Athens' part. Such detailed parallellism can hardly be a coincidence (cp. maps pp. 27, 43). Even when Athenian policy concerned itself with places that do not figure directly on our list of markets—e.g., Corcyra, Epidamnus, or Byzantium—these invariably turn out to be strategic points along some vital trade-route. Such a pattern is just what we might expect. Granted Athens' chronic shortage of wheat, timber, and other basic raw materials, it is inevitable that much of her foreign policy should have been concerned with securing adequate markets (preferably at source) and safeguarding the lines of communication between them and Piraeus—paying particular attention to such ultra-vulnerable points as straits and isthmuses. Regarded from this viewpoint, many of the curious strategic decisions made during the Peloponnesian War at once fall into place. Thucydides saw no reason to explain why a conflict between Athens and Sparta should be mostly conducted in Thrace, Chalcidice, Acarnania, Sicily, and Ionia. The reason by now should be only too clear.

If further confirmation were needed, it is supplied in equally striking fashion by the mute testimony of pottery deposits and coin hoards. Until new techniques and attitudes enabled the historian to make a fuller evaluation of this evidence, it was still possible to treat the Sicilian Expedition as an isolated, contingential phenomenon, brought about by some "unforeseen and unpredictable accident." Thucydidean generalisations are catching. When Mme. de Romilly talks of the "almost abstract mechanism of the law of imperialism," she may be clarifying Thucydides' mind, and indeed the intellectual climate of thought which he represented; but this is very different from explaining the history of the period in terms of what actually happened.

All literary source-material is, in one vital respect, extremely vulnerable as historical evidence. The process of selection and arrangement (this applies to Thucydides as to all other writers) is not only an act of historical criticism, but also an unofficial censorship. What we are presented with, in fact, is a carefully screened selection of material. You will search in vain through the pages of Thucydides for any revealing personal anecdotes such as abound in Plutarch's *Lives*. Thucydides has equally little to say to us on the vital subject of Athens' import-export trade, or her public finances. These are selective value-judgments. Our task today, then, is to search for fresh evidence which will supplement and perhaps correct his overall picture. Here we have a good deal of luck on our side. The ancillary tools of the modern historian—archaeology, epigraphy, economics, numismatics—largely by-pass the built-in screening process which makes any reliable interpretation of literary evidence so difficult a task. Inscriptions (with some obvious exceptions) were made for official public scrutiny rather than as propaganda to impress future generations. When a merchant buried his coin hoard in time of war, or a housewife or trader threw out broken pots, they did not stop to reflect that this material, carefully analysed, could give future historians much valuable information about trade fluctuations over a wide area. This kind of "hard" evidence is immune from human prejudice—except, it goes without saying, in the mind of the scholar who interprets it.

As we have seen, two of Athens' most plentiful raw materials were silver and fine clay. The fine four-drachma pieces (tetradrachms, "Attic owls") coined during the fifth century became international currency, and therefore tell us a great deal about the extent and influence of Athenian trade in foreign markets. The distribution and contents of coin hoards gives us most valuable corroborative evidence as to trading patterns in any specific area and period. Better still, it so happens that Athens' largest, most staple export was pottery—both cheap containers which carried oil, wine, or honey, and fine vases purchased abroad as *objets d'art*. Now, pottery (like plastics in our time) is virtually indestructible. Wherever Athenian traders penetrated, they left innumerable fragments of cups, pots, vases, bowls, jugs, wine-coolers, oil jars, perfume flasks, and lamps behind them. This material, properly analysed, pro-

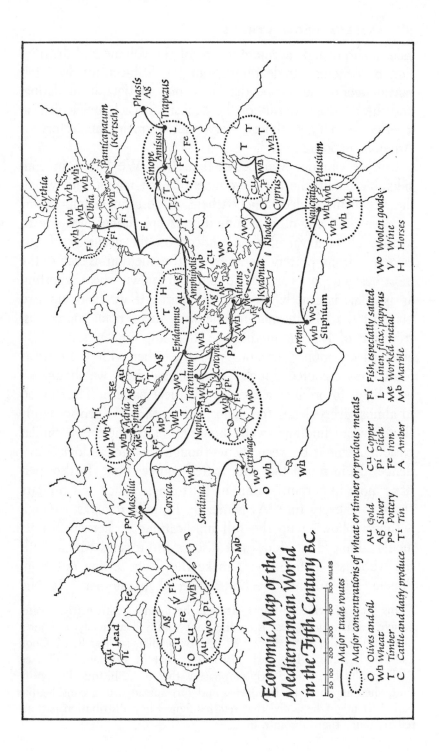

Economic Map of the
Mediterranean World
in the Fifth Century B.C.

0 50 100 200 300 400 500 MILES

⸺⸺ Major trade routes

⸺⸺ Major concentrations of wheat or timber or precious metals

O   Olives and oil   Au Gold   Cu Copper   Fi Fish, especially salted   Wo Woolen goods
Wh Wheat   Ag Silver   Pi Pitch   L   Linen, flax, papyrus   V   Wine
T   Timber   Po Pottery   Fe Iron   Me Worked metal   H   Horses
C   Cattle and dairy produce Ti Tin   A   Amber   Mb Marble

Scythia

Phasis Ag

Panticapaeum
(Kertsch)

Sinope   Trapezus
Amisus L
Olbia   Fi   Fi   Pi Fe Fe

Wh Wh Wh
Wh   Wh Wh
Fi   Wh
Fi   Fi

Fi

T   T
T   T

T   T
Wh
Wh

Naucratis   Pelusium
Wh Wh Wh   L
Wh Wh

Cyprus
Cu
O   Fi   Wh

Rhodes
Wo

Kydonia
Wo
Fe

Cyrene
Wh Wo
Silphium

Athens
Po Wh
Pi   Wh
Me

Amphipolis
Mb
Au Ag   Cu   Wo
C   Po
Epidamnus   H   Ag
T
T

Massilia
Po
V

Corsica

Sardinia

Carthage
Wo   Wh
O   Wh

Wh

Mb

Lead   Fe
Au
Ti

Ag   V Fi
Fe   Wh
Cu   O   Pi
Au Wo O

Adria   Au
Wh Wh A
V   Wh
Spina   Ag
Me
Cu
Fe   Mb
T   T
Ag
Wo   Wh

Naples
Pi Wh
Tarentum
Corcyra
Cu Pi
Wh Cu   Fi
O   V   wo

vides a surprisingly accurate record of the volume and distribution of Athenian trade throughout the fifth-century Mediterranean world (see Appendix I). From stratigraphical dating, and the relative intensity of the deposits at each archaeological level, we can trace almost every fluctuation in the history of Athenian exports.

But we can do even better than this. We know, in considerable detail, the basic products of each region with which the Athenians traded. Since Athens' largest single import, far in advance of any other commodity except timber, was wheat, we have here a valuable cross-check on the accuracy of our evidence from pottery deposits. If the method is valid[4] the most heavy deposits should be found in known wheat-exporting areas. This is exactly the case. Similarly, if we mark up two maps of the Mediterranean, one with the general source distribution of key commodities—e.g., grain, timber, salted fish, gold, silver, copper, iron-ore—and the other with those areas most hotly disputed, fought over, or colonised, we should expect them to produce a roughly identical pattern. They do so in almost every detail (cp. maps, pp. 27, 43). When we apply these overall findings to the literary record, there is a similar basic agreement between them—though the archaeological evidence fills in much that the written sources omit. It also, perhaps more importantly, illuminates foreign policy and military strategy at every turn. As Mme. de Romilly remarks (though without following up the full implications of her own statement), Thucydides "does not discuss the reasons which, with the whole sea before them, make the fleets setting out from Piraeus sail in one direction rather than another." In the

[4] This kind of evidence must naturally be handled with extreme care. I have learnt a good deal from the (not wholly convincing) strictures made against the method adopted here by scholars such as R. M. Cook and M. I. Finley. The best criticism is that of Edouard Will (see Bibliography II), who rightly emphasises that to be historically significant, sherding must be (a) heavy and (b) spread over a considerable period. It might be added that *relative* figures in a distribution pattern tell us more than absolute ones.

answer to this crucial question the whole raison d'être of the Sicilian Expedition lies concealed.

Athenian merchants had begun to exploit the Western market by the middle of the sixth century B.C., when a cut-throat rivalry developed between them and the Corinthians. From about 540 onwards we find Attic ceramic ware steadily beginning to oust that of Corinth, which for over a hundred years had enjoyed a virtual monopoly in Sicily and the towns round the Gulf of Taranto. By 520 Corinthian sherds had fallen away to a mere trickle; Athens, it is clear, had taken over this market *in toto*. "Corinth you hated; so did she hate you," exclaims one of Aristophanes' characters. The root cause of this hatred was commercial competition. However, Corinth retained her trade agreements with the predominantly Dorian cities of eastern Sicily, above all with Syracuse, where there is a significant and almost total lack of Attic pottery. Athenian trade with Sicily during the fifth century seems to have been restricted, very broadly speaking, to the non-Dorian cities of the south coast: Acragas, Camarina, and above all Gela. If she ever traded with Catana or Leontini (and there is some evidence that she did for brief periods), it was not on a large enough scale to affect the pottery-distribution pattern to any noticeable extent. This balance of influence is worth bearing in mind.

It was Athens' clash with Persia—precipitated by the Ionian Revolt (499–494) and consummated in the Persian Wars (490–479)—which first turned her statesmen's attention seriously to the West. When the Great King's slave told Darius, "Sire, remember the Athenians," it was not only invasion he planned, but also, it would seem, a highly effective brand of economic blackmail. During the period 490± to 470± Athenian trade in every area under Persian control dropped catastrophically. Rhodes, Cyprus, Phoenicia, the Black Sea, the Thraceward regions, Egypt—all tell the same eloquent and gloomy story. Attic pottery dwindles away to the merest trickle. The inference is clear: Darius barred Athenian and Ionian merchants from trading within the Persian empire, and in particular closed the Dardanelles to their shipping (though not to the vessels of their maritime rival, Aegina). The Great King, as Persian sources confirm, was very much alive to economic realities—he could hardly have governed so vast an empire otherwise—and knew better than most people just how they could be employed as formidable weapons of power politics. In particular, he both monopolised the gold supply, and kept if off the open market. The monarch who can hire mercenaries may, or may not, win all his wars; but the ruler who can outbid every competitor in the struggle for basic raw materials is certainly going to win the peace.

Many vital commodities—grain above all—were produced and controlled by remote and powerful barbarians who could demand, and get, their own chosen medium of exchange. The Scythians of South Russia, for instance, were on a perfect sellers' market, and knew it. If they opted for gold payments (which they generally seem to have done), the Great King was in a position to regulate or cut off the flow of goods from the Black Sea to the Aegean exactly as he chose. He did not need to fight to achieve this end: his agents would simply overbid their Greek competitiors at every auction, and pay in gold bullion—a gesture which the Athenians, even with the mines of Thrace at their disposal, could not possibly match.

By 494, then, the Athenians found themselves in an awkward, though not yet critical, economic position. If they were shut out from their traditional Black Sea market, they had to develop a new one without delay. There was only one direction in which they could turn: the West. Again, our archaeological evidence confirms this supposition beyond all possible doubt. At precisely the same time as Attic pottery sherds dwindle away in the Black Sea and the eastern Mediterranean, those of Sicily, Magna Graecia, and the Po Valley show a sudden and spectacular increase. This *démarche* in the West is firmly linked with the name of that far-sighted Athenian statesman Themistocles. About 492, at the beginning of his career, we find him campaigning on Corcyra (Corfu), and clearing the straits of

pirates. Clearly the main purpose of his mission was to secure
this vital Western trade-route at its most vulnerable point. He
called two of his daughters Sybaris and Italia. He also seems
to have established diplomatic relations with the tyrants of
Syracuse: the Greek embassy which approached Gelon for help
before Xerxes' invasion almost certainly did so at Themistocles'
suggestion.

When Eurybiades, the Spartan commander-in-chief, was unwilling to accept his naval strategy before Salamis, Themistocles threatened to pull out the entire Athenian contingent, put
their women and children aboard, and emigrate to Siris (or
possibly Sybaris) on the Gulf of Taranto. "It has long been
ours," he asserted, "and the oracles have foretold that Athenians must live there some day." Had it? Did they? Athens'
claim to Siris was of the flimsiest; the interesting thing is that
Themistocles made the statement at all. But after the defeat
of the Persians his political enemies—now the crisis was over—
swiftly eased him out of office. His plan for Western expansion was shelved at the same time. In 479 Athens' leaders were
far more concerned to regain control of the Dardanelles and
the Black Sea than to go adventuring beyond the Straits of
Otranto.

After the victory of Plataea the Greek allies fell out among
themselves. There now developed that deep and—as it proved
—irreparable split between the two major city-states, Athens
and Sparta. Athens' formidable display of naval expertise at
Salamis had thoroughly alarmed the Spartan bloc; from now
on they feared her as a potential rival and enemy. The creation
of an independent Athenian League (sometimes known as the
Confederacy of Delos) confirmed all their worst suspicions.
Economically, there were simply not enough markets in the
Aegean world for two major federations bent on exercising
monopolies.

The South Russian market did not, in the event, prove quite
so satisfactory a source of supply as Athens had hoped—or as
is often assumed by historians. Not until the fourth century
do the distribution figures for Attic pottery at sites such as

Olbia (Odessa) and Panticapaeum (Kertsch) take a sharp upward turn. Wherever the bulk of South Russia's exported grain was going to in the mid-fifth century, it was not to Piraeus. There was no reliable way of ensuring a quota delivery; Athens' effective authority never extended beyond Byzantium. She had to take what she could get from the Crimea, and be thankful.

The beginning of Athens' renewed interest in the West coincides with the emergence of Pericles as a young radical politician. In the 470s Athenian conservatives had been bent on exploiting Thrace, Macedonia, and the Strymon Valley, a policy which received some sharp setbacks. But about 460—by which time the economic situation must have been giving cause for alarm—we find a significant change of policy. It is now that Athens first breaks into the Campanian market, with a phenomenal rise in the quantity of Attic ware at such sites as Nola, Capua, and Cumae. At the same time Pericles negotiated an alliance with Megara, occupied her two ports of Pegae and Nisaea, and connected them to the city with long walls, very like those shortly to link Athens and Piraeus. This was a masterpiece of economic strategy; it also—and small wonder—precipitated a violent quarrel between Athens and Corinth. To achieve true independence, Athens had to secure the markets of the West beyond all possible interference from her enemies. The first step towards realising this long-term objective was to win exclusive control over the best, shortest, and safest trade-route between Magna Graecia and Piraeus. The sea passage round the southern Peloponnese was impossible during the four winter months, and hazardous at all times. The obvious route lay across the isthmus, from the Saronic to the Corinthian Gulf; but this was controlled—both politically and economically—by Corinth. The Corinthians charged heavy harbour dues on all traffic, and could refuse passage altogether if they so chose.

So long as Athenian merchants were obliged to route their goods through Corinth, Athens' entire economy hung by a thread. But in fact there did exist an alternative route across the isthmus to that provided by Corinth. The importance of this fact cannot be over-emphasised. From Nisaea on the Saronic Gulf the road ran through Megara, and then north-west to Pegae on the Gulf of Corinth. This overland link was more than twice as long as the one between Corinth's twin ports of Cenchreae and Lechaeum, and lacked their facilities for sliphauling merchantmen across the isthmus. From Athens' viewpoint, however, it had several distinct advantages, which more than compensated for transshipment and the cost of road haulage. It was, for one thing, far closer to Piraeus; indeed, virtually linked with it, since Nisaea lay immediately across the channel from Salamis. On its western side, too, the land-route was protected by the Geranean Mountains. From 460 to 446 Athens, by virtue of her alliance with Megara, controlled this route, and was thus able to keep her Western traffic moving freely, without interference or excessive overheads at the isthmus. It was a notable achievement.

Yet even now Pericles' main attention was on another market altogether. It is the Egyptian campaign of 460-459 which confirms Athens' grain shortage beyond all possible doubt. Pericles threw a vast fleet and more men than he could safely spare into achieving the conquest of this distant country. There is one reason, and one only, why any foreign power invaded Egypt during antiquity: to secure control of its immense grain supplies. Pericles is unlikely to have been any exception to this rule. He must also have calculated that Egypt was the one major wheat market—large enough, that is, to feed Attica singlehanded—which he stood the least chance of absorbing into the empire by direct military action. In this belief he was arguably correct. The only alternatives were South Russia, or Sicily with Magna Graecia. Pericles, to judge by his actions, always believed that Sicily was too tough a nut for Athens to crack; and it is doubtful—Thucydides underlines this—whether even a Panhellenic expedition could have made much headway against the barbaric chieftains of Scythia.

By 458 Pericles had every reason for confidence. The population of Athens had reached an all-time peak; but with the granaries of both Egypt and the West available, this was a problem that could take care of itself. The next year saw the annexation of Boeotia—another most valuable territorial gain, shortly followed by that of Naupactus in the Corinthian Gulf. Then, in 454, the entire structure of Pericles' new economy was thrown into jeopardy by Persia's total and annihilating victory in Egypt. Pericles could, at a pinch, afford to throw away all those men and ships; but with nearly half a million mouths to feed, the loss of Egypt's granaries was sheer disaster. By 451 the situation had become acutely critical. Athens was still technically at war with Sparta and her allies. No substitute had been found for Egypt as a regular grain market. Athenian relationships with Thrace and Macedonia were far from happy. Famine loomed over the city. Pericles was forced to swallow his pride and patch up a five-year truce with the Peloponnesian League. An emergency convoy was organised from South Russia; the truce also gave Athens the right to purchase emergency supplies of grain in markets (such as Syracuse) where Corinth enjoyed a monopoly. The famine was somehow averted; but it had been a close call.

More than ever Pericles realised that the only satisfactory solution, in the long run, was to bring an adequate source of wheat *within the limits of the empire*. In other words, Athens had to embark on a policy of imperial aggrandisement; but for a specific purpose, and with strictly limited objectives. Where was this ideal market to be found? In 450 Pericles remained of the same opinion as he had been a decade earlier: the only possible answer was Egypt. An invasion force sent out under Cimon, however, collapsed ignominiously after its leader's death, and Pericles was back to square one again. There was only one thing to be done now: a desperate measure which nothing but the direst emergency could have justified. Knowing full well the repercussions his action was bound to cause among the subject-allies of the empire (who were, after all, still bound by the polite fiction of a defensive league against Persia), Pericles opened formal peace negotiations with the Great King. This settlement, the so-called Peace of Callias, did indeed cause a storm of protest: it left Athenian imperial pretensions naked for all to see. But without it Athens might have had no imperial pretensions left to uphold; it was, by a hair's breadth, the lesser of two evils.

After the Peace of Callias, the chances of Athens obtaining *secure* access to any important source of grain, let alone of absorbing it into her empire, must have seemed very remote. Egypt was once more controlled by Persia; South Russia could not be controlled by anyone. Such grain as Pericles now obtained was on sufferance—and at the seller's price. Thrace was unpredictable, Thessaly inadequate. There was only one possible solution: for better or worse, Athens had to look westward. Until she controlled an adequate market, without fear of outside intervention, her ramshackle economy would always remain fatally vulnerable.

The need for action was precipitated by a disastrous series of events in 446, during which Athens lost Boeotia, came within an ace of being defeated by Sparta and Corinth (who struck the moment the truce ran out), and was then forced to conclude a highly disadvantageous treaty with the Peloponnesian League. From Pericles' viewpoint the most crippling condition of the Thirty Years' Peace—which shows, incidentally, how very well aware of practical economic realities the Greeks were, whatever their literary conventions—was Athens' obligation to relinquish the ports of Pegae and Nisaea. In other words, Athens was to exist, as it were, on parole: her trade with the West would depend on Corinth's good will, just as her Eastern trade depended on that of the Great King. *Control at source:* by this time the slogan must have been engraved on Pericles' heart.

CHAPTER III: *The Grand Design*

Less than seventy miles across the Adriatic from Corcyra clustered the rich Greek colonies of southern Italy; and beyond them, hymned by poets, abounding in wealth, the home of millionaire nabobs and triumphant athletes, her ranches and forests and wheatfields stretching away to some unimaginable horizon, lay Sicily. It would be a sober head indeed that could resist so intoxicating a challenge, especially when backed with the excuse of dire economic need. From about 446 a dream of Western conquest suddenly caught the public imagination. Many people, as Plutarch tells us, became "obsessed with that extravagant and ill-starred ambition to conquer Sicily, which was afterwards fanned into flame by Alcibiades and other orators." This "Western dream" was not—as one might suppose from Thucydides—based on pure speculative ignorance, a medley of myth and garbled sailors' yarns. Commercial relations with Sicily had flourished since before the Persian Wars; Athenians had daily evidence of her multitudinous riches piled high on the Piraeus wharves. The enthusiasts who "sat about in the wrestling-schools and the public meeting-places, sketching in the sand the outline of Sicily and the position of Libya and Carthage," did not make the whole picture up out of their own heads. This, it is sometimes forgotten, was a great age of trade and exploration.

Much of the pressure on Pericles at this point must have come from Athenian merchants, who were better informed than most people as to just what resources Sicily and Magna Graecia had to offer, and hoped to make a rich profit if and when Athens conquered them. There can be no doubt, either, that they pointed out, with some force, the strictly limited nature of their present concessions on the island. They could import wheat from Acragas, Camarina, Gela, Selinus, and occasionally

—if the political situation permitted—from Catana and Leontini. But this still left Athens dependent on the good will of the local authorities; she had no real guarantee of supply. Similarly, traffic through the straits to Campania was controlled by those strategically placed cities Rhegium and Messina. Such an argument, more than any other, was calculated to overcome Pericles' fundamental distaste for wild schemes such as the "Western lobby" had in mind. There was also the ever present danger of famine. The acute grain shortage recorded for 445 may well have been brought about, in part at least, by the loss of Boeotia a year earlier. But it was the second crisis of the sort in five years; some kind of decisive action had to be initiated, and without delay. Pericles could not always rely on averting disaster—as he did now—by coaxing a stop-gap consignment of wheat out of some hopeful Egyptian pretender (an act which, incidentally, was in flagrant violation of the peace treaty with Persia). There was only one course open to him, and he took it.

In 443–442 the Athenians concluded alliances "for all time" with Rhegium (Reggio) and Leontini (Lentini). Both cities were admirably placed to control the Straits of Messina, and the treaty with Leontini may also have secured Athens much-needed supplies of wheat from the eastern Sicilian seaboard. That same year saw the foundation of Thurii, a supposedly "Panhellenic" colony built near the site of long-vanished Sybaris, on the Gulf of Taranto. Thurii was promoted as an idealistic experiment, the keynote of which was cosmopolitan federalism between Dorians and Ionians: the Spartan or Corinthian lion would lie down in peace and good fellowship with the Athenian lamb. This scheme attracted considerable attention, and a glittering galaxy of VIPs was persuaded to take part in it. Its architect was Hippodamus of Miletus, who applied here the axial-grid system (symbolic of egalitarianism) which he had lately worked out for Piraeus. Empedocles and Herodotus were early visitors to the site. Thurii, in fact, was to be a showpiece; but a showpiece with a very practical underlying raison d'être. Despite the Panhellenic composition of the settlement, its leadership remained largely Athenian. Nor is it easy to believe that so outré a project was planned by a casual group of emigrants. This, surely, was Pericles' brain-child, and a highly characteristic one.

If he had decided that Athens' final security and supremacy —which implied, *inter alia*, the neutralisation of Sparta and her allies—could only be attained through the subjugation of the West, and the acquisition of its limitless resources, then it was vital to establish a bridgehead there as soon as possible. The "eternal" alliance with Rhegium and Leontini offered some control of the narrows. As an emergency alternative—treaties could, after all, be repudiated—Thurii provided a good harbour in the heel of Italy, with an adequate overland route to the Tyrrhenian Sea. It was, of course, infinitely cheaper to transport goods by sea rather than overland. But however expensive the land-route might be, it was still cheaper, and safer, than to ship freight through an unpoliced and enemy-dominated channel. Apart from the heavy tolls that Messina exacted from all shipping, there was the risk of being snapped up by pirates or privateers, who found the two-way passage through the straits a rich and inexhaustible source of booty. The only alternative sea-route meant sailing round the south coast of Sicily—a lengthy, expensive, and hazardous voyage.

But Pericles had another, equally practical reason for getting a foothold in Magna Graecia at this point. For some while now the most striking phenomenon in the West had been the steadily increasing power and ambition of Syracuse as an imperial-commercial city-state—very much along the same lines as Pericles envisaged for Athens. This process had been begun by Gelon, who turned Syracuse into the greatest single power in Sicily; it continued, step by inexorable step, with his successors. In 474 Hieron smashed the Etruscan fleet, an act which made Syracuse free of the Tyrrhenian Sea as far north as Naples and Cyme. In 453 another expedition raided Elba and set up an entrepôt on Corsica. During this decade, however, Syracuse had been severely handicapped by a large-scale rebellion of native Sicels, under their nationalist leader Ducetius. In 450, after a nine years' struggle, Ducetius was finally crushed. With her home front thus secured, Syracuse began to show dangerous and all too predictable signs of aggression. Four years later, in 446, while Pericles was making his peace with Sparta—which cost him that vital land-link across the Isthmus of Corinth— the Syracusans won a great victory over Acragas and seem to have narrowly missed defeating Gela at the same time. It is clear that they were aiming at nothing less than complete subjugation of the island.

There was also the awkward fact—which would not be lost on Pericles—that Syracuse happened to be a Dorian foundation, with a traditional ethnic bias against Athens. Her main allegiance was to her mother-city Corinth, and through Corinth to the Peloponnesian League as a whole—including Sparta. The foundation of Thurii and the alliances with Rhegium and Leontini may well have been due in part to fear of Syracusan expansion. At the same time it was vital for Athens not to upset the delicate susceptibilities of the Peloponnesian League at this early stage in the game. Hence the elaborate flummery of a Panhellenic foundation.

Whatever Sparta may have felt about it, such a move on Pericles' part was certainly calculated to cause alarm in Syracuse. Nothing could have been less welcome than this evidence of Athens' suddenly developing concern with the West. If mainland Greece was too small to contain Athens and Sparta, the Western Mediterranean, for very similar reasons, did not offer sufficient *Lebensraum* to accommodate both Athens and Syracuse. Their needs and ambitions were far too nearly identical. From now on the interests of the two powers began to clash in a way that only force, ultimately, could resolve. This Syracusan threat, moreover, must have provided the "Western lobby" with one simple and highly persuasive argument in favour of invading the island, rather than dealing with it through diplomatic or commercial channels. If Syracuse could gain control over all Sicily, then so could Athens; and indeed, if there was a danger of Syracuse doing so, it was imperative that Athens should get there first. Moreover, with Sicily subjugated, and the empire at last secure, the road lay open for yet further expansion. Was it so insane to dream of attacking Etruria and Spain and Carthage? Gelon and Hieron were both highly practical men; yet they, too, had cherished the same ambition.

In the summer of 438 Pericles suddenly took a renewed interest in Megara, lost to Athens eight years earlier under the terms of the 446 treaty. A decree was passed prohibiting the import and export of goods between Megara and Athens. This move aroused a great deal of gossip, and was popularly attributed to some petty personal vendetta on Pericles' part. The truth is less romantic. Athens had, somehow, to recover the vital overland link between Nisaea and Pegae: since these ports were taken from her, all Athenian traffic to the West had been routed via Corinth—an arrangement as hazardous as it was expensive. Pericles put out diplomatic feelers to Megara. But the Megarians—probably under heavy pressure from their Peloponnesian allies—refused all his advances. This placed Pericles in something of a quandary. He could not reduce Megara by military action; this would at once involve him in a war with the Peloponnesian League, the one thing he was determined to postpone as long as possible. Yet if Megara would not rejoin Athens of her own free will, then she had to be coerced. One way or another, the Western sea-route had to be made secure, and by-passing Corinth was an essential step in the operation. If force was excluded, perhaps economic pressure might do the trick. Hence the first Megarian Decree, freezing all import-export trade between the two cities.

In 437 Pericles secured an alliance with the Acarnanians in western Greece; another link in the chain to the West was thus made good. For the next two or three years Athenian policy was more concentrated on Thrace, Macedonia, and the Black Sea. But in 434 came an unexpected shock: some kind of Spartan-backed military coup took place at Thurii, which fell into the hands of an oligarchic junta, with strong Spartan sympathies. Pericles' showpiece of Panhellenism now became, to all intents and purposes, an outpost of the Peloponnesian League. This, surely, is why, in 433–432, we find the Athenian admiral

Diotimus sailing on a good-will mission to Naples, and carefully renewing those "eternal" alliances with Rhegium and Leontini en route. The small Athenian detachment which, a year or two later, responded to Catana's appeal for help against Syracusan aggression fits into the same pattern. With Thurii lost, it became doubly important to keep some kind of control over the straits. There was also anxiety over the Campanian market. For years now, wild Samnite tribesmen from the hills had been infiltrating Campania's fertile lowlands. Diotimus may well have been ordered to investigate this problem on the spot (after nervous merchants had spread their own panic-struck rumours round Athens) and to report on the likelihood of its holding up or otherwise endangering Athenian grain consignments.

It is also possible that Syracuse or Corinth had been deliberately undercutting Athens' prices in the open market. If Campanian wheat was being diverted to some Peloponnesian consumer, Athens had ample cause for alarm. (When the first Athenian expedition sailed for Sicily in 427, one of its declared objectives was to prevent Western grain ships reaching the Peloponnese.) Such economic pressure was both simple and effective. It scarcely required genius to see that the easiest way of thwarting Athens' imperialist ambitions was to sabotage her supplies of essential raw materials at source, and thus starve her into a more reasonable frame of mind. This, after all, was no more than Pericles himself proposed to do to Megara in 433, with the imposition of the second, more stringent, Megarian Decree. By now Athens had made an alliance with Corcyra, and become embroiled in Corcyra's fatal quarrel with Corinth. Pericles had seen war coming up out of the Peloponnese like a cloud, and from now on felt that further conciliation was pointless. At all events, his next move stirred up more violent opposition, both at home and abroad, than anything he had hitherto attempted.

In the late autumn of 433 he proposed, and the Assembly carried, new economic sanctions against Megara. By this enactment an absolute embargo was laid on all commerce between Megara and every city whatsoever throughout the Athenian

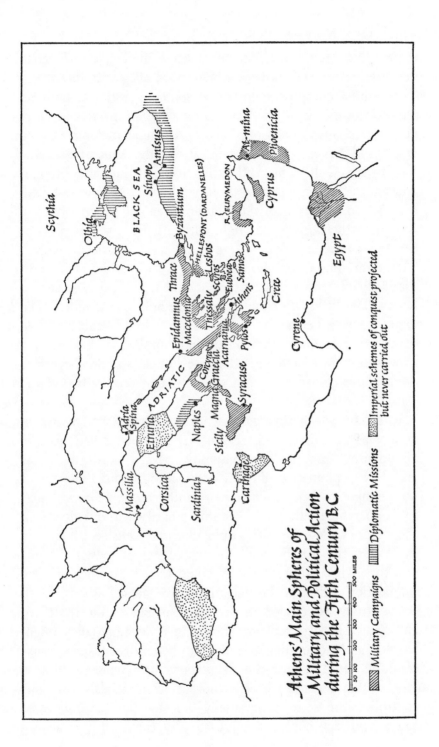

Athens' Main Spheres of
Military and Political Action
during the Fifth Century B.C.

▨ Military Campaigns   ▤ Diplomatic Missions   ▒ Imperial schemes of conquest projected
but never carried out

0 50 100   200   300   400   500 MILES

Scythia
Olbia
BLACK SEA
Sinope
Amisus
Byzantium
HELLESPONT (DARDANELLES)
Thrace
Epidamnus
Macedonia
Thessaly
Lesbos
Scyros
Euboea
Samos
Acarnania
Athens
Corcyra
Magna Graecia
Pylos
Syracuse
Sicily
Naples
Etruria
Spina
Adria
Massilia
Corsica
Sardinia
Carthage
Cyrene
Crete
Egypt
Cyprus
Phoenicia
Al-mina
R. EURYMEDON
ADRIATIC

empire. No Megarian trader might use a market, no Megarian vessel might enter a harbour which owed allegiance to Athens. To ensure a complete blockade at source, a fort was built on the north-west coast of Salamis, opposite Megara, and three vessels permanently stationed there. A similar measure of control could be exercised over Pegae by the squadron in the Corinthian Gulf. This ruthlessly stringent measure brought Megara to the verge of starvation; yet her citizens did not yield one inch to Athens' demands. Hard-pressed and famine-stricken, they nevertheless held out right through the first ten years of the Peloponnesian War, up to the Peace of Nicias in 421. That fact alone reveals how vital it was to Sparta and Corinth that Megara, with her two ports, should not fall into Athenian hands. The little city could never have held out unaided. The Peloponnesian League must have gone to considerable trouble to keep her fortified, garrisoned, and supplied with at least a bare minimum of rations; otherwise Pericles would, beyond a doubt, have gained his objective in the first year or two of the war.

In a sense, such strategy was not so much a matter of economics as of long-term siege warfare. By now it had become abundantly clear that the competitive rivalry between Athens and the Peloponnese could only be resolved by force. There were not enough markets available to permit reasonable coexistence, or to guarantee either side genuine security without depriving the other. Unless Corinth could check Athens' expansion in the West, the livelihood of the whole Peloponnesian League was threatened. Unless Pericles could secure his lines of communication against the League's disruptive tactics, Athens' Western venture was doomed almost before it had begun. If Athens and Sparta had trusted one another a little more, they might have done the one thing calculated to benefit them both: make common cause against the rising power of Syracuse. But so long as they remained hostile and suspicious rivals, those who controlled the sources of supply—not to mention interested foreign powers—could continue to play them off one against the other. The situation had reached both economic and political stalemate.

We can see now how much both Athens and the Peloponnesian League had at stake in the Adriatic when they bid against each other for Corcyra's alliance. Whoever controlled this small island would have a strategic asset of the first order at their command: mastery over the Western sea-routes both to Magna Graecia and the Po Valley, access to the Via Egnatia through Epidamnus. The Peloponnese, no less than Piraeus, depended on regular consignments of Sicilian and Campanian wheat; both sides were equally determined to prevent such supplies from reaching their enemies. Throughout 433 and 432, while Athens and the Peloponnesian League stood at the very brink of war, the topic which successive embassies debated most hotly was always the Megarian Decrees. All our sources agree that the Athenians could, as Plutarch says, "have avoided war on any of the other issues, if only they could have been persuaded to lift their embargo against the Megarians and come to terms with them." For Aristophanes and Diodorus, indeed, this is the only real issue at stake.

The Spartans, with dour insistence, sent embassy after embassy to Athens. If there was the least chance of averting war, they were determined to take it. Sparta's primitive hand-to-mouth economy, coupled with her constant obsessional fear of Helot revolts, made her shrink from the idea of a long conflict. Besides, with the Messenian plain at her disposal, and a relatively small population to feed, she was virtually self-supporting. It was only the fear of losing Corinth's alliance that drove her into decisive action. The Corinthians, after all, stood to lose far more if Athens secured a monopoly of all Western markets. "What made war inevitable," Thucydides wrote, "was the growth of Athenian power and the fear which this caused in Sparta"—a simple, accurate estimate, still given rather less credence than it deserves—yet still, as always, leaving out so much of the truth. So, in the spring of 431, hostilities were at last formally declared between Athens and the Peloponnesian League, and the Greek states' perennial struggle for economic dominance entered on a new and grimmer phase.

The general course of that unhappy conflict does not directly concern us here. What *does* concern us is Athens' doomed obsession with a "Western solution" as the panacea that would cure all military and political ills. It is this strange historical phenomenon which we must now pursue, to its final tragic climax on the blood-soaked banks of the Assinarus River. It is easy, and fashionable, to condemn Athenian imperialism out of hand as totalitarian and, worse, hypocritical: ruthless *Machtpolitik* masquerading as high-minded intellectual endeavour. Before we do so, we should reflect that, even at its most blatant, under Cleon and his successors, it was fighting for survival. Domination, in the last resort, was only a means to this end. Athens had a skeleton in her cupboard indeed, and more often than not it was that of the breadless householder.

The constant foreign aggression, the search for *Lebensraum*, the high-handed treatment of the subject-allies—all these things had as their aim the securing of desperately needed raw materials. This does not excuse much that Athens did during those terrible years; but it does make it far more understandable. For the Athenians who died in Egypt or Thrace or Sicily the spectre of hunger was at least as strong a driving force as hubris. Any abstract concept of imperial destiny looks pale and unconvincing when set beside these grimly tangible facts. A great deal of Athenian history, from Solon's day onward, is concerned, in one way or another, with the problem of securing adequate grain and timber markets. The Sicilian Expedition of 415–413 was only the last, most ambitious, and most splendidly conceived attempt to solve it.

In the summer of 427 an embassy reached Athens from the four main non-Dorian cities of eastern Sicily and the straits: Leontini, Catana, Naxos, Rhegium. Its object, predictably, was to secure help against fresh aggression by Syracuse. Leontini in particular, whose territory included such an immense and fertile arable plain, was bound to attract the attention of a city which

—powerful though it might be in other ways—did not produce enough grain for its own requirements. Nor were relations between them liable to be improved if (as seems more than likely) Leontini had begun supplying wheat to Athens.

Syracuse was now blockading Leontini by land and sea. The city might well fall to so determined an assault unless prompt and powerful reinforcements were forthcoming; and where else should Leontini seek help but from her powerful and "eternal" ally Athens? The treaty between them had been renewed six years before. More to the point, Athens' commercial interests were threatened. If Syracuse were to conquer and absorb Leontini, it was not only the wheat of the Catanian plain that would be lost, but guaranteed passage through the straits for Athenian merchantmen. Even so, the ambassadors were far from confident that Athens would honour her treaty obligations. Pericles' splendid capital, with its gleaming new temples and proud imperial fleet, had changed and suffered much since those confident, high-riding days in the 430s. Four long years of grimly frustrating warfare had gone by, with little to show for them except heavy casualty lists, rebellious allies, blackened fields, burnt-out homesteads, and the wreckage of once flourishing vineyards and olive groves.

Military morale was low, and fell still further as time went on. Citizen-soldiers had never before been called upon to face sustained and heavy losses over so long a period. There was a marked increase in desertion and column-dodging. Pericles' scorched-earth policy, his flat refusal to let Athenian troops go out and defend Attica during the Spartan army's annual invasion, his evacuation of the outlying rural districts—all this had unexpected and unwelcome consequences. The tacit admission that an Athenian hoplite could not match his Spartan opposite number in fair fight was bound to produce a bad psychological effect, to say the least of it.

But the crowding out of Athens had brought something worse still: disease. Living in cramped, insanitary hovels between the Long Walls, the country folk of Attica had been killed off in their thousands by a virulent epidemic, probably bubonic plague—though typhus and measles have also been plausibly argued—which reached Piraeus by way of Egypt and Libya, on the grain ships. The disease also spread to Athens' troops serving abroad. When the army besieging Potidaea in Thrace sailed home, it had lost 1,050 hoplites out of four thousand from the plague alone.

The physical and psychological effects of this epidemic would be hard to over-estimate. There was a serious breakdown of public morality, from which the city never quite recovered. For one short period Athens seems to have lapsed into near anarchic chaos. A wave of ugly hysteria swept through the city, to find its immediate scapegoat in Pericles, who was fined and relieved of his command. A few months later the volatile Assembly reinstated him; but by then it was too late. In September 429 he died, of overwork and disillusion and a lingering attack of the plague. With his departure, a new and brutally tough policy appears in the handling of the empire. The man behind this policy was Cleon, a merchant-tanner and new-style radical demagogue immortalised by the attacks of Aristophanes, and responsible for the notorious proposal to massacre Mytilene's rebellious citizens wholesale.

Throughout this period we find an intense concern at Athens with two related strategic concepts: the blockading of the Peloponnese, and control of the Western sea-route. Raids on the coast of Messenia and Laconia took place every year, and were supplemented by intense military activity, both at sea and ashore, in Acarnania and the mouth of the Corinthian Gulf. The Athenian blockade does, in fact, seem to have reduced grain supplies to the Peloponnese, and Sparta's establishment of a semi-compulsory "war fund" suggests that this campaign of attrition had made serious inroads on her never very healthy economy. At the same time, Spartan and Corinthian squadrons were employing very similar tactics against Athens' own supply lines. However, by the beginning of 427 it was clear that this general strategy of pin-prick raids had little more than local nuisance-value. The only thing that could seriously damage Athens at this point would be the disruption of her supply lines from Magna Graecia and the Po Valley; and the one way in which this object might be achieved was the capture of Corcyra. This island was the strategic key to Sicily and the Adriatic, a more important naval base than Gibraltar. Its acquisition by a hostile power would not only cripple Athens commercially, but might well lose her the war. The gamble was well worth trying.

The Corinthians had taken a number of prisoners from Corcyra during the early stages of the war. Most of these they sold, but with considerable foresight they kept in captivity some 250 carefully selected citizens—all right-wing conservatives of great power and influence, "whom," says Thucydides, "they treated with great consideration, hoping that a time would come when they would return and win over the island to Corinth." These men were now released (on bail, according to the official story) and at once began organising a coup d'état. Infiltration techniques were not, as is sometimes thought, invented by the Communists. The result was a violent and bloody civil war, fought out with unbelievable savagery, and actively encouraged, for their diverse ends, by Athenians and Corinthians alike. In the end the pro-Athenian or "democratic" faction prevailed. For seven days, while an Athenian squadron stood by in harbour, these "democrats" conducted a ruthless and murderous purge of their opponents. Eurymedon, the Athenian commander, waited patiently until the pogrom was complete; then he and his squadron put to sea. The gateway to the West had been made safe for Athens; Corinth's bid to secure control of the Adriatic had failed.

One episode was over; but another was about to begin. Hardly had the butchery on Corcyra subsided when the ambassadors from Leontini and her allies reached Athens. They had timed their arrival well. The Assembly's mood—inflamed by constant propaganda from the demagogues and young bloods of the "Western lobby"—was likely to catch fire at the magic name of Sicily. But this kind of enthusiasm might prove a mixed blessing. The ambassadors had no guarantee that even if Athens *did* send a task-force to Sicily, it would not be used to further her own well-publicised schemes of conquest. Pericles had been

Leontini's best guarantee: he was known to stand no nonsense from the wilder advocates of Western expansionism. But Pericles was dead now, and the guidance of Athenian affairs had passed into very different hands. Whatever people might feel about Cleon—and opinions were divided no less sharply in antiquity than they are today—no one could accuse him of a bias towards moderation. His enemies called him "the pestle of war." He fiddled his audits; he was, in Aristophanes' expressive phrase, "gorged on confiscation pasties." Worst of all, he made no bones about his attitude to the West. He was an aggressive extremist, an advocate of the "Grand Design." From his point of view, Sicily and Magna Graecia only existed as a potential source of rich pickings for Athens, a combined granary, fatstock market, and lumberyard. When he promised the proletariat wheat and fish, there is little doubt where he intended getting them.

The ambassadors knew this as well as anyone. However, in their present crisis they had no option but to seek help where they could find it, and to hope that in pursuing her own interests, Athens would also benefit them. Perhaps this is why their leading delegate, Gorgias of Leontini, had come to Athens (in a strictly private capacity) some months earlier, and had since spent much time teaching logic and filling young heads with the "lure of Sicily." It is Gorgias and his followers who are satirised by Aristophanes in *The Clouds*; he made a fortune by instructing the ambitious and unprincipled in how to make the worse cause appear the better by glib logic chopping and slanted arguments. In himself, Gorgias was a contemptible figure. What gives him symptomatic importance is the astonishing impact he made on Athenian society. His shyster techniques and bland amoralism had an almost epidemic influence: he caught on like some intellectual plague-virus. It was largely a matter of good timing. He arrived in Athens at a moment when traditional moral values, long undermined, were ready to collapse altogether. His message was exactly what the younger generation wanted to hear. If anyone could sell Leontini's case to the volatile Athenian assembly, Gorgias was the man.

He rose to the occasion with a fine flourish; his colleagues were not disappointed. After formal debate the Athenians agreed to send Leontini a squadron, "ostensibly," says Thucydides, "because of their kinship with the Leontinians, though their real aims"—surely known to every citizen in the Assembly —"were to prevent corn being brought in to the Peloponnese from the West and to make a preliminary survey to see whether it would be possible for them to gain control of Sicily." So, in the same year as the costly revolt of Mytilene, with her financial reserves at low ebb and her population still stricken by the aftermath of the plague, Athens nevertheless embarked on a hazardous and expensive venture in the West.

It was once fashionable to regard this first Sicilian expedition as a casual undertaking, virtually unrelated to the main strategy of the war. Today we know better. Megara, Pegae, Nisaea; Acarnania and the gulf; above all, Corcyra—the pattern is clear; the course of action, inevitable. On the other hand, the expedition shows disquieting signs of having been that most dangerous thing, a democratic compromise—too small to achieve concrete results, but quite large enough to cause political trouble. The conservatives and the moderate democrats probably conceded that it *might* do something to reduce supplies to the Peloponnese; the radical "Western lobby" men could console themselves with the fact that it was only an advance force. As usual, those who suffered most were the commanders: one group expected too much of them, while the other crippled them *ab initio* by allowing them a bare minimum of ships and men. If anything went wrong, it was the generals, not the voters, who would bear the responsibility. Small wonder that the demagogues of the "Western lobby" advocated their plan with such enthusiasm; the potential fringe benefits were enormous, and they had no lack of scapegoats for their own mistakes.

So in the late summer of 427 twenty ships were dispatched to Sicily, under two commanders, Laches and Chariades. The squadron sailed, not to Catana, as we might have supposed, but to Rhegium, where a permanent base was established. This great port was admirably placed for a campaign in and around the straits, but it lay over sixty miles north of Leontini, and was not even on Sicilian soil. If the Athenians really intended to rescue their beleaguered allies, they were going about it in a very odd way: the natural and obvious base for such an operation was Catana.

They managed, nevertheless, to preserve the appearances. Their own immediate interest was an invasion of the Aeolian Islands, north-west of the straits, a volcanic group which includes Lipara and Stromboli. But since the islands had no natural fresh water, the operation could not take place till after the first autumn rains. This gave Laches and Chariades about a month. While Laches set up an advance base at Catana and raised the siege of Leontini, Chariades sailed south on a diplomatic mission to Camarina and Gela. This mission seems to have met with some success. However, on his return journey to Rhegium, Chariades was intercepted by a Syracusan squadron. He put up a fight, but found himself hopelessly outnumbered, and during the engagement received wounds from which he subsequently died. His ships, together with all those aboard them, fell into the hands of the Syracusans.

It is possible that this mission scored one real and—as it turned out—momentous diplomatic success in western Sicily before losing its leader. The ambassadors from Elymite Segesta who sought Athens' aid in the autumn of 416 invoked a treaty made either (according to how we interpret Thucydides' somewhat ambiguous Greek) "with Leontini in the time of Laches and the earlier war," or with Segesta herself "in the time of Laches and the earlier Leontinian war." If the second interpretation is correct,[1] we have here a ten-year treaty originally made by Chariades, and renewed, as fresh epigraphical evidence now suggests, in 418–417.

Segesta and her southern neighbour Selinus were continually

---

[1] The balance of modern opinion thinks otherwise; but what city normally based its appeals on earlier treaties *made with other people?* Here I am content to stand with E. A. Freeman (see Bibliography), a historian who, like Grote, possesses the enviable knack of seeing more clearly than so many of his better-equipped successors.

at loggerheads. When Thucydides tells us that in early summer of 426 "the Siceliots were fighting among themselves," it is a fair assumption that Segesta and Selinus were two of the "different warring parties." Selinus, moreover, was at this point hostile to Athens—a conjunction not likely to escape the notice of an intelligent Athenian casting round, in some desperation, for potential allies. When Chariades approached Segesta, he could hardly have foreseen that twelve years later the whole fate of Athens would hang on the treaty struck with this unimportant, semi-barbarian city, so remote from the political storm-centres of Rhegium and Syracuse.

Laches was now left in sole command of the expedition. His next move—reinforced by ten extra ships from Rhegium—was against Lipara, the main island in the Aeolian group. The Liparaeans were uncommonly well placed for the interception of south-bound grain ships from Campania. If Athens wanted to establish absolute control over this vital sea lane, something had to be done about the Liparaean corsairs. Laches, however, lacked both the strength to wipe them out, and the diplomatic finesse to pressurise them into changing sides. After several abortive raids he gave up, pulled out his thirty triremes, and sailed back to Rhegium.

There was little enough to show for these three months' campaigning: one commander dead, a diplomatic fiasco, a botched invasion. Perhaps the blockade of Leontini had been raised; but this was something quite outside the main line of Athenian strategy. From the Liparaean campaign onwards (with one disastrous exception) operations were restricted to the straits and the immediately surrounding area. Laches' last operation that year was a reconnaissance raid on Locri, across on the eastern shore of the toe of Italy. The Locrians were Rhegium's chief enemies and rivals, and closely allied to Syracuse. Obviously this was another trouble spot that must be neutralised before the straits could be regarded as an Athenian monopoly. Besides, ever since the loss of Thurii, Athens must have been hoping to establish an alternative land link with

Campania, and Locri was the most obvious choice as its bridge-head.

With the end of winter Laches once more turned his mind to the immediate problem of safeguarding the straits. Athens, it was true, had an alliance with Rhegium; but Messina remained hostile, and Leontini, far away to the south, in the menacing shadow of Syracuse, was a very poor substitute. If only Athens had both Rhegium and Messina in her grasp, she would be able to exercise an absolute strangle hold over the narrows. Messina would also be highly useful as a bridgehead if at any time Athens decided on a full-scale invasion of Sicily. The Liparaean corsairs one might ignore at a pinch, but the capture of Messina was vital for any long-term policy involving control of the Tyrrhenian sea-route.

During the winter, Laches had maintained an active fifth column in Messina. This was a regular feature of Greek political and military strategy. We shall come up against it constantly during the various Sicilian campaigns, and its importance should never be underrated. It depended on two main factors: first, that there was nearly always a dissident group in any city, which, for whatever reason, would be glad to admit a foreign enemy within the walls, most often in the hope of forming a real or puppet government; and second, that fifth-century siegecraft was so primitive as to allow two ways only of reducing a town, by starvation or treachery. In the present instance Laches' agents clearly found a strong dissident group, but at the same time judged that support would be much increased by a successful display of force—something the Athenians had so far failed to achieve on the island. Laches wisely refrained from attempting an immediate frontal assault on Messina itself. Instead, he sailed some twenty miles along the coast, and landed at Mylae, which very soon surrendered on terms. This capitulation seems to have concealed a certain underlying enthusiasm, since the men of Mylae now joined Laches in his march on Messina. On the approach of this Athenian column, Messina surrendered without a blow being struck. The infiltrators had done their work well.

Here, at last, was a real triumph for Laches, and a notable step towards the realisation of Athens' Western policy. It also brought him some very welcome allies. This whole region of the north coast, below the forest-clad Nebrodes Mountains, was a stronghold of the native Sicels. For some time now they had fiercely resented Syracuse's harshly despotic colonial rule, and were only waiting for a suitable opportunity to shake it off. Shortly after the fall of Messina we find Sicels and Athenians fighting side by side. Sicel loyalty to Athens was still unshaken in 415, and persisted throughout the subsequent campaign.

With the straits now secure, Laches felt free to launch a fresh series of raids against Locri. That same autumn a full-scale expedition, with Athenians, Sicels, and the Chalcidic cities all taking part, was launched against the city of Inessa, some twelve miles north-west of Catana. Inessa had a strong Syracusan garrison, and its position made it an ideal base for raids into the Catanian plain. Laches had no great enthusiasm for this operation, and may not even have commanded it. It was a tough assignment, which called for trained hoplites rather than marines, and offered little of direct benefit to Athens even if successful. However, Laches would have found it hard to turn down a request from an ally such as Catana, especially considering how little he had done for the east-coast cities since his arrival over a year before. His relations with the Sicilian Greeks were becoming more than a little strained; he had, at the very least, to contribute an Athenian contingent to the expedition. The operation, as he must have foreseen, proved an expensive failure. Immediately afterwards Laches took all his troops and sailed off on another expedition against Locri.

This was the last straw; calculated and unblushing self-interest could hardly go further. Perhaps taking advantage of his absence—and certainly without reference to him as commander of the Athenian expedition—Leontini and her allies sent an independent mission to Athens, asking for a second, larger fleet to be sent to their assistance. They must have felt that the matter was extremely urgent; during the four winter months no one normally attempted to make the voyage between Sicily and Greece. Furthermore, such a request had to be framed with some care. It would hardly do to complain that the present squadron spent all its time advancing Athens' own interests in the straits instead of helping her hard-pressed allies. That, quite obviously, was what it had been sent out to do, and a public reminder of the fact would not be popular. The envoys can have had few illusions about Athens' motives for contracting such an alliance. It might prove equally unwise to demand Laches' replacement, since he had been confirmed in his command by the spring 426 elections.

The best line they could take in the circumstances, they decided, was to harp on the growing menace of Syracuse, and to suggest, as tactfully as possible, that Laches' squadron did not offer them adequate protection. "The Syracusans," they pointed out, "were already in control of their land"—this was undoubtedly true so far as Leontini and Catana were concerned —"and though they [the Syracusans] were being kept off the sea by a small fleet"—a little flattery never came amiss—"they were beginning to equip a fleet of their own so as to put an end to this state of affairs." Nothing could have been better calculated to stir the Assembly into action. The envoys had taken the political temperature at Athens with some skill, and they duly reaped their reward.

Cleon's real ascendency over the Athenian demos dates from the 426 elections: he could scarcely have come into prominence at a worse time. The city was just recovering from a second epidemic of plague. Supplies of food and timber were equally unsatisfactory. Athens could never go completely bankrupt while she controlled Laurium and the mines of Mt. Pangaeus; but her financial position was now precarious, to say the least. Regular Spartan raids into Attica encouraged desertion amongst slaves, and production in the silver mines had dropped appreciably. Faced with this depressing situation, Cleon seems to have had three clearly defined aims in view. First, Athens' finances must be radically overhauled. Second, the city must be provided with sure supplies of grain, timber, and salt fish. Third, the Peloponnesian League must be forced into surrender by a rigorously maintained economic blockade. As early as 427 Sparta had been suffering from a shortage of raw materials. Why settle for further years of uneasy coexistence when absolute supremacy was within Athens' grasp? It is easy—too easy—to condemn this policy as unrealistic. At the time it must have sounded remarkably convincing.

The ex-tanner set about his plan with cool efficiency. In the autumn of 426 "Boards of Collectors" were organised to extract more grain and tribute from the subject-allies. This was followed, a year later, by a drastic reassessment of their tribute rates, many of which were doubled or even trebled. The food supply was a more complex problem. Few things come in for heavier criticism from the comic playwrights than Cleon's unfulfilled promises of grain and fish. Clearly those promises were made in good faith: the food supply was far too explosive a topic to be treated lightly. When bread was short, political heads rolled. But where were the supplies to come from? Cleon's first, and most obvious plan, was to open up the West—more vigorously, and on a broader scale, than Pericles had ever envisaged. Such a course would be in line with the whole pattern of Athenian strategy since 429. His second scheme involved splitting off northern Greece from the Peloponnese, and gaining control over the wheatfields of Thessaly and Boeotia. The advantages here were obvious: strategic control of several vital land-routes, access to much-needed grain supplies, and the further isolation of the Peloponnese, perhaps leading to control over the isthmus.

Whatever failings Cleon may have had, an upper-class blind spot for the central economic realities of warfare was not one of them. He must have known very well that a widespread strategy of interception by sea meant not only less food for the Peloponnese, but correspondingly more for Athens. Every Corinth-bound grain ship captured by the Naupactus patrols, every Libyan merchantman boarded off Cythera, every Campanian convoy "run in" by Laches and his successors in the straits, would now discharge their precious cargoes—without payment—on the wharves of Piraeus. However, various complaints we find in Aristophanes' *The Knights* (424) suggest that Cleon's naval blockade did not yield quite so rich a harvest as he had hopefully anticipated. In any case, it was impossible to leave Athens' economic well-being at the mercy of such piratical windfalls. A regular, reliable source of supply, for grain, fish, timber, and other essentials, still had to be found. The problem was not so much to find a suitable market; Cleon and his friends had already made up their minds on that score. What might well prove tricky was to sell such an idea to the Assembly, and reach agreement, in detail, on the actual strategy to be carried out.

As usual, Cleon had gone one step further than Pericles. He had seen, with irrefutable clarity, that in order to carry out Athens' plans of conquest and economic self-aggrandisement it was useless to make commercial agreements or alliances. Such conventions, in the last resort, were worth nothing; they could always be scrapped when it suited one of the contracting parties to do so. Nothing less would serve than the utter subjugation of the market involved, its permanent absorption into Athens' maritime empire. There was only one place that fulfilled every requirement for this scheme: Sicily.

Such a project involved, among other things, the problem of the Carthaginian-controlled cities in the west of the island, "where the voyage from Sicily to Carthage is shortest." Cleon may well have thought it possible that the conquest of Carthage was a necessary preliminary to that of Sicily. Ever since the palmy days of the Syracusan tyrants, Greek statesmen had dreamed of breaking the hold which Etruria and Carthage maintained over the commerce of the Western Mediterranean. All of them, from Gelon onwards, assumed that the reduction of Sicily and of Carthage went hand in hand.

Which of these two steps should come first was open to debate. Cleon perhaps argued that an Athenian expeditionary force that laid hands on Carthage's Sicilian colonies might well find itself forced to fight Carthage as well as Syracuse. To hold a double front was a situation Greeks avoided like the plague if any conceivable alternative could be found. But whatever his personal preferences, Cleon knew that so farreaching and perilous a scheme was in any case bound to have a rough passage in the Assembly; and it was the Assembly as a whole, not the Western lobby, that would ultimately decide its fate.

An expedition had already been sent to Sicily; but as we have seen, it probably represented a precarious compromise between radical and conservative opinion. The time had come to see how Athens' citizens would react to the "Grand Design" itself. Cleon had no wish to be saddled with more personal opprobrium than was strictly necessary. He therefore put up one of his lieutenants, a former apprentice lamp-maker named Hyperbolus, as a stalking-horse to test public opinion. It was Hyperbolus who now proposed a measure in the Assembly for manning and dispatching a hundred triremes on an expedition against Carthage. It is quite inconceivable, at this juncture, that he could have done so except on Cleon's orders.

Conservative reactions, of course, were highly unfavourable. There is a famous passage in *The Knights* where the triremes themselves, ladies every one of them, recoil horrified at such a prospect: if this iniquitous proposal is passed, they say, they will take sanctuary at the shrine of Theseus or the Furies rather than sail on such an expedition. Yet their main objection, we should note, seems not to have been the idea per se so much as the thought of Hyperbolus having anything to do with its implementation. At all events, the scheme was prudently shelved for the time being. Perhaps Cleon had no intention of its being taken seriously at this stage. He may well have been playing that old diplomatic trick—still very popular today—of pitching his demands impossibly high in order to get just a little more than he might otherwise have done. An Athenian expeditionary force was, after all, already campaigning in and around the straits. What had to be found now was an excuse —an excuse that would convince the Assembly—for considerably enlarging it.

So when the disgruntled envoys from Leontini and the other cities of the Western Chalcidic Alliance reached Athens, in the early winter of 426, Cleon must surely have believed that the Fates were on his side. At the same time he did all that was humanly possible to ensure that the Fates made the right decision. This included soft-soaping conservative opinion in the Assembly. If reinforcements were sent to Sicily, he told them, the war would be finished far sooner. Besides, the rowers needed practice: this really came under the heading of a useful naval exercise. The Assembly, mesmerised by such glib assurances, obediently voted a second squadron of forty vessels, together with three new commanders: Pythodorus, Sophocles (not the playwright), and Eurymedon, who had presided over the liquidation of the Corcyra oligarchs. Pythodorus—a distinguished former archon who had studied philosophy under Zeno and the early Sophists—was to sail immediately with a small detachment, and supersede Laches in his command. If the fire-eaters of Cleon's own "Western lobby" began to complain (as they well might) about this Sicilian expedition's lack of concrete achievement, it would be useful to have a scapegoat ready to hand.

Early in the spring of 425 Laches, returning to base at Rhegium after a raid on Himera, found a new Athenian flagship tied up alongside the quay: Pythodorus had arrived, and was waiting to take over from him. His successor's appearance had been greeted by the first eruption of Mt. Etna in fifty years, an omen which probably gave Laches a certain amount of sour satisfaction. After handing over to Pythodorus he packed up and set sail for Athens, all too well aware that he would be liable to face prosecution on some trumped-up charge when he got there. Subsequent news from Sicily, however, may well have made him feel that, prosecution or not, he was well off out of his command. Pythodorus' first operation, a raid on Locri, failed dismally. Both Locri and Syracuse (for different but equally compelling reasons) were determined to break Athens' stranglehold over the straits; during the winter their fifth-column agents had gone to work with some effect. A month or so after Laches had gone, when the corn was beginning to ripen, a combined Syracusan and Locrian squadron appeared before Messina, and was "invited" to take over the city. Presumably Messina's pro-Syracusan faction had staged a well-timed coup.

Rhegium proved less vulnerable to such infiltration—after all, it was Pythodorus' headquarters—but even so its effective power was dangerously weakened by an outbreak of internal party squabbles. These must have been due, in the first instance, to skilful propaganda work. During the actual defection of Messina, the Locrians carried out large-scale diversionary attacks on Rhegian territory, to make sure no reinforcements were sent across the straits. Meanwhile the Syracusans, who had now finished equipping their new and much enlarged fleet, sailed north in strength to join the small advance squadron. The strategic situation had changed, literally, overnight: Pythodorus was little better off now than Laches had been when he first reached Sicily. What he needed most—indeed, the one thing that could have retrieved his losses—was the speedy arrival of the main reinforcing squadron, those forty ships earmarked for winding up the Sicilian campaign. But day followed day, and still they did not come. When Pythodorus learnt the reason for their delay, he must have wished that Laches had been confirmed in the Sicilian command.

The squadron had duly sailed from Piraeus in May—but not, in the first instance, to Sicily. During the early months of the year a dangerous situation had developed on Corcyra. The defeated right-wing party (reinforced, in all likelihood, by active support from Corinth) had taken to the hills and was now waging a highly effective guerrilla campaign against the capital. Supplies were being intercepted. Sixty Peloponnesian ships, intelligence reports claimed, had sailed to help the exiles. A serious famine existed inside the city. Conditions were dangerously favourable for a counter-revolution—the one thing Athens had to prevent at all costs. Since Corcyra lay on the direct sailing-route to Italy and Sicily, Cleon instructed Sophocles and Eurymedon to put in there en route and, in Thucydides' euphemistic phrase, "do what they could for the Corcyraeans" before proceeding to Pythodorus' assistance. Obviously the present state of affairs could not be allowed to drift on unchecked; and until news of the Sicilian setback reached Athens, it was more than reasonable to divert the relieving squadron, and deal with Corcyra's problems first.

But further delays, of a somewhat mysterious nature, now took place. Sophocles and Eurymedon were abruptly informed that a third commander would accompany them. This was Cleon's favourite general, Demosthenes. He had just got back from a successful campaign in Acarnania; though he no longer held any official position, he had been granted permission "to make what use he liked of this fleet on its way round the Peloponnese." To fritter away precious time when Corcyra might, at any moment, be lost through treachery or enemy action must have struck Sophocles and Eurymedon as sheer suicidal lunacy. Demosthenes proved both stubborn and uncommunicative; the squadron set out in an atmosphere of bafflement and bad temper. When they were still off the coast of Laconia, alarming news reached them. The sixty Peloponnesian ships not only existed, but had already made contact with the Corcyraean rebels. To Eurymedon and Sophocles this called for the swiftest action; all diversionary projects must be shelved. But Demosthenes overrode them; no doubt he was acting on Cleon's confidential orders. He had a plan to carry out at Pylos, and to Pylos the squadron must go first, emergency or no. The argument was settled by a providential storm, which blew the squadron into Navarino Bay for shelter. Demosthenes at once proposed turning Pylos into a fortified bridgehead.

Eurymedon and Sophocles by now seem to have assumed that they were dealing with an uncontrollable lunatic. They "told him that if he wanted to waste Athenian money he could find plenty of other desolate headlands round the Peloponnese to occupy, apart from this one." Demosthenes pointed out, patiently, that Pylos had a first-class harbour. He also reminded his colleagues that this was Messenian territory. The Messenian serfs would jump at any chance to rebel against their Spartan overlords. They "were capable, he thought, of doing a lot of damage if they had this place as a base, and would also be a very reliable garrison for it." Neither the commanders nor the rank and file would take any notice of Demosthenes' scheme; they dismissed it out of hand as hare-brained nonsense. In point of fact the scheme was probably Cleon's, and it turned out to be very far from hare-brained. It led, eventually, to the capture of a hundred and twenty full Spartan warriors—an event which drove Sparta to sue, unsuccessfully, for peace.

But Cleon had more in mind than this *coup de théâtre*. "Here's a jolly little cake," he tells Demos in *The Knights*, "baked with the barley-bread I brought from Pylos." The Messenian plain was Sparta's granary, worked by downtrodden and resentful peasants. If Athens could win control of it, and instigate a new revolt by the Messenians themselves, then Sparta—already under blockade—would rapidly starve, and Athenian supplies be proportionately increased. What Cleon wanted was not negotiated peace, but unconditional surrender. The gamble was well worth trying. In the end (out of sheer boredom, Thucydides says) the troops fortified Pylos as Demosthenes required. The essential work was done in a week. When the walls were complete (which seems to have coincided with the return of good sailing weather), Eurymedon and Sophocles took off for Corcyra, leaving Demosthenes five ships and their crews as a garrison. But before the Athenian squadron had got very far, the Spartans descended on Pylos in force. Their army was recalled from Attica, and their navy from Corcyra; if one of Cleon's aims had been to relieve pressure on these two vital points, he certainly succeeded.

With the vicissitudes of the seventy-two-day blockade which followed, culminating in Athens' final crushing victory, we are not directly concerned here. What matters from our point of view is the fact that Sophocles and Eurymedon turned back to relieve Demosthenes' beleaguered force, so that it was August by the time they at last reached Corcyra. Once there, however, they dealt with the situation brutally and effectively. The rebels' mountain stronghold was captured, and the rebels themselves turned over to their "democratic" opponents, who butchered them to the last man, in circumstances of peculiar savagery. The Athenians now, at last, set sail for Sicily. It was about the beginning of September.

Meanwhile the Sicilian campaign continued, with a series of indecisive engagements in and around the straits. Pythodorus, as always, was hampered by lack of an adequate task-force. He might—and did—make short work of Messina's garrison troops when they ventured outside the walls; but he could not blockade the city, let alone take it by storm. Indeed, he had barely enough triremes to patrol the straits. In the end he seems to have given up altogether. As Thucydides says, "the Hellenes in Sicily continued to make war on each other by land, but the Athenians took no part in it." Any enthusiastic support the expedition had commanded at first was now rapidly petering out. The course of events during these past two years had made it insultingly clear that the Athenians were only in Sicily for what they

could get out of it. Many Sicilian cities must have already decided that they would do better without such unpredictable
and potentially dangerous allies. The Athenians themselves can
hardly have had their morale improved by the endless delays
of the relieving squadron, first at Pylos and then at Corcyra.

For the first time, the Sicilian dream had come up against
a touch of harsh reality. This island was not a fruit ripe for
the plucking, but a collection of rich and powerful city-states
both willing and able to defend their own interests. In over
three years' campaigning, Athens had made no permanent gains,
and had lost a great deal of potential good will. Such was the
situation when, about mid-September, Eurymedon and Sophocles at last brought their squadron to anchor in Rhegium harbour. Any armchair strategist could see that the obvious thing
for this new combined force to undertake was an immediate and
energetic offensive. With forty new fighting ships in hand the
Athenians could surely have won back Messina and re-estab-
lished themselves as masters of the straits. This, in turn, would
have shown the Sicilians that they meant business—just as an
all-out attack on Syracuse would have reassured their by now
lukewarm allies, and might even have brought them some new
ones. Yet, so far as the evidence goes, Eurymedon and Sophocles
did virtually nothing from the time of their arrival until the
Congress of Gela some nine months later.

Despite their vastly increased naval force, the Athenians seem
to have envisaged nothing more aggressive than patrolling the
straits. They "carried on the war with their allies there" says
Thucydides, and that is all. Even if their Sicilian allies had deserted them *in toto*, they could have given a very good account
of themselves unaided: their fleet was now not much smaller
than the first expedition voted in 415. We are forced to consider the possibility that in Sicily—as at Pylos—Cleon was
carrying out a new policy which he found it expedient not to
publicise in advance. By 425–424 Athens held a ring of key
positions all round the Peloponnese; and after the crowning
success of Pylos, Cleon clearly felt there was a chance to smash

Sparta once and for all, by a combination of economic attrition and one final military *coup de grâce*. But if he was calculating along such lines, it is clear that he could not afford to commit Athens simultaneously to a major campaign in Sicily. Time enough to consider one "Grand Design" when the other had been achieved; it might prove vital to recall those sixty triremes from Sicily at a moment's notice, for emergency service round the Peloponnese or in the Corinthian gulf.

It is possible, then, that Cleon gave Sophocles and Eurymedon confidential orders to play a waiting game in Sicily: to police the straits, make a sufficient show of force to keep Syracuse and her Dorian allies from further aggression or expansion, and, finally, to negotiate a peace settlement on terms that would not prejudice Athens' position vis-à-vis her existing allies. Cleon knew very well that such a policy could be reversed or repudiated at any time. So long as it remained secret, those who carried it out could always be thrown to the wolves afterwards.

In *The Suppliant Women*, produced during the spring of 424, Euripides wrote, prophetically: "The man who glories in his luck may be overthrown by destiny: in that hope I rest secure." If Cleon paid any attention to this broad hint, he gave no sign of it. His secret agents were working successfully in Boeotia and Megara, the last weak links in the chain of blockade: Megara, of course, was also the key to the Western searoute. Everything had been planned out; nothing could go wrong now. However, in the best tradition of Athenian tragedy, Cleon's hubris duly reaped its reward. By the autumn of 424 Athens had suffered some of the most crushing disasters to affect any combatant power since the war began. The Athenians did succeed in recapturing Nisaea; but it was Brasidas the Spartan who occupied Megara, and this time Athens had lost her alternative isthmus crossing for good. Oeniadae, the key to the north-west land-route from Acarnania, fell into enemy hands. The Boeotian scheme—based on complex plotting with pro-Athenian elements in Thebes and Tanagra—collapsed completely after Athens' defeat at Delium. Worst of all, Brasidas made a lightning overland march through Thessaly and Thrace to capture Amphipolis, Athens' great commercial entrepôt on the Strymon.

In a few short months Cleon's policy had suffered a serious setback, and Athens found herself without one of her best and most reliable markets. The loss of Amphipolis not only jeopardised timber and grain supplies; it also meant that the mines of Pangaeus were henceforth in Spartan hands. There were plans put forward for taking over Euboea entirely, as a wheat-growing colony; and though these plans seem to have fallen through, from now on Athens' exploitation of the island was progressively increased. Emergency distributions of barley were made. In the circumstances it was only to be expected that Cleon should turn back to the old scheme of Western conquest, which he seems to have shelved at the time of his Pylos campaign.

But meanwhile the situation in Sicily had undergone a radical transformation. By now it must have become abundantly clear to the Sicilian Greeks that their internecine quarrels merely provided the great powers—Athens in particular—with a convenient excuse for getting a foothold on the island. The Chalcidic cities had found that their own claims and needs came very low in Athens' order of priorities. Laches and his successors were far more concerned with securing the straits, or establishing a commercial bridgehead in Magna Graecia, than in defending their Chalcidic allies against Syracusan aggression. When reinforcements were promised, they could be held up indefinitely on other assignments; and when they eventually arrived, they did nothing.

The Syracusans and their supporters were in a slightly different position: they had received no help from the Peloponnesian League at all, whether for ulterior motives or not. As E. A. Freeman pithily observes, from the islanders' viewpoint "the war had been a war of mutual damage to the profit of nobody." Would it not benefit all Sicilian Greeks, Dorian and Ionian

alike, to sink their private differences, and present a united front
to any power which might find it politic to meddle in Sicily's
affairs? It should now be clear why Eurymedon's call on the
Sicilian cities to prosecute the war against Syracuse met with
such a negative response.

The first diplomatic move in this campaign for reconciliation
came from Camarina and Gela. We have already seen the close
relations which, despite the accident of war, existed between
Gela and her quasi-colony. Their leaders began by negotiating
a private bilateral truce. They then sent out a joint embassy to
canvass the various other Sicilian Greek cities. What they proposed was a round-table diplomatic conference, to be held in
Gela, with delegates from every city-state attending. These delegates should be entrusted with full powers to make a general
peace settlement. Such a scheme was very uncharacteristic of
Greek politics: the more normal course would have been to invite each city to approve the truce which Gela and Camarina
had already concluded. But what its promoters aimed at was negotiation by a single body of deputies; in other words, they
intended that the Congress of Gela should, by its very nature,
symbolise Sicilian unity.

Though such a concept had obvious political advantages, it
was very hard to give it any kind of hard practical reality. For
one thing, Sicily was not exclusively Greek. It contained four
other ethnic groups, including the large Carthaginian colony in
the west of the island. "That the Greeks of Sicily were united
by living in one island," Westlake points out, "and were thereby
isolated from the inhabitants of all other lands, Greek and barbarian, was an idea that did not develop naturally and was not
easily fostered." Yet some such bond was essential if any true
co-operation was to be achieved. This is all too clear from the
opening sessions of the conference, during which the various
delegates had no other thought in mind but to urge "their
complaints and their claims in respect of matters in which they
considered they were being unfairly treated." (It must have all
been rather like a particularly acrimonious assembly of the

United Nations.) The result was pure anarchic chaos, and it looked as though the conference might well collapse for want of a common viewpoint. What saved it, seemingly at the last moment, was the speech of the chief Syracusan delegate, Hermocrates, the son of Hermon.

Both Timaeus and Polybius agree that up till their own day Hermocrates was one of the three most distinguished figures in Sicilian history. Thucydides openly idealises him. Born about 470, he was in his forties at the time of the congress, and already a leading figure in Syracusan politics. It is, however, important not to exaggerate his political virtues. Thucydides was not the last historian to draw an implicit parallel between Hermocrates and Pericles; but in fact the Pansicilianism of the one was no more disinterested than the Panhellenism of the other. Hermocrates was an aristocrat, one of the old *Gamoroi*, or titled landowners, of Syracuse; and he was addressing a congress whose delegates, for the most part, shared his own status and special interests. He derived his income from great family estates, which meant that he had a large political stake in the maintenance of the status quo, and an equally large commercial stake in the production and export of wheat. Syracuse, as a Dorian city and Corinth's foundation, maintained a regular, profitable traffic with the Peloponnesian League. Thus on at least three important counts Hermocrates would be biassed against any move by Athens to intervene in the affairs of Syracuse.

Perhaps we can go even further than this. There was a persistent rumour—which subsequent events tend to support—that Hermocrates had political ambitions, and aimed, ultimately, to take over the reins of government in Syracuse. If he did so, it would be either as dictator, or else as the head of a right-wing junta, representing both the old landed aristocracy and the new middle-class nabobs who had made a good thing out of the revolution that swept away the tyrants. He also, it appears, went out of his way to win the support of the younger generation— those who, under Syracusan law, were not yet of an age to vote in the citizen-assembly.

Now the existing government of Syracuse was, nominally at least, a democracy, though one of a very moderate sort. If the general trend of Greek political institutions is anything to go by, there must have been a strong movement among its more radical extremists for a redistribution of land. That such a group of extremists existed we know. Two of them, Athenagoras and Diocles, were among Hermocrates' chief political opponents. Diocles was further responsible for a far-reaching programme of constitutional reform which, in 412, changed Syracuse from a moderate to a radical democracy. One result of Diocles' reform was the deposition and banishment of Hermocrates *in absentia*, while commanding a Syracusan squadron in the eastern Aegean.

All this is extremely suggestive. To begin with, it shows us that the political setup at Syracuse was one which offered Athens a most promising *apertura a sinistra* if she cared to exploit it. Any Athenian agent scouting round for potential support within the walls would at once turn to Diocles, Athenagoras, and their group of radical reformers. Nor is it hard to guess the package deal Athens would promise them in return for collaboration with the invader. The oligarchic Gamoroi held a virtual monopoly over Syracuse's arable land, and in all likelihood had substantial investments in those other regions which came under the city's imperial jurisdiction. They would naturally resist to the death any programme of agrarian reform.

We have a very interesting demonstration of this only a month or two after the Congress of Gela, when, as Thucydides tells us, "the people of Leontini had enrolled a number of new citizens and the democratic party there was planning a redistribution of the land. The governing class, realising this, called in the help of the Syracusans and drove the democrats out." Nothing could be clearer or less ambiguous. Syracuse might be, in name, a moderate democracy; but it was a democracy controlled by great landowners, some of whom will certainly have had substantial interests in Leontinian territory. Deep called to deep: the propertied classes of both cities united against such a common threat to their livelihood.

It is against this loaded background that we must judge Hermocrates' motives and actions. He was at heart a conservative landlord, the spokesman of right-wing Syracusan imperialism: no one could have had more compelling reasons for preserving the regime unchanged—or, indeed, for making it more reactionary still. He regarded imperial ambitions, in themselves, as both natural and excusable. "I am not blaming those who are resolved to rule," he asserted, "only those who show an even greater readiness to submit." He could hardly claim that Syracuse was innocent of imperial aspirations, and he was all too well aware of the intense suspicions which such behaviour aroused elsewhere in Sicily. During his speech he therefore emphasised the fact that the Syracusans were prepared to be reasonable, and would willingly make concessions for the common good. "If we are sensible," he said, "we should realise that this conference is not simply concerned with the private interests of each state; we have also to consider whether we can still preserve the existence of Sicily as a whole." Here is the core and kernel of Hermocrates' policy: the plea for unity among all Greek Sicilians.[1]

A cynic might have answered that the main object of any Syracusan delegate was to get rid of the Athenians—who represented a direct threat to the Gamoroi and all they stood for— and then resume the piecemeal elimination of Syracuse's neighbours and rivals without interruption, taking over their lands and hamstringing their democratic aspirations. There was undoubtedly some truth in this. But at the same time it also remains true that Hermocrates was a genuine patriot: courageous, self-sacrificing, devoted to the cause he had taken up. The two attitudes are by no means incompatible. Hermocrates would fight to the death for Syracuse and Sicily as a whole: this does

[1] A similar powerful appeal, again based on common interests and a common threat, had been made by Themistocles at the time of Xerxes' invasion. It is the spirit which dictated Benjamin Franklin's remark to John Hancock at the signing of the American Declaration of Independence: "We must indeed all hang together, or, most assuredly, we shall all hang separately."

not imply that he was prepared to sacrifice the interests of himself or his class in the process.[2]

Indeed, he had every possible incentive to take a firm stand over Athenian intervention, since in this case what threatened the country as a whole threatened his own position even more directly. This may explain the vein of embarrassed insincerity which most scholars have professed to find in his speech. He came before the conference, he said, as "the representative of a great city, more likely to be interested in aggression than in self-defence." On the other hand, he went on, "I do not think it right to do such injuries to my enemies that I ruin myself, nor, out of a mad love of aggression, to imagine that I can control fortune, which is out of my control, in the same way as I can be the master of my own designs." As Westlake says, "this argument, which cannot have been at all reassuring, suggests that he is trying to evade an embarrassing practical issue." He was on safer ground when he diverted attention from Syracuse's special interests by concentrating on the general issues involved. "Athenian intervention," he told the conference, "has nothing to do with the races into which we are divided; they are not attacking us because they hate one or the other; what they want is the good things of Sicily which are the common property of us all." Such a blanket appeal to the delegates' sense of self-interest was not likely to fall on deaf ears.

The conference agreed, largely as a result of Hermocrates' arguments, to terminate all hostilities in Greek Sicily, and to leave each city in possession of what it controlled at the time.[3]

[2] No one, I imagine, would challenge Sir Winston Churchill's patriotism; but his attitude to, say, British India and the Labour government does not suggest that, even in his case, patriotism dissolved party allegiances (though it may have occasionally overridden them in a crisis). Similarly, Cleisthenes' democratic reforms do not seem to have precluded his watching over Alcmaeonid interests: see W. G. Forrest, *The Emergence of Greek Democracy* (London 1966) pp. 199–200.

[3] There was one exception to this rule: Syracuse—perhaps as proof of her willingness to make reasonable concessions to her less powerful neighbours—agreed to cede Morgantia to Camarina in return for a fixed sum of money.

However, though it was clear that the Siceliot cities intended to maintain complete autonomy in their dealings with one another, peace was not formally concluded until those who were allies of Athens had notified the Athenian commanders "that they were going to make peace, and that the treaty would apply also to the Athenians." Presumably it contained some clause whereby the allies of each signatory were entitled to ratify it if they so desired. Certainly the existing treaties with Athens do not appear to have been repudiated—a decision which Hermocrates, for one, can scarcely have welcomed. All the same, this was an extremely astute move. Eurymedon and his colleagues were presented with a *fait accompli*. Whatever decision they made, Leontini and their other allies would sign the Treaty of Gela regardless. To reject such an invitation was something which could not be done with impunity. If Athens' alliances in Sicily were to be preserved at all, the commanders on the spot had no option but to approve a peace treaty which, on the face of it, offered them all they had been sent out to obtain. The war in Sicily had indeed been wound up. The growing ambitions of Syracuse had, superficially at any rate, been checked. The balance of power was preserved. The fleet had gained useful battle experience, and much detailed intelligence concerning local conditions.

Athens' Sicilian allies, for their part, had no wish to lose so valuable a source of assistance altogether. The time might well come when they would once more need to appeal for Athenian support. None of them, with their long and bitter experience of Sicilian politics, was prepared to assume that the Treaty of Gela would remain in force for ever. This seemed an excellent way of hedging their bets. They also calculated, quite rightly, that in the circumstances the Athenian commanders would not have time to refer their decision back to the Assembly, as under the terms of the constitution they were obliged to do, and would therefore be more likely to endorse the treaty by way of precaution. This in fact was what happened. Eurymedon and his colleagues gave their approval, and the other signatories— amongst whom, it would appear, were some at least of the south

Italian cities—regarded themselves, in return, as now being at peace with Athens. The one exception was Locri, which refused to have any part in such an agreement. Since there was no further excuse for their continued presence in Sicily, Eurymedon and his colleagues sailed home, feeling, we may assume, that in this difficult situation they had done at least as well as could have been expected of them—a naïve view, but an understandable one.

When they reached Athens, however, an unpleasant surprise awaited them. Megara and Oeniadae had fallen by now, and Brasidas—against all expectation—was already in Thrace. Once more Athens was dangerously short of grain. How the Western extremists reacted to this patched-up Sicilian peace we can well imagine; but public opinion as a whole had come round much further, during the expedition's absence, to a policy of reckless imperial aggression than anyone not on the spot could have anticipated. So Sophocles, Pythodorus, and Eurymedon were duly tried and condemned for dereliction of duty and pocketing bribes from the enemy. Most historians assume that this was a purely vindictive prosecution, brought against the men whom it was easiest to sacrifice as scapegoats after such a setback to Athens' ambitions in the West. But to the jury the case may well have looked somewhat different. These pusillanimous commanders, with a strong fleet at their disposal, had made no new conquests and won over no fresh allies. However one looked at it, the Treaty of Gela was a humiliating dismissal, despite its concessions. Athens no longer had an excuse to interfere in Sicily; the return of the fleet was proof enough of that.

Furthermore, it looks as though the citizens at home really believed that this task-force could have captured the whole island; that nothing except wholesale bribery could explain their failure to do so. There was a hysterical mood of self-deceptive optimism in the air: the victory of Pylos had left a dangerous legacy behind it. "Such was the effect on the Athenians of their present good fortune," Thucydides wrote, "that they thought nothing could go wrong with them; that the possible and the difficult were alike attainable, whether the forces employed were large or wholly inadequate." In such circumstances the lure of the West must have seemed doubly irresistible. The "Grand Design," far from being shelved after the fiasco of this first Sicilian expedition, figured more and more prominently in the public imagination from now on; and the losses which Athens suffered during the months that followed merely sharpened men's appetites for it.

CHAPTER V: *The Phoney Peace*

Early in 423 Euripides, whose topicality so often makes him a useful sounding-board for contemporary social or political issues, produced his satyr-play *The Cyclops*. As a piece of free publicity for the Western lobby it must have been very effective. There are constant references to Sicily's richness and productivity, its abundance of cheese and meat and milk. More interesting, there is a flamboyant claim, put in Odysseus' mouth, for the Greeks who "saved freedom" during the Persian Wars: they have earned special consideration from the Cyclops—and the Cyclops, as a Sicilian, can share in their kudos, "for this whole land, under volcanic Etna,/ in whose depths you live, is part of Hellas." It is not difficult to see where such insidious propaganda was pointing. The Pansicilianism and isolation preached by Hermocrates came as a distinct embarrassment to Athens. After the Congress of Gela it was virtually impossible for her to make any move in the West without being branded as an open aggressor. The normal practice, as we have seen, was to act on some appeal for help from an ally—which might or might not have been prearranged. But since all the cities of Sicily were now, in theory at least, at peace with one another, such tactics had perforce to be abandoned. *The Cyclops—*whether deliberately or not—attacked this concept of "Sicily for the Sicilians" by appealing to the international solidarity of Greeks everywhere.

Any direct *démarche* in the West now required much careful advance groundwork. This was particularly awkward in 423. The events of the past year had once more produced a grain shortage, and with Brasidas creating havoc in Thrace and Macedonia, timber must have been hard to come by as well. Cleon was widely accused of failing, in every sense, to deliver the goods. After the loss of Boeotia the number of refugees in Athens, already dangerously high, must have reached an all-time peak. It is possible that a drastic purge of resident aliens was carried out about this time, and many expelled. Once more, as so often in Athens' history, what was needed was a breathing-space. So in the early spring of 423 a one-year truce was concluded between Sparta and Athens. The Spartans had no illusions about their enemies' motives; but then they needed a breathing-space too. Besides, they reckoned that even a year's taste of peace might blunt Athenian appetites for further campaigning. The common man, on whose vote Cleon depended, was war-weary enough already.

It is also possible that they secretly encouraged Brasidas to ignore the truce. Things were going very much his way in Thrace. When Scione revolted from Athens and welcomed Brasidas as the "liberator of Hellas," the grateful citizens bestowed a gold crown upon him.[1] A trireme arrived with a copy of the armistice; he blandly ignored it. Cleon, infuriated, proposed—and carried—a motion to destroy Scione, with all its inhabitants. Such mass reprisals seem to have been a speciality of his. An expeditionary force was sent out under the command of Nicias, whose main achievement was to lure that ambivalent figure King Perdiccas back into alliance with Athens again. His diplomatic honeymoon with Brasidas had been abruptly terminated when the Spartan took some very tough measures against Macedonian troops who panicked in battle. Much-needed Spartan reinforcements, coming to Thrace by the overland route, found Perdiccas' Thessalian friends suddenly unwilling to give them free passage through their territory.

Meanwhile there was disturbing news from Italy. In the summer of 423 a horde of Samnite hillmen captured the great Campanian city of Capua. If (as now seemed very likely) they overran the entire region, it was more than possible that Athenian wheat imports from this area would be dislocated, or even

[1] Thrace at this period was full of potential collaborators, especially among the wealthier and more prominent inhabitants, who had the reputation of being anti-Athenian, and were always being brought to trial on charges of conspiracy or "Brasidising."

dry up altogether. The Samnites cared very little for farming, let alone for a highly complex export trade. So when ambassadors from Leontini reached Athens early in 422, with news of fresh trouble between their city and Syracuse, they were assured of a more than willing welcome. Here, at last, was a chance to re-establish Athenian interests in Sicily. But it had to be exploited with extreme caution, however urgent the need; too abrupt a show of force would be fatal.

What had happened was this. After the Syracusans had assisted the landowners of Leontini to break an attempt at land redistribution by the popular party (see above, p. 70), the landowners themselves were offered Syracusan citizenship, and persuaded to abandon their own city. Since the common people had been, as Thucydides says, "scattered over the country," Leontini was now left desolate. Presumably the Leontinian magnates were invited to join some kind of real estate consortium. But this experiment ran into trouble: some of the "new Syracusans" became discontented with the scheme. They may have been homesick; they certainly resented the inevitable curtailment of their previous authority. A group of them therefore banded together and left Syracuse once more. Returning to Leontini, they reoccupied a part of the city known as the Phocaean Quarter. They also established an outpost at Bricinniae, a stronghold in the northern hills.

Very soon scattered groups of the popular party came flocking in to join them. Local patriotism triumphed over political difference and the thought of restoring Leontini was too appealing to resist. Nor should we ignore the psychological impact which this whole episode must have had, not only in Sicily, but throughout the Greek-speaking world. The Treaty of Gela had scarcely been signed; and now Syracuse—despite all her protestations—was up to her old tricks again, obviously with a view to absorbing the Catanian plain and turning the Chalcidic cities into so many Syracusan outposts. No doubt there was much talk in Syracuse itself of stopping the radical rot, of making the world safe for respectable (i.e., propertied) citizens. But the whole business, seen from outside, smelt unpleasantly of aggression and tyranny: Syracusan policy was running true to form.

This at once put the Athenians in an advantageous position; but even had it not, they would surely have been less than human had they turned down the Leontinian ambassadors' appeal. Here was a determined group of settlers, established in strongly fortified positions, and already conducting raids against Syracuse without assistance from anyone. But at the same time the Athenians were determined not to repeat their previous mistakes. Instead of a squadron, they sent out two ships only, with three accredited representatives aboard; this was to be a diplomatic mission, with no show of force.[2] Its declared purpose was to persuade, not only Athens' existing Western allies, but also, if possible, the other Sicilian Greeks, "to make a combined military effort against Syracuse in view of her lust for power, and so to save the democrats of Leontini." Everybody knew what lay behind this programme; but at least the appearances had been preserved.

The leader of this mission was a young man in his early thirties, Phaeax, son of Erasistratus. To obtain the appointment at all he must have had Cleon's backing. He is described as a "demagogue" (which may mean nothing more than a popular leader), and also as belonging to a highly distinguished family. He was, in fact, that well-known phenomenon, the radical aristocrat. (His nephew later swung over to the extreme right, and was involved in the fascist coup d'état of the Thirty Tyrants.) In 423–42 Phaeax was still at the outset of his political career— and already running into stiff competition from his contemporary Alcibiades, whose background and aims he largely shared. Two years previously Aristophanes has satirised Phaeax in *The Knights*, with a reference to "those young whipper-snappers who sit around chattering to each other in the scent-shops—'Smart fellow, Phaeax, damned clever the way he got off that capital

---

[2] It may be, too, that under the terms of the Treaty of Gela they were only allowed to enter a signatory's port with one ship, unless expressly invited to bring more: for such a condition in operation at Camarina, see below, p. 146 n.10.

charge—persuasive speaker, yes, conclusive, clear, incisive, apho-
ristic, tough line with hecklers, right?'" This suggests he had
a fashionable following among the young, and hardly bears out
Plutarch's claim that he was amiable enough, but "better at
making his views felt in conversation than at holding his own
in debate."[3]

On the face of it, Phaeax seems an unlikely choice for so
delicate and important a mission. But to have sent too distinguished an ambassador might have looked suspicious, and in
any case Phaeax was clearly no fool. He had been clever enough,
as Aristophanes' young fop reminds us, to talk himself out of a
death sentence; and though the prospect of being hanged may
concentrate a man's mind wonderfully, he has to have a mind
to be concentrated in the first place. Phaeax also possessed considerable private means—Eupolis refers to the splendid table he
kept—and seems to have possessed political backing in the shape
of a "club" (hetairia) or organised claque. Such associations,
as we shall see, came to figure more and more prominently in
Athenian public life during the last two decades of the fifth
century.

Phaeax and his team scored an unlooked-for success right at
the beginning, on their coastal voyage round the toe of
Italy. Locri, the one city which had refused to ratify the Treaty
of Gela—specifically because Athens was a party to it—now
agreed to negotiate some kind of pact through the Athenian
delegates. This was not due to any change of heart, however.
Hipponium and Medma, Locri's two ports on the Tyrrhenian
Sea, had revolted. The Locrians were engaged in a desperate
struggle to win them back, and had no time or energy to spare
for other problems. Small wonder: if the overland route passed
out of their control, they could kiss their prosperity good-bye.

From Locri Phaeax sailed south-west to Sicily; his first port
of call was Catana. He scored diplomatic successes at Camarina
and Acragas; this last was a notable achievement, since Acragas

[3] This sounds like a gloss on a pithy line by the comic playwright
Eupolis, who described Phaeax as "the best of talkers and the worst of
speakers."

had immense resources and would make an extremely valuable ally.[4] But at Gela, for whatever reason, he drew a blank. Perhaps the citizens were determined to pursue an isolationist policy; perhaps they had a secret understanding with Syracuse. Whatever the truth, Phaeax "did not go to the other states, since he realised that he would not be successful with them." This tends to suggest some kind of coalition under Gela's leadership.

Instead of returning to Catana by sea, Phaeax travelled across country through Sicel territory, probably by way of Enna, Agyrium, and Centuripae. This was a clever move. Laches and Eurymedon had probably briefed him on the qualities of the Sicels as guerrilla fighters, their fierce loyalty to their allies, their deep and abiding hatred of Syracuse. Phaeax also visited the Leontinian stronghold of Bricinniae, "where he encouraged the garrison, and then sailed back to Athens," having done about as well as could have been expected of him in the circumstances. The balance of power in Sicily and Magna Graecia was now, theoretically at least, by no means unfavourable to Athens. Rhegium was her ally, and Locri at least neutral; this probably meant that Messina would be neutral too. On the east coast of Sicily Naxos, Catana, and Leontini were pro-Athenian, as were Camarina and Acragas in the south. Segesta was already Athens' ally. This left only Gela, Selinus, Himera, and Syracuse herself among the major city-states. When Phaeax put in his report, he will surely have emphasised this.

But Athens took no immediate action of any sort. Why? Cleon, it is true, was more concerned with the situation in Thrace, and after his death there was a general movement towards peace; yet this is unlikely to be the only explanation. Phaeax must have made it very clear that Syracuse was by far the most powerful state in Sicily, and that nothing short of a major expeditionary force was capable of neutralising her. If *all* the remaining Siceliot cities had joined Leontini's anti-Syracuse coalition, they might have turned the trick unaided, and the

---

[4] We hear of a distinguished Acragantine named Phaeax; it is tempting to guess that he may have been related to the Athenian ambassador—which would also suggest one reason why our Phaeax was chosen for this mission.

terms of Phaeax's mission suggest that this was what he had been sent out to achieve. On-the-spot investigation, however, made this scheme far less attractive. In Sicily negotiated alliances always looked better on paper than they did when it came to the crunch; Alcibiades, a few years later, was very scathing about the ethnic confusion and political instability of Sicilian cities. "Such a crowd as this," he remarked, "is scarcely likely either to pay attention to one consistent policy or to join together in concerted action. The chances are that they will make separate agreements with us as soon as we come forward with attractive suggestions, especially if they are, as we understand is the case, in a violent state of party strife." Phaeax was obviously of much the same opinion. Failing a solid and reliable network of alliances, nothing could be achieved without massive military intervention.

Yet from 422 to 416 Athens appears to have abandoned the Sicilian project altogether, which suggests that such military intervention did not find favour in high places. (Even in 416–415 it formed the subject of highly acrimonious debate.) On the other hand, Phaeax must have promised his Sicilian friends some sort of quid pro quo in return for their alliance: presumably, as always, armed support in an emergency. If so, Leontini (to look no further) may well have become disenchanted with the Athenians, since, as Freeman says, "it does not appear that Athens struck a blow or spoke a word on behalf of Leontini for more than seven years to come." Such a policy, indeed, may have been due to caution and nothing more: Nicias and the moderates had a very arguable case. Phaeax's mission made it all too clear that the Greek Siceliot cities—despite the Congress of Gela—were still divided and still unpredictable. They might provide the excuse for an invasion, but they could not be relied upon as allies. If Athens still intended to break Syracuse and annex Sicily, it would have to be, in the last resort, by her own efforts.

The one-year truce with Sparta expired about the time that Phaeax left Athens. Cleon at once took a major expeditionary force to Thrace; the highly successful activities of Brasidas in this area were worrying him a good deal more than the demands of the Western lobby. But in September 422 he got himself killed during an unsuccessful attack on Amphipolis, and with his death the whole political atmosphere changed overnight. Brasidas died in the same battle; thus the two men most responsible for the prolongation of hostilities were removed from the scene at one stroke, and preliminary peace-feelers were put out by both sides almost immediately.

The Spartan government had several good reasons for wanting the war wound up. Their thirty-year peace treaty with Argos was due to expire, and no one was quite sure which way Argos would turn when it did. Cleon's war of attrition had made severe inroads on their never very stable economy. On the Athenian side, morale was lower than at any time since the great plague. Farms and homesteads lay in ruins, and their owners formed the most determined section of the pacifist group. Slaves had begun to desert in increasing numbers. Young men were evading military service whenever they could. There was a rumour circulating that Persia might, at last, intervene on the wrong side. The only cheerful people, as usual, were profiteers making a good thing out of the war itself.

Peace negotiations went on all through the winter of 422–421. Nicias, the chief Athenian advocate of a settlement, held endless conferences with King Pleistoanax of Sparta. Euripides wrote his *Erechtheus*, evoking the famous image of the spider spinning its web on the disused spear. Comic poets lashed out against the dissolute spendthrift younger generation, symbolised by Alcibiades and his friends. This did not stop them also harping continually on the material advantages and pleasures of peace—the reopening of closed markets, the renewed importation of foreign luxury goods.

By the spring of 421 everyone's patience had begun to fray. The horse-trading claims and counter-claims seemed endless. At one point Sparta ordered her allies "to prepare for building permanent fortifications in Attica—all this in order to make the Athenians more inclined to accept the terms offered." But at last, in April, Sparta and Athens reached a working arrangement. "It was agreed," says Thucydides, "that peace should be made on the basis of each party's giving back what it had acquired during the war." (One exception: Athens was to keep Nisaea, the port of Megara—though, as she did not hold Pegae, this was no great concession.) The treaty was for fifty years. Among its more important provisions were the restoration of Amphipolis to Athens, the freeing of all Spartan prisoners—including the Spartiates captured on Sphacteria—and the evacuation of several important blockade points, such as Cythera, around the Peloponnese.

The Peace of Nicias, as it came to be known, was doomed to failure from its inception. As one historian put it, "with the satisfaction of Athenian and Lacedaemonian interests, the force of principle was exhausted." Nicias and Pleistoanax had arranged things to their own advantage, and the allies of either side got very short shrift indeed. In Athens' case this made little difference: her imperial subjects were used to rough justice. But Sparta's free allies expected something better. No provision had been made for Boeotia. Megara was still left with an Athenian garrison occupying Nisaea. Most outrageous of all, there was no hint that Corinth would get back her vital possessions in north-west Greece.

It is hardly surprising that these three states, together with Elis, voted against accepting the treaty as it stood. They could argue, with some cogency, that the Ten Years' War had been —from the Peloponnesian League's point of view—a completely useless exercise. "Give the Greeks their freedom," Sparta had told the Athenians in 431; yet now Pleistoanax was agreeing to terms which merely confirmed Athens' authority over her maritime empire. Piraeus and the Long Walls were still intact. The one vital possession that had been wrested from Athens, Amphipolis, was now to be restored to her. As a superficial concession to the anti-imperialists, the treaty contained a clause specifying that Athens should not take up arms against any of her subject-allies whose cities Sparta had returned, "so long as they pay the tribute." But who would ever enforce this regulation?

The Athenians, then, had, on balance, achieved an advantageous settlement; but it still left all their major problems unresolved. The Peloponnesian League had not been eliminated; both sides would continue to jockey for every market in sight. Apart from this, the treaty depended on co-operation, and co-operation was conspicuous by its absence from the very start. Corinth and her fellow-rebels persisted in their refusal to accept the terms of the peace, despite strenuous attempts at coercion by Sparta. In the end the Spartans were forced to write their allies off altogether, and make a private *alliance* with Athens— one of the oddest political *mariages de convenance* in history.

There was also the problem of Amphipolis: as things turned out its restoration proved much easier to decree than to implement. The Spartan garrison commander, Clearidas, flatly refused to hand the town over, arguing that it was impossible to do so against the wishes of the inhabitants themselves—a neat and unanswerable point. The peace, in fact, as Thucydides saw so clearly, was no peace at all. "One has only to look at the facts," he wrote, "to see that it is hardly possible to use the word 'peace' of a situation in which neither side gave back or received what had been promised." Though this is something of an exaggeration, Amphipolis was indeed never returned—a fact which must have made many eyes in Athens turn longingly towards the great forests of Sicily and Magna Graecia once more.[5]

The events of the next six years—the "phoney peace"—are unbelievably complicated: a bewildering succession of alliances and counter-alliances, of political intrigue and chessboard manoeuvring. However, behind this clutter of detail the situation was, in essence, simple enough. There was a continuing three-way struggle—between Sparta, Athens, and the dissident members of the Peloponnesian League, such as Corinth and Boeotia—for the alliance of Argos. In Athens the main advocate of this

[5] The idea was certainly in the air still: Aristophanes' *Peace* (421) shows us Trygaeus flying off on his Sicilian dung-beetle to prepare "a new and daring adventure on behalf of all the Greeks."

"Argos policy" was Alcibiades, and its main opponent (as we might expect), the pious and conservative Nicias, who clung stubbornly to his dream of peace with Sparta, and feared that an Athenian-Argive alliance might spark off another general war.

The personal quarrel between Nicias and Alcibiades had its genesis in this head-on political clash. But the two men could never have found each other temperamentally congenial. There was no true point of contact between them. What did the young, brilliant, raffish fop, with his pet quail and his affected lisp and his endless drunken escapades, in bed or out of it, have in common with a prim, elderly teetotaller, soured by disease and pious as any old maid? Indeed, Alcibiades not only disliked Nicias, but—the thing which Nicias could never forgive or forget—on several occasions made a laughingstock of him.

In the spring of 420, after much hatchet work in the *coulisses*, Alcibiades—now elected to the Board of Generals—persuaded Argos to repudiate her treaty with Sparta, and the Athenian Assembly to accept an Argive alliance. Nicias, returning from Sparta with nothing better than a formal treaty renewal, found all his patient work undone. But it is not hard to see what Alcibiades and the pro-Argos party were aiming at. Alliance with Argos also meant alliance, now, with Elis and with Mantinea, in Arcadia. This created an anti-Spartan bloc right across the central Peloponnese, the same alignment as Themistocles had worked to achieve half a century earlier. It also suggested a possible land-route to the Gulf of Corinth, either from Argos itself or from some point on the Saronic Gulf. Athens, though she held Nisaea, was still debarred from the isthmus crossing, and still searching for an alternative route that did not involve the dangerous sea voyage round Cape Malea.[6]

One event which must have given a powerful boost to Alcibiades' policy was the destruction of Cyme, which took place

[6] It is interesting, too, and perhaps not wholly coincidental, that Argos, Elis, and Mantinea were all first-class wheat-growing areas. They could not raise enough surplus to make any substantial difference to Athens' requirements; but they might well be able to tide her over in a real emergency.

in the summer of 420. As many observers surely predicted, the Samnites in Campania did not rest content with one victory. Capua was only the prelude to further aggression. They marched on Cyme with a large army, took it by storm after a short siege, and largely destroyed its defence forces. Cyme was plundered, its men killed or sold into slavery, its women taken over by Samnite settlers. Those who managed to escape fled to Naples. It is clear that, for the time being at least, the whole Greek-based commercial economy of Campania broke down. This meant, *inter alia,* that the export trade fell into abeyance—an event which the pottery deposits faithfully record. Here was a second and most compelling reason to reconsider the "Grand Design" on Sicily.

Meanwhile there was still the need to establish a temporary land-route for Western traffic which would by-pass Corinth. In the spring of 419 Alcibiades and the Argives marched through the Peloponnese to Patrae (Patras) on the Corinthian Gulf, and built long walls from the city to its port. But an attempt to establish a fortress at Rhium, a few miles up the coast, where the mouth of the gulf is narrowest, proved less successful. The Corinthians forestalled this move, and with good reason. Holding Rhium was very like holding Messina: it gave those who did so control of the straits. At the other end of the line, as it were, the Argives invaded Epidaurus; but Sparta quickly slipped a garrison into the town. The campaigning during this period somewhat resembles a large-scale game of noughts and crosses: continual frustrated attempts to draw a line between two or three strategic points.

It was obvious, however, that sooner or later the Argive problem would provoke an open trial of strength. In the summer of 418 a major expeditionary force was assembled by the Peloponnesian League, and set out against Argos. Argos called on her allies; all of them responded promptly except the Athenians, who were held up by Nicias' delaying tactics. In the end it took Cleon's successor Hyperbolus to force the mobilisation order through, against Nicias' pious rant about unfavourable omens. Even so, the Athenian contingent turned up late, to find that

Argos, instead of fighting Agis and his Spartans, had made a four-month truce with them. The details of this undercover deal remain obscure; but the Athenians—in particular, Alcibiades, who had come with them as a special envoy—refused to accept it. They wanted a showdown; and a month later they got it—though not with the result they had so confidently anticipated. At the battle of Mantinea, Sparta and her allies inflicted a crushing defeat on the Argos coalition. It was the end of all Alcibiades' plans; it made his Argive policy obsolete overnight. There were ugly hints of betrayal and collusion. Alcibiades remained in Argos until late autumn rather than return to Athens and face the wrath of the Assembly.

Meanwhile Sparta's Argive supporters had not been idle. A successful right-wing coup took place in the city, and the new government lost no time in renouncing the tripartite alliance with Athens that Alcibiades had worked so hard to secure. In its place they proceeded to sign a fifty-year treaty with Sparta. Then, as Diodorus tells us, "they first of all seized the men who had been accustomed to be the leaders of the people and put them to death, and then, by terrorising the rest of the citizens, they abolished the laws and were proceeding to take the management of the state into their own hands."

Almost the first joint act of Argos and Sparta as allies was, predictably enough, to send a mission into the Thraceward regions to see whether King Perdiccas could be made to change sides once again; the timber shortage was general, and Perdiccas must have been doing very well all round. He cheerfully swore alliances with the ambassadors of both Sparta and Argos, but at the same time omitted to repudiate his previous treaty with the Athenians. Cumulatively, there is something very disarming about Perdiccas: his blatant and single-minded self-interest has its own gritty charm—especially when set against the high moral line which both Sparta and Athens so sedulously maintained.

By 417 Athens was feeling the pinch of hunger: grain prices had risen, and comic poets like Hermippus and Aristophanes were making jokes about empty bellies, lean cattle, iron rations. The Spartans, to judge by their strategy, knew very well what

Athens was after in the Peloponnese, and were at some pains to forestall any moves she might make there. One of the most likely—and shortest—overland routes between the Aegean and the Corinthian Gulf was the Argos-Sicyon link; Sparta (with Argive co-operation) set up a right-wing government in Sicyon as well as Argos. The Spartans also, as Thucydides blandly observes, "took various measures in Achaea, making matters easier for them there than they had been previously." This move was understandable enough: the Achaeans controlled the most vital stretch of the Corinthian Gulf, including Patrae and Rhium.

That same spring (417) a projected expedition to recover Amphipolis—the Spartans protested that they lacked the strength to enforce its surrender—had to be abandoned because of renewed double-dealing by Perdiccas. Nicias was the general chosen for this command, and rumour had it that he paid a thousand drachmas in an attempt to get out of the appointment. At the same time it looks very much as though the Athenian garrison in Aenus—permanent since 429—was suddenly withdrawn. If this is true, it is an event of capital importance. With Amphipolis lost, this great Thracian port had become doubly indispensable.

The garrison troops were normally paid in small coins known as diobols. For a decade or so before 417 large numbers of diobols turn up in excavations at Aenus. Then the flow suddenly dries up altogether and is replaced by large quantities of tetradrachms. It has been suggested that the garrison was removed as a concession to ensure friendship and loyalty, and special trading facilities granted to the local population. But this, surely, would have been to take an appalling risk. If an Athenian garrison vanished from Aenus in 417, it was, one suspects, none of Athens' doing. The grim implication is that Aenus was lost, as Amphipolis had been lost, either through a coup or by enemy action.[7] The tetradrachms (which were, in

[7] There is also the possibility that Athens' concession in Aenus was revoked by the Thracian government, perhaps as a result of representations from Sparta.

any case, international currency) would then represent what local merchants had hoarded during the Athenian occupation.

If this was what in fact took place, Athens' position in 417 could scarcely have been worse. She had lost her Campanian grain market; she was shut out of Aenus; she had failed to win back Amphipolis. Her imports from Thrace and Macedonia must have fallen virtually to nil. We can understand the stringent measures now taken against profiteers who exported goods illegally to enemy countries, not to mention the crop of narks and informers which sprang up all over Athens. But about midsummer a providential counter-revolution in Argos brought the democrats back into power. It is hard to believe that Athens did not play some part in engineering so timely a *Putsch*, especially when we see what followed. While the Spartans were still debating whether or not to march on Argos and restore the oligarchic regime (they had a convenient religious festival as a reason for not doing so), Alcibiades turned up there, with an Athenian detachment, and helped the democrats consolidate their position. He then, as Plutarch says, "persuaded the Argives to build Long Walls and so, by joining their city to the sea, to make it dependent on the sea-power of Athens." The walls of Patrae were similarly rebuilt. Thus Argos not only became immune to any land-based blockade, but also possessed a negotiable, if lengthy, overland route to the Corinthian Gulf. Alcibiades did not go so far as to bring carpenters and stonemasons from Athens without a very good reason for it.

Some anonymous cynic, who was obviously well acquainted with Athenian duplicity, warned the Argives against their over-trustfulness. Athens, he said, would gobble them up. To which Alcibiades retorted: "Maybe; but at least it will be by degrees and feet first—Sparta would swallow you head first at one gulp!" But on the whole, enthusiasm for this new Athenian entente cordiale won the day. Thucydides tells us that the entire population, women, children, and slaves included, turned out to help build the walls. Late that autumn the Spartans—who were still in touch with their supporters in Argos—at last marched against the city; they destroyed the new walls, but failed to reduce Argos itself.

There was one thing at least which could be done about this situation. In March 416 Alcibiades, who had once more been elected to the Board of Generals, sailed to Argos with a squadron of twenty ships, and proceeded to purge the city of its unreliable (i.e., pro-Spartan) elements. Three hundred citizens were rounded up and deported. A fifty-year alliance was signed between Athens and Argos. Having settled these matters, Alcibiades took off, together with his seven chariot teams, to the Olympic Games, where he proceeded to win first, second, and fourth prizes. This flamboyant display was, in part, a *réplique* to Nicias' equally lavish generosity during the religious festival on Delos the previous year. Both men were bidding for public popularity, and both succumbed to what Plutarch—rightly—describes as "a certain vulgarity and ostentation" in the process. Nicias' bronze palm-tree and gilded bridge of boats are no less culpable on this score than Alcibiades' decorated tent and endless sacrificial animals.

The same spring saw the beginning of Athens' notorious campaign against the small island of Melos, which suggests that she was concerned to develop or safeguard her trade-routes to North Africa. The Athenian garrison at Pylos conducted a series of raids into Messenia, and, says Thucydides, "captured a great quantity of plunder from Spartan territory." It goes without saying that much of this "plunder" must have been Messenia's wheat or barley harvest. The Corinthians, too, were embroiled with Athens (when were they ever not?) over what Thucydides calls "certain private differences"; but "the rest of the Peloponnesians stayed quiet." It was a brooding, ominous quietness: the lull before the storm.

All the circumstances favouring the "Grand Design" were now present. It only needed some specific impetus to set events in motion. Then, about September 416, from a remote and semi-barbarous settlement in north-west Sicily, an embassy reached Athens. It was like any one of a hundred such delegations which arrived every year; there was nothing to mark it off from the rest. Yet these undistinguished envoys were the unwitting agents of destiny. The action which they precipitated only ran its course three years later, in a bloody shambles which destroyed Athens' imperial dream for ever, and by so doing profoundly altered the entire subsequent history of Europe.

CHAPTER VI: *An Embassy from Segesta*

The quarrel between Segesta and Selinus was a typical example of that local internecine feuding which bedevilled Sicily throughout the fifth century, and which the Congress of Gela was powerless to prevent. Segesta lay in the north-west of the island, Selinus in the south-west. Both were wheat-growing states; to judge from their fine temples and public buildings they both made a good thing out of foreign trade. Selinus, until some time after the Persian Wars, had suffered badly from malaria, and her leaders consulted Empedocles, the philosopher-engineer from Acragas, on how to deal with it. Empedocles—a surprisingly modern figure in many ways—suggested a marsh-drainage scheme. This was duly carried out. But (a fact which tells us something about the Selinuntines) credit, as the coins show, went primarily to Apollo, Heracles, and the local river-gods.

Segesta was an Elymite community, though sufficiently Hellenised by 460–450 to produce Greek-type coins and, later, good Doric architecture.[1] The boundary between her territory and that of Selinus was the Cremisus River, and there are coins which show the eponymous river-god Cremisus keeping guard over his boundary mark. This was the main issue at stake between the two cities. The Selinuntines had crossed over the stream, and occupied the littoral on the Segestan side by main force. Later, as Diodorus says, "they cut off for their own a large piece of the adjoining territory, utterly disregarding the rights of the injured parties." The Segestans at first made

[1] Burford (see Bibliography) suggests that the motive for building the great unfinished Doric temple at Segesta was, primarily, to have a show of fine architecture as evidence of the city's cultural enthusiasm and for the sake of impressing the Athenians (and the Selinuntines). This seems something of an overstatement.

diplomatic representations, not only about this territorial encroachment, but also concerning what Thucydides calls, rather mysteriously, "certain marriage rights."[2] But the men of Selinus ignored their complaints, and so in the end Segesta mustered an army and expelled the interlopers. This gave rise to a full-scale war between the two cities, in which Segesta was badly beaten. The Segestans, realising that they were no match for Selinus single-handed, began touting around for allies. They seem to have won the support of Eryx, their Western neighbour; but applications to Acragas and Syracuse met, in each case, with a blank refusal. Indeed, we afterwards find Syracusan troops fighting against them, as allies of Selinus.

Having thus run through the list of potential supporters in Sicily itself, they hopefully sent envoys to Carthage, but drew blank there also. It was only when all else failed that they decided to approach Athens, despite the treaty which existed between the two cities. Such hesitation is not to be wondered at. As the events of the past decade had shown, Athens was a dangerous and unpredictable ally, whose aims in Sicily were suspect, to say the least of it. Any city which invoked her aid might well live to regret the day it did so. But the Segestans had no alternative. On the other hand, they were not the only city in Sicily anxious to secure Athenian support. The independent group holding Leontini had lately come under increasing pressure from Syracuse; even after seven years it might be that the casual promises made by Phaeax would produce aid of some sort. Segestans and Leontinians met and discussed their problems. Finally they decided to dispatch a joint embassy to Athens, appealing for support against the aggressive tactics of Selinus and Syracuse, and—as Diodorus rather ominously puts it—"promising to assist the Athenians in establishing order in the affairs of Sicily."

When the ambassadors reached Athens they found a ready

---

[2] Dover's explanation of this is surely the right one: "The right to choose a wife from another state without thereby depriving one's children of citizen rights was a subject of interstate agreement and therefore, on occasion, of interstate disputes."

audience. The moment was ripe, and men like Alcibiades and Hyperbolus had long since conditioned the younger generation with inflammatory talk of Western conquest. But at the same time there was a respectable body of opinion—moderate conservatives, middle-class landowners—which regarded any such overseas venture as highly inadvisable. After five years of peace, Athens had just about got her public finances on an even keel again, and repaired the worst of the damage to her farms and vineyards. Why risk all this now for some hare-brained scheme of aggression in the West?

The Segestans seem to have gauged the temper of the opposition with some accuracy. What they harped upon, continually, was the growing menace of Syracuse. Syracuse had already depopulated Leontini without anyone raising a finger to stop her. At this rate her leaders would soon eliminate all Athens' other Sicilian allies, reducing them piecemeal by sheer brute force. And when they were the masters of all Sicily, was it not clear what the Syracusans would do next? They were Dorians, colonists of Corinth, allied to the Peloponnesians by blood and tradition. What was to prevent them assembling a great armada and uniting with Sparta to destroy the power of Athens for ever? Would it not be wiser to destroy *them* before they grew too strong? Such arguments had a particularly insidious appeal, since they echoed, with considerable exactitude, Athens' own plans for the invasion and reduction of Sicily itself. We need hardly doubt that the Segestans knew this only too well: their subsequent actions prove them past-masters in the art of political chicanery. One point they emphasised, at various meetings of the Assembly, was their ability to make a large financial contribution towards the cost of the campaign. They also offered to fight as Athens' and Leontini's ally against Syracuse. The Leontinian ambassadors merely repeated most of these points, though they also invoked the ties of kinship over and above mere treaty obligations—something the Segestans were in no position to do.

The reaction of the Athenians was cagey, to say the least of it. Though the young might be on fire for adventure, older

and more experienced heads clearly found these proposals somewhat suspicious. No vote was taken, at this stage, either for or
against an expedition. Instead, the Athenians decided to dispatch their own ambassadors to Sicily, with two objects in view:
first, to report on the progress of the war between Segesta and
Selinus, and second, to find out whether the Segestans really
possessed, in their treasury and temple reserves, the amount of
hard cash and bullion which they said they did. How the
Segestan envoys received this somewhat insulting announcement
we are not told; probably—since Athenian suspicions, it seems,
were only too well justified—with sorrow rather than anger.

Hardly had this investigating commission left Athens[3] when
the island of Melos, under siege since the spring, finally capit-
ulated. After its surrender every adult male was slaughtered, and
the women and children sold into slavery. Five hundred Athenian settlers were sent out to repopulate the island. This barbaric action sounds like the work of Hyperbolus, Cleon's successor and imitator. On the other hand, it aroused no real
opposition. We know that Alcibiades—and probably Nicias
too—voted in favour of the measure when it was debated. Such
brutal massacres were no new thing in Athens' history—or, indeed, in Sparta's. But the quasi-genocide employed against the
Melians was unique in two respects: it happened in peacetime,
and seemingly by general consent. Twelve years earlier, when
Cleon had demanded a similar mass execution on Mytilene, the
Assembly had a change of heart and revoked their decree. But
Melos got no such reprieve: a sharp indication of the brutalising
effect which a long war and total disruption of her ancient
mores had had on Athens. It is also significant that—despite
the Peace of Nicias—not one word of protest came from Sparta.
But then Sparta, too, believed in discipline and the demands of
Machtpolitik: with similar mass executions at Plataea and Hysiae
on her own record, she was in no position to take a high moral
line against the Athenians. All the same, the mere fact of her

[3] This must have been in late September; they probably arrived in
Sicily during the first week or so of October. Another week or two, and
the weather would have made the voyage impossible.

abstention must have given the Western lobby considerable encouragement.

During the winter of 416–415 a great deal of backstairs lobbying and hatchet work went on in anticipation of the embassy's return from Segesta. No one was busier than Cleon's successor as leader of the radical party, the former lamp-maker Hyperbolus.[4] He had always—ever since proposing that expedition against Carthage in 424—regarded himself as the party's unofficial spokesman for Western expansionism. If the "Grand Design" was at last to become a reality, Hyperbolus had every intention of reaping the benefits in person. But to do so he had to neutralise not only those who, like Nicias, opposed the scheme altogether, but also dangerous rivals in his own camp. The most obvious of these were Alcibiades and Phaeax. The latter, after his diplomatic mission in 422, could with some reason style himself a Sicilian expert. Alcibiades was, quite simply, infatuated with the whole romantic idea of Western conquest (though he brought a very cool head to it) and determined, at the same time, to make a rich killing from the proceeds. Both were fluent and handsome young aristocrats with a considerable following among their contemporaries. Alcibiades, in particular, as Plutarch says, "was dreaming of Carthage and Libya, and after that of investing Italy and the Peloponnese"; the whole idea had become exciting, fashionable, a little heady and unreal.

Hyperbolus had not the least intention of being elbowed aside in this venture by some Johnny-come-lately from the *jeunesse dorée*. He therefore, about the turn of the year, proposed that an ostracism should be held in the spring.[5] It is possible that his main intention was at least as much for the

---

[4] If there is any truth in the tradition that a Syracusan embassy came to Athens during the winter of 416–415 (and most historians reject it), then it will undoubtedly have been Hyperbolus who turned down their proposed offer of alliance.

[5] The date of this ostracism has been much disputed: it has also been placed in 417 and 416. I accept the arguments in favour of 415 advanced by Raubitschek, and developed by Camon (see Bibliography).

public good as for his own private benefit. The quarrel between Nicias and Alcibiades was deep and seemingly irreconcilable. It embodied a basic division of opinion which might well paralyse the administrative powers of the Assembly altogether. In any case, Hyperbolus must have calculated that he could not lose from the result of an ostracism. If Nicias was exiled, the main opponent of Western expansion would be removed. If the lot fell on either Phaeax or Alcibiades, Hyperbolus would lose a dangerous rival. Besides, whichever of these two went, the other was bound to be easier to eliminate on his own. But the radical leader—characteristically, when we remember his origins—had failed to make allowance for one vital factor, the ingrained class-consciousness of Athenian society, which produced something very must akin to the modern Establishment.

After a month or two of private canvassing it became clear enough that the ostracism, as predicted, was bound to fall on either Phaeax, Alcibiades, or Nicias. All three, despite their personal or political differences, had far more in common with one another than with Hyperbolus. They also each possessed a claque of political supporters. What took place during the period immediately before the ostracism—despite some ambiguity in our sources—is all too clear. The moving force, from first to last, was Alcibiades. He began by approaching Phaeax, and revealing what he had in mind. If all three of them united their block votes, they would not only be safe from ostracism themselves, but in a position to pick their own victim. Two against one *might* work; three together was a certainty. Phaeax at once agreed. But Nicias, whose personal distaste for Alcibiades was a dominant factor in his decisions, might be harder to persuade. So Alcibiades and Phaeax approached him jointly, and to begin with threatened that they would unite their followers against *him*. Having thus got the old man into a corner, they offered him their alternative solution, and he accepted it gratefully.

So, as Plutarch says, "they came to a secret agreement to combine their interests, and by setting all their supporters to work, they combined to divert the ostracism from themselves."

But the best was yet to come. When the "potsherd vote" was counted, the people's choice—poetic justice, Alcibiades might have said—turned out to be Hyperbolus himself. At first this caused vast amusement: it was the kind of joke Athenians (then as now) found particularly piquant. But after a while laughter gave way to annoyance. There was a kind of distinction in ostracism: the roll-call of its victims contained some of the noblest names in Athenian history—Themistocles, Aristeides, Xanthippus, and many others. By adding Hyperbolus to their number the institution had been degraded. It was never employed again.

In March 415 Euripides produced his play *The Trojan Women*, a bitterly passionate attack on military barbarism, which must have been written with the recent sack of Melos in mind. Yet amid the pathos and the horror he still managed to slip in a quick reference to the lure of the West. Would I were in Sicily, the Chorus sings, in the land by Etna, mother of Sicilian mountains, bulwark against Carthage, or wandering through the richly watered Crathis Valley above Sybaris! The reference has no point except in allusion to current events. Clearly Euripides approved the idea of a Sicilian expedition, as he afterwards showed in his *Electra*, where we find the Dioscuri declaring: "We two must rush to Sicilian seas,/rescue the salt-smashed prows of the fleet." Putting Melians to the sword was barbarous, but presumably the men of Syracuse needed no pity from anyone. Hermocrates had preached isolation; very well, then: if they were foreigners, they could be killed like foreigners. This, of course, flatly contradicted Euripides' claim, in the *Cyclops*, that Sicily formed an integral part of Hellas; but then Euripides was almost as prone to self-contradiction as Walt Whitman.

What *The Trojan Women* makes clear—and the whole subsequent course of events confirms—is that not for one moment did anyone in Athens have *moral* qualms about the Sicilian Expedition. Many thought it rash or suicidal, but that was quite another matter. Melos produced, even if only in a minority, a sense of guilt. The prospect of raping Sicily, on the other hand, aroused nothing but excitement among the expansionists, and practical objections from moderates like Nicias. He was not against invading Sicily on principle: we may search the pages of Thucydides in vain for any hint of such scruples. He merely questioned whether the projected invasion had any chance of success.

Throughout that winter (416–415) Sparta and Athens, though not openly at war, spent much time and ingenuity encouraging one another's enemies. A Spartan force raided Argive territory, and (a significant point) proceeded to carry off the wheat harvest in wagons specially brought along for that purpose. The Athenians sent a cavalry force, together with some Macedonian exiles, to raid Perdiccas' territory from Methone. The Spartans retaliated by attempting—unsuccessfully—to make the local Chalcidians renounce their treaty with Athens and join Perdiccas. This ambivalent atmosphere of cold war and intrigue had its symbolic expression in the spring, when both Nicias and Alcibiades were re-elected to the Board of Generals. The hot-headed map-sketchers and armchair strategists had their representative; so did the cautious, non-belligerent middle classes. Only Hyperbolus had been removed from the scene, soon to be replaced by another radical named Androcles. It was now, about the first or second week in April, that the fact-finding mission sent out to Segesta reached Athens once more, together with the same Segestan ambassadors as had previously spoken before the Assembly.

They had all, it was clear, got on very well together during the winter. The Segestans brought with them sixty talents of bar silver, a month's pay for a squadron of sixty ships—which was what they asked Athens to send out. An initial meeting of the Assembly was held at once (?10 April). Having heard glowing reports from the various delegates about the wealth of Segesta, and the amount of reserve bullion in the city's temples, the Assembly voted in favour of dispatching a sixty-ship squadron as requested. After some initial uncertainty—the idea of a single commander-in-chief had been canvassed and rejected,

probably because Alcibiades was the one obvious candidate—
the Assembly further decided on a tripartite High Command,
consisting of Alcibiades, Nicias, and Lamachus. These three
generals were invested with full powers, and their official instructions were "to help the Segestans against the Selinuntines,
to re-establish Leontini also, if things went well with them in
the war, and in general to make the kind of provisions for
Sicily which might seem to them most in accordance with
Athenian interests."

It is to be noted that though the final clause more or less
gave them carte blanche to act as they pleased, there was no
open vote taken on the "Grand Design." No one, during this
first session, actually got up before the Assembly and said, in
so many words, that the aim of this expedition was in fact the
subjugation of Sicily. Everything went through smoothly, without challenge. A second debate was scheduled to take place in
four days' time; this was intended merely "to discuss the
quickest means of getting the ships ready to sail and to vote
any additional supplies that the generals might need for the
expedition." It should have been a routine debate; in the event,
it proved nothing of the sort. During those four days something had happened to make Nicias change his mind about the
entire expedition. He had not, so far as we know, spoken during the first debate; he had raised no immediate objection
when appointed to the High Command. Yet when the Assembly met again, he both claimed to have been appointed
general against his will, and gave it as his considered opinion
that the whole expedition was a fundamental mistake. What
led him to perform this ill-timed volte-face?

It is clear enough—the terms of the second debate in themselves suggest it—that during those four days the three newly
appointed commanders held their own private meeting to discuss details of strategy and logistics. At this meeting Alcibiades
will undoubtedly have outlined his plans for implementing
the "Grand Design." Marketplace fantasy was one thing, but
Alcibiades, clearly, meant every word he said. Nicias was horrified. From that moment he became a dedicated opponent of

the entire project: when the second debate was held, Nicias used it as a means of getting the question reconsidered *ab initio*. He openly declared in his speech that "the city"—a discreet generalisation—"was in fact aiming at conquering the whole of Sicily—a very considerable undertaking indeed." It could be argued that these shock tactics in one sense constituted a breach of confidence: presumably anything said at a conference of the High Command was privileged—and also top-secret. But Nicias, it is obvious, would stop at nothing in his determination to prevent the Sicilian venture taking place.

No one could deny him the courage of his convictions. The majority was dead against him, and such moderate supporters as he could find were liable to be men of slight influence. "The rich," as Plutarch observes, "were afraid of being accused of evading their contribution to the cost of the expedition and the provision of ships, and so kept silent against their better judgment." But Nicias was not deterred. He knew his own mind now. The war between Selinus and Segesta, he argued, had nothing to do with Athens, and he was determined not to let his fellow-countrymen get involved in it "on the credit of foreigners." This is an interesting phrase, and has some bearing on subsequent events.

When the expedition reached Sicily it turned out—or so we are told—that the investigating mission had been outrageously duped as to the city's financial resources. The money they saw had been borrowed, partly from Segesta's own citizens, and partly from neighbouring states. When private dinner-parties were given for the crews of the triremes, the Segestans collected all the gold and silver cups and dishes they could lay hands on, and paraded them at each banquet in turn as though they were the host's private service. The delegates, convinced by this dazzling display, reported accordingly. The episode is typical of that curious uncertainty which permeates so many events connected with the Sicilian Expedition. What at first looks plain and straightforward becomes, on investigation, increasingly ambiguous. The whole story bristles with improbabilities. To begin with, from the substantial and impressive archaeological remains still preserved today, it looks as though Segesta was far wealthier than this anecdote would imply. In any case, why should the Segestans, who were not complete fools, go to the lengths of perpetrating an elaborate hoax that would inevitably be revealed soon after the Athenian task-force reached Sicily?

There is also the curious reticence of Nicias to be considered. When the supposed fraud was revealed, Thucydides tells us that Nicias, alone of the generals, seemed to be expecting it; and from his words at the second debate it would appear that he had a shrewd idea even then of what had been going on. In that case, why did he so improbably keep this vital knowledge to himself? He could hardly have had a more powerful weapon for jamming the expedition at its very outset. The obvious conclusion is that he knew nothing—perhaps because there was nothing to know. Could it not be that the whole circumstantial story of Segesta's fraudulence was invented by Alcibiades for his own purposes? He had an excellent motive for doing so. The last thing he (or indeed Lamachus) wanted was to waste precious time and tactical advantage over Segesta's dispute with Selinus—even though this had provided Athens with her excuse for invading Sicily in the first place. If Segesta could be smeared with a double-dealing charge of this sort, then the expedition was absolved from any need to fulfil Athens' half of the bargain. To suggest that Nicias knew of the scheme beforehand—perhaps the accusation was made during discussions with Thucydides the historian, when both he and Alcibiades were in exile—would then simply be a piece of extra and gratuitous personal malice.

The bargain, certainly, never was fulfilled, despite Nicias' insistence that it should be the expedition's main object. One half-hearted attempt was made to "look into the affairs of the Selinuntines" (significantly, just after Alcibiades' defection), but this fizzled out before the expedition even reached Selinus. All that Segesta ever got out of Athens was the tiny town of Hyccara on the north coast—and even then Nicias made a packet out of selling off the inhabitants as slaves before the hand-over. After this there is only one further reference to Segesta during the whole course of the Sicilian campaign, when we find the Athenians trying to commandeer cavalry there.

If the fraud was genuine, and Nicias *did* have prior knowledge of it, it is hard to explain his silence. Perhaps he could not prove his allegations (and at such a distance it must have been virtually impossible to do so); perhaps he was afraid of the Assembly's conceivably violent reaction. Perhaps he even calculated that since nothing short of a miracle would stop the Athenians launching an expedition now, it might be useful to have a good on-the-spot excuse for withdrawal. His speech during the second debate, on the other hand, was packed with excellent and irrefutable arguments for cancelling the project *in toto*. To begin with, he pointed out that sending a major expedition against Sicily would leave Athens dangerously vulnerable at home. He had no illusions, now, as to the binding powers of the treaty that had been made in his name. He knew how explosive the situation in Thrace was; the events of the last few months had made it clear that Sparta was only waiting for a chance to stab Athens in the back. "This is no time," he remarked drily, "for grasping at a new empire before we have secured the one we have already."[6] Besides, he went on, even supposing Athens defeated Syracuse and the Sicilians, how was such a vast and distant territory to be kept permanently in subjection? (The answer, presumably, was large-scale colonisation by emigrant citizens, which would also relieve over-population.) The danger of aggression by Syracuse had been much exaggerated. More important, it was only now that Athens was beginning to recover from the serious losses in cash reserves and manpower that war and plague had between them inflicted on her.

[6] Diodorus, in his version of the speech (12.83.6) adds the cogent observation that even the mighty Carthaginians, who had made many attempts on Sicily, had never succeeded in subduing it, though their resources were far greater than those of Athens. This looks like fourth-century hindsight on the part of Diodorus' source. At the time information about Carthage was far less adequate—and optimism concerning Athens' ability to defeat her, far greater in consequence.

Then Nicias suddenly abandoned general strategic considerations, and made a venomous, totally unexpected attack on Alcibiades. This passage has the ring of remembered truth about it; it does not sound as though it was invented by Thucydides. "No doubt there is someone sitting here"—we can imagine the bitter snarl in the old man's voice—"who is delighted at having been chosen for the command and who, entirely for his own selfish reasons, will urge you to make the expedition—and all the more because he is too young for his post—" At this all eyes must have turned to Alcibiades: no one could accuse Lamachus of immaturity. Nicias went on with his tirade, attacking Alcibiades' racing stable, his profligate private life, his determination to use the expedition as a means of paying off his vast debts, the political voting claque now gathered round him. He called for the support of all older, wiser heads in the Assembly—"If any one of you is sitting next to one of *his* supporters, do not allow yourself to be brow-beaten or be frightened of being called a coward if you do not vote for war." Not once did Nicias name Alcibiades; but if Thucydides' report of his speech reflects the truth, he scarcely needed to do so.

Alcibiades had to be very careful how he dealt with this attack. Obviously one of Nicias' aims was to provoke him into some damaging indiscretion. When he replied, he gave no specific details concerning his master plan for the Sicilian campaign, nor on the armament he considered necessary to implement it. If his listeners were expecting a personal counterattack on Nicias, with sharp allusions to his age, health, indecisiveness, and pietistic pacifism, they were in for a disappointment. Instead, Alcibiades pointed out the benefits that would accrue from a partnership between the two of them. Both men, for once, were piquantly out of character. While Nicias had thrown restraint to the winds, Alcibiades had shown himself a master of moderation. Nothing was better calculated to counteract the distrust which his raffish personal habits and wild ambitions aroused in the conservative mind.

He began by justifying his extravagant way of life, pointing out (quite correctly) that such things as the chariot victories he had won at Olympia brought prestige to his country no less than to himself. Brilliant people, he remarked without rancour, are always unpopular; success always breeds envy—"and it is perfectly fair for a man who has a high opinion of himself not to be put on a level with everyone else; certainly when one is badly off one does not find people coming to share in one's misfortunes." About his political activities he could not be quite so confident. He claimed credit for engineering the Argos-Elis-Mantinea-Athens coalition; but that coalition had been destroyed by the battle of Mantinea, concerning which he remarked, somewhat disingenuously, that "though [the Spartans] were victorious . . . they have not even yet quite recovered their confidence."

But the most interesting part of Alcibiades' speech, from our point of view—and probably in the opinion of the Assembly as well—is his analysis of the political and military situation in Sicily. He pointed out that the Sicilian cities had swarming populations of mixed ethnic origins, with constant changes of government and constitution: this made for a lack of national or local patriotism. People were merely interested in getting what they could out of the regime they happened to be under; if things went wrong, they could always move on somewhere else. Concerted action was hardly to be expected from this kind of rabble. Besides, Alcibiades went on, reports of their vast reserves of heavy-armed troops had (like their aggressive policy) been much exaggerated. There were, too, large number of non-Greek Sicels ready to join any invader in attacking Syracuse. Talk of leaving Athens exposed to attack was nonsense. Sparta could invade Attica at will, whether an expedition was in Sicily or not; and the fleet left behind in Piraeus would be capable of resisting any attack a Peloponnesian squadron could muster.

Alcibiades then dealt with Nicias' suggestion that the affairs of an alien city like Segesta were no concern of Athens; and here his imperialism shows out more clearly than anywhere else. We made such cities our allies, he pointed out, not to get our-

selves reinforcements, but to annoy our enemies in the area concerned. The only way to win an empire is to back anyone
who solicits your aid. Start making finicky racial distinctions,
and you're done for. Athens has reached a point where she
must either increase her conquests or risk subjugation herself.

This speech by Alcibiades merely served to increase the Assembly's already considerable enthusiasm for the expedition.
After the ambassadors from Segesta and Leontini had come
forward and spoken as suppliants, begging for Athenian aid
and reminding the Assembly of their treaty obligations,
Nicias returned to the speaker's platform a second time. He
saw now, all too clearly, that there was no chance of getting
the main decision reversed. Accordingly he changed his tactics,
and did his best to scare the Assembly by making what he
considered a vastly exaggerated estimate of the troops and
armaments such an expedition would require. This—though he
could not have guessed it at the time—was simply to compound
disaster.

The picture he presented of Sicily was very different from
that given by Alcibiades; and in this connection we should never
forget that Nicias was Syracuse's resident proxenos in Athens,
and therefore spoke with considerable authority. These Sicilian
cities, he told the Assembly, are fiercely independent, and of
formidable strength. Their government is by no means oppres-
sive; they are most unlikely to surrender their freedom for the
privilege of being ruled by us. How many of them can we
really count on, apart from Leontini? Only Naxos and Catana.
That leaves at least seven others, all armed and equipped very
much as we are—Syracuse and Selinus above all. Nicias then
got down to logistical details, and what he said was of prime
importance for the coming expedition. These cities were well
supplied with hoplites, light-armed troops, triremes and crews.
Their financial reserves were more than adequate. "But the
greatest advantage they have over us," he pointed out, "is in
the number of their horses and in the fact that they grow
their own corn and do not have to import any." Here he hit at
the heart of the matter with a vengeance.

What Nicias was aiming at, as his subsequent recommendations show, was an expeditionary force that should be totally
independent of the country in which it operated. This shows
excellent strategical sense. He demanded a large body of heavy-
armed troops, archers and slingers; complete naval superiority,
to guarantee the expedition's supply-lines; wheat and parched
barley to be imported from mainland Greece, together with
millers and bakers; and a plentiful reserve of hard cash, since
the backing promised by Segesta "is more likely to be there in
theory than in fact." It had to be recognised, he concluded,
that Athens was going off to establish a bridgehead in enemy
territory, "and that those who do this have either to become
masters of the country on the very first day they land in it, or
be prepared to recognise that, if they fail to do so, they will
find hostility on every side."

There are one or two odd points here that deserve consideration. To begin with, Nicias does not appear to have even
considered importing a large cavalry force to match that of the
enemy. Secondly, his arrangements over the grain supply suggest that he did not expect to have any local Sicilian wheat
available at all: which is incredible. Was he so pessimistic
about Athens' allies? Did he regard it as so unlikely, too, that
the expedition would win any territory once a landing had been
made? And if, like Lamachus, he believed in the virtues of a
Blitzkrieg assault, why, in the event, did he employ such totally
different tactics? The unlooked-for implication behind all this
is that the last thing Nicias really intended the Sicilian task-
force to do was to fight; we shall return to this point later.

But the general reaction was by no means what Nicias had
hoped for: the more difficulties he raised, the more people's
enthusiasm was aroused. Excellent advice, they all said: Nicias
has a sound head on his shoulders. Instead of worrying, they
began to regard the expedition as a foregone success with so
provident a commander in charge. The young confidently
looked forward to "the sights and experiences of distant places,"
never doubting that they would return home alive. The experienced soldier—as Thucydides points out, with cool cynicism—

saw the prospect of good pay, "and of adding to the empire
so as to secure permanent paid employment in future." The
public in general thought of their daily bread. Anyone with
doubts about the venture kept quiet for fear of being thought
unpatriotic. The combination of Nicias' moderation and experience, Alcibiades' youthful daring, and Lamachus' bluff
military forthrightness was regarded as a sure-fire guarantee of
success. The lunacies inherent in such a tripartite command—
where no one commander could override the others, and nothing could be done at all until two of them agreed—were not so
apparent to the fifth-century Athenian as they are to us, or, indeed, to later Greek writers.[7]

At this stage in the proceedings a radical named Demostratus, who seems to have been one of Alcibiades' lieutenants,
came forward and addressed Nicias personally. It was time, he
said, to stop all these excuses and delaying tactics. Would the
general kindly tell them, in round numbers, exactly what troops
and armaments the Assembly was required to approve? Nicias
tried to hedge, saying that he must consult with his colleagues
first, that decisions should not be taken in such an emotionally
fraught atmosphere. When Demostratus refused to let him off
the hook, he eventually specified, as a minimum, 100 triremes,
five thousand hoplites, and the rest of the task-force in proportion. Demostratus pounced on these figures, and began a formal
motion reaffirming the decision to dispatch a fleet to Sicily,
approving the commanders' requests, and moving "that they
should be given absolute authority both at home and abroad
for the planning and conduct of the campaign." But hardly had
he started when a strange and ill-omened interruption occurred.
The day on which this second meeting of the Assembly was
held, April 15, coincided with the rites celebrating the death
of Adonis.[8] All through the city images of the god were being

[7] One is reminded of the Middle East general in World War II who
cynically described the camel as "a horse designed by a committee."
[8] The exact date of the Adonis festival has been much disputed. I follow
MacDowell (see Bibliography) pp. 186–87, who gives an admirable
summing-up of the evidence.

carried by women in funeral processions, with dirges and muffled drumbeats and loud lamentation.

The echoes of these ritual goings-on must have formed an uneasy *faux-bourdon* to all the oratory in the Assembly. But just as Demostratus was well embarked on his speech, a woman on a nearby rooftop began to keen and wail in that piercing, hysterical manner which can still be heard at any Greek or Sicilian funeral. The thud of the drums grew louder, more menacing, the harsh litany of sorrow could not be ignored. "I move that the fleet should sail for Sicily—" Demostratus began, and through his words there cut, knifelike, the dreadful *ai-eee, ai-eee*, of the woman on her rooftop, mourning the lost Adonis. It would take more than feminine hysteria to keep any good demagogue down, and Demostratus succeeded in forcing his motion through regardless. But the epidode had a very unpleasant psychological effect on the superstitious—which meant, in effect, on every member of the Assembly—so that they were "filled with misgivings for the fate of the men setting out." This, surely, was no coincidence. The whole thing sounds suspiciously like a well-organised *coup de théâtre*. Nor is it hard to guess who must have been responsible for it. Nicias was hand in glove with all the best priests and diviners in Athens. If human reason could not prevent this expedition, perhaps a series of unfavourable omens might do so.

Alcibiades, however, proved just as adroit at this kind of game as his pious opponent. There were other prophets available, if one looked around in the right places for them, and gave them a careful briefing as to one's requirements. Large numbers of supposedly ancient oracles suddenly came to light: Alcibiades personally quoted one predicting a great triumph for the Athenians in Sicily. A mission sent out to consult the shrine of Zeus Ammon in Libya came back with a prophecy that "the Athenians were destined to take all the Syracusans." It seems there were other oracles, some of which hinted at disaster; but these the messengers suppressed "for fear of uttering words of ill-omen." Alcibiades was nothing if not thorough.

But Nicias was not the only man of intelligence and judgment to believe no good would come of the Sicilian Expedition. Socrates, it is said, received a warning to this effect from his daemon, or inner voice; he told a number of close friends about it, and the story soon became widely known. There was also the strange case of Meton, the famous astronomer and land-surveyor, who had been appointed to a subordinate command, and pulled every string he knew to get out of it. When all else failed he pretended, like Odysseus in similar circumstances, to go mad: he snatched a blazing torch and set fire to his house near the Stoa Poikilé. Some sources say it was his son for whom he tried to win exemption, but the point of the story remains the same. A minority foresaw disaster in Sicily; and it was an intelligent minority.[9]

But these few men, could, it seemed, do nothing effective to counter the overwhelming tide of enthusiasm and activity which had flowed through Athens. Preparations were going ahead on all sides. Call-up lists were checked, instructions and requisition lists sent off to the subject-allies. Everywhere he went, Nicias could both see and hear signs of the expedition's steady progress towards final readiness. Somehow, he thought desperately to himself, somehow there *must* be a way of stopping this collective madness. It will soon be too late. Nicias was ill and old; in his extremity he was ready to do almost anything. The fact did not go unnoticed.

For six weeks after the second debate a battle-royal continued between the official priesthood and Alcibiades' private seers. Just how active a part Nicias himself played in this propaganda war is uncertain. (He can hardly, for instance, be held responsible for the dramatic incident of the man who bestrode the Altar of the Twelve Gods, in broad daylight, and proceeded to castrate himself.) In any case the various alarming omens and gloomy predictions—like that great clerical curse in *The Jackdaw of Rheims*—seemed to leave nobody connected with

[9] What public opinion thought of such behaviour can be judged from the treatment Meton receives at Aristophanes' hands in *The Birds* (March 414), where he gets short shrift as a pretentious quack.

the expedition one penny the worse. The atmosphere grew steadily more tense and electric. Then, abruptly, the storm broke, to leave Athens rocking from the repercussions of the most baffling and scandalous cause célèbre in her entire history.

On the morning of June 7, 415 B.C., the citizens of Athens awoke to find that a curious and well-planned piece of vandalism had been perpetrated during the night. With the single exception of the one outside the house of Andocides the orator, all the Herms in the city—square pillars which stood at street corners, surmounted by a bearded bust of Hermes, and most often with an erect phallus in front—had been mutilated, either by having their phalli knocked off, or their features hacked about, or both. To us this may seem no more than a vulgar and mildly blasphemous prank, and indeed there were some people (though not many) who took a similar view at the time. But the vast majority, as Plutarch says, "responded to it with rage and fear and believed that it was part of a daring conspiracy which aimed at far higher matters."

Athens buzzed with hysterical rumours. It was the work of Corinthian agents, some asserted, who were "hoping that the Athenians might be influenced by these portents to delay the expedition or even call it off." This was at least a plausible theory. Syracuse was Corinth's colony; Hermes was the god of travellers; and no Greek superstition was stronger than that against sailing in the same ship as a man guilty of impiety. Others, however, regarded the incident as "evidence of a revolutionary conspiracy to overthrow the democracy"—a conclusion which may reasonably strike the modern reader as something of a *non sequitur*. But whatever lay behind the episode, it had been very well organised: no mere drunken frolic was ever so efficient.

During the next few days the Council and Assembly met several times to discuss the matter, and a commission of enquiry was set up. Its members included Peisander and Charicles, two men who at the time passed for moderate democrats—and

may indeed have been so—but were afterwards deeply implicated in the right-wing *Putsch* of 411; Androcles, the new
proletarian leader who had succeeded Hyperbolus, and was
therefore an implacable opponent of Alcibiades; and Nicias'
brother Diognetus. From these names it would seem—as we
might expect—that the commission was designed to represent
all major political groupings in Athens. A former lieutenant of
Cleon's, Cleonymus, then passed a motion offering a thousand
drachmas as a reward for information leading to the arrest and
conviction of those responsible for the outrage. When this
failed to produce results, Peisander had the sum raised to ten
thousand drachmas—mainly, one suspects, to overbid the bribes
informers were getting from those with something to hide. It
looks as though even members of the commission were not
above such practices. Telecleides the comic poet specifically accused Nicias and Charicles of together handing out four thousand drachmas to one informer as a means of buying his
silence. This both suggests where Charicles' political sympathies lay at the time (i.e., with the "moderate" group), and
also raises the question of just what it might be that the
pious Nicias was so determined to hush up.

The first denunciation came on or about June 18, in somewhat unexpected circumstances, during a full session of the
Assembly held down by the docks in Piraeus. When the expedition was originally voted, it was arranged that the Assembly
should remain in permanent session for ten days prior to the
fleet's departure, and that all questions concerning the expedition should receive top priority. This meeting in Piraeus was to
hear final reports from the three generals; the last financial al-
locations had been made, and Lamachus' flagship, in fact, was
already lying off-shore at its moorings, in full sight of the Assembly. The setting and the occasion had all the making of
high drama. Yet—and this is significant—the man who got up
to cry *J'accuse!* made no reference whatsoever to the mutilation
of the Herms. His name, otherwise unknown, was Pythonicus;
and he denounced Alcibiades—who of course was present ex
officio as a member of the High Command—for having blas-

phemously parodied the Eleusinian Mysteries in the house of a wealthy resident alien named Pulytion. His accusation was then confirmed, in detail, by a slave who claimed to have been an eyewitness on the occasion in question, and who named nine other persons as having taken part in the proceedings.

Next Androcles, the popular leader, produced further slaves and aliens, who testified that Alcibiades and his friends had at various times parodied the Mysteries in a number of private houses. They also referred to other mutilations of statues (but not those of the Herms) committed by such young bloods in drunken sport. Pulytion, they said, had masqueraded as the Torch-Bearer, and Alcibiades as the High Priest, while the rest of their friends posed as initiates. In this way two completely distinct issues—the multilation of the Herms and the profanation of the Mysteries—became thoroughly confused in most people's minds at a very early point.

By now, as Plutarch says, "the people were in an ugly mood and their anger turned against Alcibiades, while Androcles, who was his mortal enemy, added fuel to the flames." Alcibiades instantly saw the danger he was in, and pressed hard for an immediate trial; needless to say, he denied the charge completely. On the credit side, he had the solid backing of the Athenian soldiers and sailors who were accompanying him to Sicily, and—perhaps more important—of the infantry from Argos and Mantinea, a thousand strong, who made it known that if Alcibiades was in any way victimised, they would withdraw from the expedition altogether.

But an immediate trial was the last thing Androcles and his radical group wanted. Without Alcibiades, many people believed, the success of the Sicilian Expedition would be seriously prejudiced; put him in court now, and he was almost bound to be acquitted, or at worst get off with a nominal fine. What Androcles wanted was to dispose of him as a political rival once and for all. His plan, therefore, according to Thucydides, "was to bring some more serious accusation against him (which they could do all the more easily when he was away) and then to send for him and bring him back to stand his trial." They

therefore arranged for certain speakers, whose active hostility
to Alcibiades was not public knowledge, to get up in the Assembly and say it was ridiculous to go to all the trouble of
appointing a general over this great task-force, and then to
hold up the departure of the fleet, just when all preparations
had been made, by "the formalities of drawing lots for jurors
and appointing times for the hearing of the case." Let him
sail now, they urged, and good luck go with him; once
the campaign is over he can come back and stand trial. The
laws will not have changed during his absence. It was a specious
but convincing argument. Alcibiades, however, saw only too
well what Androcles really had in mind: such a postponement
was activated by pure malice and nothing else. He objected,
with good reason, that "it was monstrous for him to be sent
out to command such a great force while his case was still in
suspense, and to be obliged to leave these accusations and
slanders hanging over his head." He begged once more to be
tried there and then: if he was found guilty, he was ready to
pay the penalty—which might well be death—and if acquitted,
to take up his command with no further fear of any accusations
informers might lay against him.

But the Assembly's mind was made up, and no argument,
however reasonable, could budge it. Androcles got his way. His
enemy was given sailing orders for Sicily with a capital charge
still hanging over him. About the last day of June the three
generals held a final secret session with the Council, to discuss
"what disposition they should make of Sicilian affairs, if they
should get control of the island." They agreed that Syracuse
and Selinus, the two most powerful and hostile cities, should
be taken over by Athens, and their populations either sold into
slavery or reduced to the status of serfs. The other states would
merely become subject-allies, new additions to Athens' unwieldy empire.

So next morning all Athens flocked down to Piraeus to see
the great armada set sail, not considering—in the excitement
and drama of that memorable departure—that their husbands,
brothers, sweethearts, and sons were now entrusted to the joint

mercies of a nephritic, dithering old man who thought the whole expedition a dangerous mistake; his bitterest enemy, an insolvent playboy with a serious criminal charge outstanding against him; and an indigent, boneheaded braggart soldier who was the standing butt of the comic poets. If their aim had been to sabotage the expedition deliberately, the Assembly could hardly have chosen better. Then they all trudged back home, emotionally exhausted, up the five-mile stretch of the Long Walls to the city, to find even more dramatic entertainment brewing up for them. One of the first recorded witch hunts in history was about to begin.

All those persons accused by Pythonicus and his slave—apart from Alcibiades, whose case was pending, and a member of his hetairia named Polystratus, who was caught and executed —at once (and very prudently) fled the country. This, however, should not necessarily be taken as a presumption of their guilt. From now on, anyone denounced was liable to summary imprisonment without trial. Panic and hysteria had begun to usurp cool judgment: people saw dark and tyrannous plots everywhere, and struck out in self-defence. As tends to happen on such occasions, denunciations came thick and fast.[1]

The first informer to appear after the fleet sailed (which it did about July 1) was a resident alien named Teucrus, a stonemason, who had slipped out of Athens and taken refuge in Megara. Granted immunity by the Council, he returned, and furnished the commissioners with two lists of names: those who had mutilated the Herms, and those who had profaned the Mysteries. Most of the names are otherwise unknown; but those accused by Teucrus of profaning the Mysteries included Plato's friend Phaedrus, and—somewhat unexpectedly—Nicias' brother Diognetus, who was sitting on the commission that heard Teucrus give his evidence. In the matter of the Herms, Teucrus named, amongst others, Theodorus and Meletus (both of whom had already been named by Androcles as Alcibiades'

[1] Hatzfeld (see Bibliography), discussing this point, reminds us of the Second Empire magistrate who, in a similar position, said that even if they accused him of stealing Notre Dame, he'd still make a bolt for it.

accomplices in profaning the Mysteries); Eryximachus, a friend of Phaedrus and Socrates; and Archidamus, or Archedemus, who was also a member of the Socratic circle, and a friend of Alcibiades' son. A large proportion of the accused, as before, fled the country; the remainder were arrested and put to death.

At this point the whole affair might, on the face of it, have been regarded as closed. Those responsible for both incidents —or, at least, those officially regarded as having been responsible—were either dead or on the run. But on either the fifth or seventh of July a new Council was sworn in for the next twelve months; and it is now that we find two members of the commission of enquiry, Peisander and Charicles, arguing that the mutilation of the Herms "was not the work of a small group of criminals, but an organised attempt to overthrow the popular government: and that therefore enquiries ought to be pursued as vigorously as ever." The witch hunt, in fact, was only beginning: so far the right heads had not rolled. Athens settled down to a short but extremely ugly reign of terror. The degree of panic can be gauged by the fact that when the flag was lowered to indicate that a Council meeting was in session, citizens vanished from the Agora as though by magic.

Within three days of the new Council taking office, moreover, another informer had appeared on the scene. His name was Diocleides, and he claimed to have seen about three hundred conspirators in the Theatre of Dionysus during the night of the outrage. Forty-two of these he proceeded to identify by name. They included two members of the sitting Council, one of whom, Mantitheus, afterwards served with Alcibiades in the Ionian War; Alcibiades himself; Nicias' other brother, Eucrates, and his brother-in-law Euphemus, the latter an expert on Sicilian affairs; and Leogoras, one of the best-connected aristocrats in Athens, together with his son Andocides, and other members of his family, including Critias—Plato's uncle and the future leader of the Thirty.

If Diocleides had reckoned on causing a sensation, he certainly succeeded. Peisander at once proposed that the decree forbidding the examination of citizens under torture be suspended, and the Council greeted his motion with shouts of approval. The two accused Council members furnished sureties for themselves, and then jumped bail, leaving their wretched guarantors to be racked. The point about Diocleides' revelations was that they exactly confirmed what every ordinary Athenian feared above all else: a large, well-organised oligarchic plot. All the accused were wealthy, respectable citizens, whose politics were at least right-of-centre. The Council rounded them all up and threw them into prison. At the same time (c. July 10) reports came in that a Spartan army was marching on the Isthmus, and Boeotian troops massing along the northern frontier of Attica. The alarm was sounded, and that night the citizens of Athens stood to arms—while Diocleides, hailed as the saviour of his country, was wined and dined in the City Hall.

But during the night Andocides, one of the accused, was—according to his own account—persuaded by his cousin Charmides to tell the truth about the Herms incident, mainly in order to save many wrongfully imprisoned people, including his own father. He therefore made a statement to the authorities, confirming the denunciation of Teucrus, naming Euphiletus, a wealthy landowner, as the organiser of the outrage, and adding four new names to the list Teucrus had supplied. About the purpose of the mutilation he seems to have been discreetly vague; the implication is that it was some sort of political conspiracy. The Council thereupon re-summoned Diocleides, who broke down very quickly under close cross-examination: he claimed, for instance, to have recognised the conspirators by the light of the full moon, when in fact the night of June 6–7 had been moonless. He now said he had been primed with his original story by Alcibiades' cousin. The Council promptly released all those imprisoned on Diocleides' testimony, executed Diocleides himself, and declared the emergency over.

The four men named by Andocides fled the country, while the citizens of Athens stood down and returned to their normal occupations—all, that is, except Andocides, who was kept in prison on the excuse that he had promised to furnish a slave who would confirm his story under torture, and the slave (for whatever reason) was not forthcoming. About the same time an abortive right-wing *Putsch* took place in Argos, involving several of Alcibiades' friends there, and a group of Argive hostages held by Athens were returned to the triumphant democratic government as an act of good faith—and, one may suspect, as a piece of anti-Alcibiadean propaganda. At this point things seem to have quietened down for a week or two. Then a well-born lady named Agariste (who had once been married to Pericles' music teacher Damon, and whose present husband was a member of the famous Alcmaeonid family to which both Pericles and Alcibiades himself belonged) accused Alcibiades, in very specific terms, of having performed a parody of the mysteries in Charmides' house, together with his uncle Axiochus and his close friend Adeimantus. Hard on the heels of this revelation came another, by a slave named Lydus, who claimed that the mysteries had been celebrated at the house of his master, Pherecles—already denounced by Teucrus for complicity in the mutilation of the Herms.

Axiochus and Adeimantus wisely slipped away across the border, and the imprisoned Andocides now, at last (c. August 20), either volunteered or was persuaded to give information which directly incriminated Alcibiades in the case of the Mysteries. This evidence formed the basis of the formal impeachment which Thessalus, son of the great statesman Cimon, now laid against Alcibiades in the Assembly. It was detailed, circumstantial, and plausible; and having heard it, the Assembly dispatched the state galley *Salaminia* to Sicily (c. August 25), with orders to bring Alcibiades home to stand trial. He made no resistance; but at Thurii in southern Italy he jumped ship, and made his way to Argos. He was condemned to death *in absentia*, and formally cursed by the priesthood. But Athens had not seen the last of him yet.

Nevertheless, everyone heaved vast sighs of relief: the reign of terror was over at last. The reward for information concerning the Herms went, very properly, to Teucrus, and that in respect of the Mysteries—after a certain amount of ill-natured bickering among the rival informers—to Pythonicus' slave. Both awards were presented during the Panathenaic Festival (c. September 2). The property of the Herm-mutilators was put up for auction; the case was closed. But a fog of mystery and intrigue still hangs over the whole episode. Ancient writers such as Thucydides and Plutarch frankly admitted their bafflement; the former says that "no one, either then or later, was able to say for certain who did the deed." Perhaps this is a little pessimistic.

To begin with, we must make a very firm distinction between the incident of the Herms and the profanation of the Mysteries. It is quite clear from the evidence that the latter was dragged in as a red herring, by Androcles and his friends in the popular party, with the explicit object of making some sort of criminal charge stick on Alcibiades, by hook or crook. This suggests that Alcibiades was innocent of the Herm-mutilation; it also makes it probable that Androcles had no connection with it either, but simply used the incident as a handy weapon to attack his personal enemy.

One thing it is essential to realise about the mutilation of the Herms is that those who perpetrated it (except in the unlikely event of their being mere drunken pranksters) can have had one motive, and one only, in what they did: to create an omen disastrous enough to stop the fleet sailing for Sicily. No other explanation makes any kind of sense. The mutilation of statues does not per se suggest political revolution, whether of the right or the left. The fact that many Athenians were by now hysterical enough to see the shadow of conspiracy under every bush is irrelevant to the main issue. With this in mind we can examine our list of suspects.

The most superficially attractive idea is that which attributes the deed to Corinthian agents in the pay of Syracuse. What argues against it is the fact that no one, even when the reign of terror was at its height, tried to exculpate themselves by shifting the blame outside the city: not even Andocides, who seems to have been one of the shiftiest witnesses on record, tried to produce some anonymous group of shadowy Corinthians as an alibi.

The most widespread belief at the time—no doubt fostered by the popular party for its own purposes—was that the incident somehow formed part of an oligarchic plot to overthrow the democracy. But this will not hold water either. A coup d'état demands secrecy, not adverse publicity; and in any case, the last thing in the world Athens' right-wing extremists wanted was to hold back the fleet, since its sailors were popularists and radicals to a man. It is no accident that when an oligarchic *Putsch* finally did come, in 411, the fleet was safely out of the way at Samos.

Yet another suggestion is that this was the prelude to a *left-wing* plot, organised by Androcles and his supporters, and aimed at the destruction of Alcibiades. That Androcles was out to destroy Alcibiades no one would deny; but that he intended to scotch the Sicilian Expedition in the process could only be credited by those as ready to jumble up Herms and Mysteries as were the Athenians themselves. The Sicilian Expedition was the brain-child, in essence, of the popular party. One of its main objects was to provide rich pickings, not only for the actual troops, but also for the vast army of camp-followers and speculators who sailed from Piraeus in the wake of the fleet. The last thing Androcles would ever have done was to prejudice the expedition's safe departure.

What then remains? Only the moderates, the middle-of-the-road quasi-democratic imperialists, the inheritors of the Periclean tradition, to whom all such rash expansionist ventures were anathema, and who much preferred to work for coexistence with Sparta in the intervals of cultivating their large estates and watching over investments in mining or foreign trade. Some may have been oligarchs by temperament, others intellectual radicals, others again pure rural isolationists; but they all shared a common interest in the land. The list of names given by Teucrus and Andocides (and now supported by good epigraphical evidence) amply confirms such a supposition. We possess a record of these men's auctioned goods, and it is clear that they were landed proprietors on a large scale by Athenian standards.

Insofar as we can be sure about anything in this context, then, it seems clear that the actual physical mutilation of the Herms was performed, as Andocides claims that it was, by a semi-political hetairia, or "club," of which Euphiletus was the leader. Yet the timing was too good, the organisation too perfect, surely, for the incident to have been a mere generalised protest by country landowners against ruinous aggression. Somebody was prepared to take very considerable risks to stop the fleet sailing. And if we ask—having eliminated the impossibilities —cui bono?, then one name inescapably presents itself for our consideration.

Nicias had been opposed to the expedition from the very beginning, or at least since the first High Command conference. He had argued against it vehemently and somewhat unscrupulously in the Assembly. When this line of defence failed, he had been a moving force behind the oracular propaganda designed to scare off its advocates. Both his brothers had been implicated by informers, one of participation in the Mysteries, the other (together with his brother-in-law, Euphemus), of Herm-mutilation. Perhaps the only reason why Nicias escaped indictment himself was the fear that this would give Alcibiades too free a hand. There were also, of course, the four thousand drachmas paid out to someone to stop them talking about— what? We do not know, and Teleclides carefully refrains from telling us, since, he says, Nicias knew what he was doing: "The man's a friend of mine, and I think he had his head screwed on." This is a very understandable attitude if Teleclides shared the Aristophanic attitude to rural conservatism, and sympathised with attempts to stop the Sicilian venture from taking place.

Even Nicias' well-known piety might, in the last resort, be prepared to sanction (if not to initiate) a blasphemy pro bono publico—and very much over-estimate the effect it would have on the expedition itself. (The violent political reaction, on the other hand, seems to have taken the perpetrators, whoever they were, very much by surprise.) His curious, apathetic behaviour in Sicily becomes all the more understandable if we see him as a man who not only lacked faith in his mission, but believed he was personally responsible, even if only by consent, for an act of impiety. None of this adds up to more than circumstantial evidence; the most we can say is that the incident, coming when it did, could hardly have been more convenient for him.

But whoever *was* guilty of defacing the Herms, one person most certainly was not. Alcibiades had more at stake than anyone over the Sicilian Expedition; he cannot be suspected of complicity in an affair which was bound to cause him nothing but harm. Indeed, much of the puzzlement which the whole episode has generated is due to one cause, and one only: the vicious determination of Androcles and the popular party, right from the time the scandal broke, to nail Alcibiades on any charge they could find. The red herring of the Mysteries was dragged in at the very first opportunity, by Pythonicus and Androcles in collusion. The apparently honest denunciations by Teucrus were not good enough; they named nonentities, but made no mention of Alcibiades. So right after the change of Council (which again suggests a put-up job) we have Diocleides' wild accusations, directed not only at Alcibiades himself, but also at a large sector of Athenian upper-class society. It is hard to resist the conclusion that this, too, was the work of Androcles; whether Charicles or Peisander helped him we can only surmise. On the other hand, the Council as a whole appear to have been honest men: at least they acted with commendable firmness and promptitude when Diocleides was exposed as a fraud.

But Andocides had not, as yet, sung quite the song that the popular leaders wanted. The evidence against Alcibiades had to be built up until the prosecution could go into court with an absolutely water-tight case. Clearly they could not hope to obtain this from the Herms incident; indeed, from the amount of shilly-shallying that went on, it is even possible Alcibiades had an unbreakable alibi for the night of June 6–7. They therefore concentrated on the Mysteries—of which Alcibiades had, almost certainly, performed blasphemous parodies on various occasions, together with many of his friends. (All our evidence suggests that such parodies were very fashionable at the time amongst Athens' *jeunesse dorée* and younger intellectuals.) Agariste's denunciation, coupled with the damning indictment at last brought by Andocides as the price of his release from prison, supplied exactly what Alcibiades' enemies had hoped for. Androcles had his way once more, and Alcibiades was impeached.

But the popular leader reaped a bitter victory, for himself and Athens alike. It was Alcibiades' defection to Sparta, and the diabolically good advice which he gave the Spartan government, that led in the long run to Athens' downfall. The vindictive persecution of Alcibiades did, as Thucydides implies, lose Athens the war: not because the expeditionary force in Sicily could ill spare him, as has sometimes been assumed, but because he was driven, by a mixture of self-preservation and piqued vanity, to turn and rend the country that was so implacably bent on destroying him. The incident of the Herms had wider and more lasting repercussions than anyone could have guessed at the time—least of all, perhaps, the iconoclasts who flitted through Athens' shadowy streets on that warm June night, their hammers and chisels chipping away the foundations of an imperial dream.

The Athenian armada, after leaving Piraeus, sailed round the Peloponnese by the long southern route—Corinth and Megara were firmly in control of the isthmus—and reached Corcyra, their last Greek landfall, by mid-July. Here they were joined by various local contingents: Zacynthian and Cephallenian islanders, Messenians from Pylos and Naupactus, Aetolian mercenaries, Acarnanians who had served under Demosthenes. When the whole expeditionary force was assembled, the generals held a final review, and issued detailed instructions as to how the fleet was to anchor and camp every night. Since triremes (being much more cramped than merchantmen) had no facilities for cooking or sleeping on board, this was a very necessary precaution. To begin with, they divided their armament into three separate flotillas, one under each supreme commander. "This," says Thucydides, "was so that they should not have to sail altogether, which would mean difficulties with regard to water and harbourage and supplies whenever they landed, and also so that they could preserve their order better and be easier to handle." They then sent off an advance detachment of three ships, to raise further promised funds from Segesta, and to find out which of the other Sicilian cities would receive them. After all arrangements were complete, the three great naval divisions weighed anchor and sailed out up the narrow channel between Corcyra and Epirus, bearing north-west across the Adriatic towards the heel of Italy.

The logistics of this expeditionary force are extremely interesting. It is often assumed (despite Thucydides' caveat) that it was the largest, most powerful body of ships and troops which fifth-century Athens ever sent out on a foreign campaign. We also tend to think of it as a more or less all-Athenian force. Both these assumptions are quite false. Athens supplied, in the first instance, no more than sixty fast triremes, with another forty temporarily converted[1] into military transports. Even if these forty could be used as front-line fighting ships again after they had reached their destination (and this is by no means certain), the total complement was little more than Eurymedon and Sophocles had had available in 425, and only half the number that had sailed to Egypt under Cimon. Moreover, if each troop-transport could accommodate about seventy-five soldiers, the thirty-four triremes and two fifty-oar pentekonters supplied by Chios, Rhodes, and other allies would all be required to transport the expedition's combined hoplite force. This left only Athens' sixty triremes immediately available without reconversion.

Nor did Athens make an exactly lavish contribution of heavy-armed troops. From those citizens registered in the hoplite category no more than 1,500 sailed to Sicily in 415—a striking contrast to the nine thousand who had marched out and held the Persians at Marathon, or the even larger contingent which had taken the field at Tanagra. There were also, it is true, seven hundred lower-class citizens serving as heavy-armed marines. But it was the subject-allies, reinforced by five hundred Argives and 250 Mantinean and Arcadian mercenaries, who supplied 2,900 out of 4,400 hoplites on the muster-roll. Whatever Athens was risking on this expedition, it was not, by and large, her propertied classes. Light-armed troops, including slingers and archers, provided another 1,300 men, of whom only 150 were Athenian; the rest were mostly Rhodians, Cretans, and Megarian exiles. There was one Athenian horse-transport, containing thirty horses and riders—"who were," as Freeman says, "to face the cavalry of Syracuse and all Dorian Sicily." The total combatant manpower has been calculated at 27,810, of which Athens supplied 16,780. This looks a respectable figure until we break it down. Cavalry and heavy-armed troops account for 1,530; the rest—including those seven hundred proletarian marines—are

---

[1] Probably with an upper deck: so Dover (p. 42), who has the best discussion of this problem.

the "sailor rabble," the rowers and petty officers of the fleet including metics and slaves: 15,250 in all.

The more one thinks about these figures, the odder they are. If the expedition's object really *was* the total reduction and enslavement of Sicily, they seem starkly incredible. The island, after all, was not to be conquered by cruising round its periphery from port to port. If the Athenians meant business, they would be conducting a largely land-based campaign. Once again we are forced to the conclusion that Nicias (who, after all, was responsible for the estimates voted by the Assembly) had no real intention of fighting in Sicily, whatever he may have planned to do by secret diplomacy. On the other hand, it is only too easy to see why the Assembly went along with such lopsided arrangements. The conservatives and landowners were required to make only a minimal sacrifice, while the radicals could bedazzle their own conscripts or volunteers with promises of loot, land, and glory. One concealed purpose behind the Sicilian Expedition, it would seem, was that well-tried device, large-scale colonisation. We can see this more clearly when we begin to work out the size of the non-combatant force which accompanied the fighting troops. Here we are on difficult ground. But it is hard to believe, when we add up the bakers and masons and carpenters, the hoplite and cavalry servants, the camp-followers and sutlers, the traders and merchants who accompanied the fleet in their "numerous" private vessels, that there were less than ten thousand non-combatants with the expedition. This, indeed, is an ultra-conservative estimate. Those on the official payroll must have totalled about five thousand (of whom four thousand were servants); a total figure of up to twenty thousand is by no means impossible.[2]

What such an over-all picture suggests, with some force, is

[2] Supplies, grain, tools, bakers, masons, and carpenters were carried aboard thirty merchant-vessels; the total complement of these ships, at the most conservative estimate, is unlikely to have been less than 1,500–2,000 men. There were also 100 smaller vessels (size not specified) requisitioned by the fleet, which may have accounted for a further 3,000±. This is quite apart from the private traders and camp-followers.

that the Athenians expected Sicily to be a pushover. Yet their previous experience there was hardly calculated to make them over-optimistic. Why should they suppose that this cut-price invasion force, all fleet and no army, all pomp and precious little circumstance, was competent to reduce the strongest and wealthiest Greek community in the whole Western Mediterranean? Yet the belief was undoubtedly there—not least among the speculators who crowded in the wake of the fleet. Trade, as we know, follows the flag; but it most often does so at a discreet distance until the flag has been safely planted. What produced the strange over-confidence that seems to have accompanied this particular venture from its outset, often in circumstances which—to judge by the evidence—certainly did not warrant such optimism?

Nicias and his colleagues found little enough to encourage them during their voyage round the coast of southern Italy. Diodorus, who had access to local (if often untrustworthy) sources, says that they were well received at Thurii, and obtained a market from Croton; Thucydides denies them even these small crumbs of comfort. According to him, no city provided them with a market, much less admitted them within the walls. The most they got was water and anchorage, and even these basic facilities were denied them by Tarentum, Locri, Heraclea, and Metapontum.[3] But their most unexpected setback came at Rhegium, a city which Athens had for long relied on as her "eternal" ally. Here the three flotillas, once more reunited, dropped anchor—only to find, to their astonished dismay, that the Rhegians, too, refused to allow them within the city walls. Making the best of a bad job, they beached their vessels, and set up camp in "the ground sacred to Artemis." They then opened negotiations with Rhegium, arguing that as a Chalcidic foundation she should join in rescuing Leontini from Syracuse. The Rhegian government replied they preferred to keep neutral. They would, they said, "wait for a general decision from all

[3] Both Thurii and Metapontum, however, later took part in the expedition, being forced to do so as a result of endless internal *stasis*, which left them virtually bankrupt.

the Greeks in Italy, and would then act in accordance with it."
Meanwhile the Athenians were welcome to extra-mural market
facilities if they needed them.

By now, as was inevitable, news of the expedition had begun
to filter through to Syracuse. While the Athenian fleet was
still assembling at Corcyra, a meeting of the Syracusan Assembly was convened, under the joint presidency of the city's
fifteen elected generals, to debate what counter-measures should
be taken. The oddest thing, from our point of view, is that
there seems to have been so much uncertainty as to whether this
invasion fleet was fact or fiction. Even in the fifth century,
one would have thought, international communications were
not quite so primitive. Corcyra, after all, lay no more than
seventy sea-miles across the Straits of Otranto from southern
Italy. Constant traffic came and went along the trade-routes.
How could there be any doubt about the destination and purpose of the armada lying in Corcyra roads—unless someone deliberately sowed that doubt for their own purposes? Here, of
course, the difference between ancient and modern communications *does* become apparent. News, then, travelled by word of
mouth, and could not be checked at source by picking up a
telephone or reading the foreign section of the morning paper.
One circumstantial account, therefore, was as good as another.
Start a rumour that the fleet at Corcyra was nonexistent, or
much exaggerated, or being used for some quite different purpose, and there was no reason at all why a lot of people
should not believe it—especially if it was what they wanted to
believe in the first place. But who, in Syracuse, would want to
start such a rumour, and for what reason?

Let us, before attempting to answer this question, look at
Thucydides' account—the only one we have—of the Syracusan
debate. The main point at issue, we are told, was, precisely,
whether the story of the Athenian expedition should be credited
or not. Various speeches were made, from either viewpoint, but
Thucydides only reports two of them. One is that made by
Hermocrates, the right-wing advocate of Pansicilian isolation-

ism, whom we last met during the Congress of Gela. The other Thucydides puts in the mouth of Athenagoras, an ultra-radical popularist, and the colleague of Diocles—who later, in 412, was to carry through sweeping reforms that transformed Syracuse from a moderate to an extreme democracy.[4] The speech of Hermocrates is crisp, practical, and packed with shrewd advice. I am not afraid of being thought a fool, he tells his listeners. I know what I know. The Athenians *are* coming against us, with a large invasion fleet. This talk of helping Segesta and Leontini is pure eyewash. Their first objective is the conquest of Syracuse. After that they believe the rest of the island will fall without any great effort on their part. "Do not despise the invasion, or you will be caught off your guard; do not disbelieve in it, or you will be neglecting everything that matters."

He goes on to make specific recommendations. Embassies must be sent to whip up support from the Siceliot and Italian cities, from the native Sicels, perhaps even from Carthage. Sparta and Corinth, too, must be approached for help—and encouraged to renew the war in mainland Greece. Best of all—if his listeners would accept so bold a plan—would be to collect every available ship and meet the enemy off the heel of Italy, catching them worn out after the crossing, and probably in scattered detachments, with no friendly base on which to fall back.[5] Then Hermocrates makes a remarkable statement, which has not had the attention it deserves. The Athenians, he claims, "are attacking us on the assumption that we are not going to defend ourselves." This, indeed, is just what we might suppose from a scrutiny of the expedition's logistics. But, again, why

---

[4] See above, p. 70, and below, p. 354.

[5] Modern scholars, by and large, argue that this was an impractical recommendation: Syracusan seamanship was mediocre at the time, the number of ships and trained crews available could not match up to the Athenian armada, there was no time to muster squadrons and move into position before the Athenians crossed the Straits of Otranto. Yet Hermocrates' arguments are cogent enough per se, and the mere appearance of a defence force off the Iapygian promontory might well have had incalculable psychological effect. The Athenians, as we shall see, were all too readily depressed by reverses of any sort.

should the Athenians assume any such thing? There was nothing in Syracuse's past record of tyranny, aggression, and creeping expansionism to suggest that her inhabitants would, on the Athenian fleet's approach, suddenly lay down their arms and open their gates to the invader.

Hermocrates sounds like a man trying to argue with ghosts in some Kafkaesque nightmare. "The Athenians are coming," he cries at the end of his speech, "the Athenians are, I am sure of it, already on their voyage; the Athenians are very nearly here"—but no one, or only a small minority, took any notice of him. Some thought the Athenians were not coming at all, and disbelieved every word he said. Others thought that even if they *did* come, it would be easy enough to deal with them. Others again, says Thucydides, "dismissed the idea altogether, and turned the whole thing into a joke." It was not so many years since Syracuse had been all too alive to the threat of Athenian domination, and not in the least disposed to treat it as a joke. What had produced this sudden cheerful scepticism amongst her citizens? One is tempted to answer: well-planned propaganda, over a considerable period. And once more the question poses itself: who stood to benefit by such a policy? Athenagoras' speech, as reported by Thucydides, may suggest one possible answer.

Athenagoras pooh-poohs the rumours about an Athenian invasion: the Athenians would have better sense, he says, than to embark on such a venture with the war in Greece still not properly settled. Even if they did come, it would take twice the troops they could muster to do Syracuse any real damage. They have no cavalry. They would be living in tents, and short of all supplies. It would, in fact, be all they could do to effect a landing at all. But what is most interesting about his speech is not so much the way he sets out to scotch these supposed rumours, as his explanation of how they arose and gained circulation in the first place. There is a group deliberately manufacturing such false reports, he assures his listeners. "They have reasons of their own to be frightened, and they want to put the whole city into a state of alarm, so that in the general panic they may disguise their own." Their object is to frighten the masses, and so secure the government for themselves—in all likelihood by illegal means. Athenagoras winds up his speech by attacking those young men—by implication the city's *jeunesse dorée*—who, he suggests, either want office before the legal age, or else special privileges denied to the common run of mankind. He finishes with a defence of radical democracy against reactionary and oligarchical regimes. The inference is clear: Hermocrates and his upper-class friends form a dangerous political junta, determined to seize power by any means at their disposal, and adept at disseminating false rumours to further their own ends.

But (as we know, even if the Syracusans did not) Hermocrates was in fact telling no more than the plain truth. This at once leaves us with grave suspicions as to just what Athenagoras and his radical friends were up to when they made so energetic an attempt to smear him. It is just possible that Athenagoras believed what he said; but the odds are very heavily against it. And if he did not, what were his motives? Was he, perhaps, trying to discredit Hermocrates—and divert suspicion from himself—by pinning on the conservative landowners *his own* methods of propaganda and political persuasion? If Hermocrates and his friends *were* frightened, may it not have been because they had something to be frightened of? If Athenagoras was lying, however, he was surely lying for some specific purpose. If he was responsible for the general incredulity concerning Athenian intentions, it can only have been with the object of lulling the people into a false sense of security. But the corollary is equally inescapable: the one plausible motive for doing this was to betray Syracuse into Athenian hands, by the well-tried method which fifth-century politicians found so much cheaper and easier than siege warfare.

Yet why should these ultra-democrats contemplate such an act? Here the answer is not in doubt: any Athenian fifth-column agent could have given it at once. "In return for your support when the allied fleet reaches Syracuse," we can imagine him telling Athenagoras, at some secret meeting in a dockside tavern or private house, "we will establish your party in power as the legitimate government of Syracuse. After all, you are true democrats—which is more than can be said for the present regime. You are concerned with land redistribution, are you not? Very well: we undertake that the estates of the Gamoroi shall be allocated to you and your followers. We only ask—reasonably enough, I am sure you will agree—that you cancel existing export agreements with the Peloponnesian League, and sell your surplus wheat quotas to us instead."

If this theory has even a grain of truth in it, much that is otherwise baffling falls neatly into place: above all, the curious constitution of the expeditionary force, which would not need to be designed for heavy land-based fighting; not to mention those flocks of traders and commercial adventurers, who may well have heard, through their own bush telegraph, that Syracuse was going to open its gates rather than have them battered down. The failure of the scheme—as so often, again, during this period—will undoubtedly have been due, first and foremost, to inadequate security measures. Everyone talked, in the barber's shop and out of it; sooner or later rumours would be bound to reach the ears of the government. But throughout the campaign, as we shall see, the Athenians still hoped against hope that Syracuse would fall to them by internal collusion. This false optimism perhaps did them more damage, ultimately, than any other single factor.

When Athenagoras had finished his speech, one of the presiding generals rose and formally declared the session closed. No further speakers were permitted to give their views. After deprecating the radical leader's excursus into personal party politics—it is not hard to see where this particular general's sympathies lay—he announced, briefly, that "we should be giving our attention to the reports which have reached us and seeing how we can all of us—the State as a whole and each individual in it— best deal with the invaders." Even if the rumours proved to be without foundation, the general said, sound military preparations were never wasted. Nor did it do any harm to approach one's neighbours and see where they stood. "We have seen to some of these matters already," he announced, with autocratic self-assurance, "and anything that we find out shall be brought to your notice." And on this note the Assembly was dissolved. In the general's few brief remarks we catch the unmistakable *de haut en bas* accent of the aristocratic Gamoroi; it is not hard to see how men like Athenagoras acquired such a follow-ing.[6]

But by the time the Athenian fleet arrived off Rhegium, its destination—much less its existence—could scarcely be in doubt any longer, and no amount of propaganda could disguise the reality of the threat it represented. On the other hand, active preparations for war had been delayed until the very last moment. It was only now that the Syracusan authorities began to do all the things they should have put in hand months before: garrisoning potentially treacherous Sicel cities, reinforcing the troops in their fortified frontier posts, checking stores of arms, requisitioning horses, sending out ambassadors to solicit aid from other friendly states. Yet much of the tactical advantage Nicias and his colleagues might have won from such dilatoriness on the enemy's part was thrown away. This was due, in part, to the Rhegian authorities' unexpected lack of co-operation. It would be extremely rash to launch an all-out drive against Syra-cuse (who knew whether Athenagoras and his friends could *really* be relied on?) without any adequate base to fall back on. Rhegium was neutral now; a serious Athenian reverse might tempt her to come off the fence and join Syracuse. If that happened, the expedition would be caught (almost literally) between Scylla and Charybdis, with no line of retreat available.

But what most crippled the Athenians at this critical moment was a basic difference of opinion between the three commanders over their immediate strategy. It is notoriously difficult to get accurate information about what goes on between generals or

[6] No vote was taken; the Board of Generals presumably studied the recommendations made, and acted as they thought fit. At all events, that is the last we hear of an embassy to Carthage, or, indeed, of Hermocrates' plan for meeting the Athenian armada before it reached Tarentum.

politicians behind closed doors, when the discussion is off the record. Unless Nicias, as senior general present, drafted a confidential memorandum of the debate between him and his colleagues, and dispatched it to Athens for preservation in the public archives, there is only one known source from which Thucydides could have got his account, and that is Alcibiades. Lamachus and Nicias were both dead before the exiled historian was able to consult them, and it is unlikely that at such a crucial (and probably acrimonious) discussion there were any junior officers present.

We have already seen one instance where Alcibiades may have falsified the record for his own purposes, and that is over the supposed fraudulence of Segesta. In Thucydides it is, precisely, the discovery of this double-dealing on Segesta's part which, we are told, leads to the generals' debate on strategy. The promised financial support is not forthcoming; only a further thirty talents have been produced. Because of this, and the non-cooperation of Rhegium, "the generals were at once discouraged" and "consulted on what steps to take under the circumstances." How credible are these motives? We know from epigraphical evidence that a round sum of three thousand talents was earmarked for the expedition (and in the end its total cost considerably exceeded that figure). Segesta's failure to supply more than thirty talents, though irksome, would surely not demand a complete reassessment of strategy. On the other hand, such a failure, whether true or fictional, would supply an excellent excuse for leaving Segesta in the lurch. If Athens was to get anywhere against Syracuse, she could not afford to waste time in the west of the island, tangling inconclusively with Selinus. Once again, it looks very much as though the story of fraudulence was a fabrication, designed to palliate Athens' neglect of her hard-pressed Elymite ally.

But the obstinate neutrality maintained by Rhegium was quite another matter. That alone would more than have justified the generals' council of war, since the armada had no comparable alternative base available elsewhere. There is no reason to suppose, either, that the views which Thucydides attributes to each of the three commanders are not those actually expressed at the time. Clearly the original strategy had been based on that of Laches and his successors during the 427–424 campaign, which hinged round the use of Rhegium as naval base, supply depot, and control point over the narrows. What the debate makes amply clear is that the Athenians had to find either a new base or a new policy. Nicias, as we might expect, saw this contretemps as a good excuse for contracting out of the "Grand Design" altogether. The object of the expedition—as officially laid down by the Assembly, at any rate—was, he reminded his colleagues, to regulate matters between Segesta and Selinus. If the Segestans "provided money for the whole army, then they should reconsider matters." Otherwise Athens should insist on being indemnified for a sixty-ship squadron, as agreed, and patch up some sort of truce between the warring cities. This done, they should cruise round Sicily making a demonstration of strength, and then return home—"unless," Nicias added as an afterthought, "we should happen to find some quick and unexpected way of doing good to the people of Leontini or of winning over any of the other cities to our side."

Alcibiades' reaction was immediate and uncompromising. After such a splendid beginning, he said, "they ought not to disgrace themselves by going home with nothing to show for it." But what he recommended, characteristically, was diplomatic rather than military action. Send envoys to every city except Syracuse and Selinus, he said. Make contact with the native Sicels, encourage them to rebel against Syracuse: they can supply you with good guerrilla fighters as well as with wheat. When you have approached all the cities, you will know who is likely to support you in a general war.

This was all sound enough, but too leisurely by half. On the other hand, Alcibiades did make one suggestion for positive and immediate action. Their first step, he said, should be to win the alliance of Messina, which "was the gate of Sicily and would also serve as an excellent harbour and base for the army." The element of initial surprise had already been lost. If Athens could do a quick deal with Messina, the expedition's chances

would be improved out of all measure, and Syracuse was unlikely to strengthen her defences materially before the end of
that campaigning season.

Lamachus, as might have been expected, was the only one of
the three commanders who approached the problem without
any political or diplomatic preconsiderations. He knew what the
real object of the expedition was, and how best to attain it.
Political face-saving interested him no more than complicated
fifth-column intrigue. He was an old soldier, who thought exclusively in terms of strategy and tactics. To him it seemed
abundantly clear that "they ought to sail straight to Syracuse
and fight their battle under the city walls as quickly as possible,
while the enemy were still not ready for them and were most
frightened of them." This, of course, was precisely the view
that Nicias had expressed in debate; on the spot he was far
more cautious—perhaps (that fatal ignis fatuus of the Sicilian
campaign) because he hoped to win everything without fighting, by fifth-column work and collusion. To us, Lamachus' attitude must seem the only one that had a reasonable chance of
success. He had obviously done some careful intelligence work
before propounding it. Not until the Athenians reached Rhegium had Syracuse begun to mobilise. Her fleet had not fought
in a major engagement since 453. The city fortifications dated
back to Gelon's day, and at many points were badly dilapidated.

Lamachus had also given some thought to the problem of a
new base for the fleet. Again, the solution he came up with
was by far the best one offered. A little way north of Syracuse
was the site of Megara Hyblaea, destroyed by Gelon about
483–482 and —for whatever reason—never reoccupied. It had an
admirable harbour, and was better placed, strategically speaking, for an assault on Syracuse than either Rhegium or Messina.
Since it was a ghost-town, the tricky problem of local alliances
did not arise. In all likelihood the remains of houses and harbour installations still existed there, together with material for
rebuilding and refortifying the site. This, surely, answered the
most cogent criticism of Lamachus' plan—that it was suicide to
tackle Syracuse until they had a strong base. From Megara

Hyblaea they could not only attack on the landward side, but also enforce a naval blockade. Moreover—as Lamachus did not fail to point out—if they acted quickly, and established themselves in a dominant position outside Syracuse, they stood to collect some quick, easily negotiable loot: many of the Syracusans, large landowners in particular, would be cut off on their country estates before they could transfer their goods and chattels for safe-keeping within the walls.

However, when it came to a vote, Lamachus failed to persuade either of his colleagues; and in the end, to avoid total stalemate, he agreed to the plan proposed by Alcibiades. Plutarch may or may not be right in hinting that his influence was diminished because of his poverty and lack of political *nous*; but at this stage in the game the daring strategy he advanced was not going to appeal either to Nicias or to Alcibiades. Nicias was cautious by nature; Alcibiades had no intention of running any unnecessary risks before the charge against him was cleared up. A quick victory might secure his acquittal; but any setback would be as good as a death-warrant.

Since Alcibiades' plan had been chosen, it was now necessary for him to implement it. As so often, he thought the end in view could best be achieved by charm and personal diplomacy rather than by direct military action. From the fleet's temporary base on the foreshore at Rhegium he sailed across to Messina in his own flagship, unescorted, and was given a hearing before the city's Assembly. For once his golden tongue failed to persuade. Perhaps the pro-Syracusan party was uppermost at the time; perhaps the men of Messina simply disliked the idea of having anything to do with this alien and unpredictable invasion force. At all events, they offered Alcibiades identical terms to those proposed by Rhegium: a market outside the walls, but nothing more. However, Alcibiades did not go away completely empty-handed. A group of Athenian sympathisers existed in Messina, and during his visit Alcibiades contrived to make contact with its leaders. Before he returned to Rhegium a detailed plot had been worked out between them for betraying the port into Athenian hands. It is even possible that this was really the main object of his visit, and his appeal to the Assembly (which he must have known would be rejected), a mere blind to cover his other activities.

He now proceeded to carry out the second part of his plan. At the time of the Athenians' first arrival in the strait, intelligence reports had suggested that the allegiances of the main cities were as follows. Selinus and Syracuse were actively hostile; Himera, Gela, and—surprisingly, but perhaps under duress— Catana had promised Syracuse their support; Messina and Camarina maintained a careful neutrality. Segesta and Leontini were appellant-allies of Athens, while Naxos and Acragas had at least expressed pro-Athenian sentiments. Alcibiades' first move, obviously, was to approach the Chalcidic cities, Naxos and Catana, Athens' traditional allies, and build up a solid anti-Syracusan bloc on the east coast of the island. Two generals—probably Alcibiades himself and Lamachus—put provisions aboard and sailed with a squadron of sixty triremes,[7] leaving one commander and the rest of the expeditionary force outside Rhegium. Their political forecasting had been reasonably accurate. Naxos opened its gates to them, the first Sicilian city that did so; but when they sailed on to Catana, they found a pro-Syracusan party in office, and were firmly rebuffed. They therefore cruised on some little way further, and anchored for the night at the mouth of the river Terias, close by Leontini.[8]

It must have put a severe strain on Lamachus to be so near to Syracuse, with sixty first-class fighting ships at his disposal, and not attempt that lightning assault for which he yearned. What happened the next day shows, only too clearly, how good the prospects for such a strike in fact were: Lamachus had sized

[7] These were surely the fast triremes provided by Athens; their use, in such numbers, suggests that this cruise in search of allies was not above a little quiet intimidation.

[8] Why, we may ask, did they not avail themselves of the hospitality which their Leontinian friends would surely have offered them? The answer must be that at this point Syracuse was blockading Leontini; also, of course, the town lay some way inland, and it would have been highly dangerous for the Athenians to abandon their ships.

up the Syracusan defences with a very shrewd eye. The plan which was now carried out bears the hall-mark of Alcibiades' cool bravado—yet its very success only goes to show what a unique chance was lost when Lamachus' strategy failed to win acceptance.

Syracuse and Athens were not, as yet, technically at war with one another. Syracuse had to be given a formal opportunity to do justice to the men of Leontini, whose plight formed the ostensible *casus belli* between Syracuse and Athens. The squadron therefore sailed to the mouth of the Grand Harbour, in line-ahead formation, and hove to outside it. Ten vessels were sent into the harbour itself, carrying heralds aboard. These were instructed to make a proclamation from their ships, as they sailed up, "that the Athenians had come to restore the people of Leontini to their own land, in accordance with their alliance and in virtue of their kinship with them. Any Leontinians in Syracuse should leave the city without fear, and join their Athenian benefactors." There was no response to this offer. On the other hand, there does not seem to have been any defensive counter-action on the part of the Syracusans, either. The lack of naval and military readiness in and around the Grand Harbour is almost unbelievable. There was no boom across the harbour mouth, and no patrol to guard it. If the Syracusan fleet was anywhere, it must have been either out on manoeuvres or else docked in the Lesser Harbour on the northern side of the city. The Athenians sailed in and out precisely as they pleased, and, says Thucydides, "made a reconnaissance of the city and the harbours and the general lie of the land to see where they would have to make their base for carrying on the war." Nothing could have more eloquently vindicated Lamachus' assessment of the situation.

When they were off the point of Dascon, close to the temple of Olympian Zeus, they also captured one Syracusan vessel (the only one in sight, to judge from our evidence), which had aboard the register of all the citizens, listed by tribes. This register was normally kept in the temple, but had been ordered across to Syracuse on this occasion in order to draw up a con-

scription list for those of military age (another hint at Syracuse's chronic state of unpreparedness). The generals pounced
on this valuable piece of military intelligence, but were by no
means encouraged when they discovered the large reserves of
manpower Syracuse had available.[9]

From Syracuse the squadron sailed back to Catana: the
Athenians were determined not to let so valuable a position go
by default. Careful scrutiny of the defences suggested a way in
which their object might be achieved. The authorities of Catana, as before, refused to allow the Athenian army inside the
walls. This time, however, they invited the two commanders
to come and state their case publicly before the Assembly—exactly the move that Alcibiades had been hoping for. While he
was addressing the Assembly, and most of Catana was crowding
round to hear him, some of his Athenian troops broke down a
badly dilapidated postern gate in the walls, and made their way
through to the marketplace. They did not attack anyone; they
simply strolled up and down, so far as we can tell, admiring
the view—an extremely clever move. But their mere presence
was enough to scare the small if influential pro-Syracusan party,
who obviously thought that at any moment a pogrom was liable
to take place, with themselves as its chosen victims. They therefore rapidly slipped away from the place of assembly; and the
rest "voted in favour of an alliance with the Athenians and invited them to bring over the remainder of their forces from
Rhegium." This was duly done, and the Athenians now set
about constructing a semi-permanent camp at Catana.

Intelligence reports continued to flow in, not all of equal
value. The Syracusans were said to be putting their fleet into
commission. There was also a rumour that Camarina was ready
to join Athens if approached. These two pieces of information
in conjunction seemed to justify another coastal cruise, and the
whole squadron accordingly put to sea once more. At Syracuse

[9] The episode also gave cold comfort to Nicias' diviners. There had
been a prophecy that Athens 'would capture all the Syracusans,' (see
above, p. 112) and it now looked as though (in the usual riddling way
of oracles) this prophecy had been fulfilled by the acquisition of the
city's nominal roll.

they found no sign of naval activity: the report was a false alarm. When they reached Camarina, they drew up their ships on the beach and, with some confidence, sent a herald up into the city. But here, too, Athenian intelligence seems to have been at fault. The inhabitants firmly refused to admit them.[10]

On the way home the squadron landed a raiding party in Syracusan territory, but lost a number of light-armed troops when some enemy cavalry appeared and cut off the stragglers. One way and another this second sortie was not proving at all successful. By now it was September; the campaigning season was nearly over, and they had very little to show for it. But the final blow was still in store. As the squadron sailed back into Catana harbour, the look-outs saw a newly arrived vessel lying at anchor there: a trim, fast, splendidly equipped trireme whose blazons and line instantly revealed her identity.

This was Athens' official state galley, the *Salaminia*; and no one—least of all Alcibiades—could doubt on what errand she had come.

[10] They reminded the Athenians, pointedly, of the agreement whereby "they were bound by oath only to receive the Athenians if they came in one single ship, unless they themselves asked for more to be sent."

The officers of the *Salaminia* had a delicate task to perform, and careful instructions as to how they should go about it. Alcibiades, together with certain other members of the expedition indicted on the same charge, was to be brought back home for trial. On the other hand, he was not to be placed under close arrest. The officers were "not to use violence or to lay hands on his person, but to convey in moderate language the order that he must accompany them home." Obviously it was vital to avoid any trouble with the troops in Sicily—especially the Argives and Mantineans, who had a personal loyalty to Alcibiades. But here the authorities in Athens perhaps misjudged the general mood of the expedition that autumn. Plutarch, or his source, claims that Alcibiades could, had he so wished, have produced a mutiny on his behalf; that the men suffered a loss of morale after his removal, and believed that the campaign would drag on indefinitely "now that Alcibiades who provided the spur to action had been taken away." This is highly debatable. To begin with, it was Lamachus, not Alcibiades, who provided the spur to action, such as it was; and he still remained with the fleet. Secondly, when it came to the point, not one voice seems to have been raised in objection against Alcibiades' removal.

The loss of morale, in fact, had already taken place; and we can hardly wonder at it. These two months in Sicily had been a chapter of missed opportunities, weakly erratic strategy, and irritating setbacks. The fleet had cruised in aimless fashion, to and fro, round the coastal cities of Sicily. Almost every harbour, both there and in Magna Graecia, was closed to the Athenians, including the key port of Rhegium. They had a camp at Catana, but serious naval operations, even after all this time, were still not begun. One unsuccessful skirmish ashore was the sum total of their engagements. If the officers of the *Salaminia* had marched Alcibiades off in chains, it is unlikely that any real effort would have been made to stop them. In any case, Alcibiades himself proved unexpectedly co-operative. He took the other accused persons aboard his own flagship, and declared himself ready and willing to accompany the *Salaminia* home. If the officers had known their man a little better, they might have found his attitude highly suspicious—not least since they had made it quite clear to their quasi-prisoner that the mood in Athens was one of implacable hostility to him and everything he stood for. Even before he left Catana, Alcibiades must have sized up the odds against him with icy clarity, and taken his own private decision—not only to jump trial (which was more than understandable), but also to change sides, and attack Athens as damagingly as he knew how.

The first demonstration of this switch in allegiance came soon enough, though its effects did not hit the Athenians until some little while later. While the two vessels lay at Rhegium, Alcibiades contrived to send a confidential note to the ruling party of Messina, revealing every detail of the plot he had made with the pro-Athenian group—method, strategy, names, date—to betray the city into Athenian hands. While Nicias and Lamachus were still happily convinced that the plot was proceeding according to plan, the ringleaders found themselves quietly rounded up and put to death. This was something more than mere pique on Alcibiades' part; it shows that defection was in his mind right from the beginning.

When the *Salaminia* had escorted him as far as Thurii, he decided it was time for them to part company. How well his flagship was guarded—or how well the guards were bribed—is a debatable point; neither he nor any of those accused with him seem to have found any difficulty in slipping ashore, probably at night, and losing themselves in the warren-like back streets of the port. The officers of the *Salaminia* set up a hue and cry for him, but without success. In the end they were forced to sail back to Athens empty-handed.

To someone who recognised him in Thurii, and asked whether he could not trust his own country to see justice done, Alcibiades is said to have replied: "When my life's at stake, I wouldn't trust my own mother to vote for an acquittal"—a very fair estimate of the situation, one feels. Modern notions of honour, fair play, or "facing the music" simply do not apply here. For Alcibiades to have returned to Athens at this juncture would have been tantamount to committing suicide as an obliging gesture to his political enemies. How right he was in this estimate, he learnt a month or two later, when—having slipped across to the Peloponnese in a small fishing craft—he was leading an uneasy exile's existence at Argos.

The Athenian court which had tried him *in absentia* condemned him to death, ordered the confiscation of all his estates, and finally decreed that his name should be publicly cursed by all the priests and priestesses of Eleusis—perhaps, indeed, by the entire priestly hierarchy throughout Attica.[1] Only one priestess, Theano, refused to perform this act of execration, declaring, with some dignity, that she was "a priestess dedicated to prayer, not to curses." Alcibiades' only recorded comment on the death sentence was: "I'll show them I'm still alive." Now, whatever his intentions may have been hitherto—and his betrayal of the Messina plot leaves little doubt on that score—such a ferocious, final, and vindictive sentence more or less made up his mind for him. He had no alternative left but exile; nor was it easy for him to find refuge with any neutral state, least of all one that leaned towards Athens. By condemning him in this way, his fellow-countrymen were virtually making a present of him to the Spartans.

His experiences immediately after escaping from Thurii must have shown him (if he had not already guessed) just how the land lay. He had made for the port of Cyllene, in Elis; perhaps he imagined that his brilliant Olympian victories the previous year would win him some special consideration now. If so, he was in for a disappointment. The authorities of Elis clearly found his presence an embarrassment; and so, after a very short while, he moved on to Argos. But the Argives, too, gave him

---

[1] This suggests that the court which tried him may have been a special tribunal, composed exclusively of initiates in the Mysteries.

something less than an enthusiastic welcome. Much had changed since the fine, high-riding days immediately after the Peace of Nicias. The immediate trouble was an abortive right-wing coup that had taken place in Argos only a couple of months before. During the Athenian witch hunt after icono-clasts and blasphemers, it had been alleged that Alcibiades' cousin, together with some of his close friends, were behind the plot—and, *a fortiori*, that Alcibiades himself had been mixed up in it.[2] Argive hostages had been executed; the whole incident left much rancour behind it.

It is not hard to sympathise with the dilemma of the Argive government. The charge might be (as Alcibiades no doubt claimed) a clever political invention, and, again, it might not; no smoke, they will have reflected, without fire. On top of everything else, Athenian ambassadors had now arrived in Ar-gos and were pressing strongly for his extradition. At a time when Sparta was rumoured to be considering an invasion, it would not do to offend Athens overmuch. Alcibiades' presence was really much more trouble than it was worth. Perhaps, it was suggested to him, he would—like that other distinguished Athenian, Themistocles, who had similarly sought refuge in Ar-gos—be happier, ultimately, elsewhere? It was at this psycho-logical point, we are told, that the exile finally decided to "re-nounce his country altogether." We can at least sympathise with his predicament. As matters stood, he had been made the victim of a crude political hatchet job. The chances of his ever getting back to Athens must have seemed infinitesimal. He had offended every major power group there: no one would fight on his behalf. His last remaining supporters, the young extremists of the Western lobby, were not liable to be impressed by the dismal record of the fleet in Sicily. Where *could* he turn now except to Sparta and her allies? Despite his pro-Argive record

[2] So far as we can tell, there was no truth in the rumour. It was just the kind of smear ("secret oligarch—aiming at a tyranny") which Androcles and the popular party would automatically use against him. In this case it seems to have been endorsed by the conservatives as well. Alcibiades was not particular about where he made enemies (see above, pp. 7–8).

he had long-standing family connections at Sparta; the gamble was at least worth trying.

He therefore wrote to the Spartan government, asking for a formal safe-conduct—they were unlikely to have forgotten his part in the negotiations with Argos (420), or the débâcle at Mantinea two years later—and promising, if granted asylum, "that he would render them services greater than all the harm he had done them when he was their enemy." The Spartans considered his request, and, after some hesitation, granted it. They never regretted their decision, which indeed proved a momentous turning point in the whole course of the war.

Nothing is harder for a modern individual to understand than ancient concepts of loyalty and treachery. Those who have read so far will be uncomfortably aware that patriotism, in our sense, is a quality more or less irrelevant to Greek civic morality during the fifth century B.C. On very exceptional occasions—the Persian Wars are a good example—patriotism could burst its normal partisan bounds, and become something we all can recognise; but in the ordinary way loyalty was to one's family clan, one's religious or political group, rather than to that comparatively recent institution the polis. What one scholar describes as our passion for "the transcendental power of Greek city-state patriotism" is largely the pursuit of a modern myth. There was seldom a time when an oligarchic group was not ready to betray a democratically controlled city—or vice versa—to the foreign enemy at the gates. As for distinguished individual traitors, there was no shortage of them either in Athens or in Sparta: Hippias and Pausanias are only the first two names that come to mind. The number of Spartan rulers who defected, collaborated, or plotted against the state would make a very impressive roll-call on its own.

Yet when every possible excuse has been made on this score, there still remains an unpleasantly personal flavour about Alcibiades' action—as there does about nearly all his actions. Circumstances were against him, indeed; but he reacted with a spiteful, self-centered violence that no amount of exculpation—however much we may sympathise with his position—can wholly justify. The polis, to him, was a mere stage for his personality; no other actor got more than a walking-on part—or a sleeping partnership. Ties of blood and political allegiance, then? Here we draw blank once more. Alcibiades seems not to have cared a rap for any of his kinsmen, Alcmaeonids included, much less for any specific political party; he preferred to play one off against the other, with cool and flashy cynicism, so that in the end, when the chips were down—as now after his condemnation —he stood simply and solely for himself. Themistocles may have believed he was an Athenian patriot still when he served the Great King as governor of Magnesia; but Alcibiades' protestations at Sparta have a ring of hollow and specious insincerity which nothing can disguise. He was, in the last resort, a brilliant play-actor, a professional charmer, with an immature streak that verged on the psychopathic, and a colossal vanity which required constant nursing. Nothing is more revealing about him than "his special gift," as Plutarch calls it, "which surpassed all the rest and served to attach men to him, namely that he could assimilate and adapt himself to the pursuits and the manner of living of others and submit himself to more startling transformations than a chameleon."

We all know this character: he is the classic confidence-trickster, the charming con-man, whose lack of moral principle enhances his gift for fluid self-adaptation, who lives from moment to moment, a narcissist with one eye always on the main chance, merging into his background and identifying with it in his fantasy—yet never too involved to scoop the pool when everyone is looking the other way. Such was the man—versatile, talented, irresponsible—who now, as October declined into November, set out on the road from Argos to Sparta, riding uneasily, one eye alert for patrols or ambushes, Sparta's safe-conduct folded in his wallet: a man still under forty, yet already blown, like a once-beautiful fading rose, by luxury and self-indulgence; a shallow, meretricious genius, apt instrument of Athens' fall from her imperial apogee.

With Alcibiades' removal from Sicily, Nicias became, in effect, commander-in-chief of the Athenian expedition—not an event calculated to encourage those who wanted fast and positive results. Though Lamachus was by far the more competent general, he now found himself, for whatever reason, little more than Nicias' second-in-command, "and the result," as Plutarch says, "was nothing but over-cautious and hesitant tactics." So long as Alcibiades had had any say in the matter, western Sicily remained on the very periphery of Athenian strategy. But the moment he was out of the way, Nicias—with an almost audible sigh of relief—decided to abandon Syracuse (temporarily at least) and investigate, not before time, how matters stood between Segesta and Selinus.

The entire expeditionary force was taken on this abortive excursion—an act which, if it did nothing else, gave a sharp boost to Syracusan morale. The more Athens' powerful armada frittered away its time and energies on such pursuits, the safer Syracuse became. Nicias and Lamachus divided their complement into two, and took one half each by lot. They then cruised along the north coast of the island, towards Segesta. On the way they put in at Himera—the only Greek city hereabouts—but once more found themselves refused admission by the inhabitants. They sailed on, past the Carthaginian ports of Solous and Panormus (Palermo)—no point in stirring up another barbarian hornets' nest—until they came to Hyccara, a fortified native fishing port on hostile terms with Segesta. Here they landed, and were met by a squadron of Segestan cavalry, which indicates a prearranged plan. Together they stormed the town, which seems to have offered little resistance. All moveable loot, including prisoners, went to the Athenians, while Segesta took over the town itself. Nicias, somewhat mysteriously, went on alone to Segesta, and rejoined the expedition "after receiving thirty talents and doing some other business there." It would be interesting to know just what this business was.

The attack on Hyccara was, primarily, a quick way of raising ready cash. The inhabitants would fetch a good price in the Catana slave-market, and it was desirable that they should be in good condition when they got there. For once Nicias (the bulk of whose fortune, we recall, had been made by leasing out gangs of slaves to the Laurium mining engineers) was absolutely in his element. He emptied the troop-transports, and sent the fleet straight back to Catana loaded down with Hyccaric captives. If he had ever intended to take the expedition as far as Selinus, the scheme was now abandoned. Perhaps his "business" in Segesta consisted of getting them to accept Hyccara in lieu of military aid. The army he sent home across country, most probably the way of Enna, Agyrium, and Centuripae—an exercise which gave them ample opportunity to make contact with the various Sicel leaders en route. The more guerrilla troops that were in action against Syracuse, the better. The Hyccaric prisoners were duly sold, and brought in no less than 120 talents. At an average fetching price of 150 drachmas, something not far short of five thousand slaves must have been knocked down under the hammer that day—a large haul for so small a town. Amongst them—as yet unnoticed—was a young girl who grew up to be the famous courtesan Lais.

On its way home the expedition had some trouble from the Sicel town of Hybla (Paternó), some nine miles north-west of Catana. Hybla seems always to have been ruggedly independent by nature: when the nationalist leader Ducetius tried to form a Sicel League, Hybla was the only community which refused to join it. Now the Hyblaeans were, apparently, siding with Syracuse. A hostile outpost so near to Catana could not be tolerated; for once Nicias was ready to act. Half the expeditionary force took the field, under his personal command, to bring Hybla into line. But when the summer ended, and the autumn rains came, Hybla was still holding out. Nicias had perforce to abandon the siege. This half-baked display put the finishing touch to a season's campaigning of almost unparalleled ineptitude. As Athenian morale decreased, so that of Athens' enemies in Syracuse rose day by day. The longer Nicias held off his attack on their city, the more confident the Syracusans became. After the fiasco before Hybla, their last lingering fears vanished. They now began urging their commanders to move over to the offensive, and attack Nicias' main camp at Catana. Detachments of Syracusan cavalry on reconnaissance patrols took to riding round the Athenian outposts, apparently with impunity, shouting taunts and insults at their occupants. "Re-settling that lot from Leontini in their territory, eh?" they jeered. "Looks more as if you're settling down in Catana your-selves."

It is only fair to give Nicias the benefit of the doubt when one can. Plutarch, as usual, ascribes his inactivity during the autumn to an ingrained distaste for fighting, and there may be something in this. But he was brave enough when he had to be, and by no means so dilatory as he is sometimes made out. He also had a flair for tricky strategy and tactical surprises. His object at present was to lure the Syracusans into a mood of rash over-confidence, and in this he succeeded admirably. (He may have only been making a virtue of necessity, but that is beside the point.) Such over-confidence was an essential pre-liminary to the plan which he and Lamachus had worked out between them. If the scheme was, in essence, Lamachus' idea, at least he had persuaded Nicias to go along with it—just how far, we shall see in due course. Their object, briefly put, was to establish an Athenian base on the shores of the Grand Har-bour itself. Nicias had several Syracusan exiles on his intelligence staff, and they pointed out what they regarded as the best site for such a base—the flat ground between Dascon Bay and the temple of Olympian Zeus (Olympieum), east of the road to Helorus, and on the south side of the Anapus River. Here they would be protected against Syracusan cavalry attacks—to which they were peculiarly vulnerable—by high rocky ground to their left, near the temple. They would also have the river and some swampy ground to the north of them, and a coastal salt-marsh—the present-day Salina di Siracusa—at their backs.

But to occupy this site was not such an easy matter. If they were observed bringing their fleet up, or marching in force over-land, they would find the whole Syracusan army there to fight them off. Even if they moved in under cover of darkness, they would not have time to fortify their position. Their light-armed troops and camp-followers would be particularly vulnerable to Syracusan cavalry attacks. The answer, when Nicias and Lamachus hit on it, was simple but effective: it much resembled the ruse whereby Themistocles lured King Xerxes to his downfall at Salamis. Nicias had a double agent in his service, a Catanian whom he could trust implicitly, "and who the Syracusan generals thought was on their side"—a story not unfamiliar in our own day. This man's cover story was that he belonged to the pro-Syracusan action group in Catana—men whom he named, and who were, in turn, known to the Syracusan high command. Having thus established his *bona fides*, he proceeded to bait the trap:

> He told them [the Syracusans] that the Athenians were in the habit of sleeping at night inside the city at some distance from the places where their arms were kept; if, therefore, the Syracusans would fix a day and come at dawn with their entire force to attack the Athenian expedition, their supporters in Catana would close the gates on the troops inside the city and would set fire to the ships, and then the Syracusans could attack the stockade and would easily overpower the men inside it. [Thuc. 6.64.2–3]

He also said that there were large numbers of sympathisers in Catana itself who were ready and eager to take part in such an operation, and the sooner the better.

Since the Syracusan generals had already been contemplating an assault on Catana, and since—perhaps more important—this was just the sort of story they *wanted* to believe, they did not examine it quite so critically as they might otherwise have done. Over-confidence is a catching disease. With what Thucydides rightly calls "remarkable lack of precaution," they at once arranged a day for the attack, and sent Nicias' agent back to Catana to warn his fellow-conspirators; which he duly did, though not quite in the sense they had anticipated. Nicias and Lamachus smiled to themselves, posted scouts to watch every movement on the road out of Syracuse, and waited.

When the day came, and the whole Syracusan army marched out in battle order, fast mounted messengers must have got the

news through to Catana well before noon. Nicias had to watch
his timing very carefully. The fleet must reach its destination
soon enough to set up defence-works without interruption. On
the other hand, it must not be seen by the Syracusan troops
now marching north along the coast road. This route-march
would take them two days, with a halt for the night somewhere
near Leontini; the distance was roughly forty miles. The fleet,
given a fair following wind, could cruise at an average of four
to six knots: sometimes less, seldom more. It would be wise,
therefore, to allow eight to ten hours to reach Syracuse. Given
these figures, Nicias and Lamachus had an obvious course of
action to follow. They would sail late on the first afternoon—
darkness fell about 6 P.M. in October—and pass Leontini under
cover of darkness, when their opponents were already encamped
there. This would bring them into the Great Harbour of Syracuse early in the small hours, which suited their purpose very
well. They had a full day in hand—quite sufficient for their purposes. The scheme went through exactly as planned; at first
light they began their disembarkation, at the mouth of the Anapus River, and set about fortifying the position they had chosen
as an advance base. They encountered no opposition.

The outflow of the Anapus, like all rivers near Syracuse, forms
a wide shallow estuary, with a sand-bar, and is easily fordable,
even in the depths of winter.[3] It was on the south side of
this estuary that the Athenians drew up the main body of their
fleet, though they probably detached a small squadron to guard
their rear from Dascon Promontory. This, as Thucydides admits, was their most vulnerable point, since boats could easily
be beached there, and the terrain provided no real protection.
On the promontory itself they "hurriedly constructed a fort with
stones which they picked up, and with timber." They also felled
trees and built a stockade round their ships, as protection against
a Syracusan attack across the estuary. Lastly, they broke down

[3] I found no difficulty in doing so towards the end of December. The
changing coastline has not substantially altered the outflow of either
the Anapo (to give it its modern name), the Fiume di Noto, or the Tellaro.

the bridge which carried the main Helorus road across the river. Thus, if they were holding the estuary and the flat land to the south of it, they could not be outflanked by Syracusan cavalry —not, at least, without considerable warning.

There was one obvious weakness about this plan; and here we have the first (but not the last) instance of Nicias' piety interfering with his common sense. He not only refrained from looting the treasures of the Olympieum, which was reasonable enough (even the tyrant Gelon had had similar scruples), but also kept his troops outside the limits of the temple precinct —which gave the Syracusans considerable latitude of movement. Examination of the terrain suggests that, as we might expect, a small road, little more than a track, ran direct from the Olympieum across the Anapus, probably with a footbridge crossing. (The main bridge lay to the east of this, about half a mile nearer the sea.[4]) If Nicias left the precinct untouched, he must have spared the footbridge as well. While this is unlikely to have supported cavalry, it could at a pinch be used by troops on foot —and in fact was so used, as we shall see.

The Athenians took up their position between the estuary and the Helorus road, south of the Anapus, and dug themselves in at leisure.[5] They were protected not only by the river and the high ground round the Olympieum, but also by a scatter of walls and houses on the flat ground near the estuary. This was an excellent position. It gave ample scope for infantry to manoeuvre, while at the same time ensuring maximum protection against Syracusan cavalry. (There is a silly story in Polyaenus

[4] I am assuming (as Freeman, for one, did not) that the modern road to Noto and Pachino crosses the river at much the same point as it did in antiquity: this makes far better sense of Thucydides' narrative.

[5] We can deduce their position from Hermocrates' jeering comment when Nicias broke down the Anapus bridge. Hermocrates observed— the usual canard—that Nicias' main objective seemed to be to avoid fighting; if the Athenians had been *north* of the river, as some writers have supposed, the insult would have been pointless. Hermocrates' criticism, incidentally, could just as well be applied to the invisible Syracusan garrison (himself presumably among them) who sat still and watched from behind their ramparts while fort and stockade were built.

that the Athenians scattered caltrops on the ground as an additional defensive measure: the lie of the land, and the tactics adopted, make this highly improbable.) The Athenians, moreover, could attack or refuse battle exactly as they pleased.

Meanwhile the Syracusan cavalry had reached Catana, and discovered, with some consternation, exactly what the Athenians were up to. They wheeled round at the gallop, and—barely pausing to inform the main body of their army—clattered on ahead to the Anapus, only to find the Helorus bridge down and the Athenians well dug in. Since they could not tempt Nicias into a premature engagement, and evening was coming on, they moved across the Helorus road, away from the sea, and encamped near the footbridge leading to the Olympieum.[6] Here the infantry presently joined them; and both sides bivouacked for the night. Next morning the Athenian and Syracusan commanders disposed their troops in battle formation, awaiting, as Freeman says, "the first battle between Greek and Greek on Sicilian ground of which we have any full account." Nicias put his Argive and Mantinean mercenaries on the right wing, his own Athenian hoplites in the centre, and the remainder of the allies, including the islanders, on the left—the side, be it noted, where there would be most danger from a cavalry attack. Half the total force was drawn up in this standard deployment, ranked eight deep, while the rest formed a hollow square (also eight deep) protecting the tents and the non-combatants, and with orders "to be ready to move up to the support of any part of the front line which they saw to be in difficulties."

The Syracusans had packed their entire army, allies included,

[6] Common sense suggests that it was now, and not after the subsequent battle, as Thucydides says, that they slipped a garrison into the temple, "since they were afraid that the Athenians might make off with some of the treasure there." They obviously did not know Nicias' pious temperament yet. Later they were to rectify their omission. Plutarch suggests that others—perhaps Lamachus—were anxious to occupy and plunder the temple, but that Nicias restrained them for fear of sacrilege, and deliberately allowed a Syracusan garrison to move in. One thing this whole episode proves beyond question is the existence of a second bridge.

into a heavy-armed front sixteen shields deep; the largest non-Syracusan contingent was that sent by Selinus. Their cavalry, 1,200 strong, reinforced by troops from Gela and Camarina, was drawn up on the right wing, with the javelin-throwers next to them. Clearly this was so that they might have the advantage of any open ground that was going, away from the seaward side.

The most interesting clue which Thucydides gives us to the tactics of this battle is the fact that Nicias' attack caught the Syracusans off their guard. They were not expecting it so soon; some of their soldiers, with splendidly casual insouciance, had sloped off back to the city—"which was not far distant." So the Syracusans were drawn up *north* of the Anapus, and (as we shall see) on the seaward side of the Helorus road—that is, immediately above the estuary, with the Lysimeleia marsh at their backs. The Athenians held a similar position on the south side of the Anapus; they had not moved from the defensive site they occupied the day before. This, clearly, is what took the Syracusans off their guard. They assumed that Nicias' preparations were purely defensive; that he was once more refusing battle. At the same time they were loath to attack, themselves, across terrain that gave so little scope to their cavalry. The last thing they expected was a formation attack *by way of the estuary*. But Nicias, whose strategy so often makes one weep, had few rivals as a short-term tactician; he was the perfect brigade commander, who only went to pieces when called upon to behave like a field-marshal. After a rather grim pep-talk to his troops ("Unless we win, we shall not find it easy to get away, since their cavalry will be upon us in great force"), he gave the signal for battle.

First, the light-armed troops—slingers, stone-throwers, archers—advanced in open formation, skirmishing with their opposite numbers from the Syracusan ranks. Under cover of this secondary engagement, and after the soothsayers had made due sacrifice, the hoplite phalanx moved up into position on the north bank of the estuary, facing the Helorus road, and battle was joined. For some while neither side gave way. Then, suddenly, a thunderstorm broke overhead—it was the season of the autumn rains—with lightning and a torrential downpour. The Athenians, being seasoned troops, were used to this kind of thing. The Syracusans were not. They reacted with nervous and superstitious alarm, and their line cracked.

The Argives made the first break-through, driving the enemy's left wing back towards the marshes; then the Athenians punched clean through their centre, and the Syracusan army was cut in two. This was the end of the battle. The Syracusans retreated; but the retreat never became a rout, since their cavalry remained intact, and would very soon have carved up any Athenian hoplites they found exposed ahead of the main body. After the victors had got as far as they could with safety, Nicias called off the pursuit. They set up a trophy and withdrew to their own lines.

The Syracusans halted by the Helorus road, got themselves into some sort of formation again, and went back to the city. They also seem to have reinforced the garrison of the Olympieum. However, the Athenians made no attempt to capture the temple. Next day they proclaimed a truce, and gave the Syracusans back their dead.[7] They collected their own casualties, buried them, and stored the arms they had captured aboard the triremes. This done, they struck camp, abandoned the position they had won by their own considerable skill and bravery, and sailed back to Catana. It is, at first sight, one of the most astonishing decisions in the whole course of the campaign.

Questions crowd into one's mind. If Nicias always intended to pull out of his position on the Anapus estuary the moment he had established himself there, why had he bothered to mount the operation at all? As a mere military exercise? To impress the Syracusans? Or did he have a failure of nerve once the immediate objective was gained? And was he railroaded into the operation in the first place? Though his troops undoubtedly needed practice in land-based warfare, the Syracusans were not likely to be over-impressed by such tip-and-run tactics. Failure

[7] Thucydides says the Syracusans lost 260 killed; Diodorus puts the number at four hundred. Athenian and allied casualties amounted to about fifty.

of nerve after a decision taken against his better judgment: this seems the most plausible explanation. The trouble was, of course, that Nicias—like any intellectual—could always find six good reasons for not taking positive action. His inertia was due, in part at least, to his intense awareness of all the snags and hazards surrounding any problem. Here he makes a sharp contrast with Lamachus, whose basic formula (like that of the Israelis when assaulting the Heights of Golon in Syria) was to punch through at all costs, and consolidate afterwards. Winter was approaching, he argued.[8] The expedition was not well enough equipped "to carry on the war from their base before Syracuse." They must have cavalry: this was essential. Before they could launch a real attack on Syracuse in the spring they needed more money, more wheat, more local allies.

It would be enlightening to have Lamachus' doubtless blunt and probably unprintable reactions to this summary. There are two obvious points at issue. First, why did Nicias wait till now before raising his list of objections? He was well aware of all of them before the advance base was ever established. Second, why did he so wantonly throw away the tactical advantage he had gained? An immediate all-out attack (Lamachus' original plan) would in all likelihood have had Syracuse in Athenian hands by now. The entire Syracusan army had been lured away on a fool's errand; yet the Athenians had done nothing but sit and look at the place from a safe distance. Why not? To storm and occupy Syracuse was by no means an impossibility. A determined band of mercenaries had done just that in 461, capturing both Achradina and Ortygia, their military expertise ample compensation for their lack of numbers. A large, well-equipped Athenian expeditionary force could surely have followed their example. Now it was too late; by playing safe Nicias had lost a never to be repeated opportunity of finishing off the campaign in a few months, and at comparatively little cost. His

[8] Thucydides' analysis reads as though it was taken from some dispatch of Nicias to the Assembly, perhaps that which he subsequently sent from Naxos (see below, p. 173).

own natural inclination was for slower, less flashy, more plodding methods.

It is Diodorus who tells us that what Nicias had in mind—characteristically enough—was a siege: the first time that the idea of besieging Syracuse is mentioned. What produced even this change of front in Nicias? At one moment he is doing all he can to avoid going near Syracuse at all, eager to show the flag around the coast and then return home as soon as possible. Now, with grumbling and hesitancy, we find him settling down to a long-term assault on the city he had hoped to steer clear of. It looks very much as though the officers of the *Salaminia*, when they returned to Athens, reported—among other things—on Nicias' fundamentally lackadaisical attitude; and that the Assembly, urged on by Androcles and the radicals, sent him a sharp dressing-down and some very specific orders for his future strategy.

Even though he failed to follow up his victory, Nicias had given a sharp setback to Syracusan self-confidence. The Athenian army could, it was clear, fight very well when it chose to. The Syracusans had been taken in by an elementary fifth-column trick and made to look complete fools. A day or two later Hermocrates addressed the despondent Assembly. There was nothing wrong with their morale, he said; they simply lacked discipline and experience. When it came to warfare they were amateurs, and they had been matched against the most experienced troops in Greece. It is odd that he made no boast of Syracuse's cavalry, the one arm in which Athens was at a clear disadvantage. Also, Hermocrates went on, they had suffered from too many people giving orders. A board of fifteen generals was both unwieldy and inefficient. Cut their numbers down to three, at least for the duration of the war. Give them unrestricted power to act as they thought fit, in the city's best interests. This way, he explained, the winter could be spent in organising a crash military training programme. Such training ought to be made compulsory. Arms should be provided, at the government's expense, to those who did not already possess them. Besides, a small group of military and civil leaders, with full authority to implement their decisions, would mean fewer security leaks, and fewer delays. The defence programme could be pushed through smoothly, "without the need for giving continuous explanations for what was being done"—that is, without reference to the Assembly.

There must have been violent opposition to these proposals from the radical group under Athenagoras and Diocles, and for two very good reasons. In the first place, Hermocrates was hinting, very broadly, that a group existed in the Assembly which was prepared to pass on intelligence to the enemy, perhaps even betray the city: his object in restricting the Assembly's rights of information was to deny this group access to what we would call "classified information." Nor can anyone have doubted for one moment at whom this precaution was aimed. On the other hand, Athenagoras would hardly dare to bring such a charge out into the open—least of all if it happened to be true. Much better to pursue the line he had taken before, during their debate. What Hermocrates was advocating, looked at in political terms, seemed to confirm all the worst rumours about him. It was a switch from democracy to military oligarchy, in the shape of an authoritarian junta that lay under no obligation to justify itself before the people. However, the average citizen body is liable to vote for surprising things in an emergency, especially if the emergency is war. "Temporary emergency measures" is a phrase liable to crop up, *mutatis mutandis*, during any period of hostilities.

The Syracusan Assembly, then (presumably with the consent of the Board of Generals) approved the motion put forward by Hermocrates, but compromised by not making it effective until the normal change-over at the end of the official year—that is, in the spring of 414. There is still no real note of urgency detectable in their proceedings. They duly elected three generals for the emergency—including, of course, Hermocrates himself—and invested them with full powers. They passed measures for repairing the city's fortifications, and authorised the building of a new outer wall, from the sanctuary of Apollo Temenites to the rocky heights of Epipolae. Two extra forts were constructed, one by the Olympieum, the other near Megara Hyblaea. Palisades of stakes were sunk in every beach where an assault seemed likely.

Most important of all, ambassadors were sent on a round tour, first to the Greek cities of southern Italy, then to Corinth, and finally to Sparta. Their instructions were, first, to obtain volunteer contingents for help in the defence of Syracuse; and second, to persuade the Peloponnesian League that the war in Greece against Athens should be reopened. If this was done, the Syracusans argued, Athens would either have to pull her task-force out of Sicily altogether, or else, at the very least, keep it short on reinforcements.

When these envoys left Sicily they can hardly have foreseen how unlikely and powerful an advocate they would find waiting for them in Sparta, or to what extent the advice he gave would be instrumental in saving Syracuse from destruction—and in sealing the ultimate fate of his own country.

Within a month or two of his arrival Alcibiades had acclimatised himself, in a seemingly effortless manner, to the rigorous Spartan way of life. His close family connection with Endius, a high-ranking Spartan who was subsequently elected to the Board of Ephors,[1] more or less guaranteed him diplomatic immunity, though his position was ambivalent, to say the least of it. However, as long as there was anything useful to be got out of him, the Spartans seemed unlikely to treat their Athenian guest with anything but polite circumspection.

He certainly went out of his way to show respect for local customs. People stared incredulously at this new Alcibiades, with his toughly austere manner and coarse homespun cloak: black broth, stale bread, endless physical exercise, cold dips in the icy Eurotas—he embraced the entire regime. (His hair, unkind wits observed, was long enough when he arrived.) On the other hand, nothing could keep his un-Spartan amatory urges down for long. In between his other, more manly exercises he began taking a rather less than discreet interest in Timaea, the wife of King Agis—a development which is unlikely to have gone unnoticed in high places. But no action was taken to stop the liaison—yet. It would make a useful weapon to hold in reserve against Alcibiades until the time was ripe.

There is every indication that the Athenian renegade—dazzled, as always, by his own brilliance—considerably over-estimated the personal esteem in which he was held at Sparta. "By adopting Spartan customs in his everyday life," Plutarch reports,

[1] The Ephors, five in number, were Sparta's rather sinister equivalent of the modern political commissar, with even wider powers. Amongst other functions, they could prosecute (and if need be, execute) either of the two kings, negotiate with foreign cities, convene the Assembly, and mobilise the army.

"he captivated the people and brought them under his spell," to which one is tempted to add, "or so *he* thought." In fact, the authorities seem to have watched this flamboyant ex-enemy playboy, now so zealously aping the manners of a good Spartan, with cool and cynical distrust. His performance was overdone; he protested his manliness too much. Besides, a man who turned his coat once could well do so again. The Spartans listened readily enough to his advice; no one denied that he had a clever head on his shoulders. But it is worth noting that they never allowed him to carry out that advice, or even to accompany those who did. When Gylippus sailed for Syracuse, when Agis fortified Decelea, Alcibiades himself was left behind at Sparta, a hostage in all but name, carrying on his intrigue with Timaea (we may surmise) as much out of sheer boredom as for any more positive reason.

But when the Syracusan envoys at last reached Sparta—backed now by an enthusiastic Corinthian government, which sent its own ambassadors to endorse this Sicilian appeal—Alcibiades was granted special permission to address the Spartan Assembly on their behalf. Syracusans and Corinthians had both urged Sparta to help the cause "by making war more openly on Athens in Hellas and by sending a force to Sicily," only to find the Ephors and Council infuriatingly cautious and indecisive. They were more than dubious about embarking on renewed hostilities in Greece. They shrank from the risk and expense of sending an expeditionary force to Sicily. The most they contemplated was exhorting Syracuse to hold fast and not come to terms with Athens—cold comfort for a besieged city.

When Alcibiades rose to speak, he had worked out his line very carefully indeed. First, he must justify his own highly ambiguous position. Next, he had to shock the Spartans out of their bumbling hesitancy—though without making too many financial demands on them in the process. The very real threat from Athens—to Sparta no less than Syracuse—must be offset against the prospect of easy and quick returns if they would take his advice on how to deal with it. His charm and persuasiveness had never been more needed than they were on this crucial occasion. It is possible (there is no direct evidence) that Thucydides himself was in exile at Sparta, and actually heard Alcibiades deliver his momentous speech in person. Unlike some of the speeches in the *History*, this one has a strikingly realistic and individual flavour about it.

My family, Alcibiades told his audience, has always had close ties with Sparta. For many years they looked after your interests as Spartan proxenoi in Athens. I, too, did so when your troops were held hostage there after the defeat at Pylos. I was always anxious to help you. "But when you made peace with Athens you negotiated through my personal enemies"—a neat side-swipe at Nicias—"thus putting them in a stronger position and discrediting me." It was a weak argument to defend his trucking with Argos, but perhaps the best he could muster; the justification of political action by personal pique and hurt pride is perfectly in character. Then, with a sneering allusion to the shortcomings of democracy (always calculated to please a Spartan audience), he rounded off his apologia and got down to business.

First came the bombshell, exploded without warning, and all the more effective for its lack of rhetorical flourish. Alcibiades unfolded, in flat, factual terms, the details of the "Grand Design." Yes, he said, our plans envisage the total conquest of Sicily. But that is only a beginning. Sicily, we reckon, will give us a springboard into southern Italy. From there we intend to reduce the Carthaginian empire, stage by stage, and finally overrun Carthage itself. Finally—if we bring all this off successfully—the Athenian fleet will return to Greece, bringing untold wealth, legions of Spanish mercenaries, and enough Sicilian-built triremes to enforce a total blockade of the Peloponnese. Your cities will fall to us one after another, by assault or siege. We will be the masters of all Greece—indeed, of the Mediterranean.

It is not hard to imagine what effect this revelation must have had on the Spartans. Alcibiades had hit them hard at their most vulnerable points. Moreover (whether it was true or not) he had presented the "Grand Design," not as his own private plan, but rather as Athens' official and approved policy. Now he hammered home the next point in his argument, quickly, before the violence of the shock could dissipate itself. If Syracuse fell, he insisted, all Sicily was lost. If Sicily went, Magna Graecia would follow. "It would not then be long," he continued ominously, "before you were confronted with the dangers which I have just told you threaten you from the West." *And Syracuse might well fall*—one mistake too many, a little more shilly-shallying, treachery within the walls, and the chain reaction of cumulative disaster would inevitably be set off. The Syracusans were already more or less blockaded. They lacked military experience. If the cities of Sicily were to unite and make common cause, the situation might still be retrieved; but—punch line—"what you must now realise is that, *unless you help her, Sicily will be lost.*"

Then, quickly and economically, Alcibiades outlined his positive suggestions. A force of heavy-armed infantry must be sent out (he did not say by which city) who were also qualified sailors, men who could go into action as soon as they had beached their ships, who were accustomed to amphibious operations. More important, a Spartan general should be seconded to the command of the Syracusan army—someone capable of organising an efficient defence plan, a professional soldier who would impose some discipline on these raggle-taggle amateurs, and stiffen their lamentable morale.

Having thus dealt with Syracuse, Alcibiades now turned to affairs on the home front. A cold war in mainland Greece was not enough, he argued. The Spartans must hot it up, take more open and aggressive measures. By so doing they would both show the Syracusans they meant business, and pin down Athenian reserves that could otherwise be released for service in Sicily. Also, he said, they must capture and fortify the key position of Decelea, in Attica. Now Decelea lies some twelve miles north of Athens, in a hollow commanding the pass which leads to Oropus, on the Strait of Euboea. There is a hill immediately above the site, with traces of fortification on it. Through the pass cattle and grain from Euboea were transported by the overland route to Athens. If Sparta held Decelea—not for nothing is it still known locally as Tó Kleidhi, "The Key"—she would, at one stroke, cut a vital Athenian supply-line, provide a perfect rallying point for slaves and deserters, and (as Alcibiades pointed out) isolate the Laurium silver mines, on which Athens' whole economy now depended. There was also the psychological effect of such a move to be taken into consideration. Athens' subject-allies would cease to be overawed by her. The flow of tribute would dwindle away, and finally dry up altogether. Alcibiades' plan, in effect, was to put a kind of economic half-nelson on Athens, which might well crumple her defences without the need for any final trial of military strength.

Having delivered himself of this devastating three-point programme, Alcibiades seems to have felt the need to justify himself once more, and small wonder; it would have been hard to improve on the skill and vindictiveness which he now applied to encompassing the downfall of his erstwhile homeland. "The country I am attacking," he said—how flat and forced the paradox must have sounded!—"does not seem to be mine any longer; it is rather that I am trying to recover a country that has ceased to be mine." We can imagine the dark eyes of the Spartan Ephors fixed sardonically upon him as he delivered this bromide; no one was deceived—except, perhaps, Alcibiades himself. He wound up his speech with a few embarrassed platitudes. The debate was over.

That the Spartans would follow Alcibiades' advice was never in doubt—not least since one of his recommendations, the occupation of Decelea, had a very respectable history.[2] But even now they were unwilling either to move fast, or to make more than a minimal contribution to the Syracusan campaign. The same is true, even more surprisingly, of Corinth. If the envoys from Syracuse were hoping for massive and prompt retaliation against Athens, they were out of luck. Once more Nicias had victory within his grasp; once more he frittered away the chance thus offered him. Sooner or later the gods he served so piously

[2] The Corinthians had proposed some such operation right at the outset of the Peloponnesian War, and the idea was touted round again during the winter of 422–421.

were going to tire of having their gifts ignored in this insulting manner.

The Spartans were quite happy to send out a senior officer to take charge of the Syracusan defences: such a gesture cost little, and might produce concrete results. Their choice fell on an enigmatic character named Gylippus, of whom more in due course. But they did not bother to dispatch him until the beginning of summer, when it was almost too late for him to be of any use; and even then, the forces he brought were derisory. His escort consisted of four vessels—two Spartan, two Corinthian —later reinforced by a small additional detachment of ten ships from Corinth, two from Leucas, and three from Ambracia. As for the fortification of Decelea, it was over a year before the Spartans got around to it. Seldom can such momentous and far-reaching decisions have been implemented in so casually haphazard a manner, or with so little true awareness of their ultimate importance. This debate at Sparta marks the turning point, not only of the Sicilian campaign, but also, in the long run, of the whole Peloponnesian War. It is open to doubt whether anyone present, even Alcibiades himself, had more than an inkling of the forces they set in motion on that fateful day.

Soon after the Athenian fleet's return from Syracuse to Catana (October–November 415), Nicias and Lamachus received a painful, and all too practical, reminder that their late colleague was now their dedicated enemy. They were, of course, *au fait* with his scheme for taking over Messina, with the collaboration of a pro-Athenian group inside the city. What they did *not* know was that Alcibiades had betrayed the plot to the authorities, and that the ringleaders had already been arrested and put to death. On the day arranged for the take-over, Nicias, still in blissful ignorance of what had since taken place, sailed north in strength, beached his fleet—probably near Cape Pelorus —and waited for the gates of Messina to open. He waited in vain. Those of the pro-Athenian group who had survived did, in fact, make some attempt at an uprising, even after losing their leaders, only to have the government put them down by armed force. At this the last sparks of rebellion fizzled damply out.

Yet for thirteen days Nicias waited; his intelligence service seems to have slipped up badly on this occasion—or perhaps he was being deliberately fed false reports. At last, since he was running short of stores, and his ships were being battered by autumn gales, he withdrew to Naxos—a nearer refuge than Catana—and decided to make it his winter quarters. Hangars were built for storing equipment in, and a stockade erected. It was from Naxos, when the weather cleared, that a trireme left for Athens, to ask for cavalry reinforcements and further funds in readiness for the spring campaign. Meanwhile contributions came in from Naxos, Catana, and, interestingly, Rhegium. The Rhegians would not allow their great port to be used as a base; but there was no harm in discreetly hedging one's bets.

The Syracusans, who had clearly begun to develop a cheerful contempt for Nicias, now marched out against Catana, ravaged the surrounding countryside, and burnt down the Athenians' abandoned camp. This, for some reason, brought down more criticism on Nicias' head than almost anything else. The troops' morale was getting dangerously low. There had already been one case of deliberate signalling to the enemy, which Lamachus—understandably alarmed—punished by the horrible type of execution known as *apotympanismós*, a mixture of crucifixion and slow garrotting.[3] What was needed, psychologically, was a rousing military success. Instead, Nicias undertook another abortive exercise in diplomacy.

Camarina had refused to receive the Athenian fleet on its first arrival, and had later sent a small contingent of cavalry and archers to support Syracuse. Nicias was nevertheless convinced that, on balance, her leaders sympathised with Athens. Traditionally, it is true, Camarina was no friend of Syracuse. Her

[3] Apologists for Periclean sweetness and light may be surprised to find that this was the normal punishment at Athens for homicide; see D. M. MacDowell's *Athenian Homicide Law in the Age of the Orators* (Manchester 1963) pp. 111–12.

first foundation had been destroyed by the Syracusans in 552, after less than half a century of existence, and the site left desolate until Hippocrates took it over in 495. Ten years later Gelon evicted the inhabitants and razed it a second time. Not until the general settlement of 461 was Camarina given a reasonably stable lease of life, when the settlement was recolonised from Gela.

The city had become an ally of Athens "in the time of Laches" (427). Though her Syracusan sympathisers forced a truce with Gela in 424, which led—as we have seen—to the Congress, two years later Camarina returned to the Athenian fold, and stayed there, albeit somewhat uneasily, until the arrival of the great armada. The pottery distribution figures suggest that her merchants—in marked contrast to those of neighbouring cities—had continued to do a brisk trade with Athens after 424. If (as might be deduced from this) any economic sanctions were imposed on Athens by the cities taking part in the Congress of Gela, Camarina cheerfully disregarded them, and made a killing as a result. The moral notion of blacklegging never really took root in the ancient world.

Perhaps Camarina hoped to carry on her profitable trading activities under a cover of strict political neutrality—a device familiar enough in our own day. All the same, the insignificance of her contribution to Syracuse's forces—twenty horsemen, fifty archers—encouraged Nicias no less than it alarmed Hermocrates. No harm could be done by trying a little persuasion. The men of Camarina, Nicias thought, were wavering; one determined push, and they might be brought down squarely on the right side of the fence. An embassy was therefore dispatched to argue Athens' case. But when the Syracusans heard about this, they at once sent off a rival delegation, under Hermocrates himself, to prevent Camarina breaking away. Each side, it would appear, presented its case before the Camarinaean Assembly, and Thucydides reports them in detail. Camarina, to the contending parties in Sicily, was a test case: the issue which, in Thucydides' account, most concerns both speakers is whether the Siceliot cities, generally speaking, are liable to stick with Syracuse, take a chance on Athens, or remain neutral.

Hermocrates' speech hammers away at all his favourite points. The Athenians, he tells his audience, are out-and-out imperialists, interested in nothing but their own self-aggrandisement, eager "not to resettle the Leontinians but rather to unsettle us."[4] Yet the cities of Sicily obstinately refuse to combine against this common danger. Are we, he cries, all to sit by till Athens has swallowed us piecemeal, one after the other? Neutrality will benefit no one. Camarina is well in line to be Athens' next victim.

Once more we find Hermocrates making a heavy-handed attempt to dispel fears concerning Syracusan imperialism, obviously very much aware that all the charges he brought against Athens might receive a comprehensive *tu quoque* from the next speaker. You want us weakened to reduce our arrogance, he says in effect. But you also want to lean on us when it comes to facing the aggressor. You can't have it both ways. We are all fighting for a common country, a common cause. "There is nothing [in the Athenian fleet and army] to be frightened of so long as we all stand together." If you side with Athens, or even stand aloof, Hermocrates concludes, you will be guilty of betraying your fellow-Dorians (an ethnic argument that could be emphasised or ignored as the situation demanded). An Athenian victory will merely leave you as part of the conqueror's pickings. But if *we* win—a valedictory flick of the whip here— "you will scarcely escape paying the penalty for having been the cause of our danger."

Athens' case was argued, not by Nicias or Lamachus, but by Euphemus, a man of whom very little is known. He had been archon in 417–416, and had spoken in the debate on the renewal of the Segesta treaty; so perhaps he was regarded as an expert on Sicilian affairs. What military rank he held we do not know. It cannot have been as exalted as his record might suggest, since there is no further reference to him during the whole

[4] This neat rendering is from the Loeb version by C. Forster Smith.

campaign.[5] He was, it seems, a friend of Pericles' son Paralus, and had a habit of making caustic jokes at the expense of all his acquaintances. His speech, as reported by Thucydides, has that peculiar fascination which unblushing extremism of any kind always seems to exert. It is a brazen exercise in the doctrine of pure machiavellian self-interest, which he sees as man's only true dominant motive apart from fear ("It is for our own security that we are in Sicily, and we see that here your interests are the same as ours"). Syracuse and Athens, says Euphemus, are both imperial powers: who would deny it? But Athens can guarantee Camarina protection against Syracusan dreams of conquest and exploitation: her choice is clear.

This, of course, is simply Hermocrates' argument turned inside out and given a fresh twist: the *tu quoque* gibe kicks both ways. Athens might admit, disarmingly, that her motive in keeping Camarina independent was to have a useful buffer against Syracuse; but what else was the idea of Pansicilianism (which meant, in effect, alliance with Syracuse) except a device for providing some sort of buffer against Athens? Furthermore, in both cases the independence of the small state was only guaranteed for as long as Athens and Syracuse maintained their uneasy balance of hostility; the moment either one achieved absolute power, the doctrine of self-interest advocated by Euphemus (and implied by Hermocrates) would allow them to exploit or absorb such satellites to their heart's content.

Faced with this bilateral broadside of blandishment, bullying, and pure cold cynicism, the Camarinaeans may well be forgiven for feeling that neutrality was their only possible choice. To tangle with either Syracuse or Athens at this stage spelt ruin: one preference cancelled out the other. By temperament and tradition they inclined towards the Athenians; but there was a very real danger that Athens might subjugate all Sicily. They disliked

[5] It is possible, but by no means certain, that this Euphemus is identical with the person of that name who was Nicias's brother-in-law, and implicated by Diocleides in the mutilation of the Herms: see above, pp. 120, 125.

their powerful neighbours in Syracuse; but just because they *were* their neighbours, the Syracusans became doubly dangerous, and were therefore to be placated. So finally the Camarinaeans said that since both Syracuse and Athens were their allies, but at the same time at war with each other, the only way Camarina could honour her oaths to both parties was by helping neither. This was a diplomatic evasion very much in key with the rest of the proceedings. Privately, however, they had decided that from now on, if at any time they *had* to give one side practical support, it should be Syracuse—though in no greater quantity than was absolutely essential. Athens, they sensed, might well prove an even greater menace in her hour of victory: a conclusion which the historical record does little to contradict.

From about February onwards—the time of the Camarina debate, the time of Alcibiades' speech at Sparta—Nicias began to occupy himself, in his slow, methodical way, with preparations for putting Syracuse under siege. To begin with, he launched a campaign to secure the alliance of the Sicel communities. With those on the coast he had little success; they were probably afraid of Syracusan reprisals. The mountain-dwellers of the interior, on the other hand, almost all rallied to Athens' support. They came flocking down into Naxos, bringing not only most welcome reinforcements, but also supplies of wheat and, in some cases, cash contributions. Nor was it simply a matter of waiting for volunteers. If any Sicel town up-country failed to co-operate, an Athenian column was liable to appear and pressurise the inhabitants into a more reasonable frame of mind. Nicias' only failures were in one or two remote strongholds where the Syracusans had managed to establish a garrison first. For preparations of this sort, it soon became clear, Naxos was not nearly so suitable a base as Catana; so about the beginning of March the whole expeditionary force moved back to the site of the old camp, which was now rebuilt.

From Catana a constant stream of requests and requisition orders went out to all Athens' Sicilian allies. The most crying need was for horses, which Nicias tried to raise from Segesta and the upland Sicels. His camp engineers were busy collecting bricks and iron and mortar and all the material necessary for constructing siege works. The usual embassies went the usual rounds, trying to win over unaligned cities and, in general, to drum up support wherever they could find it. The two most intriguing missions which Thucydides records are also the least expected. "A trireme," he tells us, "was sent on a mission of good will to Carthage to see if any help could be gained from them, and they also sent to Etruria, where some of the cities had offered of their own accord to join them in the war." Now, both Etruria and Carthage, as we know, were scheduled for conquest under the terms of the "Grand Design." Voluntary alliance, however, came cheaper than invasion, and in the end paid off better too. The Etruscans had a long-standing tradition of enmity with Syracuse, and were only too glad to lend her enemies a hand—especially when, as in the present case, they were, or had been, good commercial customers.

But what did Nicias hope to get out of Carthage? The mention of a good will mission in this context is suggestive. Alcibiades had described the "Grand Design" in some detail during his speech at Sparta, and what he said must have caused considerable stir far beyond the shores of mainland Greece. If a public declaration of Athens' intention to invade Carthage reached the ears of the Carthaginians—and it is hard to believe that it did not—then there was a grave risk that they might intervene in Sicily. Nicias's aim, it is clear, was to reassure them that this speech did *not* represent official Athenian policy, but was merely the irresponsible utterance, for his own selfish purposes, of a traitor and blasphemer who already stood condemned to death *in absentia.*

The whole incident, revealing in itself, also serves to highlight something far more serious—that chronic disagreement over the real nature of Athens' business in Sicily which was directly responsible for so many wasted advantages and missed opportunities during the early part of the campaign. What the Assembly voted for, what the generals discussed in secret with the Council, what the Western lobby took for granted, what the man in the street argued over in the gymnasium—all these were very different things. Which policy, when it came to the crunch, was the military High Command supposed to implement? The diplomatic promise of aid to Segesta and Leontini? The secret plan of subjugating Syracuse and turning all Sicily into an Athenian outpost? Or the more grandiose concept contained in the "Grand Design," with Sicily as a mere stepping-stone to Carthage and Spain? The trouble was that a good case could be made out for each of the three. The first might be a polite fiction, but it had, nevertheless, been publicly ratified by the Assembly. The second might not have been openly stated, but it had been agreed in private conclave before the fleet sailed. The third was upheld by at least one of the fleet's commanders (until his untimely removal), and enjoyed the widest popularity in unofficial circles. Until the winter of 415–414 nobody, either at home or in Sicily, had any clear idea of what Athens' policy was, for the simple reason that no undisputed policy existed.

By then, probably as a result of Nicias' dispatches, and various independent reports, the Athenian government had come to the belated conclusion that their only possible course was to destroy Syracuse and reduce the entire island—but not to attempt any further conquests. If this had been quite clear from the start, they might have appointed a supreme commander-in-chief and given him precise orders to carry out. As it was, they had settled for a trio of incompatible misfits who reflected (all too accurately) their own disunity and indecisiveness; and made confusion doubly sure by giving them autonomous powers. However, it was no use repining over lost opportunities. The chance of a quick, cheap success had been wantonly thrown away, and that was that. If Syracuse could no longer be stormed, then it must be taken by siege or collusion. There was to be no more time wasted over side-issues such as the war between Segesta and Selinus. Nicias may not have liked the policy he was now required to implement; but after all these months at least he *had* a policy. Progress, of a sort, had been made.

With the first coming of spring, the Athenians put to sea and sailed south from Catana. Their immediate objective was Megara Hyblaea; it looks as though Lamachus' idea of using it as a base against Syracuse had come up for consideration again. They made a landing, and ravaged the surrounding countryside, but their attempt on Megara itself proved unsuccessful. The Syracusans, with belated realisation of Megara's strategic value, had, we recall, built a fort there during the winter. Once again Nicias arrived too late. (In *The Birds* (March 414) Aristophanes coined the verb "to Niciashuffle." It is not hard to see why.) From Megara the Athenians turned back north, leaving a detachment of troops to follow them along the coast road, until they reached the Terias River, a little way beyond Leontini, in the heart of the great fertile delta. Here they marched inland, across the plain, and proceeded to set fire to the wheatfields. A small detachment of Syracusans came out and attempted to stop them, but was routed with heavy casualties. The Athenians then set up a trophy, marched back to their ships, and returned to base at Catana.

When they had supplied themselves with fresh provisions, they at once set out on a short expedition to reduce one of the main "non-co-operative" Sicel towns—Centuripae, a stronghold some twenty-seven miles north-west from Catana, in the foothills below Mt. Etna. After forcing its capitulation they returned to the coast by way of Hybla and Inessa, once more burning off the crops as they went. This suggests two things: that they had adequate supplies of wheat themselves (though not, one supposes, from the Catana-Leontini plain); and that they were deliberately attacking or destroying all sources of grain which might benefit Syracuse. In other words, they were preparing to enforce a rigorous siege.[6]

The dispatch-boat from Naxos reached Athens early in February. Although the reign of terror was over, and witch hunting for Herm-breakers and profaners of the Mysteries had largely

[6] Just how rigorous it was in the event is quite another matter (see below, pp. 214 ff.).

lapsed, an atmosphere of hysteria concerning religious matters still persisted. Pious bigots were having a field-day. A materialist philosopher from Melos, one Diagoras, known as "The Atheist," was charged with blasphemy, and wisely fled the country. The Assembly offered a reward of one silver talent to anyone who killed him on sight, and two for his return, alive and safe, to Athens. Diagoras had, it seems, been denigrating and casting doubt on the Mysteries in his lectures—a comparatively venial offence, one might have supposed. Aristophanes quoted the proclamation offering this reward in a passage of *The Birds*, and showed pretty clearly what *he* thought about it by adding: "And anyone who kills one of those old long-dead tyrants is to get a silver talent, too."

There was little evidence to show that the government took Alcibiades' speech at Sparta in the least seriously. No attempt had been made to garrison Decelea, much less to provide adequate defences or fortifications for the Laurium silver-mines. "Attic owls will never fail," remarks one character in *The Birds*; the general mood was one of defiant optimism. Indeed, the whole concept of Cloud-Cuckooland suggests that in Athens the Sicilian Expedition was still regarded as a fantastic colonisation scheme rather than as a military operation: a large-scale racket for the benefit of every crook, con-man, informer, bogus prophet, runaway slave, spurious citizen, profiteer, and fiddling bureaucrat in Attica. If you want a fight, Peisthetaerus tells one character, stop beating your poor father and take off to—not Sicily (as we might legitimately expect in 414), but *Thrace*.

The Board of Generals, armed with more inside information than the average citizen, was by no means so sanguine. Relations with Persia had been steadily deteriorating, and it now seemed a foregone conclusion that the Great King would reach some kind of agreement with the Peloponnesian League. As a result, Athens had been—at first surreptitiously, now more or less without concealment—giving aid and support to the rebel satrap of Sardis, Pissuthnes, and (after his defeat and execution) to his equally rebellious son Amorges. An Athenian general was operating from Ephesus in 414, and it seems certain (despite the fragmentary nature of the epigraphical evidence) that his activities were connected with Amorges' revolt.

There thus existed a de facto state of hostility between Athens and Persia, and the Athenian government was under no illusions as to the danger this represented. There was, too, always an outside chance that Alcibiades' recommendations had had some influence on the Spartan government (though not enough to take active measures against them), and no one could be sure how far they had been made with one eye on the Persian détente. If Sparta decided to reopen the war in Greece, *and with Persian backing*, Athens would be in a very awkward position indeed. It might prove necessary to recall troops from Sicily at something less than short notice.

Athens thus had every reason for bringing the Sicilian campaign to a successful conclusion as soon as possible, and this must have been a major factor in formulating the "tough-line" policy imposed on Nicias during the winter of 415–414. Nicias himself, paradoxically, was the person who derived most benefit from this change of front. In such circumstances no one felt inclined to quibble over his requests. The Assembly voted a new allocation of three hundred talents from the reserve fund. They also dispatched to Sicily thirty mounted archers, and 250 cavalrymen. The latter brought their own accountrements with them, but were without horses—not so odd an economy as might appear at first sight, since horses abounded in Sicily, and to transport them from Greece by the long sea-route would be a hazardous undertaking.

Since from now on the action of the narrative will take place, for the most part, in the immediate vicinity of Syracuse, a short topographical digression may help the reader to visualise the scene more clearly.[7] Syracuse was originally restricted to the near-island of Ortygia, which forms the north-east arm of the Great Harbour. From here the city slowly spread out, in a fanlike wedge, till it reached the natural barrier—and protection—of the

[7] The following section should be read in conjunction with the large-scale map of Syracuse on p. 184.

Epipolae massif. These heights (sometimes known as the Syracuse Terrace) are a natural outcrop of calcareous limestone, some three miles long from east to west, and just under two miles wide at their broadest point, narrowing sharply as they approach their western extremity. Here, at the "waist" of the plateau, is the easiest approach to the summit, a gently sloping col known in antiquity as Euryalus. Other approaches, of varying difficulty, are at Scala Greca and the Cava S. Panagia on the north face, and in the south, towards Syracuse itself, by two defiles known respectively as the Portella del Fusco and the Salita Ombra. The second of these almost certainly gave access from the plateau to the northern gate of the city. Elsewhere the cliffs are steep to sheer, and of uneven height. The south-east corner of the plateau abuts on the city wall, as it did in antiquity, leaving a narrow neck of level land between Epipolae and the sea. This coastal strip widens to the north, and provides free passage round the entire promontory, debouching finally into the open plain beyond Scala Greca.

Ancient Syracuse was divided into four main quarters: Ortygia, Achradina, Tyche, and Temenites. Of these Temenites, the area roughly south of the Greek threatre, was the most recent. Only the threat of an Athenian attack had led the Syracusans to run an extension wall across its outer limits, and thus bring it within the city's perimeter. It was, therefore, a kind of overflow suburb. Tyche, it is generally agreed, contained the dock area along the coast immediately north of Ortygia, between the Little Harbour and the city limits at I Cappuccini, and extending about half a mile inland. Tyche only seems to have been fortified about 461, at the time of the mercenaries' coup. It follows that, apart from Ortygia, Achradina was the oldest quarter—a supposition confirmed by Diodorus' regular use of the phrase "Achradina and the Island." We should therefore expect it to occupy the area immediately north of the peninsula linking Ortygia to the mainland—an area bounded on the east by Tyche, on the west by Temenites, and to the north by the cliffs of Epipolae. Yet until thirty years or so ago it was assumed, with very little question, that Achradina embraced

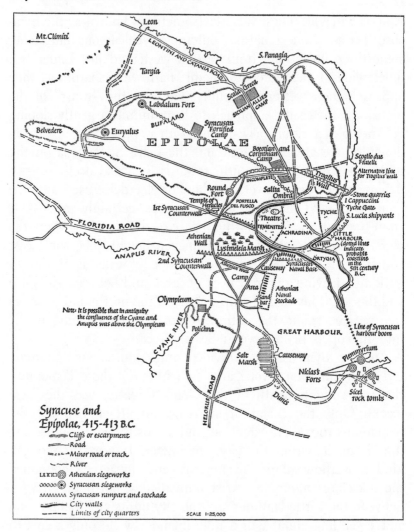

Syracuse and
Epipolae, 415-413 B.C.
᷸᷸᷸᷸ Cliffs or escarpment
══════ Road
══‑‑‑ Minor road or track
‑‑‑‑‑ River
ⅈⅈⅈⅈ◉ Athenian siegeworks
ooooo◉ Syracusan siegeworks
ᴧᴧᴧᴧᴧᴧᴧ Syracusan rampart and stockade
═══════ City walls
‑‑‑‑‑ Limits of city quarters   SCALE 1:25,000

the whole of the promontory beyond Syracuse, including all
Epipolae eastward from Scala Greca. This is a vast area for an
inhabited district, much larger than any estimate of Syracuse's
population would warrant. Furthermore, intensive excavation revealed singularly little trace of urban dwellings.

Such an assumption also makes many passages in Thucydides,
Diodorus, Livy and other writers almost impossible to interpret
without straining the text out of all recognition. How, then,

may we ask, did it persist for so long? One reason, in all likelihood, is the imposing presence of the Walls of Dionysius, which run right round Epipolae and the promontory, from Euryalus to Scala Greca, on to Ortygia, and then back by way of the Great Harbour and the southern cliff-line: seventeen miles in all, a circuit four miles longer than Aurelian's Wall in Rome, and built only a few years after the Sicilian campaign. Such walls are too often assumed to have enclosed a city, when in fact, as here, they were simply a defensive measure against possible attack.

But the main culprits in furthering the curious myth of Achradina-on-Epipolae seem to have been a couple of seventeenth-century map-makers named Cluver and Mirabella. It was they who, with more imagination than honesty, showed the entire eastern plateau as a warren of buildings and streets which do not exist now, and which, it is safe to say, never existed except in their minds' eye. It was they who transformed Epipolae into an inhabited quarter of Syracuse, though for Thucydides, and even for Diodorus, it was clearly never anything but open fields.[8] It was they who located Achradina there (this being the only quarter available for mythification), even though Diodorus, for one, leaves us in little doubt that what *he* means by Achradina is just what we might expect—that is, the flat ground on the landward side of Ortygia, immediately *below* Epipolae. For several hundred years, with muted grumbling and various ingenious topographical contortions, historians somehow contrived to interpret the Sicilian campaign in a way that accommodated this implausible piece of town-planning. Then in 1932 a Danish scholar, Knud Fabricius (see Bibliography), after a masterly summing-up of all the evidence, demonstrated beyond doubt that no occupied part of Syracuse lay on Epipolae,

[8] As Moore says (see Bibliography): "From these highly imaginative sheets of Mirabella and Cluver have descended the maps in all of our atlases, in histories (e.g., Freeman), in special works on Syracuse, in editions of Thucydides, Cicero's *Verrines*, and Livy." The willingness of scholars to take cartographical evidence on trust is touching, but occasionally, as here, quite disastrous.

that Achradina was exactly where Diodorus suggests it was, and that—by inference—every single map and discussion of the Syracuse campaign would have to be done over again from scratch.

Fabricius' monograph—perhaps not surprisingly—was received by the scholarly world in almost total silence.[9] Then, after a long and decent interval (during which his fellow-historians tried to recover face and pretend the whole thing had happened when nobody was looking) the maps were silently redrawn, and the strategy rewritten. My own account of the Syracuse campaign rests on this central thesis proposed by Fabricius. On the other hand, it adds much to his findings, and differs from them in many points of detail—mainly as the result of weeks spent walking over every inch of the terrain. One lesson I hope I have learnt from the sad yet comic myth of Achradina-on-Epipolae is that in matters topographical neither books nor maps—not even those admirable if often highly imaginative creations, the ordnance survey sheets put out by the Istituto geogràfico militare—are, in the last resort, any substitute for meticulous personal observation.

When Nicias got back to Catana from his sortie against Centuripae, he found both cash and cavalrymen awaiting him: most welcome reinforcements, on every count. His next task, obviously, was to obtain horses, since now he had the men to ride them as well as the money to pay for them. Once he possessed an efficient cavalry arm, he would be able to operate against Syracuse much more freely, without that constant inhibiting fear of having his infantry cut to pieces from the flank. Messages were sent once more to Segesta, asking not only for mounts, but also for a cavalry troop. The stables of Catana were searched for suitable horses. Naxos, the Sicel towns of the interior—all possible sources of supply were now explored.

The Syracusans learnt of these activities within a matter of hours: both camps swarmed with spies and agents. Taken in

[9] I have been able to locate only two reviews: one Italian, the other—an eminently fair and enthusiastic assessment—by the late Sir Ian Richmond.

conjunction with everything else that had been going on in the Athenian camp—especially the stockpiling of bricks and other building materials—Nicias' drive to obtain cavalry suggested that, at long last, he really meant business. Hermocrates and his two colleagues held an emergency conference to discuss what action they should take. Thucydides' account of this discussion is so curious that it will be advisable to quote it here verbatim: "They thought that, unless the Athenians could control Epipolae—the precipitous piece of ground lying directly above the city—they would find it difficult, even if victorious in battle, to build a wall to cut the city off. They *therefore* [my italics] decided to guard the approaches to Epipolae to prevent the enemy making their way up unobserved by this route, which was, indeed, the only practicable one."

There are two immediate problems here. First, what made the Syracusans so sure that Nicias intended to build a wall round the city? Such an idea had never been mentioned till now in over six months' campaigning. Secondly, if Epipolae was so vital an element in Syracuse's defences, why had it not been guarded and fortified from the first hint of an Athenian invasion —or, at the very least, during the winter that was just over? One fort had been built at Megara Hyblaea, another by the Olympieum. But on Epipolae, so far as we can tell, there were, at this point, neither forts, nor military defences of any kind, nor even look-outs posted. The conclusion is, surely, inescapable. However extraordinary we may find it in retrospect, the Syracusans were utterly oblivious to the strategic importance of Epipolae until the fact was thrust upon their notice at the last possible moment. And how, we may well ask, did this revelation take place? It looks very much as though some enterprising Syracusan agent contrived to find out, in detail, the whole Athenian plan of operation—occupation of Epipolae, siege walls, everything—and that it was this report, this immediate and specific threat, which first alerted the generals to the danger their city was in.

They certainly lost no time in taking action. At dawn (presumably on the morning after they learnt what Nicias and

Lamachus planned to do) they paraded all Syracuse's heavy-armed troops in the meadows by the Anapus River, where their earlier battle against the Athenians had taken place, and held a formal military review. Hermocrates and the other two "emergency" generals had just taken over their command; a little colour and pageantry seemed appropriate. They chose a special force of six hundred hoplites "who were to guard Epipolae and to stand by ready for action immediately wherever else they might be required."[10] They found themselves in action sooner than anyone could have anticipated.

Nicias, too, seems to have had efficient intelligence agents working for him on this occasion. At all events, he clearly knew in advance that the parade was going to be held, complete with details of place and time. Nothing could have suited him better. He embarked all his forces late in the evening, and sailed south under cover of darkness till he reached an inlet called Leon, or The Lion, nearly four miles north-west of Syracuse, and within easy reach of Euryalus, the western approach to Epipolae.[11] Here he disembarked his troops. The fleet moved a mile or two north again, to the peninsula of Thapsus. Here it cast anchor. A stockade was built across the isthmus at its narrowest point to protect the Athenians against Syracusan cavalry raids, and a semi-permanent camp set up.

Meanwhile Nicias' hoplites, like the men of Marathon, hurried across country as fast as they could, and were already in position on the heights of Epipolae when the alarm was given. If any sentries were posted on the plateau they must have kept a very lax watch. A breathless messenger galloped down to the

[10] Their commander, Diomilus, was not a Syracusan but an islander from Andros: probably a professional mercenary. Syracuse seems to have been singularly short of competent senior officers.

[11] There has been much discussion about the exact site of Leon: see, e.g., Freeman's Appendix XIII, pp. 659 ff. But it is clear that what the Athenians needed was the shortest and easiest cross-country route to Euryalus; and their natural choice for this would have been the tiny inlet a little north-west of modern Targia. This has a good beach, and offers direct access to the col over easily rising ground, up a long, shallow valley.

river-meadows with the news, and Diomilus, at the head of his six hundred men, hurried off to deal with the situation as best he could. But they had nearly three miles to go, over rough ground, and by the time they, too, had struggled up the Euryalus col they were out of breath and sadly disorganised. The Athenians saw them coming, and made their dispositions accordingly. What followed was a massacre rather than a fight. Euryalus was a good point from which to fight a defensive action, since attackers were forced to engage on a narrow front, after sweating their way up a steep hillside. Half Diomilus' force of six hundred was either killed or captured. The cavalry escorting him was also routed: it is hard to see how horsemen could have operated at all over such ground. When Diomilus himself fell, the rest broke and ran for it.

Wisely, the Athenians did not attempt to pursue them; they merely set up a trophy, and in due course gave the Syracusans back their dead under a flag of truce. The following day they boldly marched down to the gates of the city itself. No one came out to engage them. After a while they gave up and returned to Epipolae. The rest of the day was spent constructing a fort, on the northern edge of the heights, somewhere west of Scala Greca. The site was known as Labdalum; it commanded an excellent view of the plain towards Leon and Thapsus, where the fleet was now stationed. This fort was to be more than a look-out post, however; the Athenians intended to use it as a storehouse for their equipment and cash reserves while they were engaged on operations.

A day or two later—partly, perhaps, as a result of this showy victory—contributions of cavalry began to reach the Athenian camp: three hundred from Segesta, one hundred from the Naxians and the Sicel communities, together with extra horses for the unmounted Athenian contingent. When they were all assembled, Nicias found he could now count on a well-equipped cavalry arm of no less than 650 men. The enemy's one great tactical advantage had been wiped out. After a year of indecision and inaction, the battle for Syracuse was entering on a new and more dynamic phase. Those within the walls, gazing up at the now menacing heights of Epipolae, can have felt comparatively little hope about its final outcome. Many, indeed, weighing the Athenians against their own political enemies in Syracuse, had already concluded that Nicias and his men might well prove the lesser of two evils.

The whole Athenian striking force, cavalry and siege engineers included, was now established on the plateau above Syracuse. The fleet remained at Thapsus, and acted as a supply depot. Nicias seems, for no ascertainable reason, to have been chary of risking a naval engagement at this stage. The Athenians enjoyed complete superiority over Syracuse at sea, and a well-planned assault on the two main harbours would have both secured vital objectives, and have knocked out the ill-trained Syracusan navy before it had time to become a real danger. But this was not Nicias' way: he preferred more methodical and uninspired preparations. So all the stores from Catana were laboriously transferred to Epipolae, by the same route that the infantry had followed. Rations, camping equipment, timber, dressed stones, spades, axes, entrenching tools, bricks, all had to be carried up on donkeys or pack-mules, since no wheeled cart could negotiate the Euryalus col.

Nicias' nephritis had taken a turn for the worse, and he was now in considerable pain most of the time. The tactical flair and panache which the campaign occasionally displays from now on suggest that Lamachus—at long last—had been given a free hand in planning operations. If Nicias was incapacitated by illness, there would be a very good excuse for doing so. At all events, the Athenians—to the astonishment and dismay of their opponents—had suddenly begun to act like men who knew what they were about and meant to achieve their objectives with the least possible delay. The moment the Labdalum fort was complete, they moved across to the southern side of the plateau, and—with quite incredible speed, Thucydides tells us—proceeded to construct a second strongpoint, the so-called Round Fort, at a place called Syca, or The Fig-trees. To give it additional protection, they threw up a thousand-foot rampart in front of it, facing towards the city.

Thucydides does not locate the Round Fort with any precision, but it is important for us to do so if we are to get a clear picture of the subsequent operations centred on it. In point of fact—despite much scholarly disagreement, mainly occasioned by the Achradina-on-Epipolae myth—there is only one possible site which fulfils all the necessary conditions. To begin with, the Round Fort was not visible from Labdalum; this piece of information comes from Thucydides, and may have been based on personal observation. Any point towards the centre of the plateau is therefore ruled out. Strategical requirements confirm this. The Round Fort was to be a base point from which to begin wall-building operations in two directions and in each case by the shortest possible route—to the Great Harbour and the open sea. It had to be reasonably near some negotiable way down the cliffs for the benefit of those constructing the southern wall, that towards the shore of the Great Harbour. Lastly, it was close enough to the cliffs themselves for the wall on the landward side to go *north* before turning eastward across the plateau. It therefore stood immediately above the combe— scarcely a defile—known as the Portella del Fusco, just over half a mile west of Temenites and the site of the Greek theatre.

The most curious thing about these operations is the complete failure of the Syracusans to take any effective counter-measures against them. They did not attack the fleet at Thapsus, either by sea or land. Yet with all Athens' best fighting men up on Epipolae, Thapsus was surely wide open to a swift, well-directed amphibious assault. Nor, seemingly, was any attempt made to intercept Athenian supply columns between Leon and Euryalus, though here the Syracusans had open country that was ideal for cavalry patrols.

If the Syracusans were negligent, so—to a quite astonishing extent—were their opponents. Nicias may have been showing some initiative up on Epipolae; but the sea approaches to Syracuse were still open, and merchantmen carrying grain or other essential commodities could still sail unopposed into the

Great Harbour. Every day the Athenian fleet remained at Thapsus, the Syracusans could lay in more stores to ride out the siege. Why, it may well be asked, did Nicias not impose a tight naval blockade on Syracuse from the moment he got there? The only rational answer is, surely, because he was convinced (for whatever reason) that no siege would be necessary, that Syracuse would surrender without one. We shall return to this point later.

To the Syracusan generals, however, it was only too clear that unless Nicias' siege operations were stopped quickly, before they got too far, Syracuse was soon going to find itself completely cut off. The speed with which work was going forward on Epipolae produced consternation inside the city. The Athenian fleet was not going to remain at Thapsus for ever; indeed, no one could quite understand what it was doing there now. The moment Nicias' engineers had walled them off on the landward side, surely, the Athenian fleet would sail round and close the blockade by sea. Something had to be done, and without delay. The generals therefore determined to force a full-scale battle on the Athenians; it was a risk, but one well worth taking. They led their whole army up on to Epipolae (probably from the northern gate, by way of the Salita Ombra) and advanced on Nicias' camp. But when the two armies were actually drawn up and facing each other, it became clear that Syracusan discipline and morale had reached a very low ebb indeed. The men milled about in disorder. Many of them flatly refused to get into line. It is not the last time we shall meet this phenomenon among Syracusan troops; and as we shall see, there was probably more behind it than mere lack of moral fibre.

To risk an engagement in such conditions would, clearly, be suicidal. Hermocrates and his two fellow-generals therefore decided to cut their losses. The main force—that is, the citizen-infantry—was withdrawn from Epipolae, and marched back to Syracuse. The cavalry, however, remained behind, to harass working parties (these were mostly collecting rocks and large stones, which abound on the plateau) and to cut off any stragglers. They were an élite corps, recruited exclusively from the aristocratic or wealthy landowning families; Hermocrates could trust them, and knew it.

But they accomplished singularly little, notwithstanding. One tribal regiment of Athenian hoplites, reinforced by Nicias' own newly formed cavalry arm, dealt with these intruders in double-quick time, killing some and putting the rest to headlong flight. The psychological effect of such a victory must have been very great—on both sides, and for rather dissimilar reasons. If Syracusan morale was as bad as all that, Hermocrates must have argued to himself, the situation was hopeless. He told his colleagues, in very blunt terms, that it was no longer advisable to risk a full-scale pitched battle against the Athenians: the troops could not be relied upon. Instead, they should restrict themselves to limited counter-measures against Nicias' siege works.

Nicias himself interpreted this "bad morale" in a rather different way. He was still secretly in contact with Athenagoras and the radical party, and can hardly fail to have been impressed by this demonstration of non-belligerence among the Syracusan rank and file. If they were so markedly unenthusiastic about fighting an Athenian army, might not that be because they found the prospect of a truly democratic Syracuse, allied to Athens, more attractive than servitude under the present reactionary regime? Radical propaganda, it seemed, had begun to pay off. One way and another, Nicias must have reasoned, the Syracusan campaign looked as if it might reach a successful conclusion sooner than anyone had anticipated.

Next day building operations began again, with no Syracusan cavalry to hinder them. A team of pioneers began constructing a wall northwards from the Round Fort—probably as far as the east–west road across the plateau, which formed a natural turning point, and would greatly facilitate the transporting of material. Another group, says Thucydides, "collected stones and wood, which they put down at intervals in the direction of Trogilus *on the shortest line for their blockading wall* [my italics], which was to extend from the Great Harbour to the sea at the other side."

No topographical problem has puzzled students of the Syracuse campaign more than determining the location of Trogilus —or with less good reason. But so long as scholars held that Achradina extended as far north as Scala Greca, the only possible site for Trogilus was somewhere on the adjacent coast— probably at the little bay of S. Panagia. The traditional meaning of the name Trogilus was "eaten away" or "eroded"; therefore, it was argued, a bay or inlet would suit the name very well. On this interpretation, however, every bay and inlet in the world would qualify for the name Trogilus. What was there about this particular one which marked it off from the rest?

The answer is, nothing whatsoever; but once Achradina is restored to its proper place below Epipolae, S. Panagia no longer concerns us. The shortest route round the city walls between the Great Harbour and the outer sea will now, obviously, follow a very different route.[1] Its course will lie, not north, as has generally been supposed, but east-south-east, along the line of the southern cliffs of Epipolae, reaching the coast half a mile or so north of S. Lucia, in the little bay known as I Cappuccini. This, beyond any question, is the "shortest line," if we are to combine Thucydides' text with local topographical evidence; and it is here we must seek the "eroded" or "eaten away" site that is Trogilus.[2]

We do not have far to look. Anyone who has explored the coastline immediately north of Syracuse will instantly realise both where Trogilus is, and how it got its name. At several points where steps and other remains of ancient harbours can

[1] The course of the circumvallation describes a near semicircle—thus, incidentally, justifying Thucydides' use (7.2.4) of the word *kyklos* (circle) to describe the fortifications as a whole, which many scholars challenge.

[2] The only possible alternative, suggested by Piganiol (see Bibliography), is a line running slightly north of east from the road across the plateau, passing by the Grotta Santa, and reaching the coast opposite the twin rocks called I due Fratelli. But it seems most unlikely that the Tyche quarter had spread this far north by 414. Fabricius, with splendid inconsistency, having exploded the idea of Achradina-on-Epipolae, still keeps Trogilus on the north coast, placing it in the bay to the west of S. Panagia.

still be seen—including I Cappuccini and I due Fratelli—the cliffs have been eroded in the most fantastic and unusual way. Since this phenomenon can only be observed by climbing down the rocks to sea-level, it is easy to understand how visiting scholars might have missed it. A series of vast, roughly semi-circular recesses, with a flat-ceilinged overhang and a cut-back of anything up to twenty feet, are scooped neatly out of the solid rock—not by human agency, though man's shaping hand may have improved them here and there—a yard or so above sea-level. The rock is limestone schist, in flat horizontal layers, which largely accounts for the shape these open-fronted grottoes have assumed. It is probable, in fact, that Trogilus was the name, not of any specific harbour, but of the whole coastline up to a point just beyond I due Fratelli, where this odd geological phenomenon ceases.

The Athenian troops who were stockpiling timber and bricks and building stones, then, did so, we may assume, along the line of the east–west road, at intervals between I Cappuccini and the short wall running north from the Round Fort. (It is not impossible that sailors from the fleet were employed to hasten the work on from the seaward side.) Faced with this alarming threat to their lines of communication—any day now, it was clear, the Athenians would also start building south-wards, from the Portella del Fusco to the shore of the Great Harbour—the Syracusans were stung into positive action. They decided to seal off the Portella del Fusco with a counterwall and a stockade. This would not demand more men than they could spare, and the working party would have their own stock-ade to protect them as they raised each new section of the wall. On the other hand, they reasoned, if the Athenians wanted to stop this project, they would have to attack in force; and that would mean suspending all their own siege operations while they did so. The argument, if somewhat specious, at least of-fered encouragement, and work began at once.

The wall and stockade started together from a postern gate in the new extension wall outside Temenites, and ran west-ward, parallel to the cliffs, thus crossing the Athenians' presumptive line of advance at right angles. The builders cut down a number of olive trees from a nearby temple enclosure—probably that of Apollo—and used them to construct watch-towers at intervals along the wall. Once they were well past the Portella del Fusco, all they had to do was carry their double barrier under the hang of the cliffs.

For a while both sides remained intent on their own building operations, and took no military action against each other. The Athenians in particular seem to have been concentrating all their energies on completing the wall to Trogilus; they did not want to waste time skirmishing round this Syracusan stockade. After all, they still controlled Euryalus. The counter-wall was a nuisance, but no real threat. However, they kept a very careful watch on the enemy's movements. After a while, when no attacking force came out against them, the Syracusans got a little careless and over-confident. By now both wall and stockade were well advanced, and only one company was left to guard them after working hours.

It was at this point that the Athenians decided to carry out their counter-attack. They had already struck one very serious blow at those inside the city by locating, and destroying, the underground pipelines which supplied Syracuse with drinking-water.[8] Now they picked three hundred of their best hoplites, together with a few outstandingly fast runners from the light-armed troops, who were put into heavy armour for the occasion. These were to make the actual charge on the stockade. Half Nicias' remaining troops would give them cover in case of a sortie from the city. The remainder were to launch a second thrust against the stockade, at its juncture with the Temenites wall.

Nicias waited until about two o'clock in the afternoon, when

[8] We hear nothing about the effects of this move. Presumably the city also had wells, and nothing (as we shall see) was easier than to run the virtually non-existent sea blockade. But the pipes must have come down by way of Epipolae, and until Gylippus recaptured the plateau in the autumn, they presumably remained disconnected. It was the height of summer; there must, at the very least, have been severe discomfort.

the heat was most intense and most of the Syracusan pioneers had retired after their midday meal. Those who were not actually on guard duty now snatched a short siesta in their tents. Some (perhaps the married men) actually went back into the city. Even those manning the watch-towers on the wall were not liable to be at their most sharply observant. Half a flagon of wine, after a hard morning's work with spade, mattock, or sledge-hammer, under a blazing sun, must have left them drowsy and off their guard.

It was at this dead, somnolent hour of the afternoon that the Athenians launched their attack. The heavy-armed commando team charged the stockade at the double (which suggests that it was fairly close to the cliffs) and captured it with comparative ease. The defenders fled along the far side of the wall, their pursuers hot on their heels. When they reached the postern gate, Nicias' second attacking force closed in on them. Syracusans and Athenians struggled through the gateway together. But Hermocrates' garrison troops were ready for them inside, and the attackers were rapidly ejected, leaving some of their number behind, either dead or severely wounded. This was the nearest Athens ever came to taking Syracuse by storm.

The whole attacking force now re-formed its ranks and set about destroying the Syracusan counter-wall throughout its length, seemingly without any interference. The city garrison had just managed, by the skin of their teeth, to stop Athens' best hoplites from fighting their way into Achradina; they were not in the mood now to take unnecessary risks. The wall was razed to the ground and the stockade pulled up; the Athenians carried off its stakes and posts for their own use.

But the Syracusans' action, though unsuccessful, had obviously scared Nicias. Such tactics could well have crippled or seriously delayed his plans for establishing complete control over the Great Harbour. So on the day after the destruction of the Syracusan stockade, work was begun, at top speed, on the project which it had been designed to forestall—that is, the southern section of the main circumvallation, from the Round

Fort down through the Portella del Fusco and on towards the Anapus estuary. Most of this work must have been supervised by Lamachus: Nicias had had a sudden excruciating attack of nephritis, and was temporarily bedridden.

The Athenians certainly moved fast. By the time Hermocrates and his colleagues had organised a fresh counter-attack, the wall was nearly five hundred yards clear of Epipolae—an extraordinary feat. As a result, the Syracusans had no chance, this time, to operate over favourable terrain. Instead, they were forced to carry their defence-line across the great marsh of Lysimeleia, which meant that building a wall, or even an earth rampart, was out of the question. The most they could do was to dig a shallow, oozing ditch, and back it with a deep-sunk palisade. Yet even this implies a certain amount of firm ground. Lysimeleia cannot have been total swamp, but rather a low-lying area with frequent patches of bog and standing water.

The Syracusans' task was an extremely unpleasant one. Under that hot and pitiless sun they squelched through the black, stinking slime of Lysimeleia, streaked with sweat, tormented by flies and leeches, knife-keen swamp-grass slicing their hands raw, while all the time the Athenian wall moved steadily forward, and Athenian arrows came whipping through the reeds, with the quick soft hiss of a snake disturbed. The Athenians held off until they had strengthened the wall at Portella del Fusco, its most vulnerable point. Then they attacked in strength. At the same time orders went to the fleet to evacuate Thapsus and sail round into the Great Harbour. This suggests that the landward wall to Trogilus must have been far advanced —near enough, certainly, for a rumour to spread along the trade-routes that Syracuse was now totally invested. Before dawn the whole land force moved down from Epipolae. Nicias, still desperately ill, stayed behind in the Round Fort with a skeleton garrison. A similar detachment was left to guard the second fort at Labdalum.

The Athenians advanced in open order, carrying planks and old doors (where did they find *them?*) to lay down like duck-boards "where the mud was thickest and the ground firmest."

Lamachus had placed himself on the left wing, with the Argives, so that he could meet any sudden sortie from the city gates. The Athenian heavy-armed infantry, led by the same crack hoplite commando which had captured the stockade, were on the right. By daybreak they had occupied the whole of the ditch and captured most of the new stockade without a blow being struck. Then, late but willing, the Syracusans woke up to what was happening and marshalled their defences. At first they had very little success. The Athenians—wide awake and in good battle order—drove their disordered levies back on both wings. Lamachus pressed the Syracusan right wing towards the city and the Achradina gate. The Athenian hoplites punched through Hermocrates' centre like a wedge, so that the Syracusan army was split in two. Their left wing, including the cavalry, streamed away in a south-westerly direction, probably along the Helorus road, with the idea of crossing the Anapus and re-forming on high ground near the Olympieum.

At this point it looked as though the battle was over; and so, oddly enough, it might have been had the three hundred hoplites of the "special force" not decided to show off their paces once more. Fast movement was their speciality. They raced off for the Anapus bridge at the double, determined to get there before the Syracusans and cut off their retreat. In their enthusiasm they spread out—like a cross-country running pack after the first five minutes—into loose open order. The Syracusans saw what was happening, and abruptly changed their tactics. Fear of being cornered, plus the sudden realisation that here was a heaven-sent chance to swing the battle the other way, made them act with remarkable speed and precision. Their cavalry wheeled round, tore through the galloping three hundred, and made mincemeat of them. Then, nothing daunted, they charged on into the thick of the Athenian right wing, and wrought similar havoc amongst the leading ranks there. Behind them, reorganised now, came the Syracusan hoplites, a solid advancing phalanx.

Lamachus at once disengaged his Argives, rounded up a few archers, and hurried across to give what help he could; the whole right wing looked in imminent danger of crumpling up. He was not a moment too soon; by now the Syracusan hoplites were in among the Athenians, and fighting furiously. But discipline and training, not to mention a field commander who had a cool head and knew his job, saw the Athenians through. The line steadied, and then slowly began to press forward. Presumably Lamachus also brought up his own cavalry to protect his exposed right flank. Then the Syracusans cracked for the second time. Their shield line broke, the battle became a pursuit, and the pursuit a rout.

But now, fatally, Lamachus let the excitement of victory go to his head. He charged ahead after the fleeing Syracusans, accompanied by a few hoplites, leaping from tussock to tussock across the bog, splashing headlong through ditches and puddles, the great plumes waving on his helmet, his general's insignia plain for all to see. The little group, yelling and whooping, slowly drew away from the main body. They scrambled across a dyke, and then a detachment of Syracusan cavalry swept down on them, and they were cut off. A certain Callicrates, described by Plutarch as "one of the most redoubtable and daring of the Syracusan officers," spotted Lamachus standing there, and, with sporting panache, challenged him to single combat. Lamachus—forgetting, it has been argued, his responsibilities as a general—accepted the challenge. So they stood and fought among the marshes of Lysimeleia, while the tide of battle flowed past them. Then Callicrates got past his opponent's guard, and thrust home. Convulsively Lamachus grappled the Syracusan to him, his own sword driving through corslet and flesh, and the two men fell together. The few hoplites who had accompanied Lamachus were also cut down in their turn. The Syracusans snatched up Lamachus' body, armour and all, and bore it off across the river towards the Olympieum, away from the Athenian pursuit. "Then," says Thucydides, "as the rest of the Athenian army was approaching, they fell back themselves"—presumably across country.

Doubts have been cast—unjustly, I feel—on the historicity of Lamachus' heroic duel with Callicrates. Once the Athenian general was cut off, he had nothing to lose—indeed, a good deal to gain—by engaging in single combat. At least it would stop him being overwhelmed by an indiscriminate horde of Syracusans. Moreover, he would only have to keep Callicrates in play for a moment or two, and then the Athenian pursuit would catch up with them, and he would be rescued. His fault, which no one denies, was in exposing himself so rashly in the first place. Few generals can have been a greater loss, or have died less opportunely, than Lamachus, son of Xenophanes. With his removal from the scene, the Athenian expeditionary force seemed to lose all its vigour and initiative. The braggart soldier of Aristophanes, the loud-mouthed swaggering clown with the Gorgon on his shield, had showed himself no coward in his death—but he might have been better advised, like Archilochus, to throw away his shield, run for it, and live to fight, and command, another day.[4]

By now the Syracusan troops who had fled to the city earlier in the battle had recovered their confidence, and were ready for action once more. They sent a contingent back to harass the Athenians from the flank; then the rest of them, guessing that there must be hardly anyone left on Epipolae, hastened up to the plateau—probably by way of the Salita Ombra—and made straight for the Round Fort. Before anyone could stop them they had overrun the protective outer earthwork, and were advancing on the ramparts of the fort itself. At this point Nicias, hearing the noise of the attack, staggered up from his sick-bed and saw, instantly, how serious the position was. The garrison lacked the strength to fight any kind of normal defensive action. There was a real danger that the Round Fort might fall, and he himself be taken prisoner. This would drive a cart—literally as well as physically—through the Athenian siege operations. It would also cripple the expedition's leader-

[4] Yet his behaviour was not all that *outré* by fifth-century standards. The list of field-commanders killed in action during the Peloponnesian War also includes Nicostratus and Laches, the commander of the first Sicilian expedition (Mantinea, 418); Procles (Aetolia, 426); Hippocrates (Delium, 424); and Philocles (Aegospotami, 405).

ship—worse, indeed, than Nicias realised, since he had not yet learnt of Lamachus' death.

There was not an instant to lose, and for once Nicias displayed all the ingenuity and quick presence of mind which seem so singularly lacking in him on almost every other occasion of which we have knowledge. Piles of timber lay in front of the rampart, together with barrels of pitch and one or two wooden siege engines. A few shouted orders were enough. While the bulk of the garrison briefly held up the Syracusan advance, a few men ran along the rampart, dousing everything with pitch and then setting fire to it. The wood was bone-dry after days in the midsummer sun; within seconds a great crackling, belching sheet of flame and smoke roared skywards. At once the Syracusans called off their attack, not so much through fear, as our sources suggest, but because they knew this bonfire was bound to act as a warning signal to the Athenians below. The whole group withdrew to the eastern end of the plateau. By his prompt action Nicias had saved not only the Round Fort, but also a vast quantity of valuable stores.

As the Syracusans had rightly anticipated, an Athenian contingent was already on its way up the cliffs to rescue Nicias. But what really brought the whole battle to an abrupt conclusion was the timely and dramatic appearance of the Athenian fleet from Thapsus, which now came sailing, unopposed, into the Great Harbour. As the triremes rounded Ortygia and were sighted by the combatants ashore, a general Syracusan withdrawal began. From the plain and the plateau, all Hermocrates' troops now sought safety behind the city gates. Nicias found himself, when they were gone, in an extremely strong position. As the Syracusans themselves realised all too well, there was nothing to stop him extending his southern wall to the Great Harbour (or, indeed, virtually wherever he liked) in his own good time. The Athenian fleet could enforce its long-dreaded blockade, and cut all Syracuse's supply-lines. Her water-pipes had been severed already. The fortifications between the Round Fort and Trogilus were well on the way to completion. Failing a miracle, it looked as though Syracuse must fall in a few weeks at the outside.

After the battle was over, and the bodies of the fallen—including that of Lamachus—had been given back under a flag of truce, Nicias turned his main attention to the southern wall. He now had his entire force, both naval and military, united in one place, under a single command. All available men were placed on construction work. In a very short time a strong *double* wall had been built almost as far as the Anapus estuary, the walls diverging widely as they approached the seaward end, to form a kind of large enclosure or corral. Yet, for whatever inscrutable reason, Nicias now became so preoccupied with the Great Harbour that he seems to have forgotten what still remained undone on Epipolae. The two forts, with their full storerooms, should have been securely guarded. They were not—and this despite the sharp reminder Nicias had himself been given of their vulnerability in the face of a determined assault. Above all, the wall to Trogilus should have been finished without a moment's delay. Instead, several stretches were still no more than half built, and at one point at least the stones and other material were all assembled, but no courses had yet been laid.

What made Nicias so inexplicably careless? The most common theory, today as in antiquity, is that sudden and striking good fortune had turned even his sober head. Certainly nothing succeeds like success, as he now found out. Not only the hitherto recalcitrant coastal Sicels, but also many cities both in Sicily and Magna Graecia (which up till now had either backed Syracuse or else stayed prudently neutral) hastened to climb on the Athenian bandwagon. "Shiploads of grain," Plutarch remarks with nice cynicism, "appeared in his camp from every quarter." By now it must have been a rule-of-thumb cliché: *If you want to get in Athens' good books, send her a consignment of wheat.* To cap everything, three fifty-oared Etruscan galleys joined the Athenian fleet in the Great Harbour. But all this, encouraging as it undoubtedly was, still does not explain why Nicias left the blockade partially open. For one thing, his achievement had not been all *that* much to write home about. He had often done much better in the past, and there is no sign that his successes then brought on any visible accession of hyper-manic self-confidence. One is driven to consider the possibility that he may have been acting quite deliberately, and for some specific purpose.

Now, Plutarch tells us that the Syracusans were so pessimistic about the outcome of the blockade at this point that they seriously considered opening official negotiations with Nicias, and surrendering the city on terms. They felt, Plutarch tells us, "that they must come to terms *before the city was completely encircled* [my italics]." This in itself is no more than ordinary common sense. Once the trap had been closed, no besieging general in his right mind would negotiate; he merely had to sit still and wait for his victim's unconditional surrender. But Nicias, as should by now be apparent, was not an ordinary general. If he believed he could get a capitulation without any of the trouble and expense of a long siege, the odds are very heavily in favour of his having made every possible effort to do so. In that case he would have a very strong motive for leaving the Trogilus wall unfinished. Once the ring was closed, there were no further grounds for negotiation, and the Syracusan generals, with the courage of despair, might well have preferred to sit tight and sweat it out. There was always an outside chance of breaking the blockade.

If Nicias *was* banking on a negotiated surrender, what made him so sure of his ground? Agents, we are told, had been sent to him from the city with the news that Syracuse was ready to surrender on terms. Who sent them? And what was going on behind the walls as the prospect of defeat grew daily greater? One thing is immediately clear. The worse the war went against Syracuse, the more influence Athenagoras, Diocles, and their friends would exert—among the vast majority of ordinary citizens if not on the Gamoroi and the generals. Polyaenus has a story (for which there is surely some foundation) of a slave revolt in Syracuse during the siege, under a free leader named Sosistratus. Hermocrates, it would seem, dealt very neatly with this dangerous situation. He sent a cavalry officer to talk to the rebels. The generals, this officer said, admired their fighting spirit. They were to be given heavy armour, full citizens' pay, and enrolled as hoplites.

Meanwhile Sosistratus himself, the officer went on, had been co-opted on to the Board of Generals. Hermocrates would be glad to have a conference with him as soon as possible; his lieutenants were also most welcome. Sosistratus took him at his word, and turned up accompanied by about twenty of his slave-officers. Hermocrates promptly had the whole lot of them clapped in jail. Having thus, as it were, cut off the head of the rebellion at one stroke, he took six hundred armed hoplites, marched down to the open ground where the slaves had assembled (perhaps in Temenites or by the docks above the Little Harbour), and offered them a general amnesty if they dispersed and went back to their masters. Most of them obeyed like lambs; but three hundred, we are told, went over to the Athenians—which at once suggests both the story they had been fed, and just who it was that fed it to them. If this abortive slave revolt ever in fact took place,[5] the odds are that Athenagoras and Diocles were in some way responsible for it —just as they also were, I am convinced, for the near-mutinous indiscipline in the ranks which made Hermocrates withdraw his infantry from Epipolae.

Hermocrates, indeed, had survived for a long time under heavy personal pressure from the radicals. The near-encirclement of Syracuse finally gave them a lever with which to get rid of him. In any war, failure must have its scapegoat; and the obvious scapegoats on this occasion were the three generals-extraordinary. It was not hard for a skilful propagandist to channel public resentment against them. Charges of treachery were voiced: in Syracuse, as in Greece, the radical pot was always willing to call the conservative kettle black. This time

[5] In the nineteenth century the story was rejected out of hand. Nowadays, after several decades of popular revolutions, fifth-column work and infiltration techniques, we are much more conditioned to accept it—as Grosso, for one, does without question (see Bibliography).

the trick worked. By overwhelming public demand, the three generals were relieved of their duties. They were not prosecuted, however; no one—least of all Athenagoras and his friends —wanted any dirty political linen washed in public at this point. Athenagoras' sole aim in deposing them was to replace them with candidates of his own choice, and this was duly done. Two of the three replacements, Eucles and Heracleides, later turn up as Diocles' colleagues after the democratic revolution of 412. It is, indeed, not hard to guess who it was that kept Nicias informed of such matters, or why the Athenian general, despite his ill health, "felt suddenly elated by his present strength and good fortune."

At any moment, it seemed, the gates of Syracuse would be thrown open and Nicias' victorious troops march in without another blow being struck. There would be a profitable alliance with the city's new "democratic" government, an orderly and unending procession of grain ships docking in Piraeus, thunderous acclaim from the Assembly, the spectre of famine exorcised, once and for all, from Athenian soil. Athens and Syracuse would carve up the rich resources of Sicily between them, with Athens very much the dominant partner. It was, indeed, an intoxicating dream.

But Nicias and Athenagoras alike had reckoned without one man: a short, undistinguished-looking Spartan of somewhat dubious antecedents, a general who arrived in Sicily with neither fleet nor army, indeed with little to sustain him but his wooden staff and his homespun cloak and the rigorous military tradition in which he had been reared. Gylippus, son of Cleandridas —as momentous a figure, in his own improbable way, as that other unlikely hero Don John of Austria—was now approaching beleaguered Syracuse. For the second time Alcibiades had struck a blow at his countrymen in Sicily; and this time the wound was to prove mortal.

CHAPTER XII: *Enter Gylippus*

Cleandridas, the father of Gylippus, was already an experienced soldier by 466, when he fought in the Arcadian War. Twenty years later, in his late middle age, he was appointed adviser to the young Spartan King Pleistoanax during his invasion of Attica. When Pericles successfully bribed the Spartans to withdraw, Cleandridas was condemned to death *in absentia* for giving his consent to such an arrangement. He took refuge at Pericles' new "Panhellenic" colony of Thurii, where he applied for and obtained citizenship. His wife and son were still in Sparta. Cleandridas' military talents were not allowed to rust in exile: he commanded the Thurian army in several campaigns against Tarentum. More important, it was almost certainly he who, about 435, organised the right-wing officers' coup that removed Thurii from Athenian control and brought her into alliance with the Peloponnesian League. This presumably was the price of his rehabilitation in Spartan eyes.[1]

Gylippus, then, was the son of a man who had been publicly branded as a traitor. For over ten years this stigma had hung over him, while he made his way, fatherless, in the toughest masculine society that Greece knew, subject to cruel gibes and insults over and above the usual hardships which a Spartan youth had to endure.[2] To survive such treatment called for very special qualities of stubborn determination and moral

[1] Pleistoanax himself was not so fortunate. He remained in exile for nineteen years, and was only recalled in 426 as the result of an oracle.
[2] A hint of this survives in the tradition that Gylippus was a *mothax*, that is, a Helot's child brought up as a Spartan's foster-brother. His subsequent status makes the story patently false. But it is just the kind of insult which might well have been flung at him during his father's disgrace and exile.

courage. Gylippus not only survived, he rose to high rank. But the experience left its indelible mark on him. He was said to be mean, cold, harsh, and covetous. His personality sounds as dislikable as it was uncompromising—though he was not beyond admitting he was wrong on occasion. One good reason for sending Gylippus to Syracuse was, of course, his father's connection with Thurii: this might prove very helpful when looking for support in southern Italy. But we may also surmise that the Ephors were only too glad to post him overseas—especially to what looked like being a highly hazardous assignment.

Gylippus sailed towards the end of June, from Asine in the Messenian Gulf, together with a Corinthian officer called Pythen. They had four ships between them. When they reached Leucas, their last landfall before the crossing to Italy, the news they heard was very disheartening. Syracuse, it was rumoured, had been cut off by land and sea. The blockade was complete. Gylippus at once abandoned all hope of saving Sicily—an interesting confirmation of Alcibiades' strategic assessment—but decided to press on regardless; the Athenians might still be kept out of Magna Graecia. He sent a message back to Corinth, reporting on the situation and asking for the ten triremes he had been promised. They were to follow on as soon as possible, picking up some local ships en route. Meanwhile he and Pythen crossed the Straits of Otranto, and made straight for Tarentum, Sparta's one colony in the West.

From Tarentum Gylippus duly sent a representative to Thurii, reminding the government there that his father had been a distinguished citizen of their colony. But the Thurians were not impressed. (Thucydides says they despised his lack of ships, and took him for a mere freebooter.) They turned down the Spartan's request for support, and sent his messenger back empty-handed. So the city that Sparta was relying on to guarantee at least one firm alliance proved no help at all: it was not an auspicious beginning. However, Gylippus may have been anticipating a rebuff at Thuri, since he carefully avoided going there in person. This suggests that the pro-Athenian party was in control at the time. During the years 415–413 Thurii was in the throes of party stasis, with consequent rapid switches in her loyalties. Our sources suggest that during this period at least four changes of government took place, which is brisk going, but by no means improbable.

Nothing daunted by his setback, Gylippus put to sea again, and sailed on south. But off the toe of Italy the little convoy ran into bad weather, and was driven back to Tarentum by northerly gales. Further precious time went by while the ships were beached and underwent repairs. By now, too, news of Gylippus' arrival had reached Nicias in Syracuse. Like the authorities of Thurii, Nicias dismissed this four-ship Spartan general as a mere petty privateer. It is, indeed, not unlikely that Gylippus deliberately went out of his way to create such an impression, and thus ensure that no one took him seriously until it was too late. If so, he succeeded only too well.

When his ships had been refitted, Gylippus sailed on to his next "safe" port of call, Locri. Here he learnt that the blockade round Syracuse was *not*, in fact, complete, and that "it was still possible for an army to get into the city by way of Epipolae." This wholly unexpected but most welcome piece of news made him at once revise all his plans. He and Pythen held an emergency conference to discuss their next move. They could sail straight for Syracuse, running the gauntlet of the Athenian fleet. This might be a risky business, but perhaps necessary if the city was to be saved. Once Nicias had completed his walls, getting into Syracuse would be a real problem. Alternatively, they could make their way round the north coast of the island to Himera, and then march overland with as many volunteers as they could raise, both from Himera itself and among the Sicel communities they would pass on their way to Syracuse. This scheme might furnish welcome reinforcements, but was liable to lose them the advantage of surprise.

Which was more practical, of more immediate value? To have a Spartan general in Syracuse, with or without extra reinforcements—or a relief column which might not be able to enter the city? In the end they decided that the extra delay was worth risking for the very solid advantages it would confer. They therefore made Himera their immediate objective. Agents reported that Nicias, on learning of their arrival at Locri, had sent off four triremes to intercept them. But Gylippus and Pythen slipped through the straits and were on their way before this Athenian patrol reached Rhegium. It may be doubted whether Nicias was much disturbed when he learnt how they had eluded him. At this moment he was far more concerned with his private negotiations for Syracuse's surrender. Once the city had yielded, he could snap his fingers at any Spartan general. But until it did, he might have been better advised to temper his confidence with slightly stricter security.

Gylippus and Pythen reached Himera without incident, and the inhabitants gave them a warmly enthusiastic welcome. They not only agreed to send their own troops to Syracuse with Gylippus, but also offered to supply arms to those of his sailors and marines—about seven hundred in number—who did not already possess them. This in fact meant the great majority.[3] Gela promised to send a contingent. The Sicels, too, were far more co-operative after the death of their king, Archonidas, who had been staunchly pro-Athenian. Gylippus also, in his new role as supreme commander, "sent messengers to the people of Selinus, asking them to meet him with their whole force at an appointed place." This high-handed approach was conspicuously unsuccessful. When Gylippus set out from Himera, he had under him a force consisting of some three thousand hoplites and light-armed troops, with two hundred cavalry. Himera and the Sicels had each provided a thousand infantrymen, and Gylippus' own armed marines accounted for another seven hundred. Gela sent a mere hundred men, while Selinus, that great and powerful city, far from mustering her "whole

[3] The total complement of four ships would be eight hundred at most. Thus when Gylippus set out he had only 100 armed men with him. This both confirms the initial stinginess shown by the Spartan and Corinthian governments towards Syracuse, and suggests that Alcibiades' advice to double the role of hoplites and rowers had been noted and followed.

force," provided some two hundred light-armed troops and 100 armed horsemen.

It was this ad hoc but by no means negligible army which now force-marched across the island, by way of Enna and Centuripae, to attempt the relief of Syracuse.

Meanwhile the ten Corinthian vessels summoned to reinforce Gylippus had reached Leucas, where they picked up four more triremes as arranged. From Gylippus' last dispatch they had assumed that Syracuse was lost, and Sicily therefore written off, so that the war would now be carried on from Italy. But at Leucas they, too, learnt that the blockade remained incomplete. Gylippus had changed his plans and gone on to Himera. There was still hope for Syracuse. He had left instructions for the Corinthian squadron to sail there with all speed. They did so at once. Most of them followed the orthodox route, across the Straits of Otranto to the heel of Italy, and then down along the coast. But one fast vessel, commanded by a Corinthian named Gongylus, set course directly across the open sea, and thus reached Syracuse well ahead of the rest. Once again chance had intervened, literally at the eleventh hour, to save the beleaguered city; because when Gongylus dropped anchor in the Little Harbour,[4] the Assembly had already been summoned to discuss terms of surrender. His arrival caused a major sensation. Word spread to the nearby agora, and the debate was abandoned. The whole city, it seemed, now came crowding down to the waterfront to hear the news Gongylus brought them.

He told them that Gylippus was coming, that more ships were on their way. How many? someone shouted. Gongylus told him. The crowd began to murmur uneasily. Where *is* Gylippus? another voice enquired. Somewhere in Sicily, Gongylus said.

[4] It says a good deal about Nicias' notions of security that a Corinthian vessel could sail in, apparently in broad daylight, without encountering any Athenian patrols, let alone a blockade on the harbour mouth itself. As we shall see, he was scarcely more vigilant in the Great Harbour, though his fleet occupied it.

That was my last news. I've heard nothing since. Well, the same man called out, he may be; but he's not here, is he? We have the chance of negotiating on reasonable terms. You're asking us to throw that chance away. What guarantee can you offer us? Gongylus argued and pleaded. For the radical party this intervention could hardly have come at a worse time, and they must have used all their experience in mob oratory and barracking to shout Gongylus down, discredit Gylippus, and minimise his potential effect on the situation. The ordinary citizen, as I have tried to suggest, was in a quandary. He saw the advantages of surrender, yet his instinct was still to hold out if Syracuse had a chance. Athenagoras, like Cleon and his successors in Athens, probably could count on the allegiance of the "sailor rabble" and a fair proportion of the class immediately above it; but he came nowhere near controlling the citizen body as a whole.

The one thing the radicals must have tried to do was to get the debate carried through regardless, and here they failed. Gongylus persuaded the Assembly at least to postpone it. And then, with superb dramatic timing, another messenger slipped into Syracuse, from the landward side this time, which was, it would seem, no less carelessly guarded than the sea approaches. Gylippus, the messenger assured the crowd, was indeed coming to their relief, and with a large army. He was no more than a mile or two from the city. His orders, as commander-in-chief, were that the Syracusan defence forces should march out to meet him, in battle order, and ready for an engagement with the enemy. The psychological effect of this announcement is only too easy to imagine. While Nicias complacently awaited the result of the Syracusan Assembly's deliberations—a foregone conclusion, he must have told himself—the citizens, who, an hour or so before, had been preparing to endorse an instrument of surrender, now hurriedly snatched up sword and shield and sallied forth to meet their Spartan deliverer.

Since the Athenians held both the Great Harbour and Epipolae, there is only one way by which this force can have

left Syracuse, and that is through the Tyche gate, north of
S. Lucia. They then must have made their way right round the
cliffs below the bluff, keeping Epipolae always on their left,
until they passed S. Panagia and entered the main coastal plain
leading to Thapsus and Catana. Even so, the improbability of
this move does not seem to have excited as much comment
as one might have expected. There are times when the sheer
blind indifference of the Athenian forces besieging Syracuse
defies all reasonable belief. A single messenger might very
well slip through the lines unobserved. A single vessel might
just conceivably do so without attracting attention—though any
remotely competent commander would long since have established a tight blockade at every harbour mouth to stop supplies
reaching those within the walls. But what happened now was
something quite different. A large body of troops left Syracuse;
no one, it seems, either heard or saw them go. They joined
forces, in open country, with an attacking army of some three
thousand men that had advanced at least five miles without a
scrap of cover. Yet the very existence of this army does not
appear to have been known to Nicias or his men. It follows
that not only was the Little Harbour left unguarded; there were,
incredible though it may seem, no sentries posted on the seaward side to watch the Tyche gate or the line of the Trogilus
wall immediately beyond it.

From here on, it is true, the Syracusan force would be masked
for a little by the cliffs, since those Athenians who had work on
Epipolae were in all likelihood busy wall-building on the southern side of the plateau, near the Round Fort. But if a look-out
post was maintained at Scala Greca, as we might reasonably
suppose, a body of marching troops would have been in full
sight, and indeed very close, since the plain at this point has
only a narrow passage between the cliffs and the sea. No alarm
was given, so no guards can have been on duty here, either.
And what, one well may ask, about the Labdalum fort, from
which the Athenians enjoyed an uninterrupted panoramic view
of the entire northern plain, at least as far as Thapsus? The
answer, alas, is the same. Any wall-eyed sentry with his wits not

more than half fuddled with wine could have spotted Gylippus' army before the Spartan was much nearer than Megara Hyblaea, let alone a body of infantry under his very nose. Wherever the garrison of Labdalum may have been at this critical hour, it was not on look-out duty. Here, surely, we touch the very nadir of military inefficiency. Even if we assume that the Syracusan Assembly, like its Athenian counterpart, met at dawn, there is still no excuse. The Assembly was already gathering when Gongylus arrived, just before first light. More time was wasted in argument; and though the Syracusans marched out "at once" after the providential appearance of Gylippus' messenger (when did *he* show up?) it must have been broad daylight by the time the two armies met.

There is only one other possible explanation: Nicias was so sure of the city's surrender that he no longer regarded it as under siege. "For this reason," Plutarch says, "he paid no attention to Gylippus's arrival and did not even set any watch to intercept him." But even worse was to come. The men of Syracuse met Gylippus as arranged—probably in the plain near Leon.[5] Then the Spartan led his combined forces across country to the western end of Epipolae, where they silently filed up the col until they were all on the plateau itself—*still unobserved by the enemy*. So the Athenians, believe it or not, had left the vital approach of Euryalus unguarded as well—or at very best held by a sleepy guard detail that could be eliminated easily and without noise. "The sudden [!] appearance of Gylippus and the Syracusans bearing down on them," Thucydides remarks, "caused some confusion among the Athenians at first"; one can only assume they had all overslept. However, having at long last realised what was going on, Nicias' sentries sounded the alarm, and the Athenian army—professional in this at least—formed up, with swift and practised efficiency, to defend their camp and siege works. The camp probably lay in

[5] It is sometimes assumed (though Thucydides' text gives no clear support for this) that Gylippus and the Syracusans had their rendezvous on Epipolae itself; but this is to presume too far even on Athenian indifference.

the enclosed space between the southern cliffs, the Round Fort, and the east–west wall, as far as it was finished. It seems most likely that there was a gap at the point where the wall met the Epipolae cross-road, and that Nicias drew up his forces here, facing north.

Gylippus halted his army a little way off, among the grey littered stones and the wild thyme, and the Athenians eyed him warily, wondering what he was up to. Then he did a surprising thing. There came the sound of rough barked orders along the line, and with a rattle and clash his troops proceeded to pile arms. From the Spartan ranks a herald came forward, and announced that if the Athenians guaranteed to leave Sicily within five days, taking their belongings with them, Gylippus was prepared to furnish them with a safe-conduct, and to make peace.

Nicias, who by now had recovered sufficiently to take the field with his troops, stood in stony silence while this ultimatum was delivered, and made no reply to it. More than any man present, he must have been shocked by the turn events had taken; all his careful negotiations now lay in ruins. The Trogilus wall was still only half built; even the double wall down to the Great Harbour needed further work on its final section. But none of these doubts were allowed to show on Nicias' lined, impassive face as he faced Gylippus' herald. Some of his men, not realising how critical their position was, began to laugh and make coarse jokes about Gylippus, asking the herald "whether the presence of a single Spartan coarse cloak and staff had so transformed the Syracusans' prospects that they could afford to despise the Athenians." "And don't forget," some wag shouted, "it's not so long since we turned loose that bunch of Spartans we picked up on Sphacteria." "Right," said another veteran. "And every one of them was bigger than your general." "Longer hair, too," said a third.

At this the herald marched back to his own lines, and both sides prepared for battle. But Gylippus now found, as Hermocrates had found before him, that these Syracusan troops, faced with the prospect of serious fighting, tended to break ranks in a most unsoldierly fashion, "and could not be brought back into line." If the Athenians got such reluctant recruits boxed up between the Round Fort and the cliffs, there was liable to be a massacre; otherwise they would certainly break and run for it. Gylippus therefore retreated to more open ground in the middle of the plateau, and waited. But Nicias refused to be drawn. His troops stood fast, holding their defensive position. When Gylippus saw this, he decided to let well alone. There was something about the atmosphere among his own men which he did not like, and did not, as yet, understand. He therefore withdrew from Epipolae—this time, probably, by Scala Greca—and marched his three thousand men into Syracuse. There was open ground still in the newly walled Temenites quarter, and here they pitched camp for the night.

Gylippus had suffered every kind of insult in his hard and lonely life. He, if anyone, knew a hostile atmosphere when he met one. The Syracusans should have welcomed him as their saviour, and many of them, indeed, were enthusiastic enough. But there was a hard core among the rank and file which clearly regarded him as an inopportune intruder. They made endless jeering and denigratory remarks behind his back; he expected such insults from the Athenians, but not from his own troops. What lay behind it all? No doubt Hermocrates and his friends the Gamoroi very soon informed Gylippus of the real position—or, at least, of as much of it as they knew or could guess. For Athenagoras, as for Nicias, Gylippus could scarcely have arrived at a less opportune moment. The radicals had, by a skilful manipulation of popular feeling, unseated their opponents from the emergency high command, and taken it over themselves. A carefully pre-planned surrender on terms had been on the point of going through. Now the entire scheme was back in the melting-pot.

Nor is it hard to guess what the immediate consequences of that surrender would have been. Reinforced by Nicias' Athenian hoplites, the radical group and their supporters would have rounded up the Gamoroi and either thrown them into jail or murdered them out of hand, just as the right-wing party of landowners and rich merchants had been exterminated on Corcyra (see above, p. 49). A new "democratic" constitution was ready. The great estates would be carved up and redistributed among the citizens. Athens would get her grain consignments. Athenagoras and his friends would form a long-term government. Everyone would benefit in some way, except for the unfortunate Gamoroi. But now, with the arrival out of the blue of this intransigent Spartan general, at the head—worse luck—of a strong armed force, the whole situation had changed overnight. (It is interesting to speculate on what might have happened had Gylippus and Pythen sailed straight to Syracuse instead of collecting an army at Himera first.) There would be no surrender, and in all likelihood no revolution either. Gylippus and the Gamoroi were natural allies, and with Gylippus' three thousand men as well as their own retainers to back them, there could no longer be any question of eliminating them by force.

No wonder, then, that so many people had been unwilling to believe the news that Gongylus brought; they saw their brave new egalitarian world being snatched away from them. No wonder, either, that there was near-mutiny in the Syracusan ranks. Why should they fight their potential benefactors—least of all in order to re-establish Hermocrates and the great landowners, the old gang they had been working to kick out? Why should *they* shed their blood when the only result of victory under Gylippus would be to guarantee their own continued subjugation? So we have the ironic and piquant situation of Gylippus arriving, as he thought, in the nick of time to rescue Syracuse from the Athenians, only to find that a sizable proportion of the citizen body did not want to be rescued at all. He therefore not only had to perform the task for which he was sent out, but also—a far more delicate and hazardous undertaking—preserve the political status quo of Syracuse itself. That he somehow managed to achieve both objects is no small tribute to his talent, perseverance, and harsh yet impressive character.

He must, nevertheless, have had difficulty in imposing his authority—to begin with, at least. Polyaenus has a story (generally discredited by modern historians) that the Syracusan generals were against accepting him as their commander at all when he first arrived. Gylippus, he says, thereupon advised them to occupy a certain hill; passed this information secretly to the Athenians, who got there first; complained about the breach of security that had taken place; and was appointed supreme commander on the strength of it.[6] The strategem itself is an obvious and ridiculous fabrication. But that the Syracusan generals made Gylippus unwelcome there can be little doubt; after all, at least two of them (and probably all three) had been nominated by the radical group.

The Syracusan historian Philistus, who lived as an eyewitness through the siege, gave it as his opinion that it was Gylippus who "transformed the whole balance of the campaign," an opinion shared by Thucydides. The radical party was not all-powerful, and though its supporters did all they could to denigrate Gylippus, there were many others who—in the expressive phrase of Timaeus—"flocked round him, like birds around an owl, and were eager to serve under him." Yet even this partial enthusiasm on the part of the Syracusans is more than appears from now on in Nicias' camp. The Athenians and their allies had been away from home a year and more, living in primitive conditions, with equipment gradually deteriorating, and no end to the campaign in sight. Their original high enthusiasm, their expectation of a quick victory and fabulous plunder—all this had gone by the board. They had been kept going by the prospect of a negotiated surrender. Now this hope, too, was rudely snatched from them. They were trained soldiers, and did their duty when they had to. But morale in the Athenian camp was low, and became even lower as time went on.

Nicias himself, unlike his opposite number, offered no example of courage or enthusiasm to emulate: illness and disappointment had left him more depressed than any of his men. Simply and solely because of Gylippus, with his inflexible Spar-

[6] The regular argument—a perfectly valid one—against a large democratic-style high command in war-time was that it made for inefficiency and, in particular, for security leaks; Hermocrates made precisely the same points when getting the Syracusan Board of Generals reduced from fifteen members to three (see above, pp. 163–64).

tan code and his dynamic military mystique, Nicias was being compelled to fight once more—very much against his will, and now in essentially disadvantageous circumstances. (How he must have cursed himself for leaving that fatal gap in the Trogilus wall!) He had been on the point of getting all he wanted by diplomacy. Now he faced the prospect, at best, of a long, weary, and expensive siege, with, in all likelihood, little enough to show for his pains at the end of it. And supposing he failed to close the gap——? He was old and ill and tired. He yearned to be relieved of his command, and in this at least he has one's full sympathy.

Whatever his private worries about the political situation in Syracuse, Gylippus, unlike Nicias, behaved as though he had absolute confidence in himself and his mission. He certainly wasted no time. The very next morning he led out the bulk of his troops—those he had brought with him, it seems; there is no mention, this time, of the Syracusans, and small wonder —climbed Epipolae, and took up a position facing the Athenian wall, in such a manner that his opponents could not send out reinforcements to any other point without first fighting a major engagement. While Nicias' forces were thus pinned down, a commando troop of Gylippus' best men led an assault on the Labdalum fort—invisible behind the central ridge of Bufalaro see map, (p. 184) —captured it, and put the entire garrison to death.

Again, questions instantly spring to mind. Why, after the previous day's action, was there *still*, seemingly, no Athenian guard over Euryalus and the other main approaches to the plateau? Why had Labdalum, with its valuable stores and cash deposits, been left so weakly defended? Indeed, now that the fleet was no longer stationed at Thapsus, what point was there in maintaining a fort on the northern face of the plateau at all, except as a look-out post? (We have seen how efficiently its occupants carried out *that* function.) Did they even have sentries posted to warn them of Gylippus' attack? It seems most unlikely.

That same day an Athenian trireme, moored off the Little Harbour, was captured by the Syracusans: the first naval action on their part that we hear of during this campaign. What was it doing there? One can only assume that, after Gongylus had slipped in so easily, Nicias decided that this particular stable door ought to be locked, and detailed a single trireme to keep guard over the harbour entrance: not, one would have thought, a very efficient way of going about it.

By now Nicias had completed his double line of walls to the shore of the Great Harbour. Yet he did not immediately put them to any good use; nor did he, so far as we can tell, do what any man in his right mind would have done at once— that is, transfer every available man from this task to the far more vital job of pushing through the line of circumvallation between the Round Fort and Trogilus. Here building seems to have gone on, not progressively from one end, as down by the Great Harbour, but in sections, so that some stretches were complete, others half-finished, and others again scarcely begun. Each tribal regiment or allied contingent was allotted its own section, and the work went forward simultaneously at all points —the only possible method to adopt in the circumstances. Just how much of an all-out effort it was we shall see in a moment.

It was at least as important to Gylippus that the wall should remain unfinished as it was for the Athenians to complete it. There were two ways in which he could set about stopping them. The first, obviously, was by the well-tried method of a counter-wall, and this the Syracusans now began: "a single wall," Thucydides says, "which started from the city and was to go at an angle up across Epipolae." He gives no further details of its positioning. But it very probably began near the Salita Ombra—where the builders could bring material up to the plateau without difficulty and have an easy line of retreat—and ran north-west, towards the point where the roads from Euryalus and Scala Greca meet.

Gylippus also made a close study of the defences near the Round Fort (presumably while his herald was parleying with the Athenians) and observed that one section, perhaps that which

Nicias was holding against him, was still very weak. All day the Syracusans and their allies worked on the cross-wall. But at night Gylippus led a strong raiding party up to breach the defences, and perhaps, with luck, capture the Round Fort itself. The weather, unfortunately, was against him. August in Sicily can be cruelly hot, and the temperature does not drop all that far even at night. Most of the Athenians, finding their tents unbearable, were sleeping out under the stars, on the open ground beyond the wall. The noise of Gylippus' advance roused them at once. They gave the alarm, and the whole camp quickly sprang to arms. Gylippus, once the element of surprise had been lost, wisely decided not to risk a night attack, and withdrew. After this scare, the Athenians lost no time in raising and strengthening the level of the wall in this vital sector. They also from now on let no one except their own troops mount guard over it.

Once again the security and discipline of Nicias' troops seem to have been alarmingly lax. Because of their carelessness in guarding Euryalus and the other points of access to Epipolae, Gylippus now had a bridgehead on the plateau itself—the Labdalum fort. Syracusan workers could obviously come and go without overmuch difficulty to work on, or guard, the cross-wall they were constructing. Yet with enemy troops all around them, the Athenians nevertheless rolled up in their blankets and settled down for the night *outside* the fortifications, presumably relying on their light sleepers—like the geese in the Capitol—to warn them of an impending attack.

Quem Deus vult perdere, prius dementat. By now Nicias, with that steadily mounting pessimism which characterises all his actions from Gylippus' arrival onwards, had already convinced himself that Epipolae was as good as lost, and that he would do much better to concentrate on a naval blockade. The brisk efficiency which Gylippus was displaying seems to have semi-hypnotised him. Could he not see—as many of his subordinate officers must surely have urged—that to complete the Trogilus siege wall, *at whatever cost in lives or material,* was Athens' only hope, now, of forcing a Syracusan surrender? Once that enclosing ring was broken from within, and Gylippus in full command of Epipolae, it would take more than a naval blockade to reduce the city: nothing short of a miracle would turn the trick.

But Nicias appears to have believed, in some foggy way, that he had an alternative choice of strategy: that it was open to him to fight this campaign either by sea or land, as he preferred. He pottered round the foreshore of the Great Harbour; he studied the terrain; he made his decision. The fleet must be moved to a fresh base, at Plemmyrium (Penisola della Maddalena), the promontory which formed the southern arm of the harbour entrance. Plemmyrium itself was to be fortified. In this way, he argued, supplies could be brought in more easily. (But what was hindering their delivery? Not the Syracusan fleet.) Their squadrons would be nearer to the enemy, and not have to sail two miles across from the far corner of the Great Harbour whenever the Syracusans showed any signs of naval activity.

Any reasonably intelligent staff officer could have seen that this scheme was a piece of dangerous lunacy; but it takes considerable nerve to tell one's commanding officer such things to his face. If objections were raised, Nicias (who had a streak of pure mulish obstinacy on top of his other failings) must have brushed them aside. Yet a formidable indictment can be brought against his action, and it is hard to believe that he carried it through unopposed. To begin with, Plemmyrium lacked adequate supplies of water, which therefore had to be fetched in from outside, together with fuel and other essentials. When foraging parties were seen to go out regularly on such errands, the Syracusans would soon begin to intercept them with well-timed cavalry patrols. Plemmyrium, moreover, was dangerously isolated as well as being ill supplied: a desolate sandstone wilderness, eroded into grottoes, pocked with neolithic rock-tombs and cave-dwellings, about as unsuitable a site for a naval base as could well be imagined. Yet Nicias now proposed to transfer not only the fleet there, but also the bulk of stores and naval equipment—while keeping the army (except for a garrison detachment) at the opposite end of the Great Harbour.

This, surely, was to invite a land attack by Gylippus; and if all the expedition's reserve equipment fell into his hands, the loss would be crippling. Before occupying Plemmyrium himself, one feels, Nicias might have paused to speculate just why the Syracusans had never done so. If the position was as strategically valuable as he supposed, why should his opponents make him a present of it?

But the most cogent criticism of all is more closely bound up with the actual progress of the campaign. This move by Nicias was worse than stupid: it was murderously ill timed. To transfer stores and equipment, to improve the anchorage, to set up a semi-permanent camp, to construct not one but *three* forts on the headland—all this made an appalling drain on the limited pool of technicians, labourers, and building materials available. If the men who built those forts, and the stones with which they built them, had instead been available on the heights of Epipolae, the Syracuse campaign might have had a very different ending. The same argument applies to the double wall which Nicias constructed down to the Great Harbour. The main purpose of this wall—certainly the reason why it was double rather than single—was to shelter the fleet no less than to seal off Syracuse. Yet no sooner was it finished than Nicias moved the fleet elsewhere. If this wall had been single, the labour and material thus released would, once again, have substantially improved his chances of completing the circumvallation on Epipolae. However, Nicias got his way: no one contradicted him, and those who had doubts kept them to themselves—or joined the steadily increasing number of deserters who vanished into the Sicilian hinterland. When news arrived that Gylippus' Corinthian squadron was now approaching the toe of Italy, Nicias sent off a squadron of twenty ships to intercept them between Rhegium and Locri. Those chosen for this assignment were probably only too glad to be out of the way.

The rest of the fleet was duly transferred to its new station by Plemmyrium. After a little while the Syracusans—as might have been predicted—stationed one third of their entire cavalry force out at Polichna, the village by the Olympieum, "to prevent the Athenians coming out and plundering the country." These mounted troops now began to patrol the area constantly, and picked up numerous stragglers from naval working parties. Meanwhile, on Epipolae, the most crucial struggle of the entire campaign was slowly moving towards its climax. Gylippus had extended his cross-wall some little way now, a process made easier by the use of material purloined from Athenian supply dumps. While building was going on, he always had his workmen shielded by the heavy-armed infantry, drawn up ready in battle order. The Athenians stationed their own hoplites opposite them, for much the same purpose. Both sides, in fact, were engaged on a life-or-death building race, under military protection.

But the Spartan commander was always watching his opportunity, knowing that if the Athenians could once be wrong-footed, he might well get a chance to block off the Trogilus wall virtually without opposition. By now the two walls had come very close together, and it was anyone's guess as to which of them would cross the other's path first. Perhaps it was this that drove Gylippus to launch his attack. The battle was fought in a confined space between the two lines of fortifications,[7] a close-quarters affray, which meant that Gylippus was unable to make the best use of his cavalry and light-armed spearmen. The Athenians took full advantage of this tactical error, and gave their opponents a severe trouncing. The casualties were heavy. Among those killed was Gongylus of Corinth, the captain who had brought news of Gylippus' arrival in Sicily.

After his defeat this unpredictable Spartan did something very much out of character: he called his men together and

[7] Presumably, therefore, the two walls formed a re-entrant angle, with its open end towards the east: like the hands of a clock at about twenty-five past three. This suggests that Gylippus had most competition from one of the central sections, on his right, and not from the end by the Round Fort.

apologised to them, for all the world like a Communist cadre-leader performing an obligatory act of self-criticism. It had not been their fault, he said. He himself was to blame. He had allowed them to be outmanoeuvred and to fight in a disadvantageous position. Next time things would be very different. They were just as well off for arms and supplies as the Athenians, and it would be a sad day when good Dorian soldiers could not put down a mixed rabble of Ionians and islanders.

Gylippus was as good as his word. The Syracusan wall had by now almost reached Nicias' line of fortifications, "and once it was pushed past them," Thucydides says, "it would amount to much the same thing whether they fought and conquered continually or whether they never fought at all."[8] The Athenians therefore had to stake everything on winning control of both walls by force of arms, and made a spirited attempt to do so. But this time it was they who were outmanoeuvred. Nicias *had* to fight, whatever happened; and so he let Gylippus draw him too far beyond the fortifications, into open ground. His left wing was routed by the Syracusan cavalry, Gylippus' javelin-throwers kept up a steady fusillade on both flanks, and finally the whole Athenian force was driven headlong back to their camp beyond the Trogilus wall.

Gylippus, this time, had his men firmly under control. He called off the pursuit—always a difficult thing to do—and then, before the Athenians could recover themselves or take any effective counter-action, calmly set about carrying off all their stones and building material. The following night, under cover of darkness, he turned out his pioneers in force; and before dawn broke, the cross-wall had been carried well past the line which the

[8] I sometimes wonder (as did Freeman) how true, in fact, this was. After all, the Athenians had by now captured two Syracusan counter-walls that threatened their own siege works; and the Syracusans, similarly, had taken Labdalum. The task was therefore not impossible by definition. Why was it not attempted in this case? Nicias complained of the enemy's *superior numbers*; and it is true that we cannot tell how far desertion and disease—malaria in particular—had thinned the Athenians' ranks over and above their normal battle casualties.

Athenians were following. Nicias, we must presume, was so demoralised by the previous day's defeat that he set no watch over the siege works, and his men so exhausted that the busy clink of pick and shovel never disturbed their dreams.

It might reasonably be supposed that this disgraceful performance—though hardly worse than many other such incidents we have noticed—would produce an improvement in Athenian military discipline all round. An enquiry would be held, heads would roll, the whole system of guards and look-outs would be rigorously overhauled. But not a bit of it. The truth was, as Nicias hinted in his report to Athens, that he could no longer fully control his men. Any attempt to crack down on them now might well produce either mass desertions or plain mutiny.

A day or two later an even more inexplicable incident took place. The little Corinthian detachment bringing reinforcements to Gylippus had successfully eluded Nicias' intercepting squadron, and was at last approaching Syracuse. No particular blame attaches to the Athenian squadron commander who let his quarry slip through his fingers in this way. The sea is a large place, and ships can all to easily miss one another even when actively trying to make contact. But what happened next is quite another matter. The entire Corinthian contingent, led by a captain named Erasinides, now sailed unchallenged into harbour—the Little Harbour, one presumes, since thirteen enemy triremes advancing through the half-mile channel between Plemmyrium and Ortygia could hardly have failed to attract attention. Yet nobody seems to have seen them arrive; certainly no attempt was made by the Athenians to prevent their entry. What, we may ask ourselves, were the squadrons off Plemmyrium about at the time? Why had they been shifted, at great expense and trouble, from the far end of the Great Harbour if not to keep a closer eye on the comings and goings of the Syracusans and their allies?[9]

These thirteen ships meant a very considerable increase in

[9] The only possible answer is that the Corinthians slipped in by night; but this still leaves the puzzle of why no permanent blockade was kept on the Little Harbour.

manpower for Gylippus: something in the region of 2,500 extra pairs of hands, which he at once put to good use. The crews were enrolled as infantry-cum-pioneers, and joined the already vast labour force working on the Syracusan counter-wall. This was now pushed still further across Epipolae, in the direction of Bufalaro and the Labdalum fort. Gylippus' ultimate objective, clearly, was to capture and fortify the entire plateau: the raid on Labdalum had been a first move in this direction. With the extra reinforcements that had just arrived, his army—*exclusive of the Syracusans*—now totalled nearly six thousand men, mostly hoplites: enough, he calculated, to risk a direct frontal assault on the Athenian camp. The attack was duly launched. Nicias brought out his forces to fight a defensive action, but once again Gylippus proved too strong for him. This time the issue was decisive. The Athenians were beaten back with severe losses. They still held the Round Fort, but now only as an outpost of their walled camp below.

Apart from this one redoubt, Nicias was forced to evacuate Epipolae altogether, and to withdraw his entire force to the low-lying ground beside the Great Harbour. The Syracusans razed the Trogilus wall from the seaward side to within a short distance of the Round Fort: to obtain building material in the first instance, but a symbolic gesture nevertheless. The summer was over; and Athens' once-bright hopes of entering Syracuse in triumph had died with it.[10]

[10] This account of the Athenian withdrawal from Epipolae depends exclusively on Diodorus (13.8.2), who probably used Philistus or Ephorus. No other source, surprisingly, mentions it. Yet Epipolae must have been evacuated at some point, since later (see below, pp. 281 ff.) we find the Athenians making a strenuous effort to *recapture* it. Presumably the fact that they still held the Round Fort provided Nicias (and Thucydides) with a technical excuse not to admit the totality of this defeat.

During the spring and summer of 414 Sparta and Athens watched one another warily, with Argos lying between them as a combined buffer state and potential *casus belli*. The Spartans set out to invade Argos, but were turned back by an earthquake at Cleonae. The Argives, taking the intention for the deed, retaliated by raiding the border territory known as Thyreatis, and carried off twenty-five talents-worth of booty. The Spartans, understandably irritated, now launched a full-scale invasion and this time no convenient earthquake took place to give Argos a last-minute reprieve. Spartan troops marched through the Argolid, burning crops and destroying villages. This, it was clear, was no mere border raid. The Argives, in great alarm, sent an urgent appeal to Athens, as their ally, for immediate help—exactly the situation Sparta had hoped to provoke. Argos had often before suggested joint raids on Spartan territory, but the Athenians regularly turned down all such proposals. Now, at last, they gave way. A squadron of thirty vessels was dispatched to help Argos fight off this Spartan attack.

The squadron raided and burnt several places in Spartan territory—including the important iron-mining district of Epidaurus Limera. This, of course, constituted a flagrant and undeniable violation of the treaty. Sparta had often complained about such annoyances as Athens' raids into Messenia from Pylos, and her general lack of co-operation in observing the terms of the peace; but this was something different. The Spartans regarded it, quite justifiably on their own terms, as an act which left Athens and Sparta at war once more. From now on they acted on that assumption.

Sparta's motives are easy to understand. But why did the Athenians give them the excuse they wanted, now of all times? The war in Sicily had taken a turn for the worse, and reinforcements would clearly be needed there. Athens' cash reserves were falling low, and were to fall yet lower in the months that lay ahead. Persia's attitude was still highly enigmatic. The last thing on earth Athens could afford at this point, one might suppose, was to reopen hostilities with Sparta. If Pericles could not keep a Spartan army out of Attica during the first year of the war, with all his troops intact, what defence could Athens muster now? If the Spartans decided to take Alcibiades at his word, and fortify Decelea, who was to stop them? And beyond Decelea lay the silver mines of Laurium. It was sheer madness.

The bitter truth is that Athens had no conceivable alternative. By invading Argos the Spartans had got their old enemy, as they say, over a barrel. If the Athenians sat still and did nothing, they might well lose their alliance with Argos altogether. An Argive contingent was fighting in Sicily at this moment; Athens had no excuse for failing Argos in her own hour of need. If the pliable Argives did a deal with Sparta (as they had done more than once in the past) Athens would be left doubly vulnerable. On the other hand, if they honoured their debt to Argos, they could hardly hope to avoid war with Sparta. Twenty years before they had been strong enough to choose as they pleased in such a dilemma. Now it was another matter. Perhaps they felt that, on balance, Argos was a shade more dependable than Sparta; perhaps they were convinced that war was inevitable whatever happened, so they would gain nothing by sacrificing their ally, and might as well extract what initial advantage they could from making the break with Sparta themselves. Perhaps in expectation of the worst, they made another attempt—aided by Perdiccas, whose nose for failure had become less keen with advancing age—to recapture Amphipolis on the Strymon, but again without success. The gold and silver mines of Mt. Pangaeus remained tantalisingly beyond their grasp.

As autumn drew on, rumours began to circulate that the Spartans were seriously considering, not only the fortification of Decelea—an excellent motive in itself for that abortive attack on Amphipolis—but also large-scale backing for Syracuse, under the general auspices of the Peloponnesian League. It was in this

uneasy atmosphere of threatening danger and diplomatic intrigue that a long, detailed, grimly pessimistic dispatch from
Nicias reached Athens, and was read out, publicly, by the Clerk
to the Assembly.

After the capture of Epipolae, Gylippus seems to have felt,
with good reason, that he could afford to relax his pressure a
little. He had planned to establish himself on the heights before the autumn rains, and he had duly achieved his target. Nor
had he any intention of leaving the approaches unguarded, as
Nicias so inexplicably had done. Besides taking over Labdalum,
he built at least three, indeed probably four, further strongpoints on the plateau before that winter was out. One of these,
as might be expected, was placed at the summit of the Euryalus
col, where its occupants could not only defend the plateau
against immediate attack, but also had an excellent view both
of the northern plain and of the Great Harbour. The other
positions were fortified camps, and are not located by our
sources. But there can be little doubt where Gylippus, with his
shrewd eye for terrain, must have sited them: one near the
beginning of the cross-wall, above the Salita Ombra; one on
that high central rise, known today as Bufalaro, somewhat to the
west of the city; and perhaps another commanding S. Panagia
and Scala Greca.

With this distribution of strongpoints Gylippus controlled
every possible enemy approach to Epipolae. To make assurance
doubly sure, he seems to have extended the original cross-wall
right across the plateau, to the central camp and the Labdalum
fort, thus cutting Epipolae in two.[1] The three fortified sites—
Scala Greca, Bufalaro, and the Salita Ombra—Gylippus garrisoned separately, allocating Syracusans to one, other Sicilian
Greeks to the second, and overseas allies, such as the Corinthi-

[1] This has to be inferred from a confused passage in Thucydides
(7.43.4). Freeman thought the wall ran on to Euryalus; but this would
serve no useful tactical purpose, since it was from there that any major
assault was liable to come, and it would then simply be by-passed on
either side.

ans, to the third. The special force of six hundred picked Syracusan troops, now commanded by Hermocrates himself, was detailed to occupy an advanced position not far from Euryalus; its most likely base will have been Labdalum.

Having thus established himself securely on the landward side, Gylippus turned his attention to that Snark-like entity the Syracusan fleet. For all that it had achieved since Athens' invading armada first appeared upon the horizon, this modest and retiring force might as well not have existed. It sat quiet and did nothing while the Athenian heralds delivered their ultimatum. It allowed Nicias to disembark his crews and stores unhindered at the Anapus estuary. It never came anywhere near Thapsus while the enemy fleet was stationed there. At least one of its squadrons shared the northern end of the Great Harbour in apparently peaceful coexistence with Nicias' triremes, and took no action while the Athenian fleet, complete with stores and personnel, was transferred to its new base at Plemmyrium. Its one positive achievement, to the best of our knowledge, was the capture of that single isolated Athenian vessel outside the Little Harbour.

The Syracusans were frankly terrified of Athens' legendary expertise in the art of naval warfare, and had no intention whatsoever of matching their own amateur talents against these formidable professionals. It is also more than likely that the bulk of Syracuse's ultra-radical supporters were to be found, as in Athens, among the "sailor rabble," which would hardly, in this particular instance, be likely to improve the fleet's fighting morale. On the other hand, a little military success had already done wonders for the Syracusans, and probably diminished radical influence on their attitude to the war. Gylippus therefore had two problems to deal with. The fleet itself must be overhauled and enlarged, and the crews put through an intensive training programme—disciplinary as well as technical. He set about both tasks at once.

Syracuse possessed first-class docks and shipyards, and could count on unlimited supplies of timber and other shipbuilding material. The existing fleet was extensively overhauled, and numerous fresh keels were laid down. All along the Tyche foreshore the air was resonant with the sound of saw and hammer and plane; a new, clean smell, compounded of tar and resin and freshly cut wood ousted the old fishy harbour tang. The training programme was worked out, and new crews practised daily under Corinthian instructors, some of whom had probably fought against Phormio in the Gulf of Corinth sixteen years before, and had first-hand experience of Athenian naval tactics.

If Nicias chose to make this a naval campaign, Gylippus had every intention of giving the Athenians as good as he got, and perhaps better. It had not escaped his notice that while Syracuse itself had every facility for repair and maintenance work, the Athenians, ever since their fleet left Catana, had been restricted to such refitting as they could carry out on an open beach, in primitive conditions, and with inadequate equipment. This, of course, is the eternal complaint of any group condemned to hold an invasion bridgehead. But no one is expected to hold a bridgehead for more than a limited period of time.

The Sicilian venture had been planned as a comparatively short-term venture, with easy conquests and high profits. Now it had got completely out of hand. After eighteen months' continuous overseas service—and nothing tangible to show for it— troops and camp-followers alike were bored, weary, and bloody-minded. The triremes themselves had begun to deteriorate. Excessive sea-going duty, without any proper refitting or drying-out, had rotted their timbers to an alarming extent, while casualties and desertion had thinned the ranks of their crews. The much-vaunted Athenian fleet, in fact, was by no means so formidable a proposition as it had been on first arrival; and the longer it continued without proper servicing or adequate provision for its crews, the less seaworthy—and battleworthy—it was bound to become. With luck and hard training, the Syracusan squadrons should soon prove more than a match for it.

Gylippus also decided it was high time to press for futher reinforcements, both in Sicily itself and at home. Nothing succeeds like success; he could now back his canvassing with some highly concrete achievements—and that after only a month or so in command of Syracuse's defences. He himself left the city on a recruiting drive in the north of the island; it is a fair indication of his increased confidence that felt he could safely do so. Over the winter he raised a large extra contingent from Himera and the Sicels. He does not appear to have got back to Syracuse until February or March of 413.

Before he left, however, he had carefully briefed the joint embassy of Corinthians and Syracusans that was sailing for Greece. His instructions were simple: they must at all costs obtain further reinforcements. Manpower was the problem; ships were not so vital. If triremes were in short supply, Gylippus told his envoys, they could ship troops across in merchantmen, old hulks, rowing skiffs, anything that floated. He had good reason for his urgency. Reports had reached him that Nicias was contemplating an appeal for really massive reinforcements, an expeditionary force as large as that which had first appeared off Syracuse. If this were true, Gylippus reasoned, there was a very good chance that the old man would get what he wanted. The Athenians could not afford to pull out of Sicily now. It was too late; they had sacrificed too much already. Whatever the cost, they would go on. There was nothing else they could do.

The dispatch which Nicias sent to the Athenian Assembly at this point—or, to be more precise, Thucydides' version of it[2]— is a moving and pathetic document. It is also a small master-piece of self-exculpatory evasion and misleading innuendo. We can visualise the old Athenian general sitting in his tent beside the Great Harbour, plagued by marsh-flies, a dull, nagging, con-tinuous ache in the small of his back, painfully composing the report which—he hoped—would both repair his errors and send him home clear of all blame. It had to be a written dispatch.

[2] The general opinion of modern scholars, well summed up by Zuretti (see Bibliography) is that Thucydides' text (7.11–15) accurately rep-resents the substance of Nicias' dispatch (or as much of it as Thucyd-ides sees fit to reproduce) but is not a verbatim copy of the original document.

According to Thucydides (who seems here to be paraphrasing Nicias' own preamble) his reason was that messengers, however reliable, could never be trusted to convey information properly when the news was bad. Awkward facts slipped their memory. They were always anxious to say something that would please the masses. Nicias had therefore, on this occasion, put his report in writing, "thinking that in this way the Athenians would know what his views were without having them distorted in the course of transmission."

Here, already, we glimpse something of Nicias' desperately evasive skill, his gift for putting his own actions in the best possible light. He is the man who tells the unpleasant truth that no messenger dares to utter; it is only on reflection that we realise he is also concerned in case the messenger tells unpleasant or discreditable stories—and with good reason—about *him*. Hence his determination to keep the record, or his version of it, straight by means of a written dispatch. Some things, it was true, such as his private diplomatic dealings with Syracusan agents, could not safely be entrusted to paper, and here he was forced to depend on a verbal report. But his military record was quite another matter. He begins with a brisk summary of the position to date, what in modern war-time jargon would be described as a "sitrep"—initial successes, the arrival of Gylippus, the first two inconclusive battles by the Round Fort. Sooner or later, we know, he is going to have to deal with the evacuation of Epipolae. Here, in the event, is how he manages it: "Now, owing to the superior numbers of the enemy, we are forced to remain inactive and have had to give up the building of the blockading wall." The statement, as far as it goes, is quite true; but as an example of false implication by tacit omission it could hardly be bettered.

The rest of this preamble is all of a piece. Nicias complains that large numbers of his hoplites "must be employed in the defence of our own lines," but omits to mention where those lines are now drawn. He tells how the Syracusan cross-wall has been carried past his own fortifications, but merely to draw the conclusion that a blockade of the city will no longer be possible "unless a strong force could be found to attack and capture this wall of theirs." The besiegers, he says quite truly, have become the besieged. Gylippus is whipping up fresh reinforcements for an all-out attack on their camp, by sea as well as land. This leads Nicias on to a detailed apologia for the lamentable condition of the Athenian fleet. Every vessel at his disposal, he claims, is needed for the enforcement of the blockade by sea. "The slightest falling-off in the efficiency of the watch we keep would mean the loss of our supplies, which even now are difficult enough to bring in past Syracuse." This, he explains, is why the Athenian triremes have suffered so much deterioration. They can never be taken out of service for careening or repairs. In any case, he goes on, "we cannot drag our ships on shore to dry and clean them, because the enemy has as many or more ships than we have, and *keeps us in the constant expectation of having to face an attack* [my italics]."

All this is pure disingenuous moonshine. Nicias did not need over a hundred ships to enforce a blockade on two harbours. In any case the Athenian blockade—always supposing it to have existed at all—was of the most derisory kind. Anything and everything seems to have slipped through it; with the best will in the world it is hard to see how the efficiency of the watch these besiegers kept could have sunk any lower. The Syracusan navy is not all that convincing as a bogey, either. We can scarcely envisage it, on its showing so far, as a threat to anyone's supplies. As my italicised words show, Nicias avoids telling a straight lie about it. There had, of course, been no attack (unless we count that stray trireme). But, he says, there always *might* have been.

Despite such excuses, the condition of the Athenian fleet remains something of a puzzle. It was only after it left Catana, that same spring, that it lacked normal docking and refitting facilities. Deterioration would not set in to the extent Nicias suggests after a mere four or five months. Had he omitted to overhaul his triremes while he was still in a position to do so? In any case, if he could spare twenty ships to intercept the Corinthians, he could equally well have sent off, say, ten a month to be dried out and serviced in Catana. He had, so far as we know, lost only one vessel through enemy action.

Nicias then proceeds to list the obvious disadvantages of Plemmyrium as a base (see above, pp. 224–25), and the bad psychological effect these are having on the troops and sailors stationed there—but omits the crucial point that he alone was responsible for the move. Slaves, mercenaries, and conscripted foreigners are all deserting, he says: they expected rich rewards for little action, and now they are faced with an enemy who is actually going to *fight*. The Athenian trireme crews are mutinous and demoralised. He, Nicias, cannot control them. There are no replacements available. Naxos and Catana, the obvious sources, cannot supply any.

What were the overall losses on the Athenian side at this point? The most plausible estimate, that of Mastrokostas (see Bibliography), puts them at about six hundred hoplites, and up to four to five thousand rowers and petty officers of the fleet, either dead, captured, or listed as deserters. On the other hand, the loss in unskilled manpower had to some extent been made good by press-ganging prisoners from Hyccara on to the rowers' benches. Some loot-happy sailors had even "bought Hyccaric slaves and then persuaded the captains of ships to take these slaves aboard instead of themselves, thus ruining the efficiency of the fleet."

Nicias' final remarks are harsh and urgent, yet in ways as equivocal as the rest. If the Italian cities from which we obtain our supplies get a clear picture of our plight, he observes, *and know you are not sending us reinforcements*, then they may well change sides. If that happens, we shall be starved into surrender without another blow being struck. This is very odd; it looks like another excuse designed to screw some quick action out of the Assembly. That Nicias did obtain some of his supplies from southern Italy we know; but they seem to have been, for the most part, naval stores. What was to stop him getting fresh food locally, rather than crossing the Straits of Messina for it? In point of fact, as we might expect, and as a later reference makes quite clear, the Athenians also got bulk supplies from Catana.

After this extended exercise in duplicity, Nicias congratulates himself on having reported the facts, however unpalatable, rather than giving the Assembly some bromidic placebo to keep them happy. "Besides," he notes, "I know the Athenian character from experience: you like to be told pleasant news, but if things do not turn out in the way you have been led to expect, then you blame your informants afterwards. I therefore thought it safer to let you know the truth." Then comes the open statement of exculpation, at once defiant and pathetic: "*So far as the original objects of the expedition are concerned* [my italics] you can have no right to find fault with the conduct either of your soldiers or your generals." Perhaps not; but by that hedging proviso he takes away all meaning from the claim. What *were* the original objects of the expedition? Who, now, could ever be certain, much less command general assent to his views?

Nicias' own recommendations were brief and clear-cut. The Assembly must either recall the entire expedition, or else "send out another force, both naval and military, as big as the first." But to climb down now (though he did not say so) would mean an immense and almost intolerable loss of face: Nicias knew only too well that Athens would never accept this alternative. On the other hand, if a new expedition was mounted, it should, beyond doubt, be under a new commander: wipe the slate clean and start again, free from whatever errors had been made in the past. Here Nicias showed a sound practical and psychological instinct. He had to go, and he knew it. He was lucky enough (in one sense) to have a legitimate, indeed a compelling, excuse for asking to be relieved of his command. His chronic nephritis, he argued—and no modern specialist would contradict him—rendered him unfit for active service. Lamachus was dead; Alcibiades had deserted to the enemy. The whole burden of the campaign now rested on his shoulders, and they were not strong enough to sustain it.

Incredibly, this desperate *cri de coeur* fell on deaf ears. The unpredictable vagaries of the Athenian democracy provide the student of history or human nature with a very special kind of fascination—much akin to that horrified yet fascinated *frisson* which a really perverse jury verdict is said to produce in a trial judge. When Nicias' grimly evasive rendering of his stewardship had been read out, the citizens of Athens did not vote for the evacuation of Sicily—that, indeed, would have been expecting too much from them—but they did not relieve Nicias of his command, either. Instead, they promoted two of his staff officers, Menander and Euthydemus, to the acting rank of general, so that Nicias "should not have to bear the whole weight of responsibility by himself in his sickness." But this was to be no more than a temporary measure. A fresh expedition would sail in the spring of 413, commanded by perhaps the most formidable general Athens then possessed: Demosthenes, son of Alcisthenes, the victor of Pylos and Sphacteria, the seasoned veteran who had fought his way through north-west Greece and led Spartan hoplites as prisoners through the streets of Athens. If anyone could still retrieve the situation at Syracuse, and prove himself a match for Gylippus, Demosthenes was surely the man.

As his colleague in the command he was given Eurymedon, whom we last met, somewhat under a cloud, after the Congress of Gela (see above, p. 74). This was the cold-blooded butcher who had presided over the liquidation of the Corcyra oligarchs in 427, and subsequently held a command during the first Sicilian campaign. After his recall (424) he had been prosecuted and fined; presumably—unlike his exiled colleagues—he was now restored to favour. He seems to have been a tough, cruel, competent man: far from likable, but perhaps, again, a good choice in the present emergency.

While Demosthenes embarked on preparations for the new spring offensive, Eurymedon was to leave for Sicily at once, with ten ships and 120 talents of silver. By now it was mid-December, and in normal circumstances sailings to Sicily would not be resumed till March at the earliest. But this was an emergency.[3] Eurymedon's role, it is clear, was to boost morale. Besides informing Menander and Euthydemus of their promotion, and providing the expedition with fresh funds, he was deputed "to tell the troops there that help was coming to them and that their interests would be looked after." Those who have ever served in a forward area themselves may well reflect, reading this, that staff officers visiting the front do not appear to have changed their line much down the ages.

But this still does not explain why the Assembly left Nicias where he was, despite his more than reasonable plea for retirement. Generals had been executed before now (and would be again) for making a far less egregious hash of their commission than Nicias had done. Yet this time there was no word of censure—only a renewed vote of confidence. Nicias' self-exculpatory technique had proved all too successful, if not quite in the way he anticipated.[4]

The cruellest blow was that the idea of a new expedition had actually been discussed months before—probably in the spring, about the time the Athenians captured Epipolae and seemed to be carrying all before them. We can imagine the very different tone of the reports which reached the Assembly then. But, Plutarch says revealingly, "Nicias's earlier successes had aroused jealousy and hence caused a number of delays." Androcles and the popular party, to look no further, had not the slightest intention of helping a moderate like Nicias to feather his political nest at their expense.

Petty personal rivalries have always been the abiding curse of

[3] I sometimes wonder whether ancient writers did not vastly exaggerate the perils of a voyage from Greece to Sicily during the winter months. This is by no means the only occasion on which an exception is recorded. The last time I followed Eurymedon's route myself was also, as it happens, in mid-December. The weather was perfect throughout —clear blue cloudless sky, hardly any wind, and the sea like a mill-pond. Clearly one had to watch for a good spell; but the good spells existed, and were not infrequent.

[4] It could, perhaps, be argued that to keep Nicias where he was constituted a death sentence in itself, and—as things turned out—a very unpleasant one; but this was the kind of sophistication which the Assembly had not yet absorbed. Later, it would be different.

Greek politics. In this case their effect, as Thucydides saw very clearly, was catastrophic. He lays the blame for the failure of the expedition squarely on Athens' new-style popular leaders, "who . . . adopted methods of demagogy which resulted in their losing control over the actual conduct of affairs." In particular, the Sicilian venture was caused by "a failure on the part of those at home to give proper support to their forces overseas." But his key statement is this: "Because they were so busy with their own personal intrigues for securing the leadership of the people, they allowed this expedition to lose its impetus, and by quarrelling among themselves began to bring confusion into the policy of the state." We have already had occasion to notice their vicious persecution of Alcibiades during the great Herms scandal—a purely party vendetta which lost Athens one of her most talented (if most erratic) leaders (see above, pp. 116 ff.). Now they were applying the same in-fighting technique to Nicias—again, without one moment's thought for the higher claims of state over faction. Loyalty—as so often in the fifth century—went to party first and polis second.

Thucydides, it is true, places far too exclusive an emphasis on the demagogues' intrigues when analysing the reasons for Athens' failure in Sicily. Perhaps he was anxious to minimise the responsibility of the field commanders. But nothing can obscure the fact that Nicias' conduct of the Sicilian campaign was mediocre at best, falling for long periods to such startling depths of incompetence as to suggest either feeble-mindedness or else a touch of masochistic genius. Nevertheless, if a new expedition, led by Demosthenes, had arrived in the spring, not of 413 but of 414, when Epipolae was still in Athenian hands, and Gylippus had not yet set foot on Sicilian soil, this story might indeed have had a very different ending. The obstruc-tionist methods of the popular party delayed matters for six crucial months; and by then it was too late. Nicias, who knew all this better than most men, must have found a certain brutal irony—even the jealous hand of fate, or the gods—in the turn events had taken.

So the Athenians, seemingly unperturbed by the prospect of a new war with Sparta, set about collecting the ships, men, and supplies for a second Sicilian expedition that would match the first. All through the winter of 414–413, while the Spartans, ominously, "sent round to their allies for supplies of iron[5] and got ready all the other materials for building fortifications," Demosthenes' own preparations continued to go forward. Perhaps it was felt that nothing could stop a Spartan army determined to establish itself in Attica, and that Athens would therefore do better to hold Sicily at all costs. With such a base, and the limitless supplies it offered, Sparta could be dealt with later. In this assumption the Athenian government was arguably correct. Nevertheless, the prospect of still further weakening their home defences when a second front seemed imminent struck many citizens as the height of irresponsible folly. Once again Athens' popular leaders became the target for much intellectual abuse. Thucydides was by no means the only person to express serious doubts about the quality of Athenian leadership at this time.

In March 413 Euripides produced his *Electra*, which contains an intriguing and significant passage on the bankruptcy of the old criteria for judging a man's character and worth. Riches or poverty, valour or cowardice—these no longer provide any guidance, since "all our human heritage runs mongrel" and so "we can only toss our judgments random on the wind." The low-born nonentity, without breeding or family, chosen as leader though he is a mere "face in the crowd," no more possesses true moral authority than does the brainless and muscle-bound athlete—yet both, in this new society, become popular idols:

Can you not come to understand, you empty-minded,
opinion-stuffed people, a man is judged by grace
among his fellows, manners are nobility's touchstone?

[5] This suggests that Athenian raids on Epidaurus Limera may have caused serious damage to Sparta's iron-working centre there.

But the audience Euripides reproved so angrily had no intention of foregoing its right to opinions, however footling— the fundamental democratic privilege—much less of filling its "empty mind" with those high intellectual or moral principles that the playwright would have preferred to see there. "The temper of you Athenians is hard to control," Nicias wrote in his dispatch: a notable understatement.

Quite apart from the threat to Attica, it was by now common knowledge that Corinth and Sparta were, at last, on the point of sending large-scale reinforcements to Sicily. The ambassadors from Syracuse had argued their case most persuasively. The news they brought of Gylippus' latest successes produced a general reassessment of policy among the cities of the Peloponnesian League. Not only Corinth, but Boeotia, Sicyon, and Sparta herself all now promised Syracuse military aid. When this became known at Athens, twenty ships were at once dispatched to reinforce the permanent squadron based on Naupactus, the naval station near the mouth of the Corinthian Gulf. Their orders were "to see that no one crossed over to Sicily from Corinth or from the Peloponnese in general." The number of triremes at Naupactus had probably been cut back a good deal since the Peace of Nicias. This move to strengthen the standing force there is one of the first signs that Athens and the Peloponnesian League were at war again.

By March 413 two main contingents for Sicily had been assembled. The Spartans selected six hundred Helots and freedmen,[6] armed them as hoplites, and placed them under the command of a Spartan officer, Eccritus. From Boeotia came another three hundred hoplites, commanded by two Thebans, Xenon and Nicon, and Hegesander, a Thespian. This group was put aboard a small convoy of merchantmen at Taenarum, in southern Laconia, and sailed directly for Sicily across the

[6] These "freedmen," the Neodamodeis, were newly enfranchised citizens drawn, again, from the ranks of the Helots, and consisting of those who had been emancipated as a reward for distinguished war service. Sparta was never loath to thin out her more aggressive Helots; with her own Spartan warriors she was considerably less generous.

open sea, all, that is, except for Hegesander and his Thespians, who—wisely as it turned out—chose the more orthodox route, by way of southern Italy. Shortly afterwards a second contingent set out from Corinth. The Corinthians themselves sent five hundred hoplites (some from the citizen muster-roll, the rest Arcadian mercenaries; from Sicyon came another two hundred. Thus the total reinforcements now on their way to Gylippus numbered 1,600 men, all of them heavy-armed infantrymen. Nicias might be planning to fight a naval campaign, but his opponent, it is clear, had very different intentions.

To counter the threat of an Athenian blockade at the mouth of the gulf, Corinth had already sent twenty-five triremes ahead to the Naupactus area. It is not certain, from our sources, whether the merchantmen carrying troops for Gylippus sailed from Corinth through the gulf, or whether the troops marched across the northern Peloponnese and embarked at Pheia, in Elis. But in either case the Athenian squadron guarding Naupactus had to be kept occupied until the whole trooping convoy was well away into the Straits of Otranto. This operation the twenty-five Corinthian triremes carried out with considerable success.

Meanwhile what Athens most feared had come to pass. At the beginning of March—earlier in the year than ever before—a Spartan army under King Agis marched from the Isthmus and invaded Attica. For the first time in eleven years Athens' citizens saw that grimly familiar pall of black smoke hanging over the mountains, as crops and trees and homesteads were systematically destroyed by Agis' troops. If there was any opposition to the Spartan advance, we do not hear of it. The myth of invincibility still clung about these iron warriors, and it was not an Athenian army that was destined to shatter it. Worst of all, Agis followed the advice Alcibiades had given him, and made a fortified stronghold of Decelea. This outpost lay high on the western side of the Parnes range, in a hollow controlling the pass which led to Oropus and Euboea. It also dominated the whole of the Attica plain, and was, indeed, visible from Athens itself, some twelve miles away. Agis divided the work of fortification between his various allies, and installed a permanent garrison there.

The effects of this move were incalculably serious for Athens. Hitherto the grain and cattle imported from Euboea had been transported overland by way of Oropus. Now the Athenians were forced to bring it in by sea, round Cape Sunium, where there was always the chance of trouble from bad weather and Peloponnesian patrols. Also, now that the Spartans and their allies had a permanent base in Attica, they were able to do far more extensive and continuous damage to the countryside. No crops could be harvested, no seed sown. Endless raids carried off all the surviving livestock. Attica, agriculturally speaking, very soon became a non-productive wilderness. Through this waste land the enemy moved more or less unopposed, except by ineffectual cavalry patrols: the only casualties these seem to have inflicted were on their own horses, which were always going lame through being ridden far and fast over rough, stony ground.

But none of this deterred the Athenians from their fixed resolve. Early in March, at the very time that Agis was busily fortifying Decelea, and the smoke from Attica's ravaged farms and villages still rose black against a rain-washed spring sky, Demosthenes' expeditionary force was assembled in Piraeus, ready to sail for Sicily.

Spectators down by the quayside of Zea Harbour (Pacha Limani), remembering the pomp and glitter which had accompanied the departure of that first great armada two years before, must have found Demosthenes' penny-plain fleet a very poor substitute. No more than sixty Athenian vessels were allocated to it, and of these a good half were military transports rather than front-line triremes. Their total complement in rowers and petty officers was just under eight thousand men. They also had aboard 1,200 hoplites from the citizen muster-roll. Apart from the ten ships which Eurymedon had already taken across, this represented Athens' total contribution to the relief force. Demosthenes, it is clear, was expected to show considerable initiative in augmenting this modest nucleus on his way to Sicily. One obvious reason, military talent apart, why he had been appointed to the Syracuse command was because of his personal influence in north-west Greece. The only allied contingent which joined him at the outset of his journey was a modest detachment of five ships from Chios.[1]

The oddest thing of all, however, is the singular lack of urgency which seems to have surrounded Demosthenes' departure. In his dispatch to the Assembly Nicias had made it brutally clear that the fate of the whole Sicilian expedition now hung in the balance. Athens had never faced a graver emergency since the Egyptian disaster of 454 (see above, pp. 33–34). A cut-price relief force one can understand; after all, there were other equally pressing problems to be dealt with much nearer home. But once that relief force was mustered, it had a plain and paramount duty: to reach Syracuse by the fastest means at its disposal, and in any case without one moment's unnecessary

[1] Chios and Methymna were the only two remaining subject-allies with the right of supplying triremes in lieu of tribute.

delay. Here, however, we come up against a classic instance of that paralysing and apparently collective imbecility which, from time to time, descended upon the Athenian High Command. About the time scheduled for the fleet's departure to Sicily, another squadron, of thirty ships, and commanded by Charicles,[2] was likewise about to set out on an operational mission. Charicles' instructions were that he should first put in at Argos, and collect further hoplite reinforcements "according to the terms of the alliance." He was then to carry out two operations in southern Laconia.

The first of these was another raid on Epidaurus Limera, at the heart of Sparta's iron-mining district. From here Charicles had instructions to sail round Cape Malea, make a landing on the isthmus opposite Athenian-held Cythera, and fortify it. (In antiquity this little peninsula, known as Onugnathus, or The Ass's Jaw, was still linked to the coast by a narrow neck of land; today, an isthmus no longer, it has become Elaphónisi, or Deer Island.) The idea was to give deserting Helots a rallying point, and also, as Thucydides says, "so that raiding parties, *as at Pylos* [my italics], might have a base from which to operate." Somebody—one would dearly love to know who—gave Demosthenes instructions that he was to collaborate with Charicles on this mission before proceeding to Sicily. There is—as the reader will doubtless have noticed—a curious air of déjà vu about the whole business. Once again an urgent expedition (with the same destination, and even one of the same generals) is held up while Demosthenes messes about building a fort on the Peloponnesian coast. There is even another off-shore island opposite the site.

Seldom can the old best-seller fallacy—repetition the formula for success—have been more strikingly exemplified. Some anonymous noodle had got it into his head that if you put Demosthenes ashore in a deserted part of the Peloponnese and

---

[2] One of the commissioners on the board of enquiry investigating the Herms mystery (see above, pp. 115–16) and subsequently involved in the Revolution of the Four Hundred. He is almost certainly identical with the Charicles who in 404 became one of the Thirty Tyrants.

encouraged him to play bricks, remarkable results were guaranteed to follow. In 425 he had somehow brought off the best coup of the war this way (see above, pp. 63–64); duplicate the circumstances exactly, and—you never could tell—the miracle might repeat itself. The gamble was well worth trying; and while it was being carried out, Nicias could whistle for his reinforcements. There is something very disarming about such superstitious, almost Pavlovian naïvety—especially in the context of the Peloponnesian War, where, God knows, we find little enough to raise even the faintest ghost of a smile. Yet the consequences for Athens were no laughing matter. Delay followed delay. Demosthenes was held up at Aegina waiting for the ships from Chios. More time was wasted at Argos while Charicles collected his hoplites. There was the raid on Epidaurus Limera to be carried out. We can imagine, all too well, the kind of fretting impatience that gripped Demosthenes as the days went by.

Orders, however, were orders. Dutifully he sailed on to Onugnathus, sized up the terrain, planned the fortifications, supervised the initial stages of building—and then left, in a hurry. Charicles stayed on long enough to complete the task and instal a garrison, after which he took his thirty triremes home again. Meanwhile Demosthenes and the main fleet pressed on north to Corcyra, "in order to pick up allied forces from that area and then to cross over to Sicily as quickly as possible." But allied forces were not to be picked up without expending a good deal of time and trouble. Once again Demosthenes had to face facts. If he wanted a large expeditionary force, he had to build it up by his own efforts.

On his way to Corcyra he found a merchantman anchored off Pheia, in western Elis, one of the convoy being used to transport Corinthian troops across to Sicily. He destroyed the ship, but the troops were ashore, and later obtained passage in another vessel. In the Ionian islands, however, he did much better. He obtained close on a thousand hoplites from Zacynthus (Zante) and Cephallenia, and as many again from the Messenians at Naupactus. After this he left the main body of the fleet in Corcyra roads, and himself went over to Acarnania, the scene of his old campaigns, where Athens still held a couple of outposts. Demosthenes' name had not lost its magic among these wild mountaineers, many of them his veterans, who flocked to serve under him again as slingers or javelin-men.

While Demosthenes was still in Acarnania, Eurymedon, unescorted, sailed across from Italy (where he had spent much of the winter doing useful diplomatic spade work with potential allies) and made straight for Corcyra. But the news he brought could not wait; it had to reach Demosthenes at once. Eurymedon stayed only long enough to find out his colleague's whereabouts; then his flagship moved out of harbour again, and raced south towards the Ambracian Gulf. They could count on less margin of time than ever now; and already it was nearly midsummer.

Gylippus got back to Syracuse in February or March, accompanied by the reinforcements he had raised during his winter recruiting drive. He at once began pressing strongly for an immediate spring offensive. Not only that: the Syracusans, he said, were ready to try their luck in a naval engagement. An Assembly was called in order to break this novel and alarming prospect to the bulk of the populace—who would, after all, be manning the triremes that faced the Athenian fleet. Gylippus himself was brisk and laconic, with the air of someone who has a brilliant plan in his head, but no intention whatsoever of divulging it. If the Syracusans fought a sea battle, he told them, "the effect of this on the war in general would be, he expected, something well worth all the risks involved." The task of coaxing these nervous sailors into action he relinquished to Hermocrates, who made an excellent job of it. These Athenians, he said, were not born to the sea, and there was no point in being frightened of them. In fact by nature they were bigger landlubbers than the Syracusans, and had only developed a strong navy when menaced by Persia.

Hermocrates' final point was psychologically acute, and had a great deal of truth in it. Athens, he told the Assembly, very often used terrorism as a weapon, without any real superiority to back it. Why not borrow the same technique, and throw the Athenian fleet off balance by sheer bravado? Nothing more disconcerts the bluffer than to have a bold bluff played back at him. The very idea of the Syracusan navy hitting back would so disconcert these Athenians that they were bound to lose any advantage of skill and experience they might otherwise have enjoyed. When Hermocrates had finished, other speakers took up the theme. There was, so far as we can tell, no opposition to Gylippus' proposal; if there was, it certainly came to nothing. In a burst of emotional patriotism, highly diffident still, yet flattered at being wooed with such complimentary fervour, the Syracusans passed a resolution that they would fight by sea, and at once put their ships into commission. They had a fleet at least eighty strong. One squadron, numbering some thirty-five vessels, was stationed in the docks at the northern end of the Great Harbour; the remainder lay in the Little Harbour, beyond Ortygia.

Gylippus had a plan of campaign prepared which took full advantage of this disposition. Both squadrons were to descend on the Athenian naval base simultaneously, just before dawn, and force an engagement. The Athenians would thus be bottled up in the harbour mouth, under attack from both sides, and unable to manoeuvre. The scheme, as Gylippus presented it, sounded highly effective. Better still, it sounded easy. The Syracusans set about their preparations with enthusiasm. They might have felt neither so flattered nor so enthusiastic had they realised that Gylippus was using them primarily as a decoy, a side-show, to distract Athenian attention from the quarter whence the real attack would come. He was under no illusions about Syracusan standards of seamanship, even after that winter's crash training programme, and may well have assumed that their fleet—to begin with, at least—would lose every battle it fought. But that, at the moment, was not the point. All Gylippus wanted was a noisy diversion in the Great Harbour, as close to Plemmyrium as possible. The plan he had concocted would produce just this effect.

Gylippus' actions on his return to Syracuse were dictated by several urgent considerations. He knew—as everyone else must have done by now—that Demosthenes and Eurymedon were on their way with a fresh fleet, and would probably pick up massive reinforcements en route from north-west Greece and the pro-Athenian cities of southern Italy. He was also well aware of Demosthenes' formidable reputation as a general. His immediate strategy therefore virtually forced itself upon him. He must make every effort to smash Nicias before the relief expedition could reach Syracuse. If he was to achieve this object, he must first challenge, and then destroy, the still powerful Athenian fleet.

But there existed another equally compelling reason for Gylippus to finish off this campaign without any unnecessary delay. Syracuse was running dangerously short of money. There were no silver mines on the island, and it seems likely that Syracuse imported her silver from Carthage. Some optimistic scholars have argued that the supply of imported silver dried up as the result of Nicias' naval blockade; if so, it was the only commodity that did. We have already seen just how efficient a blockade Nicias maintained during these crucial months. The truth is far more simple. Ancient finances worked, by our standards, on an unbelievably short-term basis. In the fifth century, credit was almost unknown (a hundred years later it was quite another matter); we have seen how Nicias, and other generals, needed regular supplies of currency or bullion to keep going. Syracuse under siege had gone virtually bankrupt. Its normal trading operations were almost totally interrupted. Production had fallen off to nothing. The city was, therefore, living on its capital reserves.

Now, from these reserves it had not only to maintain ordinary day-to-day services, but also to feed, clothe, house, and pay the growing army of Gylippus, its potential deliverer. Corinth was happy enough to furnish reinforcements, and even Sparta was now willing to offer Syracuse more than one senior officer to command other cities' troops. But neither they nor anyone else had the slightest intention of underwriting the running

expenses of the troops they supplied. That responsibility de-
volved on the Syracusans themselves. Since the number of non-
Syracusan soldiers now fighting on Syracuse's side had reached
a total of roughly seven thousand, the drain on her resources
was enormous. By the spring of 413 the Syracusan government
had run through all its stocks of silver, and was forced to meet
the emergency by borrowing from the temple gold reserves. A
sudden plentiful issue of small gold coins, minted from dies
very like those used for the city's earliest silver currency, now
makes its brief appearance. But such a stop-gap measure was
only to be taken as a last resort, to bridge the most serious
crisis. By flooding the market with gold, the authorities forced
down the exchange rate of gold against silver to 1:13. Only
the fact that Syracuse was in desperate straits for means of
immediate payment could possibly justify this.[3]

From Gylippus' point of view, this was a doubly dangerous
situation. The moment Syracuse ceased to provide financial
backing, her army of quasi-mercenary allies would very soon
melt away. Worse still, the Syracusans themselves might well
come to the conclusion that running deep into debt in order
to fight an endless war of attrition against Athens—of all cities
—was pure lunacy. Another Athenian armada was on its way
to reinforce the first. The siege would drag on and on, its cost
would spiral astronomically. Was it all worth it? At this rate
(a point which Athenagoras and his friends were not likely to
miss when spreading their propaganda), Syracuse would scarcely
be able to afford victory even if she won it—and that was by
no means a foregone conclusion, either. The surrender on
terms they had been about to negotiate when Gylippus appeared would have cost far less, and offered prospects of solid
profit for the future. The slightest reverse now, Gylippus well

[3] One local coin hoard (Noe, 2d ed., no. 110) of this period also contains 100 Persian gold darics. It is tempting to speculate how they may
have got there. If Syracuse appealed to the Great King in 413 for financial support against Athens, she had a very good chance of getting
it: Persia was on the verge of committing herself to the support of
Sparta.

knew, would produce a violent anti-war movement in Syracuse, of which he himself—army or no army—might well be the first victim.

His immediate strategy, therefore, had two main ends in view. If possible, he wanted to deal with Nicias before Demosthenes arrived: this was the ideal solution. But Gylippus was a professional soldier, and knew how long the odds were against his knocking out the Athenian fleet in so short a time, especially with the resources at his disposal. On the other hand, what seemed essential was a victory quick and impressive enough to boost Syracusan morale—and, for preference, one which would also produce some valuable loot as a fringe benefit. There was only one obvious answer, so obvious, indeed, that Gylippus must surely have wondered whether he was not walking into some ultra-subtle Athenian trap. The three isolated forts on Plemmyrium now contained not only Nicias' naval stores and pay reserves, but also much valuable property deposited there for safe-keeping by merchants accompanying the fleet. With Plemmyrium in his hands, he could stave off the financial crisis, sever Nicias' supply-lines, impose a naval blockade on the Great Harbour, and force the Athenian fleet back on its old base, where the crews would have little room to exercise their superior tactical skill.

It sounded too good to be true; but it was true. All it called for was the possible sacrifice of the Syracusan fleet, and this risk Gylippus took without one moment's hesitation. He did not care for the Syracusans, nor they for him. They mocked him behind his back; he used them as cat's-paws. He probably had more in common with Eurymedon than with Hermocrates. He brought to the defence of Syracuse a cold brain, great technical ability, and almost total emotional indifference to the issues at stake. Gylippus was a professional doing his job. The only emotional kick he seems to have got lay in doing it successfully. As he walked the walls of Syracuse, watching the enemy's dispositions, a small, hard, nut of a man in his rough Spartan cloak, his father's shadow went before him, the moral failure for which he must still atone. The Ephors had given him this task as Eurystheus had laid the Labours on Heracles: another challenge to be faced and surmounted, another victory to be won. But the fate of Syracuse, as such, meant nothing to him.

Shortly before dawn the two Syracusan squadrons slipped their moorings and moved out to the attack. But in that dead calm which precedes a Mediterranean dawn they must have used their oars; and for once Nicias' naval look-outs were on the qui vive. The alarm was given, and sixty triremes were hastily manned. Twenty-five of them moved out to intercept the squadron now bearing down on them from the northern shore of the Great Harbour. The rest took up a defensive position against the second squadron now rounding Ortygia. Gylippus, meanwhile, had mustered his hoplites in darkness, and led them down from Epipolae by a roundabout route, to avoid rousing the Athenian camp by the Great Harbour. As dawn broke they were well beyond the Anapus, somewhere in the flat but broken countryside between the Helorus road and the sea. From the harbour mouth by Plemmyrium came a faint shout of warning, the buzz of a camp suddenly awoken, sharp barked orders, and then, blurred and distant as in dreams, the tumultuous shock and confusion of a hard-fought naval battle.

The sun was still hidden beneath the horizon, the sea lay grey and shadowed. Taking advantage of this half-light, hugging all available cover, Gylippus and his hoplites worked their way across country towards Plemmyrium. It soon became apparent that the decoy had worked to perfection. The sea beyond the headland was jam-packed with a noisy, splintering tangle of Athenian and Syracusan triremes. From what could be seen it looked, surprisingly, as though the Syracusans were getting the better of it. From their concealed position Gylippus and his men saw clusters of agitated figures hurrying down to the shore from the three forts, anxious to watch the progress of the battle, never dreaming that its true epicentre was about to form elsewhere, in the positions they had just abandoned. This was what Gylippus had been waiting for. Now he brought his troops up that last long boulder-littered slope at the double. They made straight for the largest fort, which probably stood on the high shoulder of the promontory, overlooking the harbour. By now there were few garrison troops still at their posts to defend the position, and these few were soon overcome. Any who escaped Gylippus' hoplites fled to the beach, where a number of small craft were drawn up, put straight out to sea, and made for their old camp by the Lysimeleia marsh. The occupants of the nearest guard post, seeing the main fort so easily overcome, took off without even attempting to fight.

Even above the shock and crash of the naval engagement, those down on the shore soon heard the uproar behind them which followed Gylippus' assault on the main fort. Even if they had heard nothing, the sudden appearance of numerous fugitive soldiers down by the harbour was quite enough to tell them what had happened. They turned round in amazement and horror and began hurrying towards the last surviving guard post. But before they could get there this position, too, had fallen. The whole crowd fled incontinently for the boats. When they reached the waterfront again, they found that the battle had turned in their favour. At the beginning of the engagement the Syracusan squadron coming round Ortygia had driven its opponents back past Plemmyrium into the Great Harbour. But then, in the excitement of the pursuit, its ships broke formation, and began to foul one another as they crowded through the channel.

Now, at last, professional expertise began to tell against amateur enthusiasm. The Athenians rallied, and this time it was the Syracusans' turn to retreat. The retreat swiftly degenerated into a rout. When this squadron was well on its way back to the Little Harbour, and no longer a danger, the battered Athenian line put about, and hastened to bring support to the detachment already engaged inside the Great Harbour itself. Here, too, the Syracusans had been having the best of it to begin with. (They even found time to send a fast trireme in pursuit of the small boats carrying fugitives from Plemmyrium.) But when the second Athenian squadron bore down on them, they were hopelessly outfought and outnumbered. Eleven of their ships were sunk, and the crews of eight slaughtered: Nicias' men were in no mood to be merciful. The remaining three crews, however, they took prisoner. Presumably some officer reminded them that the expedition was short of ready cash, and that slaves paid off better than corpses.

This was the end of the battle, both at sea and on land. The Athenians had won the naval engagement—their own losses amounted to no more than three ships—but they made no attempt to oust Gylippus' hoplites from Plemmyrium. They towed off the wrecks of the ships they had rammed, set up a trophy on the tiny island facing the promontory, and then withdrew to their old camp-site by the shore. There was nowhere else they could go. It was low-lying land, unpleasantly close to the marshes, with a shallow beach and a "muddy bottom on which the east wind rolls up a considerable surf."[4] But it was better than nothing.

Gylippus made no attempt to pursue them, and did not trouble his head unduly over the losses the Syracusan navy had incurred. He had got what he wanted, and with minimal losses among his own men. One of the three forts he dismantled, using its stones to repair and strengthen the remaining two. These he then garrisoned with some of his best troops. He had no intention of being caught napping like the Athenians. He then proceeded to break open all the strong-rooms and take stock of the spoils he had won. The list exceeded even his expectations. There were large reserves of grain and other commodities belonging to the Athenian merchants. There were almost all Nicias' naval stores, including spare masts, oars, sails, and rigging for no less than forty triremes. Best of all, there were very considerable cash reserves: not only the military chest, but

[4] So W. S. Ferguson, *Cambridge Ancient History*, Vol. V, p. 301. I can confirm this from personal observation. The Great Harbour is so large—over two miles from north to south, a mile and a quarter from the Anapus to the harbour bar—that it can become extremely rough in bad weather.

also the deposited capital of various merchants and the banked savings of many officers and men. It was a fabulous haul, and Gylippus had every right to feel pleased with himself.

But he was never a man to rest on his laurels. The Syracusan navy underwent immediate reorganisation, and found itself given much brisk encouragement. Their defeat, the sailors were told, "had been due to their own disorder rather than to the enemy's superior strength." All they needed was practice—and more discipline. Meanwhile they were to profit by the Athenians' mistakes. In particular, a tight blockade must be maintained over the entrance to the Great Harbour. Nicias already found it virtually impossible to bring in supplies by road: the Syracusans, mainly through their cavalry patrols, dominated every approach. Now his sea convoys, hitherto free to come and go undisturbed, would also be in peril.

With a strong Syracusan squadron waiting to intercept any enemy vessel that attempted to get past Plemmyrium, Nicias' position had become appallingly vulnerable. As Thucydides says, "it was now necessary to fight if supplies were to be brought in at all"—and from a base nearly two miles away, at that. Apart from its more practical effects, the capture of Plemmyrium had a profound psychological effect on the Athenians. They felt stunned and bewildered, and their military morale sank even lower. Envoys were now sent out from Syracuse to the various cities of Sicily, particularly in the west and south, announcing the victory on Plemmyrium, and asking for naval and military reinforcements. A new Athenian expedition was on its way; if only Syracuse could "destroy the army on the spot before the new one arrived, the war would be over." At Gela, Camarina, and Selinus the envoys obtained a favourable response. Only Acragas remained obstinately neutral. Her government announced that they would not even allow troops from Selinus to march through Acragantine territory—a decision which, as things turned out, lost Syracuse a number of valuable reinforcements.

Gylippus was also determined to attack Nicias' supply-lines at source. Twelve ships under a Syracusan commander, Agatharchus, now sailed for southern Italy. Reports had come in that a convoy of merchantmen carrying stores for the Athenians—presumably to replace those they had lost on Plemmyrium—was now setting out. Agatharchus intercepted this convoy, and destroyed the larger part of it. He then sailed on to Caulonia, where, it was said, large quantities of shipbuilding lumber were lying, ready to be shipped across for the Athenian fleet. The stacked lumber was indeed there, and Agatharchus burnt it. From Caulonia one trireme peeled off towards the Peloponnese, "with representatives aboard who were to say that in Syracuse hopes were running high and to urge the Peloponnesians to an even more vigorous war effort in Hellas." The remainder now turned back, their mission accomplished. At Locri, their first port of call, they found the merchantmen carrying Hegesander and his contingent of Thespian hoplites. They transferred these welcome reinforcements to their own vessels, and made for home.

The Syracusans had an untroubled voyage as far as Megara Hyblaea. Here they found an Athenian squadron of twenty ships lying in wait for them. (This must have been the same force which Nicias had earlier dispatched to intercept the Corinthians [see above, p. 225]. Presumably it was now on its way home.) The Athenians succeeded in capturing one enemy trireme; the remaining ten got away unscathed and reached harbour without further incident—Hegesander and his hundred-odd Thespian hoplites among them. Another piece of the final pattern had dropped into place.

In Athens, as at Syracuse, the financial situation was by now extremely serious. Apart from the heavy burden of the Sicilian campaign, there was a serious falling-off in the amount of tribute reaching Athens from her subject-allies. As reverse followed reverse, unrest grew steadily throughout the empire. In the summer of 413 it was decided to abolish the existing tribute system altogether, and to replace it with a 5 per cent duty on all goods imported or exported by each dependent state. As the allies had previously levied their own harbour dues, Athens was merely expropriating the profits for her own benefit—at more than double the rate exacted hitherto.

Just after Demosthenes and the relief force sailed, a contingent of 1,300 light-armed Thracian mercenaries reached Athens. They had been intended for service in Sicily; since they were too late to accompany Demosthenes (and in view of the present financial crisis) the Athenians decided to send them home again. At their agreed wage of a drachma a day, it was felt, they would be a prohibitively expensive luxury, even for dealing with Spartan raiders. An officer named Dieitrephes was detailed to escort them back home—doing what damage he could with them en route. The result was one of the most horrible atrocities committed by either side during the entire Peloponnesian War. Dieitrephes decided to raid the little town of Mycalessus, in Boeotia. His Thracians poured in through the open gates at dawn, taking the population completely by surprise. They were wild, uncouth savages, and now they went berserk. They broke into a large boys' school and killed all the children. They rampaged through the town like animals, brandishing their terrible short swords, butchering every living creature they met, even down to farm animals, till at last they were driven off by a force of hoplites and cavalry from Thebes.

Even the normally impassive Thucydides betrays signs of shocked emotional outrage when telling this story—though his main object, it would appear, was to illustrate the dangers of employing mercenaries. What he does not point out (it scarcely needs emphasis) is the parallel, and differences, between this outrage and, say, the massacre carried out on Melos. For the Thracians, it might be argued, there was at least the excuse of savagery and ignorance. They were brutes, and behaved like brutes. But when the Athenian Assembly passed its decree of genocide against Melos, it did so in the name of a city-state which set out to be—and in many ways was—an intellectual and moral pattern for all Greece. The corrupting influence of prolonged war can seldom have been better exemplified. Thucydides never tells an anecdote for its own sake, always to point some moral or generality; and the Mycalessus episode leaves some extremely disquieting reflections behind it.

CHAPTER XV: A *Naval Reverse*

For months on end the Athenian fleet had been stationed only a few hundred yards from a Syracusan squadron in the Great Harbour, during which time each side studiously ignored the other's existence. Now they both suddenly woke up from this long lethargy, and henceforward skirmishing was intense and continuous. The Great Harbour fairly buzzed with action —and action of just the kind we might expect when two enemy naval stations were in such close proximity. The Athenians opened this exchange by rowing across from their camp to the docks and attempting to ram some of the Syracusan vessels lying at anchor there. The Syracusans, as a counter-measure, sank a row of piles in the sea-bed, outside the docks. Nothing daunted, the Athenians came back at night in dinghies, and either broke the piles off short or else sent down divers to saw through them. The next day they brought up their biggest merchantman, a 250-tonner with a derrick on its mast, tied the block-cable to each pile in turn, and then winched it up out of the silt with a windlass. Throughout this operation the Athenians were under constant fire from the docks, and kept up a fairly brisk counter-fusillade themselves. In the end they managed to uproot most of the piles. Particularly dangerous were those that remained hidden beneath the water, with tough, sharpened points. A ship which fouled one could gash its hull badly. Expert divers were offered high rewards to go down and sever them near the bottom—a remarkable feat. But all their efforts seemed useless: no sooner was one palisade removed than the Syracusans succeeded in sinking another.

The most puzzling aspect of the whole affair is why such strategems had never been attempted hitherto. Syracusan timidity one can understand, if not the apparent indifference to harbour defences which this sudden building of a palisade would seemingly indicate. But what had there been to stop Nicias raiding the dockyards months before? Why was no attempt made to destroy the Syracusan navy before it could go into action, at a time when Athens enjoyed complete naval superiority? Again, the only possible explanation seems to be that Nicias believed the city would soon surrender on terms, and make an alliance with Athens under its new government; in that case, what point was there in risking his own men's lives to destroy useful naval equipment? Even now, it seems, he still had strong hopes of cashing in on a political coup. Messages reaching him from the ultra-democrats drew a very optimistic picture of the situation. There was little money in the Treasury—even after the capture of Plemmyrium, which had merely staved off total disaster. The people were sick and tired of this endless war. A little longer, and they would throw out Gylippus. Nicias had only to wait.

This was a plausible argument, and one well calculated to appeal to a man of Nicias' temperament. If Gylippus' quasi-mercenary army only remained a danger so long as its money lasted, there was, clearly, a great temptation to sit still, do nothing, and wait for the opposition to melt away. On the other hand, Gylippus was not a man much given to sitting still himself. He knew the score as well as Nicias did. If it was to the Athenian's advantage to play a waiting game, the Spartan had every reason to act, and act fast—whatever the public mood in Syracuse. It looked, too, as though he might very well get the chance. The ambassadors who had gone round the cities of the southern coast asking for reinforcements were doing better than they ever anticipated: the capture of Plemmyrium made highly persuasive propaganda. Camarina, after sitting on the fence for so long, at last decided to back Syracuse with her full strength. Five hundred hoplites, three hundred spearmen, and three hundred archers were, in due course, mustered and dispatched. Gela of the wheatfields agreed to send four hundred spearmen, two hundred cavalry, and the crews for five ships.

But the most positive response—and therefore the greatest danger to Nicias—came from Selinus and Himera. Between them—aided by some native Sicel levies—these two cities raised a force of at least 2,300 men: the figure may have been as high as three thousand.[1] It was plain to Nicias that he must use all his ingenuity to stop this vast contingent reaching Syracuse. It was equally plain that, cooped up as he was on the foreshore of the Great Harbour, there was very little he could do about it himself. Here, however, luck for once was on his side. Acragas, we recall, had stayed neutral; more than that, she had refused to let the volunteers from Selinus pass through her territory. This being so, there was only one route they could follow. They would have to march north-east (perhaps following the river Hypsas [Belice] and join up with the contingent from Himera. Together they would then take the familiar central route, through Enna and Agyrium and Centuripae. It was a chance in a thousand; and Nicias, for all his sickness and lethargy, at once realised the fact. Athens had a number of allies among the Sicel communities of central Sicily, and several of these—notably Halyciae and Centuripae—were well situated to control the road along which Gylippus' new reinforcements must pass. Nicias at once sent off a series of fast messengers, "asking them [the Sicels] not to let the reinforcements through, but to join up together and bar their way."

The messengers seem to have reached Halyciae too late; the men of Selinus must already have passed through en route for Himera. Otherwise the Sicels would surely have intercepted them before they joined forces with their allies, on the principle of *divide et impera*. In the event, however, this made very little difference. Somewhere in the mountains of central Sicily three Sicel guerrilla brigades laid an elaborate and highly successful ambush for the advancing column. Caught completely off their guard, the Greek troops at first could not even close ranks and defend themselves. The terrible lithe mountaineers with their knives and slings seemed to have materialised out of the rocks, like those fabulous armed men who grew from the dragon's

[1] Diodorus (13.8.4) says three thousand; Thucydides (7.32.2) mentions 1,500 survivors after eight hundred had been killed. The discrepancy may be due to his ignoring prisoners and the badly wounded.

teeth scattered in the furrow. It was only after eight hundred men had been killed that the Corinthian ambassador—the one surviving member of the whole diplomatic delegation—managed to rally the remainder. Somehow they fought their way out of the trap, and 1,500 of them, despite persistent guerrilla attacks, finally reached Syracuse.

Nicias could indeed be grateful to his loyal native allies. They had not, it is true, prevented the entire force from getting through; but then it is very doubtful whether anyone expected them to. On the other hand they *had* halved its numbers, in what was perhaps the most faultlessly executed action of the whole campaign; and, more important, they had won Nicias a few precious days' respite. Gylippus was planning an immediate attack when his reinforcements arrived. But the shattered and weary column which finally tramped through the city gates was in no condition, for the time being at least, to fight anyone. Gylippus had no option but to postpone his offensive.

Eurymedon found Demosthenes still in Acarnania, busy collecting light-armed troops and reminiscing with old comrades-in-arms. Bluntly and briefly he told him the news that had reached Italy before he crossed the straits. Gylippus had captured Plemmyrium. Nicias had lost nearly all his stores and was now himself besieged in the walled camp beside the Great Harbour. They must return to Corcyra with what volunteers they had, assemble the fleet, and sail for Syracuse at once. While they were still discussing their immediate plans, yet another senior officer appeared in Demosthenes' temporary headquarters —Conon, the commander of the naval base at Naupactus.[2] Conon reported that the Corinthian squadron at the mouth of the gulf was threatening to force an engagement. As he had only eighteen triremes to their twenty-five, he urgently needed rein-

[2] This is the first mention in history of the man who was to become Athens' greatest admiral during the period immediately after the Peloponnesian War. In 393 Conon was responsible for the rebuilding of the Long Walls, destroyed at the time of the Spartan occupation (see below, p. 355).

forcements. Demosthenes, ill though he could spare them, turned over ten of his best and fastest vessels without a moment's argument. There was good reason for what he did. Better to have a reduced fleet than run the risk of losing Naupactus. Once the cork was blown out of *that* bottle, and enemy traffic began moving freely through the mouth of the Gulf, there was no limit to the reinforcements and supplies which could be convoyed through to Syracuse by the shortest, safest route.

But Conon's request also showed how times had changed. At the beginning of the war Phormio, the great Athenian admiral, thought nothing of taking on nearly fifty enemy ships when outnumbered by over two to one. He assumed he would beat them, and he did. Sixteen years later, however, Conon was unwilling to fight without a squadron as least as strong as his opponent's, and had no qualms about weakening an operational fleet in order to get what he wanted. It is not hard to understand his position. Every year, as this long war dragged on, the Peloponnesian fleet gained further experience—which meant that an increasingly competent pool of instructors became available to train new recruits. Furthermore, those Athenian flotillas earmarked for home defence and the Sicilian campaign doubtless skimmed off the pick of what was going—the newest triremes, the best-trained crews. Conon, and others in his subordinate position, would have to put up with what was left.

Yet when all possible allowances have been made, there can be no doubt that the fighting morale of the average hoplite or sailor had fallen catastrophically since the beginning of the Peloponnesian War. Standards of training and discipline had become increasingly lax. We hear more and more of deserters and draft-dodgers and smooth young men who wangled themselves safe, well-paid diplomatic jobs instead of serving with the fleet or the infantry. Officers no less than men thought a good deal more about pay, and proportionately less of honour. The use of mercenaries was on the increase, though it had not yet reached the peak it was to attain during the fourth and third centuries.

Such were the men—eager for gain, not overfond of fighting, their pride worn down by cynicism, exhaustion, and indifference

—who now lay before Syracuse, or manned Conon's triremes off Naupactus, or watched King Agis' Spartan patrols march unhindered through the length and breadth of Attica. We shall misjudge them badly if we measure their achievements against those of an earlier, less demoralised generation.

Nicias and his force could no longer move in any direction. The Syracusan fleet controlled Plemmyrium, and Gylippus' troops were firmly established on Epipolae. The Helorus road was patrolled by Syracusan cavalry, based on Polichna, the village close to the Olympieum. Both by land and by sea communication with the outside world had been virtually severed. Yet from inside Syracuse itself secret words of encouragement still reached Nicias, urging him to hold on at all costs. Appearances to the contrary, these messages said, the Syracusans' position was worse than his. What with maintaining a large fleet and an army of mercenaries, they had already spent two thousands talents, besides running up debts that they could never repay. Wait, said the messages. Wait. It is only a matter of time.

But some of Nicias' colleagues were less patient. The newly promoted acting generals, Menander and Euthydemus, kept pressing him strongly to go out and fight. They were, naturally, ambitious; in particular, they wanted to cover themselves with glory—at Nicias' expense, for choice—before the arrival of Demosthenes. If they had done nothing by then, they were liable to be relegated to their old ranks. Against Nicias' stubborn insistence that their clear duty was to hold on, and not risk defeat before the relief expedition reached them, they "made great play with the prestige of Athens, which they maintained would be irretrievably damaged if they refused battle with the Syracusan fleet."

Hemmed in by their own walls, and the pile stockade protecting their ships, the Athenians sat idle, day after day, while the midsummer sun beat down on them, and their supplies dwindled, and the rivers shrank to a barely adequate rivulet in a wide expanse of gravel. Tempers flared; the men grew listless and apathetic, staring out to sea till their eyes dazzled, watching for the fleet that never came. At night the air was shrill with mosquitoes, and the least breath of wind brought, not freshness, but the foul and stagnant stench of the marshes. As time went by, cases of dysentery and malaria became increasingly frequent.

At Naupactus, Conon's year as commander had run out in mid-July, and he was succeeded by a newly elected member of the Board of Generals named Diphilus, who arrived with six more ships. Soon after taking over the command, Diphilus was drawn into an indecisive battle with the Corinthian squadron. Both sides, interestingly, claimed the victory. The Athenians had sunk three Corinthian vessels outright, whereas none of their own had gone down. The Corinthians, on the other hand, had *disabled* a larger number of enemy vessels. What is really interesting about this engagement (both in itself and for the effect it subsequently had on the Syracuse campaign) is the new device the Corinthians adopted, and on which their claim to victory was based. The normal method of sinking an enemy trireme—certainly that practised by the Athenians—was by ramming amidships, and all tactical manoeuvres were worked out with this end in view. Head-on ramming was regarded as the mark of an incompetent steersman.

The Corinthians had a new and revolutionary technique in mind. The regular ram of a trireme was high and sheer: strong, but not highly reinforced, and with a sharp cutting edge, as befitted its function. It was, in effect, a knife or wedge, slicing through lengths of timber broadside-on at their weakest point. What the Corinthians did was to convert the wedge into a species of battering-ram. They shortened and strengthened the prow with extra timbers, giving it a blunt, squared-off appearance. They also redesigned it so that its centre of impact was a good deal lower. But the most important change they made had to do with the catheads. In all triremes a stout beam was built laterally through the bows, so that one end projected aft of the beak on either side. These projections—sometimes also known as the trireme's "ears"—were the catheads. Their main function was as anchor-blocks, but they also gave some support to the outrigger-like superstructure, projecting beyond the hull, on which the top bank of oars vested. The Corinthians completely transformed their function. Having foreshortened the bows, they now proceeded to reinforce the catheads. Stronger, thicker timber was used, and was further strengthened to resist impact by pairs of stay-beams, each about nine to ten feet long. These ran back from the catheads into the framework of the hull itself, and were, presumably, braced against the ribs.

The peculiar advantages of this rearrangement entirely depended on prow-to-prow ramming; in other words, they made a virtue of inexperience, a point which was to prove of inestimable benefit to the Syracusans when they borrowed the same technique. At Naupactus the Corinthians found it comparatively easy to smash in the Athenian triremes' high prows; and if they missed a head-on collision, they could still inflict appalling damage with their reinforced catheads, which went ripping through the projecting superstructure as the two ships slid past each other, breaking off oars and hurling rowers into the sea. The experiment, in fact, was so successful that technicians and shipwrights were hurried over to Sicily to carry out a similar conversion job on the Syracusan navy. They worked at desperate speed, afraid lest an Athenian attack should come while their task still remained half-done. They need not have worried. Though Menander and Euthydemus pressed for a decisive naval engagement, Nicias remained obdurate. When he at last found himself forced into action, it was, as so often, too late.

If Demosthenes realised how desperate the situation at Syracuse was he gave no particular signs of it. Like Gylippus on his first arrival in Sicily, Demosthenes clearly considered that the collection of as strong a relief force as possible must have top priority. How soon he reached his destination seems to have been a matter of secondary importance. He sent Eurymedon on ahead to Corcyra, with orders to raise fifteen triremes as a replacement for the ten Conon had taken, and to round up some extra battalions of hoplites. He himself stayed on a little longer

in Acarnania, till he had gathered together all his local volunteers. It was mid-July by the time he finally sailed into Corcyra
roads, and several more days elapsed before the expedition was,
at long last, assembled for the voyage across the Straits of
Otranto to Italy. Yet even now Demosthenes—oddly, after his
initial impatience while helping Charicles—made no visible effort to speed up an uncommonly leisurely itinerary. There was
a great deal he wanted to organise in Magna Graecia. The possibility that Nicias might not last out until the relief force
reached Syracuse seems scarcely to have crossed his mind.

The fleet negotiated the straits without difficulty, and made
their first landfall at the Iapygian promontory (Capo S. Maria
di Leuca). They picked up 150 Messapian spearmen from the
off-shore islands known as the Choerades, and then put in to
harbour (probably at Callipolis) so that Demosthenes and his
senior officers could pay a courtesy call on the local chieftain.
This was one Artas, or Artos, who ruled over Messapia—that is,
most of the heel of Italy lying south of a line between Brindisi
and Taranto. We do not know exactly when the Athenians first
made contact with Artas of Messapia; but by 413 they had a
"long-standing alliance of friendship" with him. The main object of this alliance was, as we might expect, commercial. Artas
supplied the Athenians with wheat, and later with mercenaries.
For this service he was rewarded by being created an honorary
proxenos. One fifth-century comic poet, making a pun on the
king's name—*artos* in ancient Greek meant bread, or a loaf—
wrote the following passage of dialogue, perhaps with this occasion in mind:

A. From there, with a south wind, we travelled across the
sea to Italy, and the country of the Messapians, where Artos
welcomed us as his guests, and gave us bountiful entertainment.
B. A pleasant host.
A. Big and white in that area.

The whiteness of Italian bread was proverbial: both Sophocles
and, much later, the Roman encyclopedist Pliny refer to it. Artas

must have been a striking character. He made a strong impression on his contemporaries, and at least one pamphlet was written about him more than two centuries after his death.

Demosthenes and Eurymedon duly enjoyed the hospitality for which Artas was famous. They also obtained ample supplies of grain, and a large contingent of light-armed troops. Thus fortified, they cruised on along the coast, by-passing hostile Tarentum, until they reached Metapontum, where they "persuaded the people, in accordance with their alliance, to send them 300 javelin-throwers and two triremes." At Thurii they were also in luck. Yet another internal revolution had just taken place, and the party hostile to Athens had been exiled. This was a situation the Athenian commanders felt should be exploited to the full. They therefore made quite a long stop at Thurii. It seemed a suitable place to hold a final review of their forces, and, as Thucydides delightfully puts it, "see whether anything had been left behind." They also wanted time to work on the new Thurian government. Aid for the expedition was, they reckoned, a foregone conclusion. Indeed, a defensive and offensive alliance did not seem beyond the bounds of possibility. But such discreet diplomatic pressurising was not liable to achieve results in a hurry.

Whether Demosthenes and Eurymedon obtained their alliance we do not know; but the Thurians were well enough disposed towards them to furnish the expedition with three hundred spearmen and no less than seven hundred hoplites. The two generals now decided to hold a review of their troops by the banks of the Sybaris River. After this the army would march south towards the Thurian border, while the fleet cruised along off-shore towards the next large city, Croton. Demosthenes had high hopes that they would be welcomed at the frontier, and repeat the diplomatic success they had scored in Thurii. It was, indeed, a far more impressive array than that which had set out from Piraeus. Yet in one important respect Demosthenes had not noticeably improved his position. The original Athenian contingent of sixty ships had only been increased to a net seventy-three. On the other hand, his original 1,200 Athenian hoplites had become part of a heavy-armed brigade totalling nearly five thousand, and reinforced by three thousand light-armed troops. Demosthenes, unlike Nicias, clearly had every intention of fighting a land-based campaign. The total combatant force, including the trireme crews, numbered about seventeen thousand men.

Perhaps it was the sheer size of this force which alarmed the Crotonians; or perhaps they preferred to maintain strict neutrality until the issue was no longer in doubt. At all events, when Demosthenes reached the frontier river he was met by messengers from Croton, who formally forbade him and his men to march through their territory. Demosthenes did not argue the point. He led his troops downstream to the coast, where the fleet duly picked them up. Then they sailed on south, calling in at Scylletium and Caulonia, but avoiding Locri, till they rounded the toe of Italy and made their last landfall before crossing the Straits of Messina. This was at Petra, described by Thucydides as lying "in the territory of Rhegium": probably Capo delle Armi, a promontory on the south-west tip of the peninsula. The fleet does not seem to have gone anywhere near Rhegium itself, which was, of course, now neutral; but Demosthenes may also have had security considerations in mind.

Now, at last, towards the end of July, the broken coastline of Sicily lay before them. Their journey was almost over.

About the same time the Syracusans completed the adaptation of their fleet to the new Corinthian style, and were impatient to see how effective it would prove against Nicias' more conventional triremes. Faced with a direct frontal attack, they argued, the Athenians would first back off, and then employ one of the manoeuvres they knew best. They would either attempt to break through the enemy's line-abreast formation, wheel about, and take them squarely in either flank, or else try a circling pincer movement that would enable them to ram from the three-quarter position. Now, both these movements—known by the Greeks as the *diekplous* and the *periplous*—required a great deal of free space if they were to be executed with any efficiency.

If the Syracusans attacked in close line, bringing up enough ships to contain the Athenian wings, they should deprive their opponents of their one great tactical advantage—skill in conventional manoeuvre. The Athenians would not only be forced to back water, but in an area where they had very limited room for doing so—that is, immediately in front of their own camp. The rest of the Great Harbour, from Plemmyrium to the docks, was now under Syracusan control.

For several days the Syracusans and Gylippus came out offering battle, both by land and sea. The Syracusan navy cruised close inshore, while cavalry and light-armed troops ranged along the line of the walls on the landward side, jeering at the Athenians as cowards, challenging them to come out and fight. The Athenians manned the walls, but stayed where they were. Gylippus, who had been getting intelligence reports on Demosthenes' progress, was determined to force the issue before it was too late; and here, ironically enough, he had the support of Nicias' two deputy commanders. The veteran trireme captains were furious at the insults they had to swallow daily from these upstart Syracusan novices, and Menander and Euthydemus lost no opportunity of exploiting their discontent. Nicias came under increasingly heavy pressure to risk a naval engagement. Perhaps reports about these differences of opinion between the commanders reached Gylippus. At all events, after a few days he altered his tactics in one significant detail. While the Syracusan fleet remained at anchor, as though no naval attack was contemplated, Gylippus led his troops out, probably from the Achradina gate, and brought them up towards the nearer Athenian wall. At the same time a mixed force of hoplites, cavalry, and light-armed auxiliaries charged the landward fortifications, from the general direction of the Olympieum. The Athenians hurriedly manned the walls in strength on both fronts, and sent out their own light-armed troops to engage those now approaching round the marshes.

Both Nicias and his colleagues were clearly convinced that this was an exclusively land-based attack. A few moments later, to their horror, they saw the Syracusan fleet move out of its anchorage and bear down on them. The crews, who had been kept in readiness, must have gone aboard at the double and cast off in a matter of seconds. This move created just enough panic in the Athenian camp to produce the effect Gylippus wanted. Some of the trireme captains deserted the walls, and began manning their vessels. "There was," Thucydides says, "a certain amount of disturbance." Nicias seems to have been faced with a *fait accompli*; at all events he gave in, against his better judgment, and some seventy-five Athenian triremes were hastily rowed out to confront the enemy. Gylippus may indeed have intended—or have given the impression that he intended—to make a sea-borne landing. If Nicias believed this, he took the only course open to him. At all costs he had to prevent his opponents establishing any sort of bridgehead in the area of the camp itself. Labdalum had taught him that lesson the hard way.

This first engagement, however, achieved no decisive result. The Syracusans did succeed in ramming one or two Athenian ships with their new reinforced prows. But as Thucydides says, "much of the day was spent in making attacks and retiring again and trying out each other's strength." Both sides, in fact, were a little nervous. The Athenians kept warily clear of these heavy, ugly, murderous-looking triremes, while the Syracusans had not yet fully accustomed themselves to handling them.

The following day there was no sign of activity in the Syracusan lines. Nicias took advantage of this unlooked-for respite to make all his captains carry out running repairs on their ships. He also strengthened the existing shore defences. There already existed a heavy stockade, which continued the line of each wall into the water, and formed a large semicircle or rectangle, with several entrances through which the triremes could pass in and out. These entrances were spaced some sixty to seventy yards apart.[3] A trireme was eighteen to twenty feet in the beam, and at least double that width would have to be allowed for

[3] I owe this entirely convincing interpretation of Thucydides, 7.41.2, to Dover, *Thucydides VII*, pp. 31–32.

oar space; so each entrance, at the very narrowest, must have been some twenty to twenty-five yards across. The entire "pen," in order to accommodate well over 100 triremes, must have extended for a minimum distance of four to five hundred yards, especially since it is unlikely to have been carried far out into the harbour itself. The distance between the walls at the shore was probably calculated with this requirement in mind. There were, therefore, some three or four seaward entrances to the stockade.

Nicias felt, quite rightly, that these gaps—given unfavourable circumstances—might prove very hard to defend against a concerted attack. He therefore anchored a merchantman close in front of each entrance, so positioned that not more than one trireme at a time could slip round it into the "pen." To deal with any Syracusan vessels that broke through the line and tried to pursue their opponents beyond the stockade, he equipped these merchantmen with what were known as "dolphins." This crude but highly effective device consisted of a heavy iron weight, shaped like a fish, and suspended by a winch-rope from the ship's yard-arm. (Probably Nicias employed the same vessels that had been used for hauling up stakes out of the sea bed.) When an enemy trireme came near, the yard-arm was swung round over it, and the windlass released, so that the "dolphin" smashed clean through the bottom of its hull. With luck, and a strong rope, the weight might afterwards be retrieved. In any case the wrecked ship could be hauled into a position where it would effectively block the entrance.

These preparations kept Nicias busy until nightfall: the Syracusan fleet—most obligingly, one feels—decided to take a rest while his men were at work. But next morning the pattern of attack established forty-eight hours earlier repeated itself. Once again the two fleets manoeuvred in a series of inconclusive attacks and counter-attacks. The July sun beat down on the combatants; sweat, if not blood, flowed freely. At some point during the morning the Corinthian contingent's best steersman, Ariston, son of Pyrrhicus, made a suggestion to the fleet commanders. Get a priority message up to the market officials, he suggested. Make them send all the stallkeepers with provisions for sale down to the beach (probably at some point between Ortygia and the docks), so that the crews can go ashore and buy what they want on the spot. Then, the moment they have had their meal, launch a fresh attack. It will be the last thing the Athenians are expecting.

The commanders fell in with this suggestion at once. A market was set up on the foreshore. The Syracusan fleet abruptly backed water, broke off the engagement, and rowed across to the far side of the harbour, where the crews proceeded to disembark and prepare their midday meal. The Athenians got the impression, as intended, that their adversaries had had the worst of it and were giving up for that day. But instead of at once following up their advantage, as one might have hoped, they themselves "disembarked in a leisurely way, and began to attend to their various jobs, including the getting ready of their meal, in the belief that they would certainly not have to fight again that day."

In this optimistic assumption they were, unfortunately, quite mistaken. Considering the fact that they had already pulled the same trick once themselves, for their attack on the first Syracusan cross-wall (see above, pp. 197–98), they had really very little excuse for their gullibility. The Syracusans, after a quick lunch, manned their vessels again immediately and sailed out to make a second attack on the Athenian position. The Athenians, most of whom had not yet eaten, scrambled back aboard in a chaotic rush, and somehow managed to get their fleet drawn up in battle order. For a while both sides watched to see if their opponents could be persuaded to make the first move. Presently the Athenians decided it was better to chance their arm than to sit there in the sun until they were exhausted. With a rousing cheer along the line they bent to their oars, and the line of triremes surged forward.

Now the Syracusans' terrible new ramming-beaks and strengthened catheads proved their worth. They closed up and met the Athenian advance head-on, bows grinding and smashing into those high, gracefully curved stems, anchor-blocks rak-

ing along the oarbanks, crumpling outriggers like paper. Slingers and javelin-throwers poured a deadly fusillade in among the
Athenian marines, driving them back from the foredeck if the
shock of collision had not already done so. At the same time
dozens of small skiffs, loaded with archers and other light-armed
troops, moved in to support the Syracusan fleet. These boats
slipped alongside the Athenian triremes, passing under the lowest bank of oars, so that their occupants could discharge arrows
or darts at point-blank range through the rowing ports. Faced
with this savage, well-planned, and most unorthodox onslaught,
the Athenians broke and fled, racing headlong for the shelter
of the "pen," crowding past the anchored merchantmen outside every entrance, with the Syracusans in hot pursuit. But
Nicias' iron "dolphins" saved them from complete disaster. Two
over-rash Syracusan vessels had their hulls stove in, and the rest
called off the pursuit. Seven Athenian triremes had been sunk
or disabled, and most of their crews taken prisoner.

The Syracusans were jubilant, and justifiably so. They had
thrashed the redoubtable Athenian navy in fair fight—a thing
they would never have dreamed possible even six months before. They felt equally confident in their—or Gylippus'—ability
to finish off Nicias' land forces. For the first time, victory seemed
truly within their grasp. At first light the following morning,
eager to strike again before the shattered Athenians could recover from this unlooked-for defeat, they mustered their squadrons once more for a final onslaught. But as the darkness faded,
besiegers and besieged alike turned to stare at the sight that
greeted them on the horizon beyond Plemmyrium.

Out of the dawn they came, ship upon ship, ensigns lit by
the first rays of the rising sun, light glinting off helmets and
armour: a skirl of flutes, oars keeping their steady rhythm as
the boatswains called the time, massed voices raised in the
paean, a vision of imperial splendour suddenly made manifest
in all its pristine glory. At the eleventh hour—with that dramatic flair for a well-timed entry that was so characteristic of
him—Demosthenes led his glittering fleet to anchor in the Great
Harbour; and no man raised a hand to bar his passage.

The elation of the Syracusans had received a sharp setback. No one spoke of imminent victory now. If Athens, with the Spartans encamped on her back doorstep, could *still* mount such an expedition as this, when could the once more beleaguered city expect any deliverance from its sufferings? Once again the Athenian army and fleet enjoyed complete freedom of movement in and around the Great Harbour. The only troops which dared come out against them, and then only to skirmish and spy out the land, were the cavalry and light-armed troops based on Polichna.

Demosthenes was well aware of the impression he had made —his triumphal entry was planned with just that end in view —and had every intention of exploiting it before the Syracusans' terror and dismay could wear off. The combined Athenian force now totalled over forty thousand men: 9,500 hoplites, 4,800 light-armed troops, and some 27,000 rowers, marines, and petty officers. With such a formidable corps at his disposal, Demosthenes felt he could afford to take risks. He certainly wasted no time. After a quick tour of inspection to ascertain enemy positions and the general lie of the land, he went straight into conference with Nicias and Eurymedon.[1] His own views were simple enough. He had no intention of repeating Nicias' mistake, and letting things drift on without taking firm action. The original expeditionary force had looked impressive enough on first arrival, but Nicias had frittered away his advantages, both strategic and psychological, by re-

[1] It is possible that Menander and Euthydemus were also present at these staff conferences. Menander certainly survived the expedition's defeat (we find him as a commander during the last years of the Peloponnesian War) and might have given valuable information to Thucydides as an eyewitness. The description Thucydides gives of the conferences reads as though written up from minutes taken at the time.

tiring to Catana for the winter. He should have pressed home the attack on Syracuse at once, when the city was still hopelessly unprepared. If he had done so, it would have fallen—or at the least have been totally cut off—long before Gylippus could have got any troops through.

How much of this Demosthenes told Nicias to his face we can only surmise. It was no time for pointless recriminations; yet the newly arrived commander must have been appalled by the air of sick, demoralised squalor he found in the Athenian camp, and he was never a man to mince his words. Demosthenes then turned to positive recommendations. Here he was brief and cogent. They must, he said, "stake everything on a swift and decisive operation, and either capture Syracuse or else return home." The key to Syracuse was, clearly, Epipolae. Force the ascent to the heights, overpower the Syracusan strongpoints, recapture the cross-wall, and the city was as good as taken. Nicias, Plutarch says, "was alarmed at [Demosthenes'] dash and audacity and opposed any hasty or desperate attempt." In particular, he seems to have balked at the idea of a full-scale attack on Epipolae, especially since Demosthenes was anxious to make it by night. He still clung obstinately to his hope that Syracuse would fall because of internal dissension and insolvency: the messages that reached him were as optimistic as ever. But—a bad error of tactics—he did not take Demosthenes and Eurymedon fully into his confidence about these undercover dealings of his. He dropped heavy hints; he was evasive; he refused to speak out openly.

As a result, the new commanders at once assumed (and who could blame them?) that Nicias' attitude was dictated by mere cowardice; that they were in for "a repetition of the old story of hesitation and delays and endless quibbles over details." Yet they seem to have treated Nicias personally with as much consideration as possible; he was, after all, a very sick man, and they must have been shocked by the change in his appearance since their last meeting. Demosthenes even agreed to a postponement of his mass attack on Epipolae. If he could carry the cross-wall by direct assault from the Athenian camp, the plateau might then be recaptured piecemeal, without the need for a full-scale infantry battle. The plan he now evolved was, in theory, a classic, if highly hazardous, commando operation. The southern escarpment would be assaulted at various points, by specially picked companies.[2] Their main function would be to keep Gylippus' garrison troops occupied while the main attacking body, with battering-rams, stormed up the Portella del Fusco—under covering fire from the Round Fort—and made straight for the Syracusan cross-wall. A secondary diversion would be created by the cavalry, which was to raid the countryside round the Anapus River, and thus pin down the Syracusan force stationed by the Olympieum.

Like so many of Demosthenes' battle plans, this one sounded almost fool-proof; and—again like so many of them— it proved a disastrous failure in practice. The assault party with the battering-rams duly reached the wall, but beat a hasty retreat when their rams were doused with pitch and set on fire. The various groups attempting to scale the escarpment were all beaten back. Only the cavalry seems to have come through unscathed. After this fiasco Demosthenes insisted, more vehemently than ever, that their only chance was to go through with his original plan—the night attack on Epipolae—as soon as possible. Nicias was frankly pessimistic about the chances of such an operation, but in the end gave his reluctant consent to it. Demosthenes at once began to make detailed preparations. If the attack proved successful, he intended to follow it up with a crash programme of refortification. He therefore included all the stonemasons and carpenters in the assault group, and made every man carry five days' rations with him.

"Assault group" is not really an adequate term to describe the force Demosthenes led up Euryalus. If we are to believe Diodorus, it numbered ten thousand hoplites and another ten thousand light-armed troops. Since the expedition only possessed 9,500 hoplites in all, either Diodorus is giving the nearest round figure, or else Demosthenes put five hundred auxiliaries

---

[2] The heights between the Portella del Fusco and Euryalus are far from sheer in many places, and could easily be scaled by a determined assault group. Perhaps Demosthenes used his Acarnanians for this purpose. Mountain-trained guerrillas would find the rocks no problem.

into hoplite armour for the occasion. Similarly, the official roll-call of light-armed troops was less than five thousand; the second five thousand probably consisted of marines from the fleet. If these figures are even remotely accurate, it is clear that Demosthenes was putting all his eggs in one basket with a vengeance. Not a single hoplite had been spared to defend the camp in the event of a surprise attack. Nicias—who was staying behind as garrison commander—would have to make do with rowers and servants. No one could say that the victor of Pylos lacked either courage or ingenuity. Indeed, he possessed both qualities to excess. He was, very often, too clever by half; and his bravery had a habit of eclipsing his common sense.

Any general with half Demosthenes' experience—especially in the field of guerrilla warfare—should have known that a large-scale night attack is, notoriously, the most difficult of all military operations to bring off as planned. If it *does* go well, success tends to be overwhelming. But the margin of error is so great, and depends on so many incalculable factors, that to stake the future of an entire expeditionary force on one such attack must be regarded as the rashest of follies. Quite apart from the risks attaching to a night attack per se, Epipolae offered a highly unsuitable terrain for such an operation. The plateau, as we have seen, is over three miles long, and about two miles broad towards its eastern extremity. Its surface is rough and uneven, sloping up in the west to a central ridge, and strewn with large rocks and boulders throughout. Even with a good sense of direction and a large-scale map in one's mind's eye it is all too easy—*experto credite*—to lose one's bearings when walking across this featureless waste land in the dark. If Demosthenes had drawn his assault force exclusively from the men of Nicias' expedition—who, after all, had lived and fought on the plateau for several months—he might have done a great deal better. As it was, about half his troops found themselves stumbling over territory of which they had no previous knowledge, and which even now they could not make out with any degree of assurance. A better recipe for disruptive chaos it would be hard to imagine.

But Demosthenes was not quite so lacking in strategical foresight as might appear from these considerations. Indeed, what we have here is a splendid example of his over-subtle ingenuity. Like certain luminaries of the German General Staff, he had a weakness for formulating plans which depended on too many constant factors, and thus left little room for improvisation when something went wrong. The classic instance was his fantastically complex strategy before Delium in 424. Eleven years later he still had not shaken off the habit; and this time it was to prove fatal.

What he had done, as becomes apparent when one follows his movements, was to time the entire Epipolae assault in relation to the rising of the moon, which was full, or nearly full, on the night in question.[3] His first task was to move twenty thousand men from the Great Harbour camp to Euryalus without anyone observing their progress, across countryside devoid of any natural cover. Their only chance was to march this three-mile stretch at night, while the moon was still down. On the other hand, it would be almost impossible to operate effectively on Epipolae itself except by the light of the full moon; and Demosthenes, with exemplary logic, had allowed for this as well. He would so time his movements that the attacking force reached Euryalus just before the moon was due to rise. By the time they had fought their way through the first line of defences it should be well above the horizon, and give them ample light by which to storm the camps and the cross-wall.

At first it looked as though everything would come off according to plan. The army left camp as soon as it was dark, and reached the Euryalus col without being seen by anyone. Indeed, the leading detachments contrived to slip unnoticed past the Syracusans' advance post,[4] and to capture Gylippus'

[3] This dates the attack to within a day or two of July 31, since the moon was eclipsed at the full on the night of August 27. See below, pp. 295-96.

[4] Presumably (though Thucydides does not say so) these look-outs were quietly killed, or at the very least, bound and gagged. It would have been suicidal to leave them at liberty.

new Euryalus fort before the garrison knew what had hit them. But the shouts as the first men were killed woke the rest; most of them managed to get away across Epipolae and raise the alarm. Here, oddly enough, was the point at which Demosthenes' plan began to go wrong. He had clearly allowed at least half an hour, perhaps more, for the reduction of the Euryalus fort, and now by a combination of luck and judgment it had fallen in five minutes. *The moon was still below the horizon.* But the advance was under way, and nothing could stop it. There were twenty thousand men pressing up that narrow defile; and already confused shouts ahead in the darkness showed that the Syracusans had been aroused to the danger threatening them. Demosthenes could only thrust forward for his objectives as planned, and pray the gods that the moon rose quickly.

Once Euryalus and its fort had been taken, and a bridgehead established, Demosthenes' main target was the cross-wall which now ran across Epipolae, linking the fortified positions of Labdalum, Bufalaro, and Salita Ombra. His plan, it appears, was to punch through the wall's defences at two points simultaneously, midway between each of the camps. The first brigade up Euryalus—probably led by Demosthenes himself—made straight for the stretch of wall between Labdalum and Bufalaro. Here they were met by Hermocrates and his six hundred picked guardsmen, who fought bravely, but were no match for Demosthenes' veterans. The Athenians smashed through them, and pressed on to the wall. This first attack was the signal for a second. A special assault group had been left behind in the Round Fort, probably under the command of Euthydemus.[5] When it was clear, from the rumpus over the hill, that Demosthenes' brigade had broken out of Euryalus, this force launched a parallel thrust, somewhere between Bufalaro

[5] This is the only satisfactory explanation of Thucydides, 7.43.5, where it is clearly stated that a second party attacks the counter-wall *at the very outset of the action.* Besides, Demosthenes would hardly ignore the obvious tactical advantage of a bridgehead like the Round Fort when planning such an attack. Euthydemus' name is conspicuously absent from the list of those commanding on the Euryalus attack, and he is unlikely to have been left behind with Nicias.

and Salita Ombra. The garrison, caught by surprise, put up no resistance, and the Athenians began hastily tearing down the battlements and fortifications.

By now the moon was just up, low over the western hills, and—to judge from Plutarch's description—somewhat obscured by cloud: those long, curdled strips of off-white fleece which so often lie along the night horizon in Greece and Sicily, even during the height of summer. Through them the moon glowed faint and yellow—a harvest moon, in fact, and worse than useless for the task Demosthenes had set himself. His men could barely see where they were going; to cap everything they had the moon at their backs, so that they cast long shadows in front of them. What little light there was came glinting back in their eyes off the shields and sword-blades of their opponents. Even so, as long as they kept reasonably close order, and did not run into any serious opposition, the Athenians had little to fear. While Demosthenes was assaulting Labdalum and the wall beyond it, the second and part of the third brigades, under Eurymedon and Menander, had reached the top of the plateau. One column set off for the central camp on Bufalaro, the other to reinforce the assault group from the Round Fort, and if possible to capture the fortified position above Salita Ombra. Demosthenes' plan, in fact, was a straightforward three-pronged attack; and so far it had gone almost without a hitch.

The Syracusan troops who held Bufalaro were by now awake and armed, though in a state of some confusion. As Thucydides says, "the daring of this attack by night was something which they had not expected." They made a sortie, but "their charge lacked resolution," and the Athenian column quickly routed them. At the same time Gylippus and the Corinthians came hurrying up from Salita Ombra, rightly sensing that Bufalaro was where the greatest danger lay. But Gylippus had no better luck than the Syracusans. The Athenian spearhead smashed through his hastily drawn up ranks, and went on its headlong way. There was good tactical sense in these *Blitzkrieg* methods. The Athenians, convinced by now that victory was within their grasp, wanted to knock out every unit of the enemy's defending forces quickly, before they had time to recover from the sudden shock of the attack. Their plan very nearly succeeded. What defeated it, in the first instance, was a company of stolid, well-trained Boeotian volunteers: Hegesander and the men of Thespiae, so opportunely picked up by a Syracusan squadron in Locri (see above, p. 261), and brought back—the instrument of fate indeed—just in time to destroy Athens' last bid for victory.

This Thespian contingent came up from Salita Ombra some way behind Gylippus and the men of Corinth. Perhaps Hegesander was a man who refused to let himself be hurried; more probably he stopped on the way to mop up the wall party from the Round Fort—or at least hold them in check until reinforcements arrived from Scala Greca. This delay turned out to his advantage. By the time the Athenian assault column reached him it had lost all cohesion. Hegesander met it with a solid shield-wall and a phalanx of levelled spears. The Athenians hesitated; Hegesander promptly gave the order to charge. With a wild yell the Thespians surged forward. The Athenians broke and scattered, leaving many dead behind them. From this moment they were lost, utterly and completely, and the assault on Epipolae degenerated into a chaotic rout.

The fugitives went streaming back towards Euryalus, stumbling over rocks in the darkness, throwing away sword and shield as they ran. The moon was well up from the mountains now, and clear of the clouds, too: a heavy golden orb, its light shining straight in their eyes. So when, as was inevitable, the second brigade in retreat met the advancing spearhead of the third, neither side could be quite sure who these other hurrying shadowy figures were, and it took much shouting of watchwords to sort the situation out—by which time both columns were hopelessly intermingled, with fresh troops pushing forward from the rear and more fugitives crowding desperately back to escape pursuit. The chaos spread to Euryalus, since not all the third brigade had yet reached the summit, and those troops who now did so saw only a confused mass of struggling men, and had no clear idea in which direction they were supposed to go. The mass broke up into small individual groups that went wandering about in the darkness, often mistaking friend for foe and killing their own comrades. Once this had happened it was no longer possible to enforce discipline or convey orders.

Demosthenes and his brigade hurried across from Labdalum to find out what was happening, and were drawn into the general confusion. Gylippus and the Syracusans kept their own troops in firm, compact units, which constantly harried the Athenians from all quarters. So many hysterical soldiers were shouting the watchword that the Syracusans picked it up and began to use it themselves. Both sides, at different points, were singing identical war songs. In a very little while all resistance was at an end. Terrified and demoralised crowds, all discipline gone, fought and clawed and trampled their way down the narrow ascent of Euryalus. Some tried to climb down the cliffs, lost their footing, and so fell to their deaths. Others went over the edge in the darkness as they fled before some pursuing Syracusan hoplite. If Gylippus had any sense—and we have no reason to suppose he did not on this occasion— he must have blocked off the second escape-route, by the Round Fort and the Portella del Fusco.

In this hellish moonlit scene of scrambling shadow-figures and chaotic butchery it was each man for himself; and the devil indeed took the hindmost. As might have been expected, the old hands who had served under Nicias did best. They knew the plateau well, and had probably explored many of the less obvious cliff-ascents. When they reached the plain they made their way straight back to camp. The newly arrived troops of Demosthenes were not so fortunate. Many got hopelessly lost on Epipolae itself; others, who contrived to clamber down the escarpment, went wandering hopelessly round the country-side until it was light, when they were rounded up and slaughtered by Syracusan cavalry patrols.

Next day a grim, hollow-eyed group of Athenian generals and senior officers took back their dead under truce, and then sat down to count the cost of that night's work. They had lost over two thousand men killed. Many more had been seriously wounded, and "of the survivors only a handful returned with their arms." Epipolae was a litter of abandoned swords, helmets, and shields; and where, now, could replacements be obtained? If morale had been low before, it reached rock bottom after this costly fiasco. Perhaps even more dangerous than military failure was the spread of disease: in particular, malaria and dysentery. But if Nicias chose to site his camp by the very edge of the great marsh, he could hardly expect anything else.

Now, horrified by the utter disaster that had overtaken them, he rounded on Demosthenes and attacked him bitterly for his foolhardiness in ever undertaking such an operation. The result, he said, was just what he had foreseen from the beginning. Demosthenes defended himself as best he could, arguing that what had defeated them was bad luck rather than bad judgment. But they had to face facts, he insisted. After such a crippling disaster it was sheer folly to think of hanging on any longer. They were in no condition now to defeat the enemy. They need expect no further reinforcements. The campsite was a death trap, the men had reached the end of their tether. Autumn would bring a still greater diversity of sickness and epidemics.

In such a predicament they had no choice of action: they must evacuate Syracuse at once, while they still at least enjoyed naval superiority. It was criminal to stay there wasting ships and money and men's lives on this hopeless venture when they were so desperately needed for the defence of Attica. In defeat as in victory, Demosthenes was clear-cut, honest, and cogent. If his advice had been followed, the Athenians would have saved the bulk of their expeditionary force, and spared themselves untold suffering. It is possible that they might even have materially altered the whole course of the Peloponnesian War.

But now, paradoxically, it was Nicias who took a stubborn stand against the whole idea of evacuation. He admitted that the situation was bad, and that it *might* prove necessary to withdraw in the end. However, he argued, it would be a mistake to vote openly in favour of evacuation. The word would certainly get back to Syracuse, and then they were likely to have a lot of trouble keeping the move secret. As a temporising gambit this was quite effective. Thucydides claims that Nicias had not yet made up his own mind—which seems all too likely. However, he had other arguments in favour of staying put—or, at the very least, of postponing the evacuation. The Athenian Assembly, he reminded his colleagues, was not likely to react at all well if the generals carried out a withdrawal on their own authority, without referring the matter back to Athens for a formal vote. *They* might be on the spot, and in a position to evaluate the facts for themselves, without being swayed by hostile witnesses. But at home it was quite another matter.[6]

If they withdrew now, who could rely on an Athenian voter to see the truth? His judgment would be swayed by any clever speech designed to create prejudice. Besides, Nicias went on waspishly, the soldiers who were now complaining most loudly about their desperate plight would be the first—once safely home again—to turn round and accuse the generals of having been bribed to retreat. He knew the Athenian character too well, he said. Personally, he would prefer to take a chance in Sicily, and die an honourable death if he had to, "rather than be put to death on a disgraceful charge and by an unjust verdict of the Athenians."

Quite apart from this he did not foresee any immediate danger. They were still well equipped with men and ships and money. The Syracusans, on the other hand, were almost bankrupt: all the Athenians had to do was stick it out a little longer, and the enemy's troops would soon be deserting by the hundred. It was the same old story: persist just another week, or month, and all would be well. The ultra-democrats would show their hand at last, the gates of Syracuse would open, the campaign would end in triumph, and without unnecessary bloodshed.

[6] This argument, of course, was largely aimed at Eurymedon, who had acted on his own initiative after the Congress of Gela in 424, and barely escaped exile in consequence (see above, p. 74).

The details of this secret diplomacy, however, Nicias still kept to himself, and for once he was justified in doing so. Not only the generals, but every senior unit commander was present, and it was too much to hope that there would not be a leak somewhere. Once such negotiations had been made even semi-public, it would not be long before they found their way back to Hermocrates and Gylippus, thus effectively slamming the door on any chance of peace through collusion. Nicias' most powerful argument was thus denied him. All he could do was try to convince his listeners that he knew something they did not, which for reasons of security he was unable to reveal. By hints and nods he managed to convey the right impression. He was, they felt, "in the know"; he had trustworthy private sources of information. If he was so dead set against withdrawal, he must have received secret intelligence reports which fully justified such a grave decision. The general mood of the conference began to swing round in favour of Nicias' proposals. Besides, no one—least of all Eurymedon—felt much inclined to risk the Assembly's disapproval at this stage. Their record was dismal enough already without deliberately blackening it still further.

Demosthenes, sensing the change in the atmosphere, and still acutely conscious of his own personal responsibility for the Epipolae fiasco, now retreated somewhat from the extreme position he had taken up to begin with. He conceded two of Nicias' main points: that the expedition had to remain in Sicily, and that no evacuation of the island could take place unless ratified by the Athenian Assembly. But he was still adamant that they should at once withdraw their forces from the Great Harbour. Patiently he went over the arguments once more. The site was appallingly unhealthy, and far too cramped. It stank of garbage and faeces and rotting food and marsh-gas. Flies swarmed everywhere. The men were sick with fever and dysentery, and small wonder. If the position was strategically perfect they might put up with all this. But it was not. Their fleet was cooped up in one corner of the Great Harbour, with no room in which to manoeuvre. Their land forces were at a similar disadvantage, being hemmed in between Epipolae and the sea. What they should do, Demosthenes said, was transfer their forces either to Thapsus or to Catana. With either of these as a base, both fleet and army would enjoy complete freedom of movement. Better still, they could attack when they felt like it, instead of being kept eternally on the defensive. They would have a good, healthy camp-site, and plenty of open country in which to forage. It was urgent for this move to be carried out immediately, before the situation deteriorated still further. Eurymedon (who seems to have said very little during the whole debate) declared himself in agreement with Demosthenes.

But Nicias refused to give up. He dithered and argued, raising endless objections. His dream of surrender by secret negotiation had clearly become an obsession. If they evacuated the Great Harbour now, at the eleventh hour, all his planning and diplomacy would have gone for nothing. Success was so near, almost within his grasp. The gods he had honoured all his life could not let it pass from him now. Final victory would cancel all that had gone before, would atone for failure and sickness and waste and endless months of dilatory incompetence.

There was no hurry, he told Demosthenes. (No hurry!) "The question of where they should move the camp could be decided at leisure." Nicias' air of lassitude and irresolute procrastination was infectious. Demosthenes knew when he was beaten. He had no energy to continue the argument. So this crucial staff conference drifted to a close without any effective decision having been taken. Action demands effort: the Athenian expeditionary force stayed where it was. Perhaps Nicias would yet surprise them all, they argued, without real conviction. But Nicias was largely occupied by prayers and sacrifices and divination, somewhat to the neglect of his more official duties. He spent an increasing amount of time closeted with his personal soothsayer, Stilbides. August drew on, and the winds fell, and pestilence raged through the camp. Presently

Stilbides, too, fell ill and died, and Nicias was left to brood over his future alone.

Immediately after their victory on Epipolae, the Syracusans heard that Acragas—the only large city-state on the south coast which still maintained its neutrality—was in the throes of a revolution. This seemed too good a chance to miss. One of the generals, Sicanus, was sent off there with a squadron of fifteen ships to find out what was going on, and to see if he could pressurise the victorious party into an alliance. Meanwhile the promised contingents from Gela and Camarina had arrived (see above, p. 266), and the 1,500 survivors of that lethal Sicel ambush were by now recovered from their ordeal and ready for action. The outlook was something better than promising. At the same time Gylippus—never one to leave any possible source of manpower unexplored—took off on another of his whirlwind recruiting tours round the island. He let it be known, in each city he visited, that after their great success on Epipolae it would only be a matter of time before the defenders of Syracuse forced the Athenian camp. He collected a surprising number of extra reinforcements this way. Those who had prudently abstained when the upshot of the siege looked doubtful were only too eager—with equal prudence—to be in at the death.

At Selinus a pleasant surprise awaited him. The reinforcements from the Peloponnese which had set out across open sea that spring had never arrived, and were presumed lost. In fact they had been blown off course to Libya, and after various adventures had finally made the crossing to Selinus, where Gylippus found them. His forces were thus unexpectedly augmented by six hundred Spartan-led Helots and two hundred Boeotians. This windfall more than compensated him for Sicanus' diplomatic failure at Acragas. The revolution, it seemed, had gone the wrong way. It was the anti-Syracusan party that was now in power; their own friends had been exiled. But Acragas, Gylippus reflected, could be dealt with later. One thing at a time. Their first and most urgent task was to launch an all-out amphibious assault against the Athenian camp. Over three weeks had elapsed since the night affray on Epipolae. With autumn coming on they could not afford to delay much longer. Intensive preparations were put in hand at once.

Day by day more men fell sick down by the Great Harbour, and lay in their tents, feverish, sweat-sodden, while the brazen Sicilian sun beat on patched canvas and piles of evil-smelling filth and the cracked, bleached hulls of the triremes. Lacklustre eyes watched yet more reinforcements—Boeotians and Spartan-trained Helots, too!—march into Syracuse. While Gylippus increased his strength continually, their own effective numbers were dropping. Nicias prayed and muttered and burnt incense as a prophylactic against fever. Even Demosthenes seemed to have lost his old vitality. The ground-swell of apathetic grumbling throughout the camp suddenly rose to a loud and hysterical chorus of protest. *Take us home*, the men shouted mindlessly. *Get us out of here.* The noise increased until it was an incoherent baying, a mere blare of sound. Nicias called his commanders together. They were unanimous in their opinion. The men were right. What was more, they were on the verge of breakdown and mutiny.

Now, at last, Nicias was forced to acknowledge defeat. He still clung obstinately to the idea that no open vote should be taken, that security should be observed at all costs; but he was, nevertheless, ready to sanction the withdrawal of all Athenian forces from the Great Harbour. It was enough. Orders were passed down the chain of command, with as much secrecy as possible, to prepare for a general embarkation. They would sail before dawn the following day, and "at the signal not a man in the camp should be late, for he who lagged would be left behind." All that day, August 27, the Athenians worked at feverish speed, sick and well alike, packing stores and equipment, loading the triremes, hauling up yard-arms. By the time darkness fell, the entire expeditionary force was ready for departure. A message had been sent to Catana, cancelling all standing orders for supplies. A great sense of relief and finality spread through the camp. The moon rose, full once more, and hung clear among the summer stars. Some men slept; others, sick and sweating, lay in the open air for coolness' sake, staring idly up at the night sky.

It was they who, about 10 P.M., first saw the black shadow begin to creep across the moon's silver disk, spreading and spreading till nothing remained but a faint ghostly penumbra. If the stars in their courses fought against Sisera, the moon's ecliptic was, with equal fatality, the unwitting instrument of Nicias' destruction.

CHAPTER XVII: *Death by Water*

By the end of the fifth century B.C. it was more or less accepted—at least among educated people—that a solar eclipse was "caused in some way or other by the shadow of the moon." But a lunar eclipse was still a thing of mystery and terror, hard to explain in rational terms, and for the vast majority of the population, as Plutarch put it, "a supernatural portent and a warning from the gods that fearful calamities were at hand." Nor, paradoxically, were people over-anxious to be convinced otherwise. Philosophers like Anaxagoras might make bold scientific speculations on the causes of such phenomena, but remained very chary of publishing their conclusions, except among close friends who thought as they did. The pious were convinced—and with some reason—that such persons "belittled the power of the gods by explaining it away as nothing more than the operation of irrational causes."

It would be hard to find a more striking proof of the sheer blind superstitious terror which an eclipse of the moon produced during this period than the reaction among the Athenian rank and file on the night of August 27, 413 B.C. For weeks now they had been importuning their officers to get them out of this hell-hole by the Grand Harbour. Yet when they had at last prevailed, when the fleet was on the very point of sailing, a shadow passing across the moon could still send them en masse to Nicias and Demosthenes, demanding that the date of departure be postponed. Nicias, of all people, was not likely to treat such a request with the contempt that it deserved. Indeed, by all accounts he was in a greater lather of panic and agitation than any of his men. The death of Stilbides, "who had done much to hold his superstitious fears in check," left Nicias dependent on various lesser soothsayers. Had some of these perhaps been suborned by Syracusan agents? It would not be surprising. Nicias' dependence on soothsaying and divination was well known. Anyone anxious to influence his decisions (or even to obtain secret information) would hardly ignore so obvious an opening.

Suspicion becomes near-certainty when we examine Nicias' reaction to the eclipse, and the advice on which he based it. The normal practice in such cases, according to our ancient authorities, was to suspend action for *three days only*. Yet Nicias' diviners recommended that he should wait, not three, but "thrice nine" days—i.e., a whole lunar cycle. Furthermore, as Philochorus[1] pointed out, for men contemplating a withdrawal—which requires concealment rather than light—eclipses counted as a *favourable* omen, a fact which any professional diviner should have known quite well in the first place. It looks unpleasantly as though those twenty-seven days were a device to give the Syracusans time to prepare for a major assault. "They manned their ships," says Thucydides, "and put the crews into training for what seemed to them the right number of days." Demosthenes and some others may have suspected the truth; in any case they urged Nicias to ignore so monstrous a ruling. But Nicias was adamant. Until the prescribed period had elapsed, he said, "he would not even join in any further discussion on how the move could be made." Demosthenes had either to climb down or risk a prosecution for impiety. He climbed down.

Whether or not the Syracusans were responsible for that fatal delay, they took the fullest advantage of it. The moment they learnt (from deserters, it is said: a revealing detail) that Nicias had been planning to pull out his entire expeditionary force, they set about preparing a vigorous offensive. To contemplate evacuation was an open confession of inferiority. On the other hand, if the Athenians made a successful withdrawal, they would in all likelihood carry on a war of attrition from some other base, such as Catana, where it would be far harder to defeat them. Gylippus and the Syracusans therefore made

[1] A fourth-century Athenian historian who was also a trained seer and diviner.

it their aim, as Thucydides says, "to force the Athenians to fight at sea as quickly as possible, in a position where the advantages were on the side of Syracuse"—that is, from their stockade on the shore. While Nicias spent more and more time with his soothsayers, and the Syracusan fleet went into strict training, Gylippus slowly tightened the blockade round his opponents' camp.

All initiative had now passed to Syracuse. Her cavalry patrols controlled the entire plain from Epipolae to Plemmyrium. Her ships sailed insolently round the Athenian "pen," the crews laughing and jeering at these cowards who refused to come out and fight like men. After a while, even boys in fishing-boats would row across to challenge the Athenians and to fling well-chosen insults at them. The blockade had become a cruel and contemptuous game. But it was a game with an ulterior purpose. As before, Nicias was determined not to fight if he could possibly avoid it. Gylippus did not, even now, feel strong enough to carry the Athenian walls and stockade by direct assault. He therefore had either to starve the defenders into submission or else tempt them out to fight. The first course he never seems to have contemplated. It was not, for one thing, his style of fighting; and he probably felt that to seal off so large an area effectively enough to prevent *any* supplies getting in, even at night, would require more men than he could well spare. What he did not know was that the Athenians had cancelled the dispatch of stores from Catana altogether—and were, apparently, unable to get a second messenger through to countermand their original order. He therefore set about a deliberate policy of irritation: the jeers and insults and provocative gestures, the pin-prick raids, the insolent indifference to any possibility of Athenian reprisals—all this was directed to one specific end. Sooner or later, and in all likelihood sooner rather than later, someone behind that stockade was bound to lose his temper.

Gylippus' first success came when he got a mixed force of Athenian hoplites and cavalry to make a sortie from the walls and engage the Syracusan troops based on Polichna. The Syracusans cut off Nicias' hoplites and drove them back in head-long retreat. The Athenian cavalry proved no match for Syracuse's formidable mounted squadrons. A mass of fugitives struggled through the narrow postern gate into the camp, leaving their horses behind to be rounded up by the victors. It was a promising start to Gylippus' new campaign; and he followed it, the next day, with a full-scale amphibious assault. While the Syracusan cavalry and light-armed troops advanced from Polichna towards the western Athenian wall, a body of hoplites, under Gylippus himself, emerged from the Achradina gate and moved along the line of the bay in the direction of the stockade. They were helped by a causeway which ran a good way round the Great Harbour, between the muddy fore-shore and the Lysimeleia swamp.

Meanwhile the Athenian fleet had at last been tempted into action. A young Syracusan boy named Heraclides, from one of the city's most distinguished aristocratic families, volunteered to act as stalking-horse. He rowed over to the stockade, and shipped his oars right outside one of the entrances. From this daring vantage-point he then proceeded to tear off so filthy a stream of abuse that one trireme commander took the bait, manned his vessel, and set off in pursuit of him. This was the signal for ten triremes—no more as yet—to sail across from the Syracusan lines and rescue the boy: obviously he could not outdistance an Athenian man-o'-war in his dinghy.[2] Perhaps the same number of Athenian vessels now took off to support their own colleague. Before anyone quite knew how it had happened, the Athenians found themselves committed to a full-scale naval engagement. It was an early and classic case of escalation.

[2] This Syracusan detachment is traditionally supposed to have been led by the boy's uncle, Pollichus, which seems plausible enough. The entire story is queried by most historians in its present context. Freeman arbitrarily transferred it to the final battle in the Great Harbour. But Plutarch is quite specific; the incident either took place now or not at all, and on balance—though by a very small margin, I must confess—I am inclined to accept it.

The Syracusans brought up seventy-four triremes; the Athenians finally mustered eighty-six. Their line of battle was roughly parallel to the stockade. Eurymedon commanded the right wing, with Agatharchus the Syracusan against him. In the centre, Menander's squadron faced that of Pythen the Corinthian, who had accompanied Gylippus on his original momentous voyage to Sicily. The Athenian left wing under Euthydemus was opposed by Sicanus of Syracuse, just back from his unsuccessful diplomatic mission to Acragas. It was Pythen who first broke the Athenian line, driving their centre back shorewards, his heavy, blunt-prowed triremes smashing into the hulls of Menander's vessels. Some of the Athenians managed to retreat inside the "pen"—presumably the iron "dolphins" were once more primed and ready—but others were forced aground, among the shoals and shallows that lay between the stockade and the Syracusan docks.

When Sicanus, the commander of the Syracusan right wing, saw all these stranded, wallowing vessels, he hurriedly called up a fire-ship which he had in readiness—an old merchantman full of pitch-soaked firewood, mostly pine faggots. The wind was in the right quarter. Sicanus set the fire-ship alight, and let it drift down on the beached Athenian squadron. One or two of the nearest triremes went up in flames, but somehow Nicias' sailors managed to push the fire-ship off and extinguish the blaze before it spread further. Euthydemus' wing was now in much the same plight: Athenian vessels were strung out, more or less disabled, all along the foreshore. This was exactly the kind of situation for which Gylippus had been waiting. He and his troops advanced along the causeway, hoping to catch the Athenian crews as they stumbled on to the beach, and kill them before they could put up any kind of defence. This would also make it easier for the Syracusans to tow off the triremes without interference. Gylippus seems to have been a little careless or excited; his troops were, we are told, "advancing in disorder," and this gave their opponents a splendid opening. The landward approaches between the stockade and the city were being guarded by those rather improbable allies of Athens, the Etruscans. The moment they saw what was afoot, they charged along the beach to the rescue.

Gylippus' men had already found out, to their great dismay, that these trireme crews were anything but helpless victims. They fought off all attempts to dislodge them, with a fierce and Ajax-like determination. Now, while the struggle still raged among the ships, up came the Etruscans, and rapidly routed the whole of Gylippus' advance column, which they proceeded to chase into the Lysimeleia marshes. But the main body of Gylippus' army was still intact. In the end, fearful for his ships, Nicias sent out his own hoplites to engage the enemy. The risk, if it was a risk, paid off. The Athenians drove back their opponents, with some losses, and managed to rescue most of the stranded ships—though not before the Syracusans and their allies had captured eighteen, and butchered every man aboard them. There was no quarter given in this engagement. The Athenians, reasonably enough, felt that by and large they had had the better of the fighting on land. Afloat, however, it was a very different matter.

Here the Syracusans could claim a complete and overwhelming victory. They had forced the Athenian left wing and centre ashore, with heavy losses. The right wing fared no better. At the outset of the engagement Eurymedon had attempted to outflank Agatharchus' squadron and make an attack from astern —the *periplous* manoeuvre. But Agatharchus, by a skilful counter-movement, cut Eurymedon off from the main fleet, with six other ships, and forced him to retreat into Dascon Bay, about a mile south of the stockade. The Athenian commander was completely encircled, with no available leeway in which to attempt a break-out. All he and his little detachment could do was run their vessels ashore and try to escape on foot. But once again the Syracusans moved faster than he did. So Eurymedon, the butcher of Corcyra, met his own end, struck down among the melancholy Dascon sea dunes: it is hard to feel overmuch sympathy for him. All seven of the ships cut off with him were destroyed. It was after this that the Syracusans fighting the main engagement "drove back the whole Athenian fleet and forced the ships ashore."

The effect of this crushing naval defeat on the Athenians may well be imagined. After Demosthenes' arrival, they felt they at least had complete mastery at sea. Now even this comfort was taken from them. They fell into a state of total despondency, unable to credit what had happened, wishing like children that the expedition had never taken place. For once, Thucydides remarks severely, the imperialists of the Aegean were up against cities "of the same type as their own": that is, "democracies like themselves, and places of considerable size, equipped with naval and cavalry forces," cities which could neither be bullied nor suborned. Fifth-column efforts were useless; no promises of a change of government would work on such people; superiority of numbers had brought the besiegers no advantage. This, of course, is something of a rhetorical exaggeration. Syracusan democracy, as it existed in 413, was hardly democracy at all. The city's cavalry was excellent; but—until an undemocratic Spartan took them in hand —neither its fleet nor its infantry had been much to write home about. It was true that Nicias' fifth-column diplomacy had failed in the event, but on at least one occasion it came within a hair's-breadth of success. The change of government had not, as yet, taken place; within a year, however, Diocles and his friends were to put it through without external assistance.

The one indisputable claim which Thucydides makes is that the Athenians had not been able to exploit their superiority in numbers and material resources. Indeed, the margin of superiority had itself been much whittled away. Between Demosthenes' arrival and the aftermath of this latest disaster, the Athenians had lost about nine thousand men, in battle or by illness, and not less than twenty-five triremes, probably more. "Now, after this wholly unexpected defeat at sea," says Thucydides, "they were at their wits' end." The Syracusans, on the other hand, were riding very high indeed. Their unlooked-for and overwhelming naval victory had filled them with aggressive confidence. They suddenly realised that the long emergency was over. They were not, now, fighting to save Syracuse: Syracuse was already saved. Their main object was "to prevent the enemy from saving himself." Visions of fame and glory throughout the whole Greek-speaking world shimmered enticingly before them. Now, with exultant determination, they gathered their strength to deliver the *coup de grâce*.

They had complete mastery over the Great Harbour. Their ships sailed to and fro without fear of attack, while the demoralised Athenians remained inside the stockade, patching up their battered triremes as best they could. Presently the Syracusans embarked on a project which must have struck cold fear into every Athenian heart: they set about constructing a boom across the harbour mouth, the three-quarter-mile stretch between Ortygia and Plemmyrium.[3] To do this they anchored two groups of triremes, merchantmen, and other craft broadside-on, end to end, and lashed them securely together, leaving a small gap in the middle for their own ships to pass through. Presumably they were obliged to unstep their masts in order to do so, since the vessels on either side of the gap were linked by iron chains, and a bridge of planks spanned the entire structure. This operation was completed in three days, between September 6 and 8—a remarkable feat.

Once the harbour mouth had been sealed, the fate of the Athenians became a virtually foregone conclusion. The degree of their demoralisation can be judged from the fact that at no point during those three days—or nights—did they make any attempt to force the passage while there was still a chance of their doing so unimpeded. To get away after the end of that period would mean both fighting a major naval engagement *and* breaking down the boom.

[3] Why had the Athenians never attempted so obvious and highly effective a manoeuvre, especially during the early stages of the campaign, when they (like the Syracusans now) enjoyed complete naval superiority? If one begins asking this sort of question, there is no end to it—and precious little satisfaction. One can only say, "For the same reason, presumably, as they never guarded or fortified Epipolae," and leave it at that.

Once again—and now for the last time—chronic indecision turned out to be Nicias' undoing. When his troops saw the Syracusan engineers begin work on the boom, they all "clamoured for their generals to begin an immediate withdrawal by land." Nicias could not bear the thought of sacrificing his fleet, which still numbered about 150 effective vessels apart from merchantmen[4]; but neither was he willing to risk the hazardous night action which might have saved them. In the event he did what his instinct was always to do: procrastinated until it was too late. Only when the bridge of boats was anchored in place, and the last chains had been riveted home, did Nicias finally summon his fellow-generals and battalion commanders to a council of war, to determine how they should extricate themselves from the trap that had been drawn round them. It must have been a singularly gloomy meeting. Provisions were running out, and unless they could regain naval superiority, there was scant prospect of obtaining any more. Further delay would be fatal. But Nicias still balked at the idea of abandoning the fleet.

In the end the Athenians resolved to do what they should have done three days earlier. The Round Fort and the upper walls (to a point well below the Portella del Fusco) were to be evacuated. A new cross-wall was to be built between the two existing ones, as close to the shore as possible, leaving enough room only for the reserve stores, the sick, and a small garrison. Every available ship, whether fully seaworthy or not, was to be put into commission. All the best officers and hoplites, and as many archers and javelin-throwers as possible, were to be packed aboard. The remainder would be stationed on land, along the shore. With this powerful naval task-force they would make one last supreme effort to destroy the Syracusan navy,

[4] The first expedition had a total of 134 ships, later reinforced by ten more under Eurymedon, and three Etruscan pentekonters, making 147 in all. The Athenians lost thirteen on various occasions, and perhaps another ten seriously disabled. Thus when Demosthenes arrived they had about 124, and his seventy-three brought the total to 197. In the latest sea battle twenty-five were destroyed, and probably twenty more disabled, leaving a putative 152.

and batter their way through the harbour barrier to freedom. If they succeeded, they would sail for Catana. If they lost the day, and only then, they would burn their ships (or what was left of them) and set out on foot for the nearest friendly place, whether Greek or Sicel, that they thought they could reach.

At dawn the next day, September 9, they had 115 triremes manned and ready for action. They could have put still more into commission, but their stock of oars was exhausted—the spare reserve, like so much else, having been lost with the capture of Plemmyrium. Even so, of 6,500 hoplites and about 3,300 light-armed troops still available, the great majority was somehow packed aboard: perhaps nine thousand men in all. With 16,000 rowers this made a total assault force of some 25,000 men, or about 217, on average, to a vessel—overloading by normal standards, but on the present occasion speed did not have first priority. Eight to nine thousand further combatants (of whom not more than a thousand were primarily land-fighters, the rest being surplus rowers), together with something like twenty thousand camp-followers and civilians of all kinds, were left behind to guard the stockade and watch the course of the battle. They were not the only spectators. In Syracuse, too, it was known what was afoot. The sea-walls of Ortygia and Achradina were crowded: every balcony and roof-top in the city with a view out over the Great Harbour had not an inch of spare standing-room.

But these onlookers were different. A large proportion of them were women—wives, mothers, daughters, or sweethearts of the grim-faced men now manning the city's fleet, amateur sailors no longer, but seasoned veterans. There were children, nervous, giggling excitedly; and old men whose fighting days were over; and many more who were crippled or maimed, their scars barely healed yet—"all of them," says Diodorus, "watching the conflict in great agony of mind, since this was the decisive moment of the entire war."

The Syracusans mustered no more than seventy-four triremes, against the Athenians' 115; but they also had numbers of dinghies operating beside the larger vessels, their job (see above, p. 280) being to slip under the oarbank of an enemy ship, and attack the rowers from close quarters, with arrows or sling-stones. On this occasion the dinghies were manned by boys still too young for service aboard the triremes, but who never-theless found a way to fight at their fathers' side.

Watchers in the city had observed Nicias' withdrawal from the Round Fort, Athens' last bastion on Epipolae. This was a particularly happy omen for the Syracusans. Close to the foot of the escarpment, beside the Portella del Fusco, there stood a temple sacred to Heracles. Nicias had lost some of his religious scruples, it would seem, since the time when he kept so meticulously clear of the Olympieum: this temple had been incorporated into the walls themselves. For many months now, in consequence, it had been impossible for the citizens to honour Heracles with sacrifices according to custom. Now no enemy stood in their way, and they were free to approach the temple once more. By a strange coincidence, this turn of events had taken place on the very day of the god's festival. Heracles was their national hero: it seemed an excellent omen. Priests and generals led a procession (probably from the postern gate in the new Temenites wall) to make sacrifice while the ships were being manned for battle. After due inspection of entrails the diviners prognosticated a glorious victory—"provided that the Syracusans did not seek battle, but remained on the de-fensive, for this was the way in which Heracles overcame his enemies, simply by defending himself when he was attacked."

While these preliminaries were going on, Nicias delivered the customary exhortation to his men before sending them into battle. One cannot, somehow, envisage Nicias putting fire into anyone's belly; and the version of his speech given by Thucyd-ides merely confirms this. It is earnest, sincere, practical, and deadly dull. Like any conscience-stricken bureaucrat, Nicias is checking off points on his fingers, talking aloud in self-justifica-tion. All possible provisions have been made, he says. We have consulted with the steersmen. This time we are carrying large numbers of hoplites and spearmen on deck. Our aim is to fight a land battle at sea. We have taken steps to counter the effects of those heavy prows—all ships will be provided with grappling-irons,[5] so that once an enemy vessel has charged, it will not be able to back off again. This is very much to our advantage when the enemy holds the whole harbour area outside our encampment.

"Remember this," Nicias tells his troops, "and fight it out to the limit of your strength." Then—we can almost hear him clear his throat before proceeding, in a precise, old-maidish way—he emphasises that so far he has been talking to the hoplites rather than the sailors. It is *their* business to fight. When he turns to the rowers, he says something very surprising: "Think of the pleasure it is and how much worth preserving, that all this time you, *though not really Athenians* [my italics] have, through knowledge of our language and imitation of our way of life, been considered as Athenians and been admired for it throughout Hellas." So the rowers in 413 were (for the most part at any rate) not native Athenians, not even drawn from the subject-allies—since these are described as showing them "respect"—but either metics (resident aliens), slaves, or hired mercenaries.[6]

Such remarks as Nicias does address to his fellow-Athenians, though grimly cogent, are not calculated to elate the spirits of those about to join battle. All he has to offer is the courage

[5] Where did these grappling-irons come from? If they formed part of Nicias' equipment, why do we not hear of them being used before? If they were a new idea, where were they obtained—under siege conditions, with no hope of importing stores? Perhaps the Athenian cavalry had their own blacksmith; even so, he would have been kept busy forging over two hundred grappling-irons in twenty-four hours. Another mystery.

[6] Cf. the remark, by a Corinthian, that "Athens' power is purchased, not native" (Thucydides, 1.121.3). Dover, *Thucydides VII*, p. 54, has a valuable note on this passage. Yet surely Nicias' remark is an exaggeration? What had become of the vast "sailor rabble" of Piraeus? Surely they would and did flock to join the Sicilian venture? Or was a place on the rowing benches regarded, by 413, as something too much like hard work? See above, p. 239, for the practice of using slave substitutes.

of despair. Athens has no more triremes like these, he says, and her reserve of trained hoplites is exhausted. If you fail now, your victorious enemies will at once sail against Athens— and how can Athens hope to withstand both them and Sparta together? If Syracuse breaks you, Sparta will break your fellow-countrymen. Their fate, like yours, rests upon this one battle. Then, suddenly, at its very conclusion, this drab speech flares into a brief moment of splendid and all too prophetic rhetoric. "Now, if ever, is the time to stand out firm and to remember, each and all, that those of you who are going to go aboard the ships are the army and navy of the Athenians, the whole state that remains, and the great name of Athens." From half a century and more before, there comes the memory of another conflict, when Athens' triremes again sailed forth to face fearful odds, and a "great shout" rang out:

On, sons of Greece! Strike for the honour and freedom
Of country, children, wives, graves of your forefathers,
Ancestral gods: all, all are now at stake.

But the struggle in the Great Harbour was a far cry from that splendid and immortal moment. Then, Athens was fighting for the freedom of Greece; now, a band of failed invaders were trying to save their own skins. Syracuse was not, could never be, a second Salamis. Yet in another sense Nicias' words were all too true. Though Athens was to survive for almost another decade, it was here in the Great Harbour, on a September morning in 413 B.C., that her fate—and perhaps the whole future of Europe—was ultimately decided.

When he had delivered his speech, Nicias gave the command to man the ships. Yet even now, "realising how much was at stake and how imminent already the hazard," as Thucydides says, he felt he must do still more to fire his men's hearts for the approaching conflict. He could not bear to stand idle ashore; he called for a boat, and in it he passed slowly down the line of Athenian triremes, addressing each captain formally by name, stretching out his hands, appealing to them, reminding them of the great responsibility they bore. In the agony of the moment it is the old, well-worn clichés that have most power over us. Nicias urged the valorous to preserve their high honour, and the sons of distinguished fathers not to betray their family pride. He begged them to remember their wives, their children, the gods of their native land. He spoke of the glory won at Salamis; he "reminded them of their country, the freest in the world, and of how all who lived there had liberty to live their own lives in their own way." Let them not sully the bright fame of their fatherland. Let them not succumb like slaves to these men of Syracuse.

Words, inadequate words; after his tour of the fleet Nicias still felt he had failed, that the encouragement he offered was at most barely adequate to so momentous an occasion. But he could do no more. When he landed, he gave orders for the troops still ashore to spread out in as long a line as possible, so that they could give every encouragement to their comrades. There was silence now except for the shuffle of feet, water slapping and knocking against the piles of the stockade, the occasional creak of an oar on leather.

In the Syracusan lines similar preparations were going on. Someone had found out about the Athenian grappling-irons, and now, as a last-minute counter-measure, they were busy spreading hides over the prows of the triremes, so that the spikes would slide off without getting a proper grip. Gylippus, Hermocrates, and other commanders went from ship to ship, reminding the men that these Athenians had come to enslave Sicily, and deserved no quarter; that they were now in a state of utter desperation, anxious only to save themselves from the final disaster. Let the men of Syracuse go forward with righteous anger in their hearts; let them taste the supreme pleasure of taking vengeance upon the aggressor.

Now the Syracusan fleet and army moved out to their battle stations. One squadron guarded the bridge of boats at the harbour mouth. The remainder split up into detachments, which took up positions all round the harbour, so that they could attack the Athenians from all quarters at once. Gylippus had similarly posted companies of infantry "ready for action at all points along the shore where ships might put in."

Silence still: tension that was almost unbearable. Then, suddenly, the high clear call of a trumpet, followed by the lash and thrust of oars moving at the boatswains' command. The whole Athenian fleet put out at once, in classic order, and began their fateful dash for the harbour mouth. At the nearest point, close under Ortygia, the distance was one and a quarter miles. From the stockade to Plemmyrium was almost half a mile further. While the crews bent to their oars, the troops on deck all sang the Athenian battle hymn. It must have been a splendid and awe-inspiring sight.

Perhaps in obedience to the word of the soothsayers, no attempt was made to intercept the Athenians' advance. The first blow must be struck by them. They converged on the centre of the barrier at its weakest point—the gap spanned by the bridge, with its iron chains—smashing through the cordon of ships that guarded it, working frenziedly to clear a passage. While they were thus occupied, "the Syracusans and their allies bore down on them from all sides, and soon the fighting was not only in front of the barrier but all over the harbour." It is not certain whether this first Athenian attack actually forced the gap or not. Diodorus, with the eyewitness account of Philistus before him, claims that it did: Thucydides suggests the reverse. But in any case there was no major break-out. If a few Athenian triremes cleared the gap, they were soon driven back again. The whole battle was fought and won inside the Great Harbour.

The Syracusans seem to have closed in on the Athenian fleet from three directions: the city walls, the beach towards Dascon, and the middle of the harbour. They thus drew off the majority of the vessels engaged in the attempt to force the boom: the Athenians backed water rapidly and wheeled about to face their attackers, and a whole series of separate engagements took place, with groups of triremes fighting it out all over the Great Harbour. Never before, as Thucydides says, had so many vessels fought together in so confined a space: nearly two hundred of them jammed in an area of less than two square miles.

A solid mass of vessels still lay tangled at the barrier, an inextricable mess of splintered masts and oars and trailing rigging, while hoplites fought grimly across their heaving decks, and the air was loud with whirring arrows, the dry racket of javelins, the smash and cheer as some fresh ship joined the pack and discharged its troops to join in the general mêlée. But the bulk of the fighting took place in more or less open water, where speed and manoeuvrability counted for a great deal. There was seldom enough room for the Athenians to employ their favourite technique, ramming amidships; and in any case their heavy, overloaded vessels left them at a severe disadvantage when dealing with triremes attacking from several quarters at once. Many of them—the nucleus of the original attack—still lay huddled together even after their retreat from the barrier, so that the Syracusans sailed round and round in clear water, driving them in until they began to foul each other.

The Athenians had also made a bad tactical error by cramming their vessels with archers and spearmen. These were, for the most part, men unaccustomed to fighting at sea. As Ariston the Corinthian said, with professional scorn, they "will not even find out how they are to throw their weapons from a sitting position."[7] The tossing and wallowing of the ships also made it extremely difficult to aim an arrow or a javelin with any real accuracy, since the points could so easily be deflected. The Syracusans preferred to bombard their opponents with stones, "which did equal damage at whatever angle they struck."

The hand-to-hand fighting throughout the harbour reached desperate heights of heroism. Collisions, often accidental, were frequent, as one ship crashed into another while trying to avoid a third, or was rammed itself while actually ramming an oppo-

[7] Why, it may be asked, should they thus handicap themselves even aboard ship? The answer is not very clear. Perhaps Ariston was referring to those who defended the lower oar-ports against attacks by small boats.

nent. A constant rain of spears, arrows, stones, and javelins sang through the air. Oarbanks snapped off like so many twigs, masts fell with a jarring crash, prow hit grindingly into prow. The sheer volume of sound alone must have been quite terrifying. Apart from the splintering crash as ships collided, there was the ubiquitous uproar of battle, the incoherent grunts and shouts of men locked in desperate combat, the sharp clatter of sword against shield. Boatswains blew their whistles and screamed orders which no one heard, or could obey if they did. Cheers and groans from the spectators ashore blended with the shrieks of dying men, on the decks or in the water. Limbs thrashed and contorted, the sea was churned into a bloody froth. Often a ship would go down taking its entire complement with it.

Sometimes the hides on the prows of the Syracusan vessels saved them from the Athenian grappling-irons; sometimes they did not, and the two triremes would roll in the swell, locked together, while their marines fought out a land action afloat. Some men sprang on to the deck of an enemy vessel as their own boat sank, were cut off, and died fighting. Others, more fortunate or more skilful swordsmen, beat back the enemy crew, either killing them or pushing them overboard, and took over their trireme themselves.

Those ashore were in an agony of suspense, cheering or groaning at each individual victory and defeat, more worked up, if it were possible, than those actually taking part in the engagement. Some, Thucydides says, "were looking at some part of the battle where there was nothing to choose between the two sides, and, as the fight went on and on with no decision reached, their bodies, swaying this way and that, showed the trepidation with which their minds were filled." Sometimes a Syracusan trireme was destroyed under the very walls of the city, and parents or wives would see their sons and husbands butchered before their eyes.

Yet it was here, under Ortygia, that the Athenians first cracked. To the cheers of the crowd on the walls, and desperate encouragement—slowly turning to angry curses—from their own friends ashore, they were forced back and back, till finally, all order gone, they put about, and fled headlong for the stockade. Then the next ships in line, their flank now exposed, also began to back off, and in a moment the whole Athenian formation crumpled and broke, each trireme running ashore where it could, the crew leaping out and making for the shelter of the camp.

The Syracusans pursued them with great shouting and cheering, hauling off their abandoned triremes, pouring a hail of arrows and javelins into the survivors as they scrambled through the shallows. Gylippus and his infantry detachments cut off the stragglers, or skirmished with the Athenian troops who came down to help their friends. The Great Harbour was thick with wreckage and floating bodies. Sixty Athenian triremes had been destroyed or captured. Syracuse had lost no more than eight vessels sunk outright, and sixteen badly damaged. It was the end of all Athens' hopes. Nothing remained now but ignominious retreat.

CHAPTER XVIII: *The Last Retreat*

The camp by the stockade was a scene of hideous and demoralised hysteria. While the victorious Syracusans removed
their wrecks and their dead, and were welcomed home by the
cheers of the entire city, those Athenians who had survived
thronged round the generals' tents, clamouring to be led away
overland, now, that very night. They made no attempt—an event
without parallel in the whole war, and one which eloquently
demonstrates their condition—to take up their own dead under
truce. They left them to rot where they lay, or to drift with
the wind, amid broken spars and cordage, on the blood-red surface of the Great Harbour. What had been a proud expeditionary force was now a mere panic-stricken mob.

Demosthenes went to Nicias privately, and urged him to hold
on. He pointed out that the Athenians still possessed something
like sixty ships, whereas Syracuse, even with her light losses,
now had under fifty. The barrier was either breached or, at the
very least, severely damaged. If they delivered a surprise attack
at dawn they might still force their way out. Nicias fell in with
this proposal;[1] but when they put it before the troops they met
with a flat refusal. "The sailors," says Thucydides, "would not
go on board, being so demoralised by their defeat that they no
longer regarded victory as a possibility." Faced with this im-
passe, Nicias and Demosthenes had no option but to agree to
an overland retreat. They decided to march that same night,
under cover of darkness, and the men at once set about striking
camp and gathering their belongings together. They also burnt
some of the ships—a stupid mistake, since it merely advertised
their intentions to the enemy. But Syracuse, from a comparatively early hour, had been a scene of triumph and feasting

[1] Diodorus (13.18.2) says that he was in favour of an overland retreat
from the start.

and celebration, with wine flowing in rivers, and hymns of thanksgiving to Heracles for bringing the city this great and unprecedented victory.

It would have taken stronger men than the Syracusans to keep grimly sober in this moment of high triumph and deliverance. At long last the shadow of enslavement had passed from them. They had fought like giants, and now they would take their ease like gods. We can scarcely blame them. But two men in Syracuse kept their wits about them on that fateful night: Gylippus and Hermocrates. Both realised that the Athenians were almost sure to attempt a break-out during the night. They therefore went to the authorities—appointees, one remembers, of the ultra-democrats (see above, pp. 206-7 ff.)—and proposed that the entire Syracusan army should march out, as soon as possible, to set up road-blocks and occupy all the passes. It would, they said, be a very serious thing if so large a force was allowed to escape to some other part of Sicily, and to keep up their campaign against Syracuse from a new base.

The magistrates saw the force of this argument. In theory, they said, they completely agreed with the proposal put forward. But it might prove a little difficult to persuade the rank and file to obey orders just now. They were relaxing after their splendid naval victory. They were all exhausted, and many of them, perhaps the greater number, had more or less serious wounds. They were holding the festival of Heracles, and, to be quite blunt, by now most of them were very drunk indeed. The last thing anyone could make them do at present was march out and build road-blocks in the dark. The magistrates were apologetic, but firm.

At this point Gylippus seems to have abandoned the project. Plutarch offers us a brief glimpse of him later on that evening, a dour figure amid all the jollity, moodily watching while the Syracusans swilled and sacrificed. His Spartan sense of discipline, it seems, was outraged by the knowledge that he "could neither compel nor persuade them to cut short their festivities and attack the Athenians as they withdrew." Hermocrates, on the other hand, did not give up so easily. He summoned some of his trusted young aristocratic friends, members of the élite cavalry corps. Ride down to Nicias' camp as soon as it gets dark, he told them. Pass yourselves off as friends of his, men from Leontini.[2] Tell him not to withdraw tonight—say the Syracusans have set ambushes for him, that all the roads and passes are guarded. Tell him to organise the retreat in his own time, without hurrying, and with ample preparation. Say he should march out by daylight, when he can see what he's doing and will have adequate warning of any attack.

It was a fairly transparent ruse, the best that Hermocrates could think up at short notice; and perhaps he was as surprised as anyone when the Athenians fell for it. Here, after all, was a group of unidentified horsemen who appeared outside the camp for a brief moment, delivered a most implausible message, and vanished into the night again. Did no one think to challenge their *bona fides?* The Athenians did not detain them, or even ask for their credentials. They did not—the obvious course— send out scouts to find if the story was, in fact, true. From their camp they could clearly hear sounds of revelry going on inside the victorious city, but not even then did they stop to ask themselves if it was likely that the roads had really been blocked. They swallowed every word of what they had been told; with guileless credulity they put off the retreat until another day. Then, worn-out by their sufferings, they fell asleep. If they had marched that night as planned, they would have got clean away.

The following morning, despite their junketings, the Syracusans were up and about at first light. What had been an outrageous bluff was rapidly converted into sober truth. Cavalry

[2] These must have been the landowners who were invited to take up Syracusan citizenship in 423 (Thucydides, 5.4.4), some of whom afterwards seceded (see above, p. 79), on the grounds that they did not receive their proper dues in Syracuse. Such men would be natural recruits for the ultra-democrats. According to Plutarch, Hermocrates' friends "pretended that they came from the party inside Syracuse with which Nicias had long been in secret correspondence." The episode suggests that Hermocrates knew a great deal—more than we might otherwise have assumed—about Nicias' collusionist activities.

and infantry hastened out into the surrounding countryside, crapulous but full of purposeful energy. While the cavalry patrolled all open areas, the infantry posted guard detachments by fords and other river crossings, broke down the bridges, built barricades on every road the Athenians were likely to take, and sent special detachments to seize the nearby passes and defiles. While all this was going on, naval patrols sailed up alongside the Athenian stockade, and towed away the fifty or more triremes that still lay abandoned on the foreshore. No one from the camp made the slightest effort to stop them. There was also the matter of the Athenian dead. Perhaps five thousand unclaimed corpses lay there on the strand or floated among the shallows, with kites and vultures already fighting over them. If Nicias would not honour his debt to the fallen, those who had slain them must do so, and without delay. Corruption was swift; September brought diseases enough already without adding plague to them.

How did they dispose of these bodies? In 1890 Paolo Orsi, the great Italian archaeologist, was excavating on Plemmyrium, and found the whole promontory honeycombed with primitive Sicel rock-tombs. Many of these tombs had been forced open, and filled with dozens of bodies thrust in pell-mell—mass graves with scarcely a sign of formal burial. The stone slabs had been replaced, and the tombs covered up again. It was here, on Plemmyrium, above the Great Harbour, where they fought that last desperate battle, that the Athenian dead found their anonymous resting place.

All that day and the following night the Athenians lay up and rested, to recover from their ordeal as best they could before setting out on what promised to be a harsh and hazardous retreat. They knew, now, how they had been duped; they knew that in order to survive they would have to fight their way across every river-bed and mountain pass, constantly harassed by cavalry patrols, pursued and sniped at every inch of the way. But there was no other course open to them except abject surrender. On the morning of the third day, September 11, they were ready to move. The whole force numbered some forty thousand men, of whom about half were non-combatants and civilians.[8] They were drawn up in two elongated hollow squares, under the command of Nicias and Demosthenes. The fittest hoplites were stationed at the front and rear of the column, the pack-animals and the walking wounded in the centre. Hoplites and cavalry, contrary to general practice, carried their own packs and rations. Many of their servants were dead or had deserted, and they did not trust those who remained. In any case there was little enough food to carry.

It was a terrible scene: one from which almost every shred of human dignity had been stripped away. These bandaged and bloody scarecrows were a far cry from the proud conquistadors who had sailed from Piraeus on a summer morning three years before, shields and armour newly burnished, trumpets blaring as the sails filled and they moved out in open formation, hull down for Aegina, spray flying in the wind, gilded figureheads dipping proudly in the chop and cross-waves of the Saronic Gulf. All lost now, the dream and the glory, the lure of the West that had drawn them and broken them and left them to slow death among the Sicilian ravines. They stood silent, in shame and dishonour, not meeting each other's eyes, waiting for the command to march. The dead lay sprawled and stiff, chapfallen, dust on their blank, accusing eyes. But worse than the eyes of the dead were the hoarse prayers and lamentations of the living: the wounded and limbless who crawled or hobbled down the ranks, seeking friends, comrades, tent-companions, officers, any to whom they could voice their heart-rending appeal: *Don't leave us. Take us with you. Take us away from this place.* Some were too weak to move, some groaned in delirium, or howled like mad dogs.

[8] The total figure is Thucydides' estimate. A fighting strength of over forty thousand at the time of Demosthenes' arrival had been halved by casualties and disease. The minimum non-combatant figure when the relief force reached Syracuse was some 29,000. Since *their* losses were due almost entirely to disease, they were proportionately much less— but nine thousand is still a shockingly high figure.

Nicias stood at the head of the column, yellow, emaciated, yet somehow suggesting greater reserves of power and endurance than the strongest man there. Some individuals need defeat in order to find their full moral stature, and Nicias was surely one of them. "It was clear to all," Plutarch wrote, "that he persisted in his duty not in his own interests, nor because he clung to life, but because for the sake of the men under his command he refused to give up hope." He never complained. "No man strove harder, by his tone of voice, his expression, and his bearing to show himself superior to his misfortunes." That is a high tribute indeed. Forgetting his own plight, he walked up and down the ranks, cheering and encouraging his men, holding out what hope he could for the future. The gods had taken sufficient toll of them by now, he said. "Other men before us have attacked their neighbours, and, after doing what men will do, have suffered no more than what men can bear." They still had plenty of fine infantrymen among them. There would be help from the Sicels along the way.

Nicias raised his voice louder and louder as he reached his peroration, perhaps to shut out the appalling clamour of the sick and dying who were being left behind. "Let this one thought be in the mind of every man among you," he cried, "that on whatever spot of ground he is forced to fight, there, if he wins it, he will find a country and a fortress . . . It is men who make the city, and not walls or ships with no men inside them." (This last aphorism was at least as old as Alcaeus, the sixth-century lyric poet from Lesbos; but it had a good rhetorical ring about it, perhaps all the more comforting through long familiarity.) It is curious, and rather endearing, that in this moment of extreme emotion he did not lose his fussy, old-maidish preoccupation with tidiness and detail. While he was addressing the troops he could not help observing the way their ranks were dressed, "and wherever he saw that they were not in close formation or were out of order, he brought them together and set them in their correct positions."

Then, at last, he gave the order to march.

The retreating army's destination—almost inevitably—was Catana.[4] To get there they had to choose a route where it would be hard for the Syracusans to pursue them, and in particular where they could avoid the attentions of the terrible Cossack-like Syracusan cavalry. This is pecisely what Nicias and Demosthenes attempted to do. They had a hard task. The Syracusans armed all the crews of their triremes to help hunt down and destroy the enemy column. "For three days," says Diodorus, "following close on their heels and encompassing them on all sides they prevented them from taking a direct route towards Catana, their ally." That statement, probably based on the account given by Philistus, could hardly be more specific. It is also, I believe, quite true. The discrepancies which historians profess to find between this version of events and that given by Thucydides turn out, on close examination, to be more apparent than real.

On the first day the Athenians marched westward from their camp, more or less along the line of the modern road to Floridia. They reached the Anapus River at a point just under four miles from Syracuse, the site of the present Capocorso bridge. Here they found a detachment of Syracusan and allied troops awaiting them. They attacked and routed this force, and then pushed on slowly through open country. The Syracusan cavalry made endless attacks on their flanks, while light-armed troops harassed them with arrows and javelins. In the end they halted after proceeding less than another mile, and made their camp on a little hill, between the road and the Massa Artiglieria. The next morning they set off early, marched another two miles, and, says Thucydides, "descended to some level ground." Here they camped again, and went foraging. The area was inhabited, and water was plentiful. The commissariat parties went round collecting food from various houses. We do not hear of its being

[4] We could have deduced this even if Diodorus (13.18.6) had not stated so categorically. I only emphasise the point here because almost all modern scholars take it for granted that their destination was some unidentified Sicel stronghold lying more towards the west. I shall return to this point later (see below, pp. 323–24).

paid for. The water-containers were all filled, "as for many furlongs in front of them, in the direction which they intended to take, the supply of water was not plentiful."

Meanwhile the Syracusans had gone on ahead of them, and fortified the pass which they were clearly planning to negotiate. Thucydides describes this as "a steep hill with a rocky defile at each side of it." It was known as the Acraean Heights, and its identification provides an interesting problem in ancient topography. Acrae itself, the modern Acremonte, near Palazzuolo, lies about twenty miles due west of Syracuse. Scholars have generally assumed (a) that the Athenians, *from the very beginning of their march*, were making for the general area of Acrae; (b) that the Sicels whom they contacted when they changed their plans had, similarly, been their liaison target *ab initio*; and (c) that the Acraean Heights must be sought in the vicinity of Acrae itself, or along the direct route thither. These three propositions are, of course, interdependent.[5]

The pass which the Syracusans fortified is therefore traditionally assumed to have been the modern Cava Spampinato or Calatrelli, a mile or so west of Floridia. But there is something very amiss with this identification, hallowed though it has become over the years.[6] There is no open level ground close to the Cava Spampinato, much less a plentiful supply of water (as I found to my cost when exploring it in midwinter). There is no

[5] One of the few scholars to concede that the Athenians were making for Catana is Freeman (p. 701). However, as he places the Acraean Heights on the route to Acrae, he is led to remark, with understandable puzzlement, that the Athenians seem to have chosen a roundabout way of reaching their destination.

[6] Dover, the latest commentator, seems aware of the difficulties (see *Thucydides* VII, pp. 66–67); he knows, for instance, that Syracusan cavalry could not possibly operate anywhere near the Cava Spampinato, and opts for a route slightly further south, through the Contrada Raiana. He admits, however, that this "suits Thucydides' description of the Syracusan tactics better but his description of the ground less well." He also confuses the Cava Calatrelli with the nearby (but very different) Cava Culatrello Cirino, which perhaps handicapped him somewhat in forming a judgment.

terrain suitable for cavalry operations. There is a long, shallow, winding gorge, but this is anything but steep. Most important of all, there is nothing here which even remotely resembles Thucydides' description of the Acraean Heights.

Suppose, however, that the Athenians were not making for Acrae at all, but for Catana, as Diodorus[7] says they were. Suppose, too, that the Acraean Heights had *no* immediate geographical connection with Acrae, but—as that redoubtable topographer Colonel Leake assumed—lay "in a north-westerly direction, and not more than ten or eleven miles distant from Syracuse." Where, then, would we look for them? The answer is never in doubt. As we scan the north-western horizon, whether from the coastal plain or the heights of Epipolae, one feature of the landscape instantly rivets the eye. Nicias and Demosthenes, while pondering over their escape-route, must have been acutely conscious of it. This is the great white limestone massif known as Monte Climiti, a formation not unlike Epipolae in type, but on a far grander and more impressive scale: a vast plateau tapering to a high cliff-face some eight miles north-west of Syracuse. At its south-west corner there are two great ravines, the larger and more centrally placed being known as the Cava Castelluccio. Immediately below these cliffs the Anapus River pursues its leisurely way; the land around it broadens out at this point into a flat, lush, roughly triangular plain, with lower hills rising on all sides of it.

A two-mile march from the site of Nicias' previous camp takes one into the centre of this little valley. Here is the "level ground" to which the Athenian column descended. Here is the plentiful supply of water. And here, vast, lowering, are the Acraean Heights, with the pass which Nicias intended to force clearly visible, and the second ravine a little away to one side. At some period an earthquake has shaken down great quantities of rock half-way up the gorge, but it is still negotiable, and must

[7] And, in my submission, Thucydides: at 7.80.2 it is the *new* route they are taking which is "not in the direction of Catana [implying that the earlier one had been] but towards the other side of Sicily, to Camarina and Gela . . ."

once have been far easier of ascent: no more difficult, say, than the Samaria Gorge leading to Sphakiá, in the White Mountains of western Crete. Once one has reached the summit of the plateau, it becomes clear what Nicias intended to do. The old track is still there, winding away over the hills, till it eventually joins the road from Molilli to Sortino, and continues on its way, metalled now after a fashion, but still twisting and doubling back in hair-pins and *virages*, down into the valley between Monte Pancali and Monte Cassara, bringing the traveller— weary perhaps, but still in good shape—to the outskirts of Le- ontini. Leontini remained friendly to Athens (or at any rate was not overtly hostile, even in 413) and formed the regular stopping point between Syracuse and Catana.

This was a bold, even a desperate plan; but it was well worth trying. Once Nicias had forced the pass, and gained the summit of the Acraean Heights, he would have no more to fear from Syracusan cavalry until he reached Leontini. Indeed, it was very much a moot point how far the enemy would keep up the pur- suit at all in this wild and mountainous terrain, where the only inhabitants were Sicel tribesmen friendly to Athens, and water —another minor confirmation of Thucydides—singularly hard to come by.[8]

The next day—the third of the retreat—the Athenians set out towards the Cava Castelluccio. (We are not told on which side of the Anapus they pitched their camp; but the enemy made so much trouble for them that it looks as though they were held up at the ford.) The Syracusan cavalry, which had ample room to operate in these flat river-meadows, kept up constant charges on their flanks. Volleys of javelins rained in among them from the light-armed troops. After a long and exhausting struggle the Athenians gave up the attempt for that day and returned to their old camp-site. They could no longer forage for provisions, since "it was now impossible to leave the camp because of the enemy cavalry."

[8] I noted one natural spring at the summit of the Cava Castelluccio, but no other constant source of water until the junction with the Molilli–Sortino road.

Nicias, as we have seen, could be as mulish on occasion as he was vacillating in the ordinary way of things. He ought to have realised that his only real chance of forcing the Cava Castelluccio was to get there before his pursuers, and hold the pass with a rear-guard action while the bulk of his two columns made the ascent. But once Nicias got an *idée fixe* in his head it was singularly hard to dislodge it. On the fourth day, accordingly, he returned to the attack. This time his troops fought their way into the ravine itself—only to find (as they might have expected by now) that the Syracusans had built a rough wall across it from side to side, at the point where the gorge narrowed for the final ascent. Behind this wall the enemy infantry waited— "many shields deep," as Thucydides says. High on the rock-face to right and left perched Gylippus' archers and slingers. It was a sight to daunt the toughest troops on earth.

But the Athenians were fighting now for survival. The shocked mood of despair and collapse which followed the last battle in the Great Harbour had been replaced by a blind, irrational ferocity. They charged the wall. Javelins, arrows, sling-stones plummeted down on them from point-blank range: it was almost impossible to miss. A deep, bristling shield-wall barred their way. They were fighting uphill, in a narrow space where they could not deploy their full strength. After a long and fruitless struggle they retreated a little way, and rested. As they sat there, sweating and dispirited, there came a rumble of thunder, a few heavy drops of rain. The blue sky had suddenly clouded over. The Athenians grew even more depressed, "for they saw in all these events omens of their own destruction." It was mid-September, and the first autumn rains were due: those brief but torrential Mediterranean storms, monsoon-like in their intensity, which can, within half an hour, turn the driest desert into a flooded quagmire.[9] The old hands on the expedition must have scanned

[9] In Greece this phenomenon is known as the *protovróchia*. I have seen it produce a torrent of water at least two feet deep down the steep stepped street on the side of Mt. Lycabettus, in Athens, where I live, and—on another occasion—float a motor-coach off the ground and across the road.

the sky anxiously at this premonitory sign. Another three or four days at most, and the floods would come, wiping out tracks, filling each dry, stony stream-bed with a roaring, brown, turbulent spate of water, making movement across country almost impossible.

While the Athenians rested, Gylippus brought up a working party to the foot of the Acraean Heights, with the ingenious idea of cutting off Nicias' retreat by means of a second rampart or wall. But the Athenian rear-guard saw what was being done, and took strong counter-measures. After this the entire column moved back into the plain and bivouacked for the night.

Nicias and Demosthenes were now convinced that it was impossible, as things stood, to force an ascent up the Cava Castelluccio. They therefore decided to advance up the line of the Anapus, in a north-westerly direction, with the Monte Climiti escarpment on their right flank.[10] This was a logical move in the circumstances. They were still advancing in the same direction, and though the ground between the Anapus and the cliffs was dangerously flat and exposed, there was always the chance of their finding a new way up to the plateau that the Syracusans missed.

On the morning of the fifth day since the retreat had begun (September 15) they struck camp and began their march once more, through the river-meadows known today as the Massa Puliga. The Syracusans, realising what their aim was, attacked in full force, never letting up, but never standing firm when the Athenians attempted to charge them. The cavalry swooped down again and again, thundering across the open flats beside the river. Gylippus concentrated especially on the rear-guard, to see if he could cut off any lagging detachments, and thus

[10] Those who place the Acraean Heights somewhere up the Cava Spampinato—e.g., by the Massa Monasterella—make very heavy weather of this move; they are forced to assume that the Athenians turned *south* in order to by-pass the gorge. Anyone who could get an army across country from north to south through the Contrada Raiana must have been a genius of the first order.

"cause a panic throughout the whole army."[11] Despite all his efforts the Athenians moved on, slowly and doggedly. Many of them were wounded by spear or arrow; all were exhausted, from shortage of food and these repeated, futile charges they made against a too elusive enemy. Finally, after advancing little more than half a mile, they called a halt and rested. The Syracusans seem to have been flagging by now, too; at all events they called off the attack and withdrew to their own camp.

That night Nicias and Demosthenes held an emergency conference. It was quite clearly impossible to go on. The route they were following left them exposed to attack on all sides; nor did it offer any immediate prospect of obtaining fresh provisions, which they desperately needed. Somehow this crippling pursuit had to be shaken off. They therefore planned to march secretly back to the coast during the night, and then backtrack inland along the line of the Cacyparis (Cassibile) River. A messenger was sent off across country under cover of darkness—travelling, probably, by the old road between Solarino and Palazzuolo—to warn the local Sicels of what was happening, and to arrange a rendezvous somewhere on the upper reaches of the Cacyparis. With this escort, the Athenian army, or what was left of it, could make another attempt to reach Leontini, perhaps over the mountains from Buccheri. Another possible solution was to march inland as far as Enna, recuperate there, and then return to Catana by a good road and through friendly territory: Agyrium, Centuripae.

Throughout the camp, fires were banked up with plenty of fuel, to convince the Syracusans that their quarry was still *in situ*—an old device, but a surprisingly effective one. Then the entire force set out, in two main columns as before, with that of Nicias leading. During the night the two groups became

[11] What, it may be asked, was the *Athenian* cavalry doing all this while? Singularly little, it would seem. We know the cavalry accompanied the retreat, since they got away afterwards (see below, p. 337); but they seem to have provided scant protection against Gylippus' hit-and-run tactics.

separated: Nicias kept his men in better order, and set the standard marching pace, so that the rear-guard under Demosthenes lost contact with them. It looks, too, as though Demosthenes had been saddled with the worst troops and the walking wounded.[12] His men lagged far behind the advance column, and, as Thucydides says, "marched in some disorder." The line of their retreat must have run from the Anapus to Taverna and Floridia, and then more or less along the existing road as far as the little town of Cassibile. Here, instead of branching off at once in the direction of the river, as the modern highway does, the ancient route continued towards the coast, where it joined the Helorus road close to the little bay now known as Porto Gerbo, about a mile and a half from the Cassibile river-crossing. This exactly accords with Thucydides' description.

The distance from the Athenians' last camp by Monte Climiti to the junction with the Helorus road is just about twelve miles. Thucydides makes it clear that Demosthenes' rear-guard, despite its confusion during the night march, managed to reach the coast by dawn—that is, about 5 A.M. If we allow an average marching speed for the rear-guard of two mph, with ten-minute breaks each hour, this places the time of departure from Monte Climiti at about 10 P.M., and Demosthenes' arrival at the Cacyparis shortly before 6 A.M. Nicias, on the other hand, if he marched his troops at a steady three mph, could have reached the Cacyparis at any time after three o'clock in the morning. His plan, clearly, was to attack the Syracusans guarding the ford while it was still dark, and eliminate them before advancing up-river. As it was, he had to wait until Demosthenes caught up with him, which not only precluded any hope of surprise, but gave the Syracusans a few valuable hours in which to block his route.

When dawn broke, and the two halves of the army were once more united, they marched on to the Cacyparis and found it, as Nicias had feared, strongly guarded. They forced

[12] Thucydides (7.80.4) says that the rear-guard numbered "half or more of the whole," which would seem to confirm this.

the passage of the ford, and routed the troops sent to hold it against them. But their advance scouts now reported a further obstacle. Some two miles upstream, where the Cacyparis enters the rocky gorge known as the Cava Grande, the Syracusans were busy barricading the gorge itself, driving piles into the stream-bed to form a stockade, and walling off the passage on either side.[13]

Nicias had no intention of facing another obstacle of this sort after his disastrous attempt to force the Cava Castelluccio. His local guides told him that he could obtain his objective equally well by marching on to the next large river, the Erineus, and turning inland there instead. The route would be harder going, but still viable. Nicias agreed to this suggestion. One thing, however, which he saw very clearly was that he must not, this time, let himself be anticipated by a Syracusan defence force. He had to reach the upper gorges of the Erineus before any ingenious group of sappers could put a wall and stockade up to block this line of retreat as well. Time was vital. Nicias had no intention of being out-manoeuvred yet again as a result of sitting down to wait for the rear-guard to catch up with him. He therefore decided to press on at full speed. If he established himself on the Erineus, he could hold the way open for Demosthenes. Demosthenes in return could prevent the Syracusans by-passing his column along the direct route, and if need be fight a rear-guard action to hold them off. The two columns now separated. Some soldier who feared the outcome of the retreat seems to have buried his cash for safety before leaving: a hoard of this period found near the Cacyparis contains fourteen Athenian tetra-

[13] This seems the only reasonable interpretation of Thucydides, 7.80.6–7, an otherwise puzzling passage. A wall-and-stockade complex is clearly intended to be built *across the river*. Such a device is useless in open country, and doubly so at a ford-crossing, which lies at right angles to the stream. The mouth of the Cava Grande is the obvious place to block any anticipated march up-river, and a wall and stockade the perfect way to do so. This also explains Nicias' change of plan. Otherwise, having defeated the guard at the ford, why did he not proceed as arranged?

drachms, eight Syracusan coins, plus one or two from Rhegium, Catana, Gela, and Leontini.

Meanwhile the main Syracusan pursuit force, encamped below Monte Climiti, had awoken at dawn to find the Athenians gone. They lost a good deal of time in footling recriminations against Gylippus, whom they accused—interestingly—of having allowed Nicias to escape. But once they had struck camp and sent out scouts it was not difficult to find out which route the Athenian forces had taken, and they hurried off in pursuit, leaving Monte Climiti by 7: 30 or 8 A.M. at the latest.

Now by noon, Thucydides says, Nicias was about fifty stades ahead of Demosthenes: that is, just over six miles. His march for the day took him to the Erineus River, which he crossed, and then encamped on high ground a little beyond it. This at once reveals the much-debated identity of the Erineus: it is, and can only be, the Fiume di Noto, or Falconara, which intersects the old road almost exactly ten kilometres (6+ miles) from the modern Cassibile bridge. The high ground where Nicias made his camp for the night is equally unmistakable: a large, gently sloping knoll about one kilometre from the Fiume di Noto ford, just short of the road to Calabernardo. His total day's march from the Cacyparis, then, was eleven kilometres, or almost exactly seven miles.[14]

The Syracusans who had set out that morning from Monte Climiti caught up with Demosthenes about noon. If they struck camp at 7: 30 A.M. and marched without breaks, at an average three mph, they would by midday have covered some

[14] I must apologise here for challenging yet another hallowed tradition, since virtually all historians take it for granted that the Fiume di Noto is the Assinarus, a view now sanctioned by the ordnance survey map of the Istituto geogràfico militare. But to make this equation they are obliged to resuscitate minute and virtually non-existent watercourses such as the Cavallata, visible only to the eye of faith; more important, they must tacitly ignore the distances as recorded by Thucydides. My views are substantially those of Leake (pp. 87–88) and Ettore Pais *Italia antica* (pp. 218 ff.: see Bibliography). Pais made a habit of checking all local names with the peasants, *"ben sapendo quanto pòco ci sia da fidarsi, per la parte toponomastica, delle carte dello Stato Maggiore italiano"* (p. 225).

fourteen miles, and have reached a point rather less than a mile beyond the Cacyparis. If Nicias was at that time 6+ miles ahead of Demosthenes, he must have already crossed the Erineus, and established himself on the knoll where he bivouacked that night—a perfectly feasible supposition. The distance was only seven miles; he could have marched it in under three hours without the slightest trouble.

There remains the problem of why Demosthenes, at noon, was still less than a mile beyond the Cacyparis crossing. The answer seems clear enough: by the time Nicias had moved on ahead, the Syracusan forces guarding the entrance to the Cava Grande (probably reinforced by cavalry patrols) had realised what was happening, and promptly marched out in pursuit. Demosthenes first of all fought a delaying action against them, and then set off along the road Nicias had taken. But the progress of the rear-guard was reduced to a snail's pace by constant pressure from the Syracusan cavalry and light-armed troops: we have already seen, on several occasions, just how effective this technique could be.

When Demosthenes saw the main pursuit force approaching, he formed up in battle order to make a last stand. But he took a little too long redeploying his exhausted troops, and the enemy had time to surround him. He took up his position in a large walled olive grove, which stood in the angle between two roads, and was known as the "estate of Polyzelus."[15] There is just such an olive grove, in just such a position, about one kilometre beyond the Cacyparis, near the Contrada Gallina; if the "estate of Polyzelus" was not here, it must have been somewhere close by.

Hour after hour, all through that long September afternoon,

[15] Polyzelus was the brother of Gelon, tyrant of Syracuse; when Gelon died in 478–477 he left a potentially explosive situation by bequeathing his power and sovereignty to Hieron, his other brother, but entailing his widow Demarete (Theron's daughter) to Polyzelus. Hieron tried, unsuccessfully, to get rid of Polyzelus by sending him into the forefront of the battle, like Uriah the Hittite. Eventually a reconciliation took place between the brothers, and Polyzelus returned to Syracuse, where he died.

the Syracusans kept up a deadly fusillade of missiles against Demosthenes' position. They had no intention of engaging in hand-to-hand combat with such desperate men. The siege was over: why should they risk their lives in the moment of victory? The sun moved slowly down the sky; the shadows lengthened; and still there came that deadly, unpredictable *zip* as arrow or sling-stone flashed down between the olive trees, and, all too often, found its mark.

When Gylippus and the Syracusan commanders judged that their victims were at breaking point, they issued a proclamation through a herald. If any of the "islanders"—that is, Athens' subject-allies—would come over to them, their lives and liberty would be guaranteed; "and," says Thucydides, "a few cities did so." Afterwards, terms of surrender were offered to the remainder. If they laid down their arms, they would be guaranteed immunity from summary execution, death by starvation, and life-imprisonment. (We shall see in due course how well these guarantees were honoured.) Demosthenes thereupon surrendered on behalf of his men. But he did not intend to be led captive himself. As Gylippus and the Syracusans approached, he made an attempt to commit suicide by falling on his sword. But a group of enemy officers "quickly surrounded and seized him before he could kill himself." The victor of Pylos was a prisoner now; what thoughts went on in his mind, and that of the Spartan Gylippus, as they stood, at last, face to face?

Of over twenty thousand who had set out with Demosthenes on that nightmarish retreat, not more than six thousand survived to take advantage of Gylippus' offer. This sadly reduced body was now drawn up in column of route, under escort, for the journey back to Syracuse. As they passed a certain point, each man was required to throw all the money he possessed into an upturned shield by the roadside. Four shields were filled to the brim in this way. Syracuse might have triumphed over her enemies; but she was still in dire need of negotiable currency.

The Syracusan cavalry caught up with Nicias early next morning, as he was striking camp. They told him Demosthenes and the rear-guard had surrendered, and suggested that he follow their example. But Nicias had already been tricked once by a bogus message from the enemy camp, only a week before, and with catastrophic results. He refused to believe this story without demonstrable proof. A truce was therefore arranged, and Nicias sent off a herald with the Syracusans, escorted by an Athenian cavalry detachment, to see if there could possibly be any truth in what they said. The party set off at a gallop on the sixteen-mile journey to Syracuse. Nicias' herald was back before noon, visibly shaken, with the news that Demosthenes had indeed surrendered, and all his men with him.

Nicias then made his last appeal to Gylippus. He asked for an armistice, and permission to withdraw his troops from Sicily under safe-conduct. In return for this, he would make an agreement with Gylippus, in the name of the Athenian people, to reimburse Syracuse for all expenses the city had incurred as a direct result of the war. Until this debt was discharged, he offered to leave hostages with Gylippus, in the proportion of one man to each talent owed.

This offer Gylippus and the Syracusans treated with angry contempt. They had no intention of letting their prey go now, however tempting the bribe. The moment Nicias' herald returned to the Athenian lines, and the truce was over, the Syracusans hemmed them in from all sides, and proceeded to give them the same treatment as they had dispensed to Demosthenes. They did not attempt a direct infantry assault, but wore down their opponents' nerves—and numbers—by a constant battering hail of stones, darts, arrows, and javelins. This ordeal continued until evening.

But Nicias' men proved tougher than their unfortunate

comrades of the rear-guard. They withstood this fusillade without any thought of surrender, though by now they were half-starved and suffering acutely from thirst. It was the end of a long summer, and the Erineus was dry, or nearly so. This may have been one reason why Nicias abandoned his plan for striking inland. The Tellaro, the next river to the south, runs dry less often than the Fiume di Noto, and his guides probably informed him that he would find water there. Nicias decided to attempt a break-out, as before, under cover of darkness. He probably buried part of the military chest before leaving: Orsi records a cache of two thousand silver pieces discovered here, and connects this exceptionally large hoard with the Athenians' final retreat. Two other hoards from the Fiume di Noto area, containing Athenian coins and Persian gold darics, as well as local currencies, may represent private fortunes similarly buried during the final stages of the march.[1]

At some time during the night, then, Nicias struck camp and prepared to move off. But the Syracusans, who were encamped all around, heard suspicious sounds of activity from the enemy lines, and promptly stood to arms, singing their battle hymn. The Athenians stayed where they were—all except a body of three hundred men, who broke through the cordon and vanished into the night; they were subsequently rounded up by Syracusan cavalry patrols.

Dawn broke heavy and clouded. Nicias' men awoke parched with thirst, eyelids gummed together, tongues rough and dry. Thunder muttered on the horizon, but still the rain did not come. Slowly and wearily they formed up and set out once more, huddled behind their shields, the Syracusans pressing them hard the whole time, "showering missiles and hurling javelins in upon them from every side." Their immediate objective was the next river, the Assinarus (Tellaro),[2] just over

---

[1] Orsi, pp. 345–47; Jongkees, p. 42; Noe, 2d ed., nos. 109, 110. (See Bibliography.)

[2] For the identification see especially Leake, pp. 87–88, and Pais, *Italia antica* pp. 217–25, who points out that local peasants from Noto call the Tellaro the Atiddaru, a very possible corruption from Assinarus. But the whole problem—in particular that of rivers with two or even three names, e.g., Helorus-Assinarus—is too complex to discuss here.

three miles further on. All the way the Syracusans kept up their unremitting attacks, using cavalry, infantry, and light-armed troops indiscriminately, goading and tormenting the exhausted Athenians as picadors will goad a bull. Then, when they came within sight of the river, Nicias and his men saw that both bridge and ford were blocked by strong Syracusan forces.[3] Too weak to fight another action, almost past conscious thought now, held together only by ingrained discipline and the dogged will to survive, they turned inland—as perhaps they had always intended—following the line of the river, chivvied away from it by Syracusan cavalry patrols, burning with thirst, struggling on, more and more slowly now, the last reserves of their will almost exhausted. Clouds piled higher, spread across the brazen sky. The air was heavy and still.

It had become a horrible cat-and-mouse game, a slow attrition of the human spirit. Perhaps for three miles the column lurched forward. The Assinarus ran through a deep cut here, and its precious water seemed further away than ever. Then, close to the tiny modern hamlet of S. Paolo, the Athenians cracked. They forgot order and discipline, they forgot the Syracusans, they forgot everything save their torturing and insupportable thirst. The men at the head of the column broke ranks, and went scrambling down the river-bank in a blind, frenzied stampede. As they did so there came a peal of thunder from overhead, and the rain, too long delayed, came sluicing down in torrents.[4] A scene of unutterable chaos ensued. Hundreds of men were now crowded into the narrow cut, and more followed every moment. The Syracusans quickly brought up

[3] It is generally assumed that the final disaster took place as soon as the Athenians reached the Assinarus. The present account takes account of two factors which argue against this: (1) the Tellaro runs through flat country near the coast, but has steep and precipitous banks about three miles inland; (2) a possible burial-place recorded by Orsi lies precisely at the point where the banks are steepest. Both these points are discussed below in the text.

[4] The Erineus had been too dry to provide water, yet the Assinarus was in spate, and capable of sweeping men away. The only possible explanation of this is that the autumn rains broke just about the time of the disaster.

detachments along the far bank, and began to slaughter the hysterical mob in the river-bed, with every weapon they could lay hands on. Arrows and javelins discharged at point-blank range were reinforced by rocks picked up from the bank itself. The Athenians fought and clawed for space, trampling each other underfoot, gulping greedily at the fouled and bloody water. Syracusan cavalry patrols on the northern side of the river herded more of them over the edge like so many Gadarene swine. Some fell on their own spears, and were disembowelled. Some fought each other in their frenzy. Some, as the rain poured down and the river began to rise in spate, were swept away in a tangle of arms and baggage, often still struggling.

By now the stream-bed had been churned into a mess of blood and filth, and the dead lay piled in heaps, skewered with arrows, skulls egg-smashed by rocks, the torrent foaming round them in a horrible pinkish froth. Those few who struggled up the bank were cut down by Gylippus' waiting butchers, and most of those who fled across the fields rather than join the holocaust were soon rounded up by cavalry patrols. The Athenian expeditionary force had ceased to exist.

Nicias saw the horror in the Assinarus, and knew the end had come. It was more than a defeat; it was a defilement. There, mindless, brutish, and terrified, dying like animals, without dignity or pride, were Pericles' countrymen, citizens of the greatest imperial power Greece had ever known. In that moment of destruction by the Assinarus Athens lost her imperial pride forever. The shell of splendid self-confidence was shattered: something more than an army died in Sicily.

Then, at last, Nicias made his way to where Gylippus stood, wrapped in his blood-red cloak, and surrendered. He flung himself down at the Spartan's feet, begging him to stop this dreadful and bestial slaughter. He asked nothing for himself: Gylippus and the Spartans, he said, could do what they pleased with him. Gylippus was moved by this appeal; he remembered, too, how long and patiently Nicias had worked to bring about peace between their two countries. He raised the old man to his feet, and passed the word to his officers that the Athenians should be given quarter. The killing was to stop; all enemy troops who had survived were to be taken prisoner.

But this order was more easily given than enforced. It took a long while to pass on to every detachment, and was not immediately obeyed even when received. By then many more of Nicias' men had fallen. Even when Gylippus managed to get the blood-bath under control, the total count of prisoners secured by the state remained small, since large numbers of Athenians were carried off and concealed by individual captors. Diodorus states that 18,000 were killed at the Assinarus and seven thousand taken prisoner; but this second figure, as we know from Thucydides, includes the six thousand who had already surrendered with Demosthenes. The Assinarus death roll was almost certainly exaggerated by Syracusan field officers, partly to increase their kudos, partly to conceal the number of Athenians who had been made private prisoners;[5] but even so it was an immense slaughter, the greatest of its kind—not excluding the massacre on Melos—which we know to have taken place during the whole course of the Peloponnesian War. Survivors were few, and mostly from among the better-armed or more technically qualified troops: hoplites, cavalry, the trierarchs and steersmen of the fleet.

Perhaps a thousand hoplites, and nearly all the cavalry, smashed their way through the Syracusan lines and got to Catana, from which base they subsequently kept up continual raids against Syracusan territory. The cavalry commander, Callistratus, after shepherding this mixed force to safety, nevertheless felt that for himself, personally, a life preserved by fleeing the field in such circumstances was not worth living. So he rode back to Syracuse, alone, and made his way round by Euryalus until he reached the Athenians' abandoned camp. He found it being systematically stripped by Syracusan looters, and managed to kill five of them before he was finally overpowered.

[5] Diodorus is frequently blamed for this kind of numerical distortion; but Thucydides, too, was also accused, in antiquity, of consistently inflating Athenian losses.

The Syracusans herded their prisoners together along the river-bank, and set up two trophies, with the armour of Nicias and Demosthenes suspended from them. Nicias' shield, which bore an elaborate interwoven design of gold and purple, was afterwards removed to one of the temples in Syracuse, where it remained on display till Plutarch's time, five centuries later. All the tallest and finest trees beside the river were hung with the Athenians' captured weapons, their shields and helmets and corslets. The Syracusans crowned themselves with wreaths, decorated the trappings of their own horses, and cropped the manes and tails of any they had taken from the enemy. Then they set out on their slow but triumphal homeward procession. "They had," says Plutarch, "triumphed in the most brilliant campaign ever fought between Greeks, and by a prodigious display of courage and enterprise they had gained the most annihilating of victories."

When they were gone, an uneasy silence settled over the Assinarus, broken only by the clink and rattle of tree-hung weapons turning in the breeze, the *drip-drip-drip* from rain-sodden foliage, the low roar of the river. Presently the sun came out again, and the clouds passed away. Steam rose from the earth. Here and there a body with some lingering spark of life still in it twitched once, and lay motionless. Black dots circled against the light, grew in number, descended like obscene Furies. Soon the whole battlefield was a mass of kites and vultures, flapping and tearing and fighting over the pale bodies of the dead, in a hideous parody of the death-struggle which had so lately taken place there.

Where were these Athenian dead buried? Once again the question poses itself with some insistence. Buried they must have been; so many thousands of corpses, whether close to human habitation or not, would have caused an appalling pestilence if simply left to rot where they fell. Besides, such behaviour—as we have already noticed after the last battle in the Great Harbour—was basically repugnant to the Greek mind; and the Syracusans, we should never forget, were themselves colonial Greeks. With such a vast number of bodies to be disposed of, it is reasonable to assume that interment took place as near as possible to the scene of their slaughter. Now, the modern Tellaro's banks, as we have seen, form a steep and striking cut about three miles inland. Here, then, or hereabouts, is where we should look for the bodies of Nicias' comrades; and here, recorded in the long-forgotten back files of the Italian archaeological journal *Notizie degli Scavi*, is where the answer to this puzzle may conceivably be found.

In 1890–91 work was going forward for the construction of the Noto–Licata railway. This involved building a bridge across the Tellaro just by the hamlet of S. Paolo, opposite the cut. While the foundations for this bridge were being dug, the engineers came upon a number of Sicel rock-tombs, buried some seven metres under alluvial silt, their entrances covered by slabs. When Orsi examined the site, pottery in the tombs enabled him to date the last burials there to the closing decades of the fifth century. The tombs apparently formed part of a large necropolis, but owing to the immense deposit of silt above them were not properly excavated. What struck Orsi as odd was that no known historical site, Sicel or Greek, could be connected with this area. The nearest possibilities, Casmenae and Helorus, both lie some miles away. Orsi, like the vast bulk of his contemporaries, took it for granted that the Assinarus was to be identified with the Fiume di Noto. Perhaps this is why he never seems to have asked himself—even after his very similar discovery at Plemmyrium—just who, in the last years of the fifth century, would have been most likely to utilise an ancient, long-abandoned Sicel necropolis on the banks of the Tellaro River, and for what purpose.

One archaeological discovery links up with another. A few years ago workmen digging in Peristéri, a northern suburb of Athens, found some ancient slabs of marble that had been used to construct an early Christian sarcophagus. These slabs dated from the fifth century B.C., and were covered with lists of names. As the Greek scholar Mastrokostas has conclusively shown, they were originally memorial plaques, and formed part of a cenotaph to the Athenian citizen-hoplites who died during the Sicilian Expedition.

We know too little of the anonymous, uncelebrated heroes of history, the men who passed through great events, whose sweat and blood helped to shape the world we inherit, yet who died and were forgotten as though they had never been, leaving no memorial to posterity. Throughout this story we have been concerned, inevitably, with the men who were *not* forgotten, the politicians and commanders who took the decisions that others carried out. But now, for one brief moment, the curtain is lifted. Here, passing in silent order, like the names on any war memorial in any age, are the heavy-armed infantrymen who toiled and fought and died on the heights of Epipolae or during the long agony of that final retreat. 2,950 Athenians of hoplite rank fought in Sicily. Between 700 and 1,200 of them died in action. Of these casualties, 169 names, from fine tribal regiments, are preserved on the Peristéri stelae:

Of the Hippothontid regiment:

Philion	Pistias	Philetaerides
Isodemus	Philostratus	Philargus
Aeschines	Agasicles	Damasias
Leochares	Nicomachus	Nicon
Aeschylion	Demophanes	Polyeuches
Mnesibolus	Oenophilus	Lysonides
Menippus	Egemachus	

Alethus	Tharreleides
Telephanes	Phyromachus
Theomnestus	Euages
Theodorus	Lysimachus
Polites	Charigeiton
Aristophilus	Socrates

[Certain names of steersmen, regimental commanders, archer-captains, trierarchs, and *peripolarchoi*—roughly equivalent to National Guard officers—have been lost here: they were normally inscribed at the head of the list.]

Of the Aeantid regiment:

Eucleides [regimental commander]

Phayllus	Archidamus	Eucrates
Demochares	Diocles	Sophronius
Chaerephanes	Epitimides	Xenocrates
Cleocritus	Polycrates	Callias
Chariades	Himeraeus	Daesias [trierarch]
Pyelion	Demetrius	Phanias
Xenocles	Peisippus	Carpides
Phoryscus	Xenochares	Harmonides
Thoenilus	Egesias	Blepyrus
Antistates	Eucrates	Eutimides
Teisias	Sostratus	Ergotimus
Hagnodemus	Smicrus	

Isodicus [archer-captain]

Telesicrates	Manteiades
Lysidemus	Leostratus
Andron	Theorus
Sosippus	Callicles
Mnesibius	Demoteles
Callicles	Neaeus
Demotes	Lysinus
Diocles	Phanias
Nausistratus	Chaeredemus
Aeschylus	Anthemion
Thrasylochus	

Of the Antiochid regiment:

L[aches]	L-m--	Phil--
Callimachus	Oenopion	Poseidippus
Nicomachus	Euphiletus	Apollodorus
Hagnostratus	Agasicles	Epicrates
Epicles	---menes	----res
---odorus	Demagetus	Sophocles
Neocles	Demosthenes	Demodocus
Ergotimus	Nicasion	Philocedes

Pasiteles	Philodemus
Eulampides	Athenades
Lysidemus	Aristophanes
Proteas	Phrynus
S[ocr]ates	---lochus
Philomelus	Polymedes
Epichares	Aristeides
Phoryscus	Euthyphron

Of the Leontid and Acamantid regiments:

Eumelus	Chariades	Hierocleides
Philochares	Philocleides	Theopompus
Phileas	Telesias	Aleximachus
Lysicles	Epicharinus	Nicoteles
Hierocles	[C]ephisidorus	Leand[r]us

Glaucippus	Charicles
Leucippus	Poseidippus
Aeschines	Alcaeus
Ecphantus	Eraton
Phrynichus[6]	

[6] Such a list as this shows up, all too clearly, the limitations of our historical knowledge, and the danger of speculating too boldly on the identity of A[1] (literary source) and A[2] (inscription) simply because they both happen to be called A. (If both can be shown to belong to the same tribe or deme, the chances of identity are greatly increased in probability.) Even in the fragments which survive, duplications of name are quite common. It scarcely needs saying that the Aeschines and

These were the men who sailed to Sicily with high hope of glory and gain in their hearts, who were determined to win for Athens the wheat and timber she so desperately needed, and safeguard the livelihood of the wives and children and mistresses and parents they left behind them. These were the men who fought and marched and bivouacked from Catana to Syracuse, from Syracuse to that last scene of carnage by the banks of the Assinarus. Many of them, I believe, lie to this day no more than a stone's throw from the scene of their destruction, seven yards deep beneath the S. Paolo bridge, among the quiet fields where now no trumpet blows, no marching feet are heard. *Requiescant.*[7]

When the Syracusans returned home after their victory, the whole city, we are told, offered sacrifice to the gods in gratitude for this deliverance. It is like Shakespeare's King Henry after Agincourt: "Let there be sung *Non nobis* and *Te Deum.*" Various special victory issues of coins were struck, including one which showed Syracuse's tutelary nymph Arethusa triumphant over Athena Parthenos, wearing the latter's triple-crested helmet and—supreme insult—the terrible Gorgon from her aegis. Other cities followed suit: Selinus produced a tetradrachm bearing the device of a winged Victory. To the gods the honour and praise; but when thanks had been duly given, there was still justice to be done. In particular, there remained the problem of what fate should be reserved for the two captive generals. The next day an extraordinary meeting of the Assembly, open not only to Syracusans, but to all the allied cities that had fought against Athens, was held to decide this im-

---

Demosthenes mentioned here have nothing to do with the orators, or the Leucippus with the atomic philosopher; the same applies to such names as Socrates, Callicles, Euthyphron, Aeschylus, Sophocles, Aristophanes, Alcaeus and Phrynichus.

[7] Re-examination of the terrain now suggests to me that Nicias may have struck inland immediately after leaving the Erineus, following the old track, which only meets the Tellaro at S. Paolo. But it is impossible to decide such a point with any certainty.

344 ARMADA FROM ATHENS

portant issue. There must have been a good many men in Syracuse, Athenagoras and Diocles first among them, who felt very uneasy about Nicias in particular, and, as Thucydides says, "were afraid that this fact [his having been in contact with them] might lead to his being examined under torture, and so bring trouble on them at the very moment of their success."

It is, then, perhaps not surprising that Diocles ("a most notable leader of the populace," Diodorus calls him) made the first speech in the Assembly, hoping, one presumes, to settle the whole matter out of hand. He began by suggesting that the day of the victory (September 18) should in future be kept as a religious festival, known as the Assinaria, and celebrated with public games.[8] Next, he moved that the Athenians' servants and subject-allies should be treated as spoils of war, and sold into slavery. Free Athenian citizens, together with any free Italiots or Sicilian Greeks who had fought at their side, should be imprisoned in the stone-quarries, and rationed to one pint of barley meal a day. The generals—we can almost hear Diocles pause as he came to the most critical item in his brief—the generals should be executed as common felons.

The Assembly was on the point of ratifying these proposals without discussion, exactly as Diocles had hoped. Men's minds were still intoxicated by the heady atmosphere of triumph and revenge. But then both Hermocrates and, unexpectedly, Gylippus rose to enter a plea for mercy. Hermocrates realised that mere vindictiveness could not further reduce Athens' broken dream of imperial expansion, and might have unfortunate political repercussions abroad.[9] He remarked that "it

[8] This proposal was duly carried out. At the first Assinarian Games the prizes consisted of captured Athenian arms and armour, together with commemorative decadrachms, of medallion size, specially struck off from dies designed by Euaenetus and Cimon, the most remarkable coin-designers of this period.

[9] Syracuse had by no means abandoned her own dream of controlling all Sicily: some Syracusan coins minted about this time bear the head of Koré ("The Maiden"), otherwise Persephone. Koré and Demeter were national Sicilian deities *par excellence*, "in whose common worship all of the cities were united" (Baldwin-Brett, pp. 2–3).

was more important to use a victory honourably than to win it," a remark absolutely characteristic of the man in its imposing moral rotundity, and one which, not surprisingly, produced an uproar of disapproval in the Assembly. Gylippus, on the other hand, made no attempt to cloak his motives in a fog of high-minded sentiment. What he wanted was to enhance his own glory and kudos, and he cared very little who knew it now the war was over. He therefore asked for the generals to be turned over to him, so that he could take them back alive to Sparta. It was this, I suspect, which finally sealed Nicias' and Demosthenes' fate. The Syracusans had never cared for Gylippus, and they disliked him more openly now they no longer stood in need of his help. They distrusted his motives: Spartans were proverbially dodgy characters when they became involved in international politics. Besides, these prisoners were rightfully theirs, and Gylippus had no claim on them. Success, it is clear, had gone to the Assembly's collective head. Sentence of death was formally pronounced upon both generals—in Demosthenes' case, at least, with flagrant disregard for the promises made to him at the time of his surrender.

So Nicias and Demosthenes were executed, perhaps after torture,[10] and their bodies thrown outside the gates of the city— "as a public spectacle," Plutarch says. The Corinthians apparently were scared that Nicias, being a rich man and *persona grata* with the Spartans, might escape through bribery and work them further mischief—though Nicias' character, let alone his state of health, hardly warranted such a fear. One can only hope that the sight of that old, emaciated, disease-ridden body gave them some satisfaction. Yet, curiously, the harshest verdict pronounced on Nicias—though seldom taken as such—is that of Thucydides. Perhaps this should not surprise us. The Athe-

[10] This is implied by Diodorus' phrase "execution with ignominy." A doubtful reading in Plutarch suggests death by stoning, which our other testimony does not support. Nor is there any reason to believe the story Plutarch got from Timaeus, according to which Hermocrates gave both prisoners the chance to commit suicide in prison. It may be that his plea got the original sentence mitigated to normal execution. The best discussion is still Freeman, pp. 711–14.

nians left Demosthenes' name on their war memorial to the fallen, presumably on account of his attempted suicide. But that of Nicias they omitted, because he had surrendered voluntarily, and was thus regarded as an "unworthy soldier"—a distinction which may strike the modern mind as somewhat harsh.

Throughout the *History*, Thucydides makes no bones about Nicias' ineffectuality; and we know that Thucydides was a man who did not suffer fools gladly. Moral criteria are hard to find in his pages. What he admires above all is success, the glory of power, *dynamis*, military, political, or financial domination. Like so many intellectuals, he is fascinated by naked *Machtpolitik*. The one unforgivable crime for him is failure: perhaps because, as a participant in the drama, he failed so strikingly himself. However smooth the irony, however veiled the barb, Thucydides could hardly help giving Nicias very short shrift indeed. He sums him up as "a man who, of all the Hellenes in my time, least deserved to come to so miserable an end, since the whole of his life had been devoted to the study and the practice of virtue." The historian might have permitted himself a brief sardonic smile had he known how many people would take that double-edged tribute as an undiluted compliment. In fact, it is about as merciless an epitaph as the wit of man could devise—an epitaph not on the man alone, but on the whole way of life which he represented. Patriotism, said Edith Cavell, is not enough. Nor, says Thucydides grimly, is virtue; and here his Sophistic training shows through. Goodness, he is saying, cannot survive stupidity. Nicias was an honest, pious, sincere man. Yet for all his piety and virtue, his unflinching courage, his cultivation of the good life, he died hideously, because he was also a bumbling ass with no sense of judgment, who brought down on his own head the fate he endured with such stoic resignation.

Before the last retreat Nicias reminded his men that his own life had been spent in dutiful regard for the gods and just and blameless actions towards men. *Because of this*, he said, his hope for the future was still undimmed. But Thucydides, who had absorbed the right-is-might ethics of the Sophists, knew better. Nicias was an anachronism. From now on the world belonged to a different breed of man: tougher, crueller, more egocentric, whose conscience had no truck with the scruples Nicias knew. Those who still honoured the old ways contracted out of the political life more and more as time went on; and politics became immeasurably the worse for their absence.

Perhaps it would have been a kinder fate for the remainder of the Athenian expedition had they suffered a quick death as Nicias did. Instead, they were herded into the main Syracusan stone-quarry, outside the Tyche gate, known today as the Latomie dei Capucini. Here they remained for ten weeks on end, all seven thousand of them, packed together in a narrow place without any sort of roof over their heads. They were burnt by the sun all day, and at night, especially as winter drew on, they suffered increasingly from cold, with sudden violent changes of temperature at dawn and dusk. They had no sanitary facilities of any sort. Their diet was a pint of meal and half a pint of water a day. They died of pneumonia and starvation and their bodies were left to rot where they lay, among piles of ordure. The Syracusans, who seem to have regarded this hideous spectacle as a side-show somewhat akin to a bear pit, jeered at their victims from the edge of the quarry as they passed by. But presently the number of corpses grew so great, and the stench so disgusting, that this pastime began to pall. For pure vindictiveness the whole episode can have few parallels.[11] Demosthenes records that one Epicerdes of Cyrene gave a hundred *minas* to the prisoners, "and this . . . became the chief instrument in saving them from all perishing of hunger," an act for which Athens voted him special privileges and immunities.

After ten weeks had elapsed, all the surviving prisoners except for free Athenian, Italiot, and Greek Sicilian citizens were sold off as slaves, each one being branded on the forehead with the koppa mark normally reserved for horses. The residue endured a

[11] The Athenians later retaliated in kind: when they captured four Syracusan triremes off Ephesus, all free citizens among the crews were put to hard labour in the Piraeus quarries.

further six months of this barbaric treatment. They were then removed from the quarries and put to hard labour in prison, with an increase of rations. Some, by special arrangement, were farmed out to young aristocratic masters. The more intelligent of these contrived to do very well for themselves, either being set free or at least treated with decency and respect. As always, education brought its own peculiar benefits. Well-read Athenian prisoners, or those with a good grounding in music and mathematics were much sought after as tutors for Syracusan children. A grim catch-phrase later passed into common use at Athens when news of some missing person was sought: "He's either dead or teaching school." Perhaps the oddest advantage conferred by a training in literature—and the one which most clearly reveals the Sicilians' colonial streak—was the special consideration accorded to anyone who knew some part of Euripides' work by heart.

"Even the smallest fragments of his verses," says Plutarch, "were learnt from every stranger who set foot on the island, and they took delight in exchanging these quotations with one another." So it fell out that various Athenian citizens, condemned to slavery after the disaster at the Assinarus, had earnt their freedom by teaching their master all they could remember from Euripides' plays. Others, starving and foot-sore after the battle, had been taken in and fed in return for reciting a choral lyric or two. Some of these—such as the closing words of the *Hecuba*—had an all too bitter applicability to their own plight:

Files to the tent,
file to the harbour.
There we embark
on life as slaves.
Necessity is harsh.
Fate has no reprieve.

Many strange things there are in this world, Euripides' fellow-poet Sophocles declared, but none come stranger than Man. It

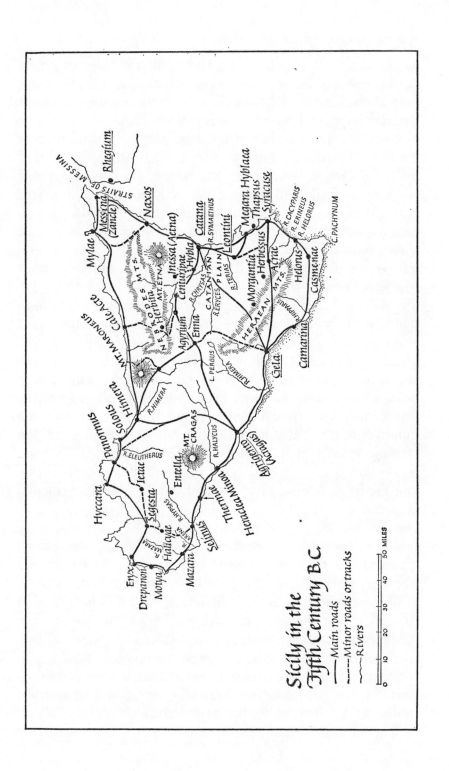

Sicily in the
Fifth Century B.C.

——— Main roads
– – – – Minor roads or tracks
~~~~ Rivers

0   10   20   30   40   50 MILES

is pleasant to think that when these battered veterans finally made their way home, they sought out Euripides in his lonely retreat on Salamis, and thanked him for having been, however unwittingly, the means of saving their lives.

What was the final fate of the remaining Athenian prisoners in Sicily? Polystratus, a middle-aged gentleman who had served with the cavalry, both during the retreat and subsequently at Catana, claimed that their raiding activities after the defeat brought in enough loot to ransom all the troops still held captive by Syracuse. It would be pleasant if we could believe this. But Polystratus made the statement while on trial, to emphasise his patriotism; and the total sum raised (to judge from the tithe paid to Athena) was precisely five talents. At the going purchase-price for a highly qualified slave, this would have ransomed only about 100 men. Perhaps what Polystratus meant was *cavalry* troops; the élite always tended to look after its own.

It is possible that some prisoners held by the Syracusan government (as opposed to those in private hands) gained their release in this way. Even so, Polystratus obviously exaggerated his raiding group's achievements and influence to gain the jury's sympathy. The hard truth surely is that most of the prisoners—apart from a lucky minority—never left Syracuse again, but lived and died there in resentful servitude, acting out the harsh fate they had planned to inflict on their colonial masters.

When news of the disaster first reached Athens, people refused to believe it. It was some casual stranger who first told the story when he landed at Piraeus: sitting in a barber's chair, glad to be ashore, expansive, discussing what had happened as though it was common knowledge. To his amazement, the barber said nothing, but threw down razor and towel and hurried out of the shop. The stranger waited, with increasing irritation, but the barber did not return. This was not surprising, since he had gone straight off up into Athens, a matter of five miles, to tell his tale to the magistrates.

The result was a quite extraordinary uproar. The magistrates called an emergency session of the Assembly, and made the now half-hysterical barber repeat his story. When he was cross-examined as to how he came by it, he appears to have relapsed into total incoherence. With uncommon speed the Assembly—scarcely less hysterical than their victim, and clearly anxious to exorcise what they most feared—condemned the hapless barber as "a rumour-monger and public agitator." He was actually being tortured on the wheel when messengers reached Athens with a full, circumstantial, and all too convincing account of the expedition's end.

The Athenians were—are—a curious and paradoxical people, unpredictable, volatile in their emotions, yet capable of great and stoic endurance. On the day that the disaster became public knowledge, a comedy called *The Battle of the Giants*, by Hegemon of Thasos, was being performed. As word ran through the audience, the author-producer's first thought was to stop the show. But then he saw that not one person had left the theatre, though almost everyone there must have lost a relative in Sicily. The jokes got louder laughs than ever. No Athenian was going to let any foreigner in the audience see how deeply this calamity had affected him. The play went on without interruption; no public tears were shed, then or later. In Aristophanes' *Lysistrata* (411) the heroine exclaims: "We have borne sons and sent them out as hoplites—" But she is at once cut short by the Commissioner for Public Safety: "Hush, woman! Do not remind us of past misfortunes!" For some time, indeed, people could not bring themselves to face the truth at all, much less discuss it. There are some disasters so appalling that the mind cannot accept their existence. "They thought," says Thucydides, "that this total destruction was something that could not possibly be true."

When the full horror was borne in on them, past all denying, they turned on the politicians and demagogues who had advocated the expedition, the soothsayers who had prophesied its success—anything to find a scapegoat for what their own will and necessity had decreed. This is scarcely to be wondered at. The disaster was complete and absolute, its practical consequences incalculable. None of the expedition's aims had been achieved. Timber and grain were as hard to come by as ever; more so now that the cash to purchase them was running out.[12] Trade with the West, far from expanding, had been severely disrupted. As a direct result of the expedition, and the resultant drain on Athens' military and financial resources, Sparta was now entrenched at Decelea, the Laurium mines were lost, and the never failing "fountain of silver" with them. The empire was bankrupt; the subject-allies stood on the very brink of revolt.

"Comrade, look not on the West," Housman wrote, "'twill have the heart out of your breast." In pursuit of their ignis fatuus, and with steadily increasing obstinacy as failure followed failure, the Athenian people had sacrificed over 29,000 fighting men; had spent at least 3,420 talents, and probably much more, of a total income for this period not exceeding 5,784 talents; had lost nearly two hundred triremes, the best the city possessed; had, in fact, squandered—and all for nothing—Athens' accumulated reserves of men, material, and bullion, leaving themselves penniless, under-defended, without either hope or provision for the future.

And then, with that incredible resilience which characterises the Athenian in every age, they pulled themselves together, tightened their belts, and set out to salvage what they could from the wreckage. They took measures of economy and reform. They somehow scraped together enough timber to build new ships. They amnestied most of their exiles; even, after several years' hesitation, Alcibiades. Immediately after the disaster they set up a ten-man Committee of Public Safety, which numbered Sophocles amongst its members. On the very edge of starvation, their manpower crippled, their fleet decimated, their mines and farmland occupied by the enemy, fearing imminent invasion from Syracuse and a general revolt among their own allies, these indomitable people nevertheless determined to fight on and win.

[12] Eupolis the comic poet, writing during the autumn of 413, mentions severe food shortages and profiteering by urban entrepreneurs at the expense of the country districts. See Page, *Select Papyri III*, pp. 202 ff.

They did not win in the event, though—typically—they threw away at least one golden opportunity of doing so. But they continued to hold out for nearly another decade. The final disaster of Aegospotami did not come until 405; neither Sophocles nor Euripides lived to see it.

Yet after that black day in September 413, Athens was never the same again. The shock had gone too deep, proved too traumatic. Perhaps this change emerges most clearly in the comedies of Aristophanes. Gone forever, after *The Birds*, are the savage, laughing, satirical self-confidence and pride of plays like *The Knights* or *The Wasps*. From now on Athenian comedy slides slowly but steadily into fantasy, black farce, and literary jokes. Political issues give way to the domestic minutiae of private life. There were no more political issues that bore writing about. Gone were the days when quick-witted Athenian amateurs could pass two controversial laws before breakfast, win a battle by midmorning, and invent a new theory of the universe while exercising in the gymnasium. Athens' imperial pride had been destroyed, and her easy self-assertion with it. Aegospotami merely confirmed the ineluctable sentence imposed on the banks of the Assinarus. Pindar's violet-crowned city had been cut down to size, and an ugly tarnish now dulled the bright Periclean charisma. The great experiment in democratic imperialism—that strangest of all paradoxes—was finally discredited, and extremists from right and left alike hastened to fill the gap it left behind.

Yet Athens' heritage, despite everything, persisted. Her democracy might be short-sighted, anarchic, volatile, and totally unprincipled; but democracy, of a kind, it stubbornly remained, and in the event proved harder to dislodge than any totalitarian thinker could have foreseen. In 411 there took place that right-wing oligarchic coup known as the Revolution of the Four Hundred. Yet less than a year later, after the naval victory off Cyzicus, popular government had been restored. In 404, after the humiliation of defeat, when the Long Walls had been torn down and Spartan troops occupied the Acropolis, a fascist junta, the so-called Thirty Tyrants—complete with purges, torture, secret police, and all the rest of the sickeningly familiar apparatus essential to modern totalitarianism—imposed itself on Athens. By February 403 it had been overthrown; in September of the same year Athens once more became a full democracy.

Athens' defeat in Sicily had been, first and foremost, a defeat for the "sailor rabble" and hence for the popular party. It is no coincidence that what followed was a right-wing coup. In Syracuse, however, the situation was reversed. Here the rowers had triumphed, and in the end (ironically enough) it was this victory, rather than any collusion with Athens, which a year later (412) swept Diocles, Athenagoras, and their ultra-radical party into power.

Thucydides, characteristically, is dazzled by the glorious achievement of Syracuse's victory. Had she not conquered the greatest armada sent forth by the most imposing naval power of all Greece? What catches his admiration is the manifestation of *dynamis*, superior force. The lamentable consequences of this victory do not really concern him. Syracuse in fact had little joy of her deliverance and unlooked-for triumph. The effort expended on defeating the Athenian invader had left the entire island war-weary and vulnerable. Across the water Carthage, having long bided her time, now decided to strike at an advantageous moment.

In 409 the Carthaginians launched an invasion which resulted in the destruction of Selinus and Himera. Three years later a second expedition also destroyed Acragas. It was only the rise to power of that remarkable military genius Dionysius which prevented Syracuse from suffering a similar fate. The ultrademocrats did not enjoy their brand-new regime for long. Syracuse, the city which would go down to history as the rock on which Athens' imperial ambitions foundered, ended the century as she had begun it—under the autocratic rule of a dictator.

The characters in the drama—those of them who survived—mostly came to unhappy or violent deaths sooner or later. Alcibiades was received back in triumph by the city which had exiled him, only to be exiled a second time, and perish at the hands of Persian assassins shortly before Athens' final downfall. Gylippus, having done so brilliantly, was convicted of embezzlement soon after Aegospotami, and ended his days, like Alcibiades, in exile and disgrace.[13] Hermocrates, after a military career of great distinction, for which he got very little thanks, was killed during a stupid and clumsy attempt to take over the government of Syracuse by force.

By a curious turn of fate, the grain Athens had fought so desperately to obtain came pouring into her granaries from the first decade of the fourth century. In 393 Conon engineered a rapprochement between Athens and Persia. The Long Walls were rebuilt, and it was Persian gold that financed their construction. With the Great King's co-operation Athenian merchants obtained all the vast Black Sea wheat consignments that Pericles had so long and vainly struggled to control.[14] It was, indeed, a merchants' century that was dawning now, a world of individuals and great kingdoms, of science and philosophy, where the city-state was an odd anachronism, surviving most vigorously in the nostalgic minds of conservative intellectuals. Yet anachronism or not, men were still willing to die for it, as we know from the brilliant, vituperative speeches of Demosthenes. The tragedy is that the Athenians who went down before Philip's Macedonian pikes at Chaeronea, in 338, were fighting for a chimera: the Athenian polis had run its course three quarters of a century before. Though the slogans it had generated

[13] He was entrusted with the Athenian public funds and Lysander's personal prizes, done up in sacks under seal, and ordered to take them back to Sparta. He slit each sack open at the bottom and abstracted some of the contents (mostly "Attic owls") for himself, not knowing that they all contained a tally showing the total as checked. The Ephors were puzzled by the discrepancies until Gylippus' servant was heard to remark, cryptically, that there were far too many Attic owls roosting in his master's roof.

[14] There were still famines: see M. N. Tod, A Selection of Greek Historical Inscriptions, Vol. II (Oxford 1948), nos. 198 and 200; also M. Rostovtzeff, A Social and Economic History of the Hellenistic World (Oxford 1941), Vol. I., p. 95 with reff. But these were caused, for the most part, either by profiteering and inflation, or else by the expansionist activities of Macedonia.

still echoed on (some of them remain in use today), all it stood for lay bleached and dry among the white-picked bones of Athens' dead soldiers in Sicily. The spring had gone out of the Periclean year, and the high summer, too, and not all the brilliant sophistries of the Hellenistic Age would ever bring them back.

DISTRIBUTION-FIGURES FOR ATTIC RED-FIGURE POTTERY OVERSEAS IN THE FIFTH CENTURY B.C.

[Note:— These figures are largely compiled from the provenience indexes in Beazley's Attic Red-Figure Vase-Painters (2d ed.), with occasional supplementation from more recent publications. An asterisk * indicates significant change.]

Date / Area	490-460	460-430	430-410	410-390	After 390	
Adriatic						
ADRIA	117	— 71	*— 13	— 3	+ 10	
SPINA	35	*+ 232	+ 310	*— 165	*+ 286	
Etruria						
ETRURIA (gen.)†	678	+ 746	*— 272	*— 45	— 20+	Incl. Clusium, Bologna, Caere, Falerii, Numana, Volsinii, Tarquinia, Todi, Veii, Vulci.
POPULONIA	9	+ 20	— 5	— 2	2	Figs. do not suggest much trade in iron, though other cities may have acted as middlemen.
Campania						
CAPUA	44	*+ 95	— 45	*— 2	+ 17+	
CUMAE	10	+ 27	— 24	*— 2	+ 8+	
NOLA	59	*+ 228	— 184	*— 9	+ 11+	
NEAPOLIS]		+	+	*—	+	
PAESTUM]	5	13	22	5	30	
SORRENTO]						
Magna Graecia†	11	*+ 66	+ 73	*— 22	+ 37	†Incl. Apulia, Ceglie, Egnatia, Metapontum, Padua, Rhegium, Suessula.
LOCRI	22	*— 148	*— 27	— Nil	Nil	
TARENTUM	20	+ 27	— 22	*— 4	4	
East Sicily†	5	+ 17	+ 19	*— Nil	˙?1	†Incl. Acrae, Catana, Leontini, Megara Hyblaea, Ragusa, Syracuse. A minimal increase at Syracuse for the period 430-410 must be attributed to the presence of Athenian troops.
S. Sicily						
ACRAGAS	22	+ 38	— 23	*— 4	Nil	
CAMARINA	1	*+ 39	+ 60	*— 5	Nil	
GELA	74	*+ 225	†— 189	*— 2	2+	†Incl. 108 pieces from Vassallaggio reported by Prof. Trendall
Area S. Sicily (cont'd)						
SELINUS	10	+ 24	— 10	Nil	Nil	W. and N. Sicily give a nil return, except for one or two scattered pieces at Segesta and on the Lipara Is.—both, again, presumably due to the Athenian troops there.

Date	490-460	460-430	430-410	410-390	After 390	
N. Africa†	13	+ 20	+ 27	− 20	*+ 59	†Incl. Carthage, Cyrene, Egypt, Naucratis.
East Med.						
AL-MINA (Posideium)	3	*+ 24	+ 33	− 31	− 29	
CYPRUS†	Nil	12	− 9	− 4	+ 6	†Marium, Salamis, misc.
RHODES†	14	*+ 68	− 37	*− 4	+ 10+	†Camirus, Ialysos, Lindos.
Aegean						
AEGINA	· 3	+ 7	− 2	− Nil	?1	
DELOS	8	*+ 32	− 28	*− 1	+ 3	
MELOS	Nil	1	Nil	2	+ 4	
Greece						
BOEOTIA†	11	*− 41	*− 8	*− 4	*+ 44	†Incl. Tanagra, Thebes, misc.
CORINTH	6	+ 23	− 15	− 5	− 1	
EUBOEA†	9	*+ 75	*+ 103	*− 17	− 2+	†Chalcis, Eretria.
MEGARA	1	1	1	Nil	Nil	
SPARTA	Nil	Nil	Nil	Nil	Nil	
West. Med.						
AMPURIAS (Spain)	11	*+ 60	*− 16	⊥ 6	+ 9	
FRANCE†	1	+ 9	+ 11	+ 17	+ 20	†Marseilles, Beziers.
Area						
North Greece						
MACEDONIA	Nil	1	Nil	Nil	2	
OLYNTHUS	Nil	8	5	1	*+ 72	
THASOS	Nil	5	Nil	Nil	+ 6	
Pontus and S. Russia						
KERTSCH (Panticapaeum)	4	+ 12	− 5	+ 11	*+ 47	
OLBIA	3	2	1	2	3	
CRIMEA and S. RUSSIA (misc)	4	5	5	3	*+ 46	

Note: Some of these areas (e.g., Macedonia) are misleadingly blank owing to lack of excavation; but even in adjacent areas that *have* been well dug, such as Olynthus and Thasos, the picture is not all that much different. The *relative* fluctuations throughout are surprisingly consistent. The first general point that strikes one is the consistent decline in all areas of Athenian trade during the last decades of the fifth century, and its equally marked recovery at the beginning of the fourth. For areas where we have literary testimony—south Russia is a good case in point—this resurgence is confirmed.

Spina in the Adriatic retains the highest rate of trade throughout. Etruria declines abruptly after the failure of the Sicilian Expedition. It is interesting to note that Athens' enemy Locri did so much trade with her until the 430s. The absence of trade with eastern Sicily, and its catastrophic falling off with cities such as Acragas and Gela is discussed in the body of the text. Perhaps the most impressive confirmation of this method's historical accuracy comes from the figures for Euboea, which precisely echo the pattern of events in the fifth century.

POPULATION AND GRAIN CONSUMPTION FIGURES IN FIFTH-CENTURY ATHENS

CATEGORY	480-479	457	431	425-422	415	411	393
HOPLITES (muster roll)	?9-10,000	?16,000	13,000 [Th]	?10,000	?11,000	9,000	?9,000
VETERANS (aet. 40-59)	?8,100	?13,400	?10,700	?8,000	?8,900	?7,100	?7,100
EPHEBES (aet. 18-19)	?900	?2,000	?2,300	?2,000	?2,100	?1,900	?1,900
CAVALRY	?500+	?1,500	1,000[Th]	?750	?1,000	?500+	?500+
METICS (Hoplite Status)	?1,000	?3,500+	3,000[Th]	2,500	?2,500+	?2,000+	?2,000+
ROWERS [cits.] (sub-hoplite category)	19,500	?30,000	?35,000	c.22,000 [incl. lt-armed troops]	?24,000	12,000 [losses Sic. Ex.]	?12,000
ROWERS [met.] (sub-hoplite category)	18,000	?24,000	?22,000	?24,000	?20,000	?22,000	?22,000
SLAVES	?54,000	?110,800	?115,000	?83,000	?95,500	?87,200	?100,000+
TOTAL CIT. POPULATION (x4 adult males)	39,000 x4 = 156,000 (30,000 Hdt.)	?254,000	c.248,000	?171,000	?188,000	?122,000	122,000 (30,500x4)
TOTAL METIC POP. [x4]	?76,000	?110,000	c.100,000	c.66,000	?100,000	?98,000	?196,000
OVERALL TOTAL	286,500	?474,000	463,000	320,500	?383,500	?307,000	?418,000
TOTAL GRAIN CONSUMPTION +300,000 med. fodder	2,019,000	3,144,000	3,078,000	2,223,000	2,601,000	2,142,000	2,808,000

Note: The daily ration of a rower in the fleet was 1 *choinix* (1.92 pts). At 48 *choinices* to the *medimnus* (about a bushel and a half) this gives an annual consumption of between 7 and 8 *medimni*. Slaves and women and non-manual labourers consumed much less: allow an overall requirement of 6 *medimni* per annum. Add an average of 300,000 *medimni* for cattle fodder. This will be a conservative estimate, since clearly the number of cattle must have varied in proportion to the population.

SICILIAN CITIES: PRODUCTION AND CONSUMPTION
IN THE FIFTH CENTURY B.C.

AREA	ACREAGE AND PRODUCTION	POPULATION AND CONSUMPTION
ACRAGAS	768,000 acres [Scramuzza 259, n.2] inland as far as Vassallaggio. ?200,000 acres arable land, 150,000 acres in production. Max. yield (x21) = 3,150,000 med. Low yield (x10) = 1,500,000 med.	20,000 adult cits. = total (x4) of 80,000; with metics and slaves prob. overall total about 300,000 (cf. figs for Athens). Diod. Sic. 13.84.90; Diog. Laert. 8.2.63, who claims total fig. 800,000. Cf. Freeman 2.392-7. Need 2,100,000 med.
CAMARINA	Holds Morgantia from Syracuse: Th. 4.65. ?30,000 acres productive, ?25,000 under cultivation at any one time. x21 = 525,000 med. x10 = 250,000 med.	Unknown: perhaps about the same as Catana (60,000+). Holm, GS 2.402-3 estimates 70,000. 360,000 med. needed: allow 70,000 for fodder, total requirement 430,000 med.
CATANA	Controls area between city and mouth of Symaethus R. ? 45,000 acres, 40,000 under cultivation at one time. x21 = 840,000 med. x10 = 400,000 med.	10,000 adult male cits. [Diod. Sic. 11.49.1] x4 = 40,000 total cit. body. Holm, ibid., estimates 70,000.x 6 (Beloch) = overall pop. ?430,000 annual consumption in med.
GELA	?105,000 acres arable land, 100,000 always available. x21 = 2,100,000 med. x10 = 1,000,000 med.	Unknown. Holm, ibid., estimates ?70,000+ ?overall pop. = ?1,200,- 000; add fodder, total c.1,500,000 med.
LEONTINI	?100,000 arable land, with 80,000 under cultivation at any one time. x21 = 1,680,000 med. x10 = 800,000 med.	20,000 adult male cits [Diod. Sic. 11.49] x4 = 80,000 total cit. body, x6 (Beloch) = 120,000 overall pop. This produces a fig. of 720,000 med. annual need. Add 60,000 med. for fodder, total = 780,000 med.
SELINUS	200,000 acres total domain [Bernini 321] ?50,000 acres arable land, 40,000 under cultivation at any one time. x21 = 2,520,000 med. x10 = 1,200,000 med.	23,600 adult male cits. [Diod. Sic. 13.54-59] x 4 = 94,400 total cit. body. Holm, ibid., estimates 100,000.x6 (Beloch) = 141,600 overall pop. This indicates annual consumption of 850,000 med. Add 100,000 med. fodder, total = 950,000 med.
SYRACUSE	200,000 acres total domain (Bernini 321). ?50,000 acres arable land, with 40,000 under cultivation at one time. x21 = 840,000 med. x10 = 400,000 med.	? 400,000 [Bernini 321] : more reasonable than Holm's 800,000, based on old concept of Achradina- on-Epipolae: see above, p. 182 – 86. Accepting Bernini still produces annual consumption of 2,400,000 med. without fodder: add 300,000, total then = 2,700,000.

SELECT BIBLIOGRAPHY I: *Ancient Sources*

B—Collection Guillaume Budé   L—Loeb Classical Library
P—Penguin Classics   T—Teubner Text
Ed—Edition   Tr—Translation

Aeneas Tacticus   R. Schöne. Leipzig, 1911 (T, Ed).
Illinois Greek Club. London, 1923 (L, Ed, Tr).
L. W. Hunter. *Aineiou Poliorketika*. Oxford, 1927
(Ed, Tr).

Aeschines   C. D. Adams. *The Speeches of Aeschines*. London,
1919 (L, Ed, Tr).

Andocides   G. Dalmeyda. *Andocide: Discours*. Paris, 1960 (B,
Ed, Tr).
D. MacDowell. *Andocides on the Mysteries*. Oxford,
1962 (Ed).
K. Maidment. *Minor Attic Orators* Vol. I. London,
1941 (L, Ed, Tr).

Aristophanes   V. Coulon and H. Van Daele. *Aristophane*. 5 vols.
Paris, 1960–64 (B, Ed, Tr): Vol. I, 7th rev. imp.;
Vol. II, 5th rev. imp.; Vol. III, 6th rev. imp.
B. B. Rogers: *The Acharnians* (London, 1910);
The Knights (London, 1910); *The Clouds* (London, 1916); *The Wasps* (London, 1915); *The Peace*
(rev. ed., London, 1913); *The Birds* (London,
1906); *Lysistrata* (London, 1911); *The Ecclesiazusae* (London, 1902) (Ed, Tr).

Aristotle   H. Rackham. *Aristotle: Politics*. (London, 1932);
Ed, Tr). *Aristotle: Athenian Constitution*. etc. London, 1935 (L, Ed, Tr).

Athenaeus   C. B. Gulick. *Athenaeus: The Deipnosophists*. 7
vols. London, 1927–41 (L, Ed, Tr).

Cornelius Nepos   J. C. Rolfe. London, 1929 (L, Ed, Tr).

Ctesias   J. Gilmore. *Fragments of the Persika of Ctesias.*
                   London, 1888 (Ed).
                   R. Henry. *Ctésias: La Perse, L'Inde, Les Sommaires
                   de Photius.* Brussels, 1947 (Ed, Tr).

Diodorus Siculus   C. H. Oldfather. Vols. IV–V, London, 1945, 1950
                   (L, Ed, Tr).

Euripides   G. Murray. *Euripidis Fabulae.* 3 vols. Oxford, 1902–
                   13 (Ed): Vol. 2, 3rd ed., 1913; Vol. 3, 2d ed., 1913.
                   D. Grene and R. Lattimore. *The Complete Greek
                   Tragedies,* (Vols V–VII). New York (Modern Li-
                   brary), 1956–59 (Tr).

Herodotus   A. D. Godley. 4 vols. London, 1920–25 (L, Ed, Tr).
                   C. Hude. *Herodoti Historiae.* 2 vols., 3rd ed. Oxford,
                   1926 (Ed).
                   Aubrey de Selincourt. *Herodotus: The Histories.*
                   London, 1954 (P, Tr).

Isocrates   G. Norlin and LaRue Van Hook. 3 vols. London
                   (L, Ed, Tr).

Justin   E. Chambry and Mme. Thély-Chambry. *Justin:
                   Abrégés des Histoires Philippiques de Trogue Pom-
                   pée.* 2 vols. Paris, 1936 (Ed, Tr).

Lysias   W. R. M. Lamb. London, 1930 (L, Ed, Tr).

Pausanias   W. H. S. Jones, H. A. Ormerod, and R. E. Wycher-
                   ley. *Pausanias: Description of Greece.* 5 vols. Lon-
                   don, 1918–35 (L, Ed, Tr): Vol. V, rev. ed., 1955.
                   J. G. Frazer. *Pausanias' Description of Greece.* 6
                   vols. London, 1898 (Ed, Tr).

Pindar   L. R. Farnell. *The Works of Pindar.* 3 vols. London,
                   1932 (Ed, Tr): Vol. II (Commentary), repr. Am-
                   sterdam, 1961.

Plato   E. R. Dodds. *Plato: Gorgias.* Oxford, 1959 (Ed).
                   W. R. M. Lamb. *Plato: Laches,* etc. London, 1924
                   (L, Ed, Tr).

Plutarch   B. Perrin. *Plutarch's Lives*. Vols. 1–4, London, 1914–
                  16 (L, Ed, Tr).
                  Ian Scott-Kilvert. *Plutarch: The Rise and Fall of
                  Athens. Nine Greek Lives.* London, 1960 (P, Tr).

Polyaenus   J. Melber. *Polyaenus, Strategemata.* Leipzig (T,
                  Ed).

Polybius   W. R. Paton. 6 vols. (L, Ed, Tr).

Strabo   H. L. Jones. *The Geography of Strabo.* 8 vols. Lon-
                  don, 1917–32 (L, Ed, Tr).

Thucydides   K. J. Dover. *Thucydides Book VI and Thucydides
                  Book VII.* Oxford, 1965 (Ed).
                  C. Forster Smith. *Thucydides' History of the Pelo-
                  ponnesian War.* 4 vols. London, 1919–23 (L, Ed,
                  Tr): Vol. I, rev. imp., 1928; Vol. II, rev. imp., 1930.
                  H. S. Jones, rev. by J. E. Powell. *Thucydides His-
                  toriae.* 2 vols. Oxford, 1942 (Ed).
                  J. de Romilly, *Thucydide:Histoire de la guerre du
                  Péloponnèse.* 4 vols. with R. Weil and L. Bodin.
                  Paris, 1953–62 (B, Ed, Tr).
                  Rex Warner. *Thucydides: The Peloponnesian War.*
                  London, 1954 (P, Tr).

Xenophon   E. Kalinka. *Die Pseudoxenophontische* Ἀθηναίων
                  Πολιτεία. Berlin, 1913 (T, Ed, Tr).
                  E. C. Marchant. *Xenophon: Memorabilia and Oe-
                  conomicus.* London, 1923 (L, Ed, Tr).
                  ———. *Xenophontis opera*, Vol. V, *Opuscula.* Ox-
                  ford, 1920 (Ed).

Miscellanea   G. Coppola. "Una pagina del Περὶ Σικελίας di Fi-
                  listo," *Riv. Fil. Class.* 8 (1930), pp. 449–70 (Ed).
                  W. Dittenberger. *Sylloge Inscriptionum Graecarum.*
                  1915–24 (Ed).
                  J. M. Edmonds. *The Fragments of Attic Comedy*,
                  Vol. I, *Old Comedy.* Leiden, 1957 (Ed, Tr).
                  J. J. Hondius and A. G. Woodhead. *Supplementum
                  Epigraphicum Graecum.* Leiden, 1923–   (Ed).
                  G. F. Hill, *Sources for Greek History*, B.C. 478–431.

New ed. rev. by R. Meiggs and A. Andrews. Oxford, 1951 (Ed).

F. Jacoby. *Fragmente der griechischen Historiker* (FGrHist), Vol. III B, section 69 ("Sizilien u. Grossgriechenland"), pp. 540–688, paras. 554–77, Leiden, 1950; Commentary (1955), pp. 479–612 (Ed).

Th. Kock. *Comicorum Atticorum Fragmenta.* Leipzig, 1880 (Ed).

D. L. Page. *Select Papyri III: Literary Papyri.* Rev. ed. London, 1950.

M. N. Tod. *Greek Historical Inscriptions.* Vol. I, 2d ed., Oxford, 1946.

R. Meiggs and D. M. Lewis. *A Selection of Greek Historical Inscriptions to the end of the Fifth Century B.C.* Oxford 1969. (Note: this edition replaces Tod, but was published too late for me to utilize in the present work.)

SELECT BIBLIOGRAPHY II: *Modern Literature*

KEY TO THE ABBREVIATED JOURNAL NAMES

Ant. class	*L'Antiquité classique*
AJA	*American Journal of Archaeology*
AJPh	*American Journal of Philology*
Cl.Phil.	*Classical Philology*
Cl.Rev.	*Classical Review*
Harv.Stud.Class.Phil.	*Harvard Studies in Classical Philology*
JHS	*Journal of Hellenic Studies*
Riv.Fill.Class.	*Rivista di filologia e di istruzioni classica*
TAPhA	*Transactions and Proceedings of the American Philological Association*

ABBOTT, G. F. *Thucydides. A Study in Historical Reality.* London, 1925.

ACCAME, S. "La politica estera di Pericle nei primi anni del suo predominio," *Studi Calderini-Paribeni* I (Milano, 1956), pp. 39–49.

ADAMASTEANU, D. "L'Ellenizazione della Sicilia ed il momento di Ducezio," *Kokalos* 8 (1962), pp. 167–98.

ADCOCK, F. E. *Thucydides and his History.* Cambridge, 1963.

ALFIERI, N. "Problemi tecnici, storici, archeologici e museografici posti in luce dagli scavi di Spina," *Cisalpina* 1 (1959), pp. 89–102.

ALFIERI, N., and ARIAS, P. E. *Spina.* Munich, 1958.

ALLEN, Ruth. "The Mutilation of the Herms: A Study in Athenian Politics." Dissertation, Univ. of Cincinnati, 1951.

AMIT, M. "Le Pirée dans l'histoire d'Athènes à l'époque classique," *Bulletin de l'Association G. Budé* (1961), pp. 464–74.

——. *Athens and the Sea: A Study in Athenian Sea Power.* Coll. Latomus, Vol. 74. Brussels, 1965.

AMYX, D. A. "The Attic Stelae, Pt. III," *Hesperia* 27 (1958), pp. 163–310.

ANDREADES, A. M. *A History of Greek Public Finance.* Vol. I., rev. ed. Cambridge, 1933.

ANDREWES, A. "Thucydides and the Persians," *Historia* 10, (1961), pp. 1–18.

ARDAILLON, E. *Les Mines de Laurion dans l'Antiquité.* Paris, 1897.

ARGENTATI, A. "La spedizione in Egitto (459–454? a.c.) nel quadro della politica estera ateniense," *Acme* 6 (1953), pp. 379–404.

AWDRY, H. "Note on the walls of Epipolae," *JHS* 29 (1909), pp. 70–78.

BAKER, W. "Ricerche subacquee nel Porto Grande di Siracusa," *Atti del II Congresso Internazionale di Archeologia sottomarina* (Albenga, 1958), pp. 85–89.

BALDWIN-BRETT, A. *Victory Issues of Syracuse after 413 B.C.* (Numism. Notes and Monogr. no. 75). New York, 1936.

BARRECA, F. "Nuove osservazioni sul Castello Eurialo," *Archivio Storico Siracusano* 2 (1956–57), pp. 146–151.

BARRON, J. "Milesian politics and Athenian propaganda c. 460–440 B.C.," *JHS* 82 (1962), pp. 1–6.

———. "Religious propaganda of the Delian League," *JHS* 84 (1964), pp. 35–48.

BARTOLETTI, V. "Potenza della Sicilia e ardore degli Ateniensi in Tucidide," *Studi Italiani di Filologia Classica* (1937), pp. 227–35.

BEAUMONT, R. L. "Greek Influence in the Adriatic Sea before the Fourth Century B.C.," *JHS* 56 (1936), pp. 159–204.

———. "Corinth, Ambracia. Apollonia," *JHS* 72 (1952), p. 62–75.

BEAZLEY, J. D. *Attic Black-Figure Vase-Painters.* Oxford, 1956.

———. *Attic Red-Figure Vase-Painters.* 2d ed., 3 vols. Oxford, 1963.

———. "Spina e la ceramica greca," *Spina e l'Etruria Padana* (Atti del I Convegno di Studi etruschi) (Firenze, 1959), pp. 47–58, pls. xi–xvi.

———. "The Excavations at Al-Mina, Sueidia, III. The Red-figured Vases," *JHS* 59 (1939), pp. 1–44.

BELOCH, K. J. "Die grosse athenische Expedition nach Sizilien," *Griechische Geschichte* II², 2, pp. 290–311.

BÉRARD, J. *La colonisation grecque de l'Italie méridionale et de la Sicile dans l'antiquité.* 2nd rev. ed. Paris, 1957.

———. *Bibliographie topographique des principales cités grecques de l'Italie méridionale et de la Sicile dans l'antiquité.* Paris, 1941.

BERNINI, F. "Ermocrate Siracusano," *Athenaeum* 5 (1917), pp. 320–47; 6 (1918), pp. 108–21.

BOARDMAN, J. *The Greeks Overseas.* London, 1964.

———. "Greek Archaeology on the Shores of the Black Sea," *Arch. Reports for 1962–63* (*JHS* supplement), pp. 34–51.

BOGAERT, R. "Le cours du statère de Cyzique," *L'Ant. class.* 32 (1963), pp. 85–119.

BOWRA, C. M. *Pindar.* Oxford, 1964. (See Ch. III, "Echoes of Politics," esp. pp. 99–158.)

BOYSAL, Y. "Ueber die alteren Funde von Sinope u. die Kolonisationsfrage," *Archäologischer Anzeiger* 1959 (1960), pp. 8–20, p. vii.

BRADEEN, D. W. "The popularity of the Athenian empire," *Historia* 9 (1960), pp. 257–69.

———. "Athenian Casualty Lists," *Hesperia* 33 (1964), pp. 16–62.

BREA, L. B. *Sicily before the Greeks*. London, 1957.

BREWSTER, F. "The Arrangement of Oars in the Trireme," *Harv.-Stud.Class.Phil.* 44 (1933), pp. 208–11.

BRUNT, P. A. "Thucydides and Alcibiades," *Revue de Etudes Grecques* 65 (1952), pp. 59–96.

———. "The Megarian Decree," *AJPh* 72 (1951), pp. 269–82. (See also under WENTKER, H.)

BULLOCK, C. J. *Politics, Finance and Consequences*. Harvard Univ. Press, 1939.

BURFORD, A. M. "Temple-building at Segesta," *Cl.Q.* 11 (1961), pp. 87–93.

BURN, A. R. *Persia and the Greeks*. London, 1962.

Cambridge Ancient History, The.

Vol. IV, *The Persian Empire and the West*. Rev. imp. Cambridge, 1960.

Vol. V, *Athens 478–401 B.C.* 5th imp. Cambridge, 1958.

Plates, Vol. II. Cambridge, 1960.

CAMON, F. "La demagogia di Iperbolo," *Giornale Italiano di Filologia* 15 (1962), pp. 364–74.

———. "Le cariche pubbliche di Iperbolo," ibid. 16 (1963), pp. 46–59.

———. "L'ostracismo di Iperbolo," ibid, pp. 142–62.

CARCOPINO, J. *L'ostracisme athénien*. 2d ed. Paris, 1935.

CARY, M. *The Documentary Sources of Greek History*. Oxford, 1927.

———. *The Geographic Background of Greek and Roman History*. Oxford, 1949.

———. "The sources of silver for the Greek world," *Mélanges G. Glotz* 1 (1932), pp. 133–42.

———. "On the Egyptian Expedition of 459–4 B.C.," *Cl.Q.* 7 (1913), pp. 198–201.

CARY, M. and WARMINGTON, E. *Ancient Explorers*. London, 1929.

CASSON, Stanley. *Macedonia Thrace and Illyria: Their relations to Greece from the earliest times down to the time of Philip son of Amyntas*. Oxford, 1926.

CAVAIGNAC, E. "Athènes et le seapower au Ve siècle," *Bulletin de l'Association G. Budé* (1962), pp. 194–7.

CAVALLARI, F. S. *Zur Topographie von Syrakus*. Göttingen, 1845.

CAVALLARI, F. S. and C., and HOLM, A. *Topografia archeologica di Siracusa*. Palermo, 1883; Appendice. Torino, 1891.

CHAMBERS, M. H. "Thucydides and Pericles," *Harv.Stud.Class.Phil.* 62 (1957), pp. 79–92.

CHAMOUX, F. *Cyrène sous la Monarchie des Battiades*. Paris, 1953.

CHRIST, K. "Historische Probleme der griechisch-sizilischen Numismatik," *Historia* 3 (1954–55), pp. 385–95.

CIACERI, E. *Storia della Magna Grecia*. 3 vols. Città di Castello, 1925–32.

CHROUST, A. H. *Socrates: Man and Myth*. London, 1957.

CICCIO, G.de *Gli aurei siracusani di Cimone e di Eveneto*. 2d rev. ed. Rome, 1957.

CIRAMI, G. *La monetazione greca della Sicilia antica*. Bologna, 1959.

COHEN, R. "Quelques mots sur Nicias," *Mélanges G. Glotz* I (1932), pp. 227–39.

COLOMBIN, G. "Le portrait de Nicias." Thèse de licence, Univ. de Liège, 1936–37. Cf. *Revue Belge de Philologie et d'Histoire* (1938), p. 577.

COLUMBA, G. M. "La prima spedizione ateniese in Sicilia (427–424 av. Cr.)," *Archivio Storica Siciliano* NS 10 (1887), pp. 65–94.

COMPERNOLLE, R. van. *Etude de chronologie et d'historiographie siciliotes: Recherches sur le système chronologique des sources de Thucycide concernant la fondation des colonies siciliotes* Etudes de Philologie, d'Archéologie et d'Histoire anciennes publiées par l'Institut historique belge de Rome, Vol. V. Brussels/Rome, 1959.

——. "L'hellénisation de la Sicile antique," *Rev.de l' Univ. de Bruxelles* 12 (1960–61), pp. 296–329.

——. "Ségeste et l'Hellénisme," *Phoibos* 5 (1950–51), pp. 183–228.

——. "La vitesse des voiliers grecs a l'époque classique (VIe et Ve siecles)," *Bull. de l'Inst. hist. belge de Rome* 30 (1957), pp. 5–30.

CONDURACHI, E. "Les statères de Cyzique et les routes commericales du Helléspont au Danube," *Eirene* I (1960), pp. 61–67.

CONGRESS. *Deuxième conférence internationale d'histoire économique, Aix-en-Provence 1962*. Vol. I., *Trade and Politics in the Ancient World*. Paris, 1965.

CONNER, W. R. "Charinus' Megarian Decree," *AJPh* 83 (1962), pp. 225–46.

COOK, A. B. "Triremes," *Cl.Rev.* 19 (1905), pp. 371–77.

COOK, J. M. *The Greeks in the East*. London, 1962.

CORNFORD, F. M. *Thucydides Mythistoricus*. London, 1907. Cf. J. P. Postgate, *Cl.Q.* 1 (1907), pp. 308–18.

CRISPO, C. F. *Contributo alla storia della più antica civiltà della Magna Grecia.* Tivoli, 1940.

CROISET, M. *Aristophanes and the Political Parties at Athens.* Tr. J. Loeb. London, 1909.

DAVIES, O. *Roman Mines in Europe.* Oxford, 1935.

DELEBECQUE, E. *Euripide et la Guerre du Péloponnèse.* Paris, 1951.

——. *Thucydide et Alcibiade.* Aix-en-Provence, 1965.

DICKINS, G. "The True Cause of the Peloponnesian War," *Cl.Q.* 5 (1911), pp. 238–48.

DODDS, E. R. *The Greeks and the Irrational.* Univ. California Press, 1951. (See Ch. VI, "Rationalism and Reaction in the Classical Age," pp. 179–206.)

DOVER, K. J. "Problems in Thucydides VI and VII," *Proceedings of the Cambridge Philological Society* 183 (1954–55), pp. 4–11.

DROYSEN, H. *Athen und der Westen.* Berlin, 1882.

DUNBABIN, T. J. *The Western Greeks.* Oxford, 1948.

EARP, A. J. "Athens and Miletus ca.450 B.C.," *Phoenix* 8 (1954), pp. 142–47.

EHRENBERG, V. *The People of Aristophanes: A Sociology of Old Attic Comedy.* 2d ed. Oxford, 1951.

——. *Society and Civilisation in Greece and Rome.* Martin Classical Lectures XVIII. Harvard Univ. Press, 1964.

——. "The Foundation of Thurii," *AJPh* 69 (1948), pp. 149–70.

——. "Polypragmosyne. A Study in Greek Politics," *JHS* 67 (1957), pp. 46–67.

——. "Pericles and his Colleagues," *AJPh* 66 (1945), pp. 113–34.

FABRICIUS, K. *Das antike Syrakus. Eine historisch-archäologische Untersuchung.* Klio Beiheft XXVIII. Leipzig, 1932. Cf. I. Richmond, *Cl.Rev.* 47 (1933), pp. 16–17.

FAZELLI, T. *De rebus Siculis decades II.* Panormi 1558–60. The best annotated edition is that printed in Catania, 3 vols., 1749–53.

FEHR, W. L. "Ships and sea fighting in the Peloponnesian War," *The Classical Bulletin* 41 (1965), pp. 81–85.

FERGUSON, W. S. *Greek Imperialism.* Boston, 1913.

——. *The Treasurers of Athena.* Cambridge, Mass., 1932. "Sparta and the Peloponnese" and "The Athenian Expedition to Sicily," *Cambridge Ancient History* 5 (1927), pp. 254–311.

FINLEY, M. I. "Athenian Demagogues," *Past and Present,* 21 (1962), pp. 3–24.

——. *A History of Sicily.* Vol. I: *Ancient Sicily.* London 1968.

——. "The Black Sea and Danubian regions and the slave trade in antiquity," *Klio* 40 (1962), pp. 51–59.

——, ed. *Slavery in Classical Antiquity. Views and Controversies.* Cambridge, 1960.

FORBES, R. J. *Metallurgy in Antiquity.* Leiden, 1950.

FORREST, W. G. "Aristophanes' Acharnians," *Phoenix* 17 (1963), pp. 1–12. "Note on the closing sections of Pseudo-Xenophon's *Constitution of the Athenians,*" *AJPh* 68 (1947), pp. 309–12.

FREEMAN, E. A. *The History of Sicily from the Earliest Times.* 4 vols. Oxford, 1891–94.

FREEMAN, K. *The Presocratic Philosophers. A Companion to Diels,* Fragmente der Vorsokratiker. Oxford, 1946.

FRENCH, A. *The Growth of the Athenian Economy.* London, 1964.

FRISCH, H. *The Constitution of the Athenians: a philological-historical analysis of Ps-Xenophon's treatise de re publica Atheniensium.* Classica et Mediaevalia, dissertationes II. Copenhagen, 1942.

FROST, F. J. "Pericles, Thucydides, son of Melesias, and Athenian Politics before the War," *Historia* 13 (1964), pp. 385–99.

——. "Pericles and Dracontides," *JHS* 34 (1964), pp. 69–72.

FUKS, A. "The Old Oligarch," *Scripta Hierosolymitana* I (1954), pp. 21–35.

GATHY, A. "La topographie de Syracuse en 413 av.j.c. d'après les livres VI et VII de Thucydide." Thèse de licence, Univ. de Louvain. Cf. *Revue Belge de Philologie et d'Histoire* 25 (1946–47), p. 369.

GERNET, L. "Approvisionnement d'Athènes en Blé au Ve et au IVe Siècle" (Univ. de Paris, Bibliothèque de la Faculté des Lettres: Mélanges d'Histoire ancienne XXV, pp. 271–391). Paris, 1909.

GIGANTE, M. *La costituzione degli Ateniesi: Studi sullo Pseudo-Senofonte.* Naples, 1953.

GILLIE, D. "Collusion at Mantinea," *Rendiconti dell'Istituto Lombardo.* 97 (1963), pp. 199–226.

GOMME, A. W. *A Historical Commentary on Thucydides.* 3 vols. Oxford, 1945–56.

——. *Essays in Greek History and Literature.* Oxford, 1937.

——. *More Essays in Greek History and Literature.* Oxford, 1962.

——. *The Population of Athens in the Vth and IVth Centuries* B.C. Oxford, 1933.

——. "The Old Oligarch," *Athenian Studies presented to W. Ferguson* (*Harv.Stud.Class.Phil.Suppl.*, Vol I., 1940), pp. 211–46.

——. "Notes on Thucydides Book VI," *Cl.Rev.* 34 (1920), pp. 81–85.

——. "Four passages in Thucydides," *JHS* 71 (1951), pp. 70–80.

GOOSSENS, R. "Autour de l'expédition de Sicile," *L'Ant. class.* 15 (1946), pp. 43–60.

GORBUNOVA, K. S. "Red-figure Kylikes from the excavations of the Olbian Temenos," *Olbia* (Moscow. Leningrad, 1964) p. 188.

GRAHAM, A. J. *Colony and Mother-City in Ancient Greece.* Manchester Univ. Press, 1964.

——. "The fifth-century cleruchy on Lemnos," *Historia* 12 (1963), pp. 127–28.

GRIFFO, P. and MATT, L. von. *Géla: destn d'une cité grecque de Sicile.* Geneva and Paris, 1964.

GROSSO, F. "Ermocrate di Siracusa," *Kokalos* 12 (1966), pp. 102–43.

GRUNDY, G. B. *Thucydides and the History of his Age.* 2d ed. 2 vols. Oxford, 1948.

GUEPIN, J. P. "Sophists and Coins," *Bulletin van de Vereeniging tot Bevordering der Kennis van de Antieke Beschaving* (Leiden) 35 (1960) 56–62.

GUIDO, M. *Syracuse: A Handbook to its History and Principal Monuments.* London, 1958.

HAMMOND, M. "Ancient imperialism: contemporary justifications," *Harv.Stud.Class.Phil.* 58–59 (1948), pp. 105–61.

HAMMOND, N. G. L. *A History of Greece to 322 B.C.* Oxford, 1959.

HASEBROEK, J. *Trade and Politics in Ancient Greece.* Trs. L. M. Fraser and D. C. Macgregor. London, 1933.

HATZFELD, J. *Alcibiade: Etude sur l'histoire d'Athènes à la fin du Ve siècle.* 2d ed. Paris, 1951.

HAUVETTE-BESNAULT, A. *Les Stratèges athéniens.* Paris, 1885.

HAVERFIELD, F. "Two notes on Syracuse," *Cl.Rev.* 3 (1889), pp. 110–12.

HEICHELHEIM, F. M. *An Ancient Economic History.* Vol. II: *The Classical Age of Polis Economy.* Tr. Joyce Stevens. Leiden, 1964.

HEITLAND, W. E. "Thucydides and the Sicilian Expedition," *Journal of Philology* 23 (1895), pp. 45–75.

——. "Topography of Syracuse," *Cl.Rev.* 8 (1894), pp. 123–24.

HENDERSON, B. W. *The Great War between Athens and Sparta.* London, 1927.

HIGGINS, R. A. *Greek and Roman Jewellery.* London, 1961.

HIGNETT, C. *A History of the Athenian Constitution to the End of the Fifth Century B.C.* Oxford, 1952.

HILL, G. F. *A History of Cyprus.* Vol. I. Cambridge, 1940.

——., and WALKER, J. *A Guide to the Principal Coins of the Greeks.* 2d ed. London, 1959.

HOCHHOLZER, H. "Zur Geographie des antiken Syrakus," *Klio* 29 (1936), pp. 164–72.

HOLM, A. *Geschichte Siciliens im Alterthum.* 3 vols. Leipzig, 1870–98.

——. "Zur Topographie des Rückzuges der Athener von Syrakus 413 v. Chr.," *Verhandlung der Versammlung Deutscher Philologen* (1882), p. 262.

HOW, W. W., and WELLS, J. A *Commentary on Herodotus*. Rev. ed., 2 vols. Oxford, 1928.

HUETTL, W. *Verfassungsgeschichte von Syrakus*. Prague, 1929.

HUXLEY, G. L. *Early Sparta*. London, 1962.

JARDÉ, A. *Les céréales dans l'Antiquité*. Paris, 1925.

JONES, A. H. M. *Athenian Democracy*. Oxford, 1957.

JONGKEES, J. H. *The Kimonian Dekadrachms: A Contribution to Sicilian Numismatics*. Utrecht, 1941.

KAGAN, D. "Argive Politics and Policy after the Peace of Nicias," *Cl.Phil.* 57 (1962), pp. 209–18.

KARYŠKOVŠKY, P. "Olbia and the Athenian Sea-League," *Archaeological Material from the North Coast of the Black Sea* 3 (Odessa, 1960), pp. 57–100 (in Russian).

KENT, R. G. *A History of Thessaly*. Pennsylvania, 1904.

KIENAST, D. "Der innenpolitische Kampf in Athen von der Rückkehr des Thucydides bis zu Perikles' Tod," *Gymnasium* 60 (1953), pp. 210–29.

KIRCHNER, J. *Prosopographia Attica*. 2 vols. Berlin, 1901–3.

KIRTLAND, L. "Nicias, his family, and the tradition of his great wealth," *Dissertation, Princeton* 1938. Cf. *Classical Weekly* 32 (1939), p. 220.

———. "Nicias' display of great wealth at Delos" (résumé), *TAPhA* (1938), p. xli.

KLEVE, K. "*Apragmosyne* and *Polypragmosyne*: two slogans in Athenian politics," *Symbolae Osloenses* 39 (1964), pp. 83–88.

KNOKE, F. "Zur Topographie von Syrakus," *Neue Jahrbücher für das klassische Altertum* 16 (1913), pp. 365–8.

KRAAY, C. M. "Hoards, Small Change and the Origins of Coinage," *JHS* 84 (1964), pp. 76–91.

LABARBE, J. *La loi navale de Thémistocle* (Bibliothèque de la Faculté de Philosophie et Lettres de l'Université de Liège, 143). Paris, 1957.

LABAREE, B. W. "How the Greeks sailed into the Black Sea," *AJA* 61 (1957), pp. 29–33.

LAISTNER, M. L. W. *A History of the Greek World, 479–323 B.C.* London, 1936.

LAMB, W. R. M. *Clio Enthroned*. Cambridge, 1914.

LANG, M. "The Revolution of the 400," *AJPh* 69 (1948), pp. 272–89.

LARSEN, J. A. O. "The *Acharnians* and the pay of Taxiarchs," *Cl.Phil.* 41 (1946), pp. 91–98.

LAUFFER, S. *Die Bergwerkssklaven von Laureion*. 2 vols. Mainz, 1956–57.

LEAKE, M. "Topographical and historical notes on Syracuse," *Transactions of the Royal Society of Literature* (Vol. 3, 2d series) (London, 1850), pp. 239–376. Also issued as a separate pamphlet, n.d.

LORETI, L. "La ceramica attica e i commerci greco-padani del sec. V a.c.," *Emilia preromana* 2 (1949), pp. 13–50.

LUPUS, B. *Die Stadt Syrakus im Alterthum.* (German trs. of CAVALLARI, F. S. and C., and HOLM, A., *Topografia archeologica di Siracusa*, q.v.) Strassburg, 1887.

MACDOWELL, D. "Aigina and the Delian League," *JHS* 80 (1960), pp. 118–21.

——. "Theagenes of Peiraieus," *Rheinisches Museum für Philologie* 114 (1961), pp. 229–36.

MCGREGOR, M. F. "The Genius of Alcibiades," *Phoenix* 19 (1965), pp. 27–46. See also under MERITT, B. D.

MCIVER, D R. *Greek Cities in Italy and Sicily.* Oxford, 1931.

MAGIE, D. *Roman Rule in Asia Minor.* 2 vols. Princeton, 1950.

MANNI PIRAINO, M. T. "Atene ed Alicie in IG i² 20," *Kokalos* 6 (1960), pp. 58–70.

MANSUELLI, G. *La politica estera di Siracusa, dalle origini a Dionisio II.* Ed. M. T. Galli R. Oppi. Bologna, 1958.

MASTROKOSTAS, E. Ἡ στήλη τῶν ἐν Σικελίᾳ πεσόντων, *Arch.Ephem.* 1955 (1961), pp. 180–202 (in modern Greek).

MATTINGLY, H. B. "The Growth of Athenian Imperialism," *Historia* 12 (1963), pp. 257–73.

——. "Athens and Euboea," *JHS* 81 (1961), pp. 124–32.

"The Athenian Coinage Decree," *Historia* 10 (1961), pp. 148–88.

"The Peace of Callias," *Historia* 14 (1965), pp. 273–81.

MAUCERI, L. *Il Castello Eurialo nella storia e nell'arte.* Syracuse, 1939.

MAY, J. M. F. *Ainos: its History and Coinage, 474–341 B.C.* Oxford, 1950.

MAZZARINO, S. "Per la cronologia della spedizione 'periclea' in Sicilia," *Archivio Storico per la Sicilia Orientale* 42–43 (NS 11–12) (1946–47), pp. 5–15.

——. "Tucidide e Filisto sulla prima spedizione ateniense in Sicilia," *Bollettino Storico Catanese* 4 (1939), pp. 5–72. (This is the same periodical as *Arch.stor.Sic.orient.*)

MÉAUTIS, G. *L'aristocratie athénienne.* Paris, 1927.

MEIGGS, R. "The crisis of Athenian imperialism," *Harv.Stud.Class.-Phil.* 67 (1963), pp. 1–36.

——. 'The Dating of Fifth-Century Attic Inscriptions', *JHS* 86 (1966) 86–98.

MERITT, B. D. *Athenian Financial Documents.* Univ. of Michigan Studies, 27. Univ. of Michigan Press, 1932.

———. *The Athenian Year.* Univ. of California Press, 1961.

———. "The departure of Alcibiades for Sicily," *AJA* 33 (1930), pp. 125–52.

———. "The Battle of the Assinarus," *Cl.Phil.* 27 (1932), pp. 336–42.

———. "The Athenian Alliances with Rhegion and Leontinoi," *Cl.Q.* 40 (1946), pp. 85–91.

———. "Athens and the Delian League," *The Greek Political Experience* (Princeton, 1948), pp. 93–108.

———. "Athens and Carthage," *Harv.Stud.Class.Phil.Suppl.*, Vol. I (1940), pp. 247–54.

———. "Greek inscriptions," *Hesperia* 26 (1957), pp. 198–270, pls. 50–63. See esp. pp. 199–200.

———. "The Alliance between Athens and Segesta," *Bulletin de Correspondance Hellénique* 88 (1964), pp. 413–15.

———., and WADE-GERY, H. T. "The dating of documents to the mid-fifth century," *JHS* 82 (1962), pp. 67–74; 83 (1963), pp. 100–17.

———., WADE-GERY, H. T., and MCGREGOR, M. F. *The Athenian Tribute Lists.* 4 vols. Vol. I, Cambridge, Mass.; Vols. II–IV, Princeton, N.J., 1939–53.

MICHELL, H. *The Economics of Ancient Greece.* 2d ed. Cambridge, 1957.

———. *Sparta.* Cambridge, 1952.

MILNE, J. G. "Trade between Greece and Egypt before Alexander the Great," *Journal of Egyptian Archaeology* 25 (1939), pp. 177–83.

———. "The early coinages of Sicily," *Numismatic Chronicle and Journal of the Numismatic Society* 5ˢ 18 (1938), pp. 36–52.

MINNS, E. H. *Scythians and Greeks.* Cambridge, 1913.

———. "Thirty Years of Work at Olbia," *JHS* 65 (1945), pp. 109–12.

MIRONE, S. "Monnaies historiques de la Sicile antique II," *Aréthuse* 3 (1927), pp. 101–25.

MOMIGLIANO, A. "Le cause della spedizione di Sicilia," *Riv.fil.-class.* 7 (1929), pp. 371–77.

———. "Il nuovo Filisto e Tucidide," *Riv.fil.class.* 8 (1930), p. 467–70.

———. "La spedizione ateniese in Egitto," *Aegyptus* 10 (1929), pp. 190–206.

MONGAIT, A. *Archaeology in the U.S.S.R.* Tr. David Skvirsky. Moscow, 1959.

MONTANARI, G. B. "I problemi sulla diffusione e sul commercio della ceramica attica nell'Italia settentrionale," *Cisalpina* 1 (1959), pp. 293–308.

MOORE, F. G. "The topography of Syracuse": Appendix to Vol. VI of the Loeb ed. of Livy (Bks. XXIII–XXV), pp. 505–10. London, 1958.

MORRISON, J. S. and WILLIAMS, R. T. *Greek Oared Ships, 900–322 B.C.* Cambridge, 1968.

MURRAY, H. A. "Two notes on the evaluation of Nicias in Thucydides," *Bulletin of the Institute of Classical Studies* 8 (1961), pp. 33–46.

MYRES, J. L. *Geographical History in Greek Lands.* Oxford, 1953.

NENCI, G. "Una ignorata revisione delle liste dei cittadini ateniese nel 424/23 A.C.," *Riv.fil.class.* NS 42 (1964), pp. 173–80.

NESSELHAUF, H. "Untersuchungen zur Geschichte der delisch-attischen Symmachie," *Klio* Beiheft 30 (N.S. 17) (Leipzig, 1933).

NICOSIA, G. *Aristofane ed il pensiero politico del V sec. A. C.* Rome, 1939.

NOE, S. P. *Bibliography of Greek Coin Hoards.* 2d ed. (Numismatic Notes and Monographs no. 78). New York, 1937.

———. *The Thurian Dix-Staters.* (Numism. Notes and Monogr. no. 71). New York, 1935.

———. "Hoard evidence and its importance," *Hesperia* Suppl. Vol. VIII (1949), pp. 235–42.

NOVIKOVA, T. F. 'Le développement économique de Syracuse au Ve siècle," *Memoires de l'Institut pédagogique, Série historique* 7 (1956), pp. 152–65 (in Russian). Résumé in *Bibl.Class.Orient.* 8 (1963), pp. 19–21.

ODERMANN, E. *Der Festungskrieg vor Syrakus in dem Jahren 414–13 v.Chr.* Leipzig, 1927.

OKAL, M. "Aristophane et l'année athénienne," *Eirene* 1 (1960), pp. 101–24.

OLDFATHER, W. A. "The alleged avarice of Sophocles," *AJPh* 47 (1926), pp. 358–60.

OLMSTEAD, A. T. *A History of the Persian Empire.* Chicago, 1948.

ORLANDINI, P. "L'espansione di Gela nella Sicilia centro-meridionale," *Kokalos* 8 (1962), pp. 69–121.

ORSI, P. "Scoperte di antichità nel territorio siracusano" (XVI, Avola; XIX, Nota), *Notizie degli Scavi di Antichita* (1891), pp. 345–48.

PACE, B. *Arte e Civiltà della Sicilia antica.* 4 vols. Milano, 1936–39. 1st vol. 2d ed., 1958.

PAIS, E. *Storia della Sicilia e della Magna Grecia.* Vol. I. Torino, 1894.

———. "La disfatta degli Ateniesi all'Assinaro," *Italia antica* (Bologna, 1922), Vol. I, pp. 217–26.

PARETI, L. *Sicilia antica.* Palermo, 1959.

——. *Contributi alla scienza dell'Antichità.* Vol. 1, Studi Siciliani e Italioti. Firenze, 1914.

PARKE, H. W. "A note on the topography of Syracuse," *JHS* 64 (1944), pp. 100–2.

PEREMANS, W. "Thucydide, Alcibiade et l'expédition de Sicile en 415 av. j.c.," *L'Ant. class.* 25 (1956), pp. 331–44.

PERROTTA, G. "Il papiro fiorentino di Filisto," *Studi italiani di filologia classica* (1930), pp. 311 ff.

PETRE, Z. "La théorie sophiste de l'égalité naturelle," *Studii Clasice* 5 (1963), pp. 69–91 (in Rumanian: French résumé).

PIGANIOL, A. "Deux notes sur l'expédition de Sicile," *Revue des Etudes grecques* 50 (1937), pp. 1–14.

PIPPIN, Anne. "The *Demioprata* of Pollux X," *Hesperia* 25 (1956), pp. 318–28.

POUILLOUX J. *Recherches sur l'histoire et les cultes de Thasos, de la fondation de la cité à 196 avant j.c.* Vol. I. Paris, 1954.

PRESTEL, G. *Die antidemokratische Strömung im Athen des 5. Jahrhunderts bis zum Tode des Perikles.* Breslau, 1939.

PRITCHETT, W. K. "The Attic Stelae," *Hesperia* 22 (1953), pp. 225–99 (cf. *Supplementum Epigraphicum Graecum XIII*, pp. 12–22); *Hesperia* 25 (1956), pp. 178–317.

——. "Five new fragments of the Attic Stelai," *Hesperia* 39 (1961), pp. 23–29.

PUSEY, N. M. "Alcibiades and τὸ φιλόπολι," *Harv.Stud.Class.Phil.* 51 (1940), pp. 215–31.

QUINN, T. J. "Thucydides and the unpopularity of the Athenian empire," *Historia* 13 (1964), pp. 257–66.

RANDALL. R. H. "The Erechtheum Workmen," *AJA* 57 (1953), pp. 199–210.

RAUBITSCHEK, A. E. "Athens and Halikyai," *TAPhA* 75 (1944), pp. 10–14.

"Theopompus on Hyperbolos," *Phoenix* 9 (1955), pp. 122–26.

"Theopompus on Thucydides son of Melesias," *Phoenix* 14 (1960), pp. 81–95.

RAVEN, E. J. P. "The Leucaspis type at Syracuse," *Congress internationale de numismatique* (Paris, 1953), Vol. II, pp. 77–78.

REHM, A. "Ueber die sizilischen Bücher des Thukydides," *Philologus* 89 (1934), pp. 133–60.

RICCIONI, G. "Problemi storici e archeologici di Adria preromana," *Cisalpina* 1 (1959), pp. 208–19.

ROBERT, L. "Le serment des Ephèbes athéniens," *Etudes Epigraphiques et Philologiques* (*Bibliothèque de l'Ecole des Hautes Etudes*, 272), Paris, 1938, pp. 296–307.

ROBINSON, E. S. G. "The Athenian Currency Decree and the Coinage of the Allies," *Hesperia* Suppl. Vol. VIII (1949), pp. 324–40.

———. "The El Mashkuta Hoard of Athenian Tetradrachms," *Numismatic Chronicle and Journal of the Numismatic Society* 7 (1947), pp. 115–21.

———. "Coins from the Excavation at Al-Mina, 1936," *Numismatic Chronicle and Journal of the Numismatic Society* 5⁸ 17 (1937), pp. 182–96.

ROEBUCK, C. *Ionian Trade and Colonization* (Monogr. on Archaeol. & Fine Arts, IX). New York, 1959.

———. "The Grain Trade between Greece and Egypt," *Cl.Phil.* 45 (1950), pp. 236–47.

ROHDE, H. *De Atheniensium imperio quid quinto quartove a.Chr. n. saeculo sit iudicatum. Dissertatio Inauguralis*, Göttingen, 1913.

ROMILLY, J. de. *Thucydides and Athenian Imperialism*. Tr. Philip Thody. Oxford, 1963.

ROOS, E. "Athens Vertragsverhältnis zu Egesta im 5. Jahrh. v. Chr.," *Opuscula Atheniensia* 4 (1962), pp. 9–29.

ROSTOVTZEFF, M. *Iranians and Greeks in South Russia*. Oxford, 1922.

STE CROIX, G. E. M. de. "The character of the Athenian Empire," *Historia* 3 (1954–55), pp. 1–49.

SALMON, P. "La politique égyptienne d'Athènes (VIe et Ve siècles avant J.C.), *Mémoires de l'Académie royale de Belge, Classe des Lettres*, Vol. 57, fasc. 6. Brussels, 1965.

SANCTIS, G. de *Storia dei Greci, dalle origini alla fine del secolo V.* 2 vols. Firenze, 1961.

———. *Ricerche sulla storiografia siceliota*. Firenze, 1958.

———. "I precedenti della grande spedizione ateniense in Sicilia," *Riv. fil.class.* 7 (1929), pp. 433–56; reprinted in *Problemi di Storia antica* (Bari, 1932), pp. 109–36.

SARTORI, F. *Le Eterie nella vita politica ateniese del VI e V secolo a.c.* Rome, 1957.

SCATURRO, I. *Storia di Sicilia*. Vol. I, *Dalle origine al 264 av. Cr.* Rome, 1950.

SCHECHTER, S. "Two notes on Diopeithes the Seer," *Cl.Phil.* 58 (1963), pp. 115–18.

SEAGER, R. "Alcibiades: the charge of aiming at Tyranny," *Historia* 16 (1967), pp. 6–18.

SÉCHAN, L. "Deux grandes figures athéniennes: Thucydide, Alcibiade," *Revue des Etudes grecques* 79 (1966), pp. 482–94.

SELTMAN, C. *Greek Coins*, 2d. ed. London, 1955.

SHEAR, T. L. "Koisyra: Three Women of Athens," *Phoenix* 17 (1963), pp. 99–112.

SIMONE, C. de. "Un caduceo di bronzo proveniente da Brindisi," *Archeologia Classica* 8 (1956), pp. 15–23, figs. 1–2, pls. vii–viii.

SMITH, Sidney. "The Greek Trade at Al-Mina," *The Antiquaries Journal* 22 (1942), pp. 87–112.

SMITH, S. B. "The economic motive in Thucydides," *Harv.Stud.-Class.Phil.* 51 (1940), pp. 267–301.

STERN, E. von. "Die griechische Kolonisation am Nordgestade des schwarzen Meeres im Lichte archaeologischer Forschung," *Klio* 9 (1909), pp. 139–52.

——. "Die politische und sociale Struktur der Griechencolonien am Nordufer des Schwarzmeergebietes," *Hermes* 50 (1915), pp. 161–224.

SUTHERLAND, C. H. V. "Corn and coin: a note on Greek commercial monopolies," *AJPh* 64 (1943), pp. 129–47.

TALBOT, J. F. "Aristophanes and Alcibiades," *The Classical Bulletin* 39 (1963), pp. 65–68.

TARN, W. W. "The Greek warship," *JHS* 25 (1905), pp. 137–56; 204–24.

TAYLOR, A. E. "On the date of the trial of Anaxagoras," *Cl.Q.* 11 (1917), pp. 81–84.

TREU, M. "Athen und Karthago und die thukydideische Darstellung," *Historia* 3 (1954–55), pp. 41–59.

TORR, C. *Ancient Ships.* Cambridge, 1895.

TÖTTÖSSY, Cs. "Lysistrate and the oligarchic coup d'Etat," *Acta Antiqua Academiae Scientiarum Hungaricae* (Budapest) 10 (1962), pp. 273–82.

TRENDALL, A. D. "Archaeology in S. Italy and Sicily, 1961–63," *Arch. Reports for 1963–64 (JHS)*, pp. 33–50.

TUSA, V. "Frammenti di ceramica con graffiti da Segesta," *Kokalos* 6 (1960), pp. 34–48.

——. "An archaic sanctuary at Segesta," *Illustrated London News* (Archaeological Section no. 2153), Oct. 19, 1963, pp. 632–35.

VALLET, G. *Rhégion et Zancle: Histoire, commerce et civilisation des cités chalcidiennes du détroit de Messine.* Paris, 1958.

——. "Athènes et l'Adriatique," *Mélanges d'Archéologie et d'Histoire* 62 (1950), pp. 33–52.

——., and VILLARD, F. *Megara Hyblaea.* Vol. 2 (text). Paris, 1964.

VAN BUREN, A. W. "News Letter from Rome," *AJA* 57 (1953), pp. 211–18, pl. 65, fig. 16.

VILLARD, F. *La Céramique grecque de Marseille (VIe–IVe siècle):* *Essai d'histoire économique.* Paris, 1960.
See also under VALLET, G.

WADE-GERY, H. T. "Thucydides the son of Melesias," *JHS* 52 (1932), pp. 205–27.

——. "The ratio of silver to gold during the Peloponnesian War; IG i² 301," *Numismatic Chronicle and Journal of the Numismatic Society* 5⁸ 10 (1930), pp. 16–38, 333.
See also under MERITT, B. D.

WALLACE, W. P. "The Egyptian Expedition," *TAPhA* 67 (1936), pp. 252–60.

——. "Thucydides," *Phoenix* 18 (1964), pp. 251–61.

WARMINGTON, E. H. *Greek Geography*. London, 1934.

WEBSTER, T. B. L. *Political Interpretations in Greek Literature*. Manchester Univ. Press, 1948.

WENTKER, H. *Sizilien und Athen. Die Begegnung der attischen Macht mit den Westgriechen*. Heidelberg, 1956. Cf. P. A. Brunt, *Cl.Rev.* 7 (1957), pp. 243–45; A. W. Gomme, *JHS* 78 (1958), pp. 156–58.

WEST, A. B. "Pericles' Political Heirs," *Cl.Phil.* 19 (1924), pp. 124–46, 201–28.

WESTLAKE, H. D. "Athenian aims in Sicily, 427–4 B.C. A study in Thucydidean motivation," *Historia* 9 (1960), pp. 385–402.

——. "Hermocrates the Syracusan," *Bulletin of the John Rylands Library, Manchester* 41 (1958–59), pp. 239–68.

——. "Thucydides' Narrative of the Sicilian Expedition" (résumé), *Proceedings of the Classical Association* 50 (1953), p. 27.

——. "Nicias in Thucydides," *Cl.Q.* 35 (1941), pp. 58–65.

——. "Thucydides 2.65.11," *Cl.Q.* 52 (NS 8) (1958), pp. 103–10.

——. "Thucydides and the Athenian disaster in Egypt," *Cl.Phil.* 45 (1950), pp. 209–16.

——. "Athenian food supplies from Euboea," *Cl.Rev.* 62 (1948), pp. 2–5.

——. "Alcibiades, Agis and Spartan Policy," *JHS* 58 (1938), pp. 31–40.

——. *Individuals in Thucydides*. Cambridge, 1968.

WHIBLEY, L. *Political Parties in Athens during the Peloponnesian War*. 2d ed. Cambridge, 1889.
Greek Oligarchies: Their Character and Organisation. Cambridge, 1913.

WHITMAN, C. H. *Aristophanes and the Comic Hero* (Martin Classical Lectures, Vol. XIX). Harvard Univ. Press, 1964.

WILL, E. "Archéologie et histoire économique," *Etudes d'archéologie classique* 1 (1955–56), pp. 147–66. Paris 1958.

WILLIAMS, B. H. G. "The Political Mission of Gorgias to Athens in 427 B.C.": *Cl.Q.* 25 (1931), pp. 52–56.

WILLIAMS, G. W. "The curse of the Alkmaionidai, III: Themistokles, Perikles and Alkibiades," *Hermathena* 89 (1952), pp. 58–71.

WINTER, F. E. "The chronology of the Euryalus Fortress at Syracuse," *AJA* 67 (1963), pp. 363–87.

WOODHEAD, A. G. *The Greeks in the West*. London, 1962.

——. *The Study of Greek Inscriptions*. Cambridge, 1959.

——. "Thucydides' portrait of Cleon," *Mnemosyne* 13 (1960), pp. 289–317.

——. "Peisander," *AJPh* 75 (1954), pp. 131–46.

——. "Greek Inscriptions," *Hesperia* 17 (1948), pp. 54–60.

——. "IG 1^2 95 and the ostracism of Hyperbolus," *Hesperia* 18 (1949), pp. 78–83.

WOOLLEY, L. *A Forgotten Kingdom*, 2d ed. London, 1959. "Excavations at Al-Mina, Sueidia. I–II," *JHS* 58 (1938), pp. 1–30, 133–70.

ZIEHEN, L. "Das spartanische Bevölkerungsproblem," *Hermes* 68 (1933), pp. 218–37.

ZIMMERN, A. *The Greek Commonwealth. Politics and Economic in Fifth-century Athens*. 5th ed. rev. and with preface by Russell Meiggs. Oxford, 1961.

——. "Thucydides the Imperialist," *Solon and Croesus* (Oxford, 1928), pp. 81–104.

ZUNTZ, G. *The Political Plays of Euripides*. Manchester Univ. Press, 1955.

ZURETTI, C. O. "La lettera di Nicia (Tucidide 7.11–15)," *Riv.fil.-class.* (1922), pp. 1–12.

GENERAL INDEX

Acarnania, 25, 41, 48, 51, 62, 66, 129, 252, 268, 273, 283 n.2

Achaea, 11–12, 90

Acrae, 322, 323

Acraean Heights, 322–24, 326 and n.

Acragas (Agrigento), 11–12, 21, 22, 29, 37, 40, 81–82, 95, 96, 143, 260, 268, 294, 301, 354, 360

Adeimantus, 122

Adonis, 2, 111, 112

Adriatic, 21, 37, 45, 49, 129

Aegean, 15, 30, 70, 90, 303

Aegina, 10, 30, 251, 319

Aegospotami, 353, 355

Aenus, 90 and n.7, 91

Aeolian Isles, 52, 53

Aetolia, 129, 202 n.4

Africa, North, 20, 92

Agariste, 122, 127

Agatharchus, 261, 301–2

Agis, King, 89, 167–68, 246–47, 270

Agyrium, 82, 154, 267, 327

Alcibiades, 3, 4, 13, 37, 80, 83, 84, 91, 97, 98, 99–101, 102, 105, 107–9, 110, 111–14, 116, 120, 122, 125, 126, 139, 140, 142, 143–45, 146–52, 153, 172, 181, 207, 210, 212 n.3, 232, 239, 243, 246, 352, 355; Argive Policy, 86–89, 91–92, 108; Background, 6–8; Death, 354; "Grand Design" and, 103–4, 169–70, 178; Mysteries and, 8,

116–18, 119–24, 126–27, 150; Spartan Defection, 127, 150–52, 167–72, 177–78, 181

Alcmaeonidae, 7, 72 n.2, 122, 152

Ambracia, 172, 252

Amisus, 19

Amorges, 181–82

Amphipolis, 67, 84–86, 90, 91, 232

Anapus River, 155, 157–61, 188, 199, 200, 204, 234, 257, 283, 321, 323, 326, 328

Anaxagoras, 13, 297

Andocides, 115, 120–24, 125, 126–27

Androcles, 102, 116–18, 119, 123, 124, 126–27, 150 n.2, 163

Apollo, 95, 164, 197

Arcadia, 87, 130, 209, 246

Archidamian (Ten Years') War, 4, 85

Archidamus, 120

Archonidas, 212

Arethusa, 343

Argos, Argives, 84, 86–90, 91–92, 102, 108, 117, 122, 130, 147, 149, 150, 151, 159, 161, 200, 231–32, 250, 151

Aristeides, 101

Ariston, 278, 312 and n.7

Aristophanes (Playwright), 5–6, 29, 45, 48, 50, 58, 60, 63, 80, 81, 86 n.5, 89, 113 n.9, 125, 180, 181, 202

Artas, 273–74

Artemis, 132

Asine, 210

Assinaria, 344 and n.8

Assinarus (Tellaro) River, xi, xiv, 46, 157 n.3, 330 n.14, 334 and n.2, 335–36, 337–39, 343 and n.7, 348, 353

Athen, 1, 343, 350

Athenagoras, 70, 134, 135–37, 138, 164, 194, 205–7, 214, 218–19, 255, 344, 354

Athens, Athenians, xiii, 1–10, 16–23, 25, 29, 42, 44, 47, 53, 54, 60–62, 65, 69, 74, 77, 79–81, 85–86, 88–90, 96, 102, 104, 106, 109, 110, 112, 115, 120, 129, 139, 144, 146, 147–49, 151, 155, 159, 163, 168, 171, 173, 175–76 and *passim*; Acropolis, 13, 353; Assembly, 1, 2, 4, 5, 7, 8, 10, 18, 42, 48, 49, 51, 56, 58, 59, 60, 89, 98, 100, 102, 103, 106–7, 109, 111–12, 115, 116, 118, 119, 122, 125, 131, 143, 162 n.8, 163, 178–79, 181, 182, 207, 233, 236, 239–40, 242, 249, 262, 291–92; Casualties, 161 n.7, 239, 289–90, 303, 314, 318, 319 n.3, 337, 340–42, 352; Cavalry, 109–10, 130, 177, 186–87, 189, 194, 201, 247, 299–300, 308 n.5, 319, 327 n.11, 337, 350; Council, 1, 2, 115, 118, 119, 120, 121, 126, 178; Demos, 57, 63; Economics, 14ff., 28–29, 41–45, 171; Finances, 18, 57, 97, 106, 232, 261–62; Foreign Policy, xii, 18, 24–25, 28; High Command, 1–10, 103–4, 110–11, 117, 125, 138–42, 179, 250; Hoplites, 9, 47, 55, 111, 130, 159, 160, 161, 188, 194, 197, 200–1, 218, 226, 237, 269–70, 272, 283, 299–301, 309, 319, 337, 340–42; Imperialism, xii, xiii, 8, 34–35, 42–46, 58, 127, 131; Long Walls, 1, 47, 85, 119, 268 n.2, 353, 355; Markets, 26–35, 41–45, 57–58, 84, 91; Morale, 47–48, 84, 173, 220, 225, 227 n.8, 235, 239, 260, 269–70, 282, 295; Ostracism, 99–101; Piraeus, 1, 2, 10, 25, 28, 32, 33, 37, 38, 45, 48, 58, 62, 85, 108, 116, 118, 129, 207, 247, 274, 308 n.6, 319, 347 n.11, 350; Plague, 4, 47–48, 51, 57, 106; Population, 18, 33–34, 106, 359; Resident Aliens (Metics), 1, 18, 78, 117, 119, 131, 308; Subject-Allies, 1, 9, 46, 57, 85–86, 113, 118, 130, 171, 279 n.1, 261–62; Tetradrachms, 16, 26, 90, 181, 329–30, 355 n.13; Tribute, 16, 57, 86, 171, 249 n.1, 261; Triremes, 1, 2, 3, 7, 9–10, 19, 59–60, 64, 111, 129, 130, 143, 169, 203, 212, 234, 238, 239, 249 n.1, 257–59, 271–72, 275–80, 314, 337; Western Policy, xii, xiii, 1, 8, 10, 29–35, 37–46, 48–51, 55, 58, 59–60, 65–66, 67, 74–75, 77, 83–84, 88, 92–93, 97–98, 99–100, 101–2, 103, 150, 178–79

Attica, 14ff., 47–48, 57, 64, 84, 108, 121, 149, 170, 209, 232, 244, 245–46, 247, 270, 290

Axiochus, 122

Barley (Gen.), 14, 16–18, 67

Black Sea Region, 19, 29, 30, 31, 41, 355

Boeotia, 14–16, 34, 35, 38, 58, 66, 77, 85, 86, 121, 245–46, 262, 288, 294–95
Brasidas, 66, 67, 74, 77–78, 84
Bricinniae, 79, 82
Byzantium, 20, 32

Cacyparis (Cassibile) River, 327, 328, 329–30, 331
Callias, Peace of, 34–35
Callicrates, 201
Callipolis, 273
Callistratus, 337
Camarina, 29, 37, 52, 68, 72 n.2, 80 n.2, 81, 82, 143, 145, 146, 160, 173–77, 260, 266, 294, 323 n.7, 360
Camicus, 11
Campania, 21, 32, 38, 42, 45, 53, 54, 58, 78, 88, 91
Capua, 32, 78, 88
Carthage, 23, 37, 41, 59–60, 68, 96, 99, 101, 106 n.6, 134, 138 n.6, 153, 169, 178, 179, 254, 354
Casmenae, 339
Cassibile, 328, 330
Castelluccio, Cava, 323, 324 and n.8, 325, 326, 329
Catana, 22, 23, 29, 38, 42, 46, 51–52, 55, 56, 81, 82, 109, 143, 145, 146, 147, 148, 153, 154–57, 159, 161, 172, 173, 177, 180, 186, 191, 215, 235, 238, 239, 240, 282, 293, 295, 298, 299, 306, 321 and n.4, 322 n.5, 323–24, 327, 330, 337, 343, 350, 360
Caulonia, 261, 275
Cenchreae, 33
Centuripae, 82, 154, 180, 213, 267, 327
Cephallenia, 129, 251

Chaeronea, 355
Chariades, 51, 52, 53
Charicles, 115, 116, 120, 126, 250 and n.2, 251, 273
Charmides, 121, 122
Chios, 130, 249, 251
Choerades, 273
Cimon, 34, 122, 130
Cleandridas, 207, 209
Clearidas, 86
Cleisthenes, 72 n.2
Cleon, 46, 48, 50, 57, 58, 59–60, 62, 63–67, 77–78, 80, 82, 83–84, 88, 98, 99, 116, 214
Cleonae, 231
Cleonymus, 116
Clubs, Political (Hetairiai), 6, 81, 100, 107, 119, 125
Cnossos, 11–12
Cocalus, 11
Coins, Coin-Hoards, 13, 16, 25, 26
Colonisation, 13, 28, 37, 106, 131, 181
Conon, 268 and n.2, 269–70, 271–72, 355
Copper, 16, 20, 21, 23, 28
Corcyra (Corfu), 21, 25, 30–31, 37, 42, 45, 51, 65, 129, 133, 251–52, 268, 272, 273; Civil War on, 49, 60, 62–64, 218–19, 241, 302
Corinth, Corinthians, 9, 29, 32, 33–35, 38, 40, 41, 42, 44, 45, 48–49, 58, 62, 69, 85, 86, 88, 92, 97, 115, 123, 129, 134, 165, 168, 171–72, 210, 212 n.3, 214, 225, 226, 228, 233, 235, 236, 238, 245–46, 251, 254, 261, 268, 271–72, 275, 278, 287, 288, 301, 308 n.6, 345; Gulf of, 32, 33, 34, 44, 48, 87, 90, 235, 245–46, 269

Cremisus River, 95
Crete, Cretan, 11–12, 130
Crimea, 19, 25, 32
Croton, 132, 274, 275
Cyllene, 149
Cyme (Cumae), 32, 39, 87–88
Cyprus, 20, 29
Cyrene, 20 and n.3, 347
Cythera, 58, 85, 250
Cythnos, 16
Cyzicus, 353

Daedalus, 11
Damon, 122
Dardanelles (Hellespont), 20, 30, 31
Dascon, 144, 155, 157, 302, 311
Decelea, 168, 170, 171 and n.2, 172, 232, 246–47
Deforestation, 13, 15
Delium, 67, 202 n.4, 285
Delos, 31, 92
Demeter, 22, 344 n.9
Demosthenes (General), 62–64, 129, 241, 243–44, 247, 249–50, 251–52, 254, 256, 262, 268, 269, 270, 272, 273, 274, 275–76, 280, 281–94, 295, 297, 298, 303, 305 n.4, 315, 319, 321, 323, 326–32, 333, 338, 345–46
Demosthenes (Orator), 347, 355
Demostratus, 111–12
Diagoras, 181
Dieitrephes, 262
Diocleides, 120–21, 126, 176 n.5
Diocles, 70, 134, 164, 205–6, 207, 303, 344, 354
Diodorus Siculus, xii, 12, 45, 89, 95, 96, 106 n.6, 132, 161 n.7, 163, 183, 184, 185, 229 n.10, 267 n.1, 283, 306, 311, 315

n.1, 321 and n.4, 323, 337, 344, 345 n.10
Diognetus, 116, 119
Diomilus, 188 n.10, 189
Dionysius I, 185, 354
Diotimus, 42
Diphilus, 271
Dorians, 38, 40, 66, 67, 69, 97, 130, 175, 227
Dover, K. J., xiv, 96 n.2, 130 n.1, 227 n.3, 308 n.6, 322 n.6
Ducetius, 39, 154

Eccritus, 245
Economics, Ancient, 13, 24–25, 26–35, 254. See also s.v. Athens and Syracuse
Egypt, Egyptians, 12, 13, 18, 20, 29, 33–34, 35, 38, 46, 48, 130, 249
Elba, 21, 39
Eleusis, 16, 149
Elis, 85, 87, 108, 149, 246, 251
Empedocles, 38, 95
Enna, 82, 213, 267, 327
Ephesus, 181, 347 n.11
Ephorus (Historian), 229 n.10
Epicerdes, 347
Epidamnus, 20, 21, 25, 45
Epidaurus, 88
Epidaurus Limera, 231, 244 n.5, 250, 251
Epirus, 129
Erasinides, 228
Erineus (Fiume di Noto) River, 157 n.3, 329–30 and n.14, 331, 334, 335 n.4, 343 n.7
Erosion, Soil, 13, 15
Eryx, 96
Eryximachus, 120
Etna, Mt., 21, 61, 77, 101, 180

Etruria, Etruscans, 20, 21, 39, 41, 59, 178, 204, 302, 305 n.4
Euboea, 17, 67, 170, 246–47
Eucles, 207
Eucrates, 120
Euphemus, 120, 125, 175–76 and n.5
Euphiletus, 121, 125
Eupolis (Playwright), 81 and n.3, 352 n.12
Euripides (Playwright), 66, 77, 84, 101, 244–45, 348, 350, 353
Eurotas River, 167
Eurybiades, 31
Eurymedon, 49, 60, 62, 63–64, 65, 66, 68, 73–74, 82, 130, 241–42, 249, 252, 254, 256, 268, 272, 274, 281, 282, 287, 291 n.6, 292, 293, 301–2, 305 n.-4
Euthydemus, 241–42, 270, 272, 276, 281 n.1, 286, and n.5, 301

Famine, Food-Shortage, 18 n.2, 34, 38, 44, 77, 89–90, 207, 355 n.14
Fifth-Column, Espionage, Propaganda, 1, 5, 9, 54, 61, 70, 135–38, 141, 142–43, 151, 156, 163–64, 194, 205, 206 n.5, 237, 255, 270, 291–92, 303, 317 n.2
Fish, Salt or Pickled, 19, 28, 50, 57
Floridia, 321, 322, 328
Four Hundred, Revolution of, 250 n.2, 353
Freeman, E. A., xi, xii, 52 n.1, 67, 83, 130, 158 n.4, 159, 185 n.8, 188 n.11, 227 n.8, 233 n.1, 300 n.2, 322 n.5, 345 n.10

Gela, 22, 29, 37, 40, 52, 68, 82, 143, 160, 174, 212, 260, 266, 294, 323 n.7, 330, 360; Congress and Treaty of, 65, 68–74, 77, 79, 80 n.2, 81, 83, 95, 134, 174, 241, 291 n.6
Gelon, 31, 39, 41, 59, 141, 158, 174, 331 n.15
Gold, 13, 19, 20, 28, 30, 232
Gongylus, 213–14, 216, 219, 222, 226
Gorgias, 50–51
Grain (Gen.), 15, 16–18, 21, 24, 28, 30, 35, 46, 57, 77, 192, 204, 355, 359–60
Great King (of Persia), 20, 23, 29, 30, 34, 35, 152, 181, 255, 355
Gylippus, 168, 172, 197 n.3, 207, 209–13, 216–29, 233–36, 241, 243, 245–46, 252–61, 266–68, 272, 276, 277, 280, 282–83, 285, 287–88, 289, 292, 294, 295, 298, 299, 300, 301–2, 310, 314, 316, 325, 326, 327 n.11, 330, 332, 333, 336, 337, 344, 345, 353–54 and n.13

Halyciae, 267
Hegesander, 245–46, 261, 288
Helorus, 155, 158, 159, 160, 161, 200, 257, 270, 328, 334 n.2, 339
Heraclea, 132
Heracleides, 207
Heracles, 95, 307, 316
Hermes, Herms, 2–3, 115, 116, 117, 119, 120, 121, 122, 123–27, 180–81, 243, 250 n.2
Hermippus (Playwright), 89

Hermocrates, 69, 70–74, 77, 101, 133, 134–35, 136, 138 n.6, 158 n.5, 163–64, 174–76, 187, 188, 193–94, 198, 199, 200, 203, 205–7, 217–18, 219, 220 n.6, 233, 252–53, 256, 286, 292, 310, 316, 317, 344, 345 n.10, 355

Herodotus (Historian), xiii, 20, 38

Hieron I, 39, 41, 331 n.15

Himera, 21, 61, 82, 143, 153, 211, 212, 213, 219, 236, 266, 267, 354

Hippocrates (Sic.), 174, 202 n.4

Hippodamus (Architect), 38

Hipponium, 81

Hybla (Paternó), 154, 180

Hyccara, 105–6, 153–54, 239

Hyperbolus, 8, 59–60, 88, 97, 98, 99–101, 102, 116

Hypsas River, 267

Hyria, 12

Hysiae, 98

Iapygia, 11, 134 n.5, 273

Illyria, 15, 20

Inessa, 55, 180

Ionia, Ionians, 25, 29, 38, 67, 227

Iron, 16, 19, 21, 23, 28, 231, 244, 250

Italy, 99, 129, 132, 133, 134, 210, 211, 213, 252, 268, 275

Koré (Persephone), 344 n.9

Laches, 51–56, 58, 60, 61–62, 67, 82, 140, 174, 202 n.4

Laconia, 16, 48, 62, 245, 250

Lais, 154

Lamachus, 3, 7, 103, 105, 107, 110, 111, 116, 119, 139, 141, 142, 143, 144, 147, 148, 153, 155–57, 159 n.6, 162, 172, 173, 180, 188, 191, 199, 200, 203, 204, 240; Background, 5–6; Death, 201–2; Poverty, 5–6, 9, 142

Latium, 21

Laurium (Mines), 4, 16, 18, 57, 153, 171, 181, 232

Leake, M., xi, 323, 330 n.14, 334 n.2

Leogoras, 120

Leontini, 22, 23, 29, 38, 39, 40, 42, 46, 47, 51, 52, 53, 54, 55, 56, 60, 70, 73, 79–80, 82, 83, 96, 97, 103, 109, 132, 134, 143, 144, 155, 157, 175, 179, 180, 317, 325, 327, 330, 360

Leucas, 172, 210, 213

Leucon, 18

Libya, 37, 48, 58, 99, 112, 294

Lipara, 52, 53

Locri, 53, 54, 61, 74, 81, 82, 132, 211, 225, 261, 275, 288

Lycia, 20

Lydus, 122

Lysander, 355 n.13

Macedonia, Macedonians, 19, 32, 34, 41, 77–78, 91, 102, 355 and n.14

Magna Graecia (Southern Italy), 15, 20, 30, 33, 37, 39, 45, 49, 50, 67, 82, 86, 147, 165, 169–70, 204, 210, 239, 246, 254, 261, 273

Magnesia, 152

Malea, C., 87, 250

Mantinea, Mantineans, 87, 89, 108, 117, 130, 147, 151, 202 n.4

Mantitheus, 120

Marathon, 9, 130, 188

Mediterranean, 20, 23, 30, 40, 59, 132, 169, 257

Medma, 81

Megara, 32, 33, 41, 42, 51, 66, 74, 85, 119, 129, 130; Megarian Decrees, 43–45

Megara Hyblaea, 141, 142, 165, 180, 187, 216, 261

Meletus, 119

Melos, 92, 98, 101, 181, 262, 377

Menander (General), 241–42, 270, 272, 276, 281 n.1, 287, 301

Messapia, 273

Messenia, 14, 15, 45, 48, 63–64, 92, 129, 210, 231, 251

Messina (Zancle), 21, 22, 38, 39, 54, 55, 60, 61, 64, 65, 82, 88, 140–41, 142–43, 148, 149, 172–73, 275; Straits of, 38, 39, 42, 47, 52, 53, 55, 58, 64, 65, 67, 143, 239, 275

Metapontum, 132, 274

Methone, 102

Methymna, 249 n.1

Meton, 113 and n.9

Miletus, 38

Minos, Minoan, 11–12

Monte Climiti, xiv, 323, 326, 328, 330

Morgantia, 72 n.2

Mycalessus, 262–63

Mycenae, Mycenaean, 11–12

Mylae, 54

Mysteries, 8, 116–17, 119–20, 122, 123–27, 149 n.1, 180–81

Mytilene, 48, 51, 98

Naples (Neapolis), 39, 42, 88

Naupactus, 34, 58, 129, 245, 246, 251, 268, 269–70, 271–72

Naxos (Sicily), 46, 82, 109, 143, 162 n.8, 173, 177, 180, 186, 239

Nebrodes Mountains, 21, 55

Nicias, 3, 4, 5, 8, 9–10, 13, 78, 83, 84, 85, 87, 88, 90, 92, 98, 99–101, 102, 105, 106, 107, 108, 109–11, 116, 119, 120, 125–26, 131, 138, 139, 140, 141, 142, 145 n.9, 148, 152–63, 169, 171, 172, 173, 176 n.5, 177–78, 179, 182, 186–90, 191, 193, 194, 197–98, 202–5, 207, 211, 212, 214–25, 227–29, 243, 251, 254, 256, 257, 260, 266–68, 270, 273, 275–76, 277–78, 280, 281–82, 283, 284, 289–94, 295, 297–98, 302, 305, 307–8, 309–10, 315, 317, 319–20, 321, 323–24, 325–38, 339, 343 n.7, 344, 347; Background, 4–5; Bribery, Alleged, by, 90, 116, 125; Death, 345–47; Dilatoriness, 4–5, 161–63, 180, 204, 293; Dispatch by, 233, 236–43, 245, 249; Nephritis, 4, 119, 192, 199, 220, 239, 282; Peace of, 84–86, 98, 150, 245; Piety and Superstition, 4, 112, 125–26, 158, 159 n.6, 171–72, 297–99; *Proxenos* of Syracuse, 4–5, 109; Slave-Owner, 4–5, 153–54

Nicon, 245

Nicostratus, 202 n.4

Nisaea, 32–33, 35, 41, 51, 66, 85, 87

Nola, 32

Oeniadae, 66, 74

Olbia, 32

Olives, Olive-Oil, 17, 21, 26

Olympic Games, 7, 92, 108, 149

Omens and Prophecies, 2, 111–14, 125, 145 n.9, 297–98

Onugnathos, 250, 251

Orontes River, 13
Oropus, 170, 246–47
Otranto, Straits of, 21, 31, 133, 134 n.5, 210, 213, 246, 273

Paeonia, 19
Pais, E., xi, 330 n.14, 334 n.2
Pangaeus, Mt., 19, 57, 67, 232
Panhellenism, 38, 40, 41, 69, 209
Panormus (Palermo), 153
Panticapaeum (Kertsch), 32
Paralus, 176
Parnes, Mt., 246
Patrae (Patras), 88, 90, 91
Pegae, 32, 33, 35, 41, 44, 51, 85
Peisander, 115, 116, 120, 126
Peisistratus, 13
Peloponnese, 32, 42, 44, 45, 48, 51, 58, 62, 65, 85, 87, 88, 89, 90, 99, 129, 149, 169, 245, 246–47, 250, 261, 294
Peloponnesian League, 24, 34, 35, 40, 41, 44, 45–46, 57, 62, 63, 67, 69, 85, 86, 88, 92, 97, 108, 137, 165, 181, 209, 232, 245–46, 269
Peloponnesian War (Gen.), 19, 21, 24, 25, 44, 45–46, 47–49, 66–67, 171 n.2, 202 n.4, 251, 262, 268 n.2, 269, 281 n.1, 290, 337
Pelorus, C., 172
Perdiccas II, 78, 89–90, 102, 232
Pericles, xii, xiii, 4, 7, 10, 13, 19, 32, 33–34, 35, 37, 38, 39, 40, 41, 42, 44, 47, 48, 49, 50, 58, 69, 122, 124, 173 n.3, 176, 209, 232, 353, 355, 356
Persia, Persians, 14, 20, 29, 30, 31, 34, 35, 38, 84, 130, 181–82, 232, 252, 255 n.3, 334, 354, 355; Persian Wars, 14,

16, 17, 19, 29, 37, 77, 95, 151
Petra, 275
Phaeax, 80–83, 96, 99–101
Phaedrus, 119, 120
Pheia, 246, 251
Pherecles, 122
Philip II, 355
Philistus (Historian), 12, 220, 229 n.10, 311, 321
Philochorus, 298 and n.1
Phoenicia, 20, 24, 29
Phormio, 235, 269
Pindar, 20, 353
Piracy, Pirates, 30–31, 39, 53, 54
Pissuthnes, 181
Pitch, 21
Plataea, 31, 98
Plato (Philosopher), 7, 15, 119, 120
Pleistoanax, King, 84, 85, 209
Plutarch of Chaeronea, xii, 6, 9, 26, 37, 45, 81, 91, 92, 99, 100, 104, 115, 117, 123, 142, 147, 152, 153, 155, 159 n.6, 167–68, 201, 204, 205, 216, 242, 282, 287, 297, 300 n.2, 316, 317 n.2, 320, 338, 345 and n.10, 348
Polyaenus (Military Writer), 158–59, 205–6, 219–20
Polybius (Historian), 69
Polystratus, 119, 350
Polyzelus, 331 and n.15
Pontus, 19
Portugal, 23
Potidaea, 48
Pottery, Sherding, 13, 26–32, 88, 174, 357–58
Po Valley, 13, 20, 21, 30, 45, 49
Protagoras, 13
Pulytion, 117

Pylos, 63–64, 65, 67, 74, 92, 129, 169, 231, 241, 250, 284, 332

Pythen, 210, 211–12, 219, 301

Pythodorus, 60–62, 64, 74

Pythonicus, 116–17, 119, 122, 126

Rhegium (Reggio), 38, 39, 40, 42, 46, 51, 52, 53, 61, 65, 82, 132–33, 138–39, 140, 141, 142–43, 145, 147, 148, 173, 212, 225, 275, 330

Rhium, 88, 90

Rhodes, 29, 130

Rome, 20, 185

Romilly, J. de, 25, 28

Russia, South, 13, 19, 20, 30, 31–32, 33, 34, 35, 355

Salamis, 9, 15, 31, 33, 44, 156, 309, 310, 350

Samnites, 42, 78, 79, 88

Samos, 124

Sardis, 181

Saronic Gulf, 10, 32, 33, 87, 319

Scione, 78

Scylletium, 275

Scythia, Scythians, 30, 33

Segesta, x, 1, 52, 53, 82, 92–93, 94–95, 97–98, 99, 102, 103–4, 105, 106, 108, 109, 110, 129, 134, 139, 140, 143, 153–54, 175, 177, 179, 186, 189

Selinus (Selinunte), 1, 22, 37, 52, 53, 82, 94–95, 103–4, 105, 109, 118, 139, 140, 143, 153–54, 160, 179, 212, 260, 266, 267, 294, 343, 354, 360

Sicanus, 294, 301

Sicels, 39, 55, 82, 108, 134, 138, 140, 154, 177–78, 180, 186, 189, 204, 211, 212, 236, 267–68, 294, 306, 320, 321 n.4, 322, 324, 327, 339

Sicilian Expedition (427–424), 42, 51–55, 60–62, 64–66, 67–75, 202 n.4

Sicilian Expedition (415–413), xi, 1–10, 12, 46, 102 and passim; Alcibiades' Analysis of, 169–70; Fleet's Role in, 3–4, 9–10, 110–12, 129–32, 191, 234–35, 238, 239, 257–59, 265–66, 269, 271, 279–80, 301–3, 305–14; Logistics of, 9–10, 111–12, 129–32, 134; Radicals and, 124; Speculators and Merchants on, 2, 124, 131–32, 137

Sicily (Gen.), 1, 2, 5, 8, 11–12, 20, 24, 25, 29, 30, 37, 39, 46, 49, 50, 51, 52, 55, 59, 61, 62, 64, 66, 67, 74, 81, 83, 86, 94–95, 96, 101, 103, 105, 108, 109–11, 112, 131, 140, 147, 152, 165, 169, 181 and passim; Cattle and Dairy Produce, 21–22, 37, 77; Fish, 22; Greeks of, 67–74, 77, 80, 83, 108, 109, 132; Slave-dealers, 5; Timber, 21, 37; Wheat, 22–23, 33–35, 37, 45

Sicyon, 90, 245–46

Siege-Warfare, 5, 44, 136, 163, 170, 177–78, 186 and passim

Silver, 16, 19, 20, 23, 26, 28, 171, 232, 254, 255

Sinope, 19

Siris, 31

Slaves, Slavery, 1, 5, 17, 18, 57, 84, 105–6, 117, 121–22, 131, 153–54, 171, 205–6, 239, 308, 347

Socrates, 7, 18, 113, 120

Solon, 13, 14, 17, 46

Solous, 153

Sophocles (Playwright), 273, 348, 352, 353

Sophocles (General), 60, 62, 63–64, 65, 66, 74, 130

Sosistratus, 205–6

Spain, 20, 23, 41, 169, 179

Spampinato (Calatrelli), Cava, 322, 326 n.10

Sparta, Spartans, 4, 16, 24, 25, 31, 34, 35, 38, 39, 40, 41, 45, 47, 48, 57, 63–64, 66, 67, 78, 83, 84, 85–86, 87, 88, 89–90, 91, 97, 98, 102, 106, 108, 121, 124, 134, 150, 151–52, 165, 167–72, 178, 207, 209, 211, 214, 217, 219, 231–32, 241, 244, 245–46, 247, 250, 254, 255 n.3, 268 n.2, 270, 281, 309; Ephors, 167, 168, 171, 210, 256, 355 n.13; Helots, 45, 209 n.2, 245, 250, 294–95

Sphacteria, 85, 217, 241

Stilbides, 293–94, 297

Strabo (Geographer), 21

Stromboli, 52

Strymon (Struma) River, 19, 32, 67, 232

Sunium, C., 247

Sybaris, 31, 38, 101, 274 (River)

Syracuse, 1, 4, 5, 9, 22–23, 29, 31, 34, 42, 47, 52, 53, 54, 59, 61, 65, 66, 68, 71, 79, 82, 96, 99 n.4, 101, 106, 108, 109, 112, 115, 118, 123, 130, 132, 133, 134, 135, 138, 140, 141, 142, 143, 144, 145–46, 153, 154, 155–57, 161, 162, 165, 168, 171, 172, 173, 175–76, 177–78, and *passim* thereafter; Achradina, 162, 182–86, 192, 195, 200, 276, 300, 306; Agrarian Reform, 70, 79, 137; Bufalaro, 221, 229, 233, 286, 287; Casualties, 161 n.7, 314; Cavalry, 22, 109, 110, 130, 135, 138, 154, 155, 158, 159, 160, 161, 163, 189, 192, 193–94, 201, 224, 226, 227, 260, 270, 276, 281, 289, 300, 303, 317–18, 321, 324, 326–27, 331, 333–34, 335–36; Epipolae, xi, 165, 183, 184, 185, 187–88, 189, 190, 191, 192, 193, 195, 197 n.3, 199, 202, 204, 206, 211, 214, 215, 216–18, 221, 222–23, 225, 226, 229, 233, 237, 242, 243, 257, 270, 282–90, 292, 295, 299, 304 n.3, 307, 323, 340; Euryalus, 183, 185, 188, 189, 191, 192, 197, 216, 221, 222–23, 233–34, 283, 285–86, 288, 289, 337; Finances, 254–55, 266, 270, 291, 332; Fleet, 191, 222, 234–35, 236, 252–60, 265–66, 270, 271–72, 276–80, 301–3, 305–14; Gamoroi, 69, 70, 71, 137, 138, 205, 218, 219; Government, 70, 79, 133, 137–38, 163–65; Grain Shortage, 23, 46–47, 360; Great Harbour, xi, 144, 155, 157, 185, 192, 193, 195, 196, 198, 199, 203, 204, 214, 217, 222, 224, 225, 228, 229, 233–34, 253, 256, 257–58, 259 n.4, 265, 267, 268, 275, 280, 281, 285, 292–93, 295, 297, 300, 304, 306, 309, 311, 314, 315, 318, 325, 338; Hoplites, 200, 201, 206, 229, 259, 276, 303; I Cappucini, 183, 195–96; Imperial Ambitions, 39–40, 42, 44, 46, 55–56, 67, 71, 73, 79–80, 97, 135; Labdalum, 189, 191, 215–16, 221, 223, 227 n.8, 229,

233–34, 277, 286, 287, 289; Leon, 188 and n.11, 189, 192, 216; Little Harbour, 144, 183, 206, 213–15, 222, 228, 234, 253, 258; Lysimeleia (Marsh), 160, 199, 201, 258, 259, 300, 301; Morale, 193–94, 206, 217–18; Olympieum, 155, 158, 159, 161, 165, 187, 200, 201, 226, 270, 276, 283, 307; Ortygia, 162, 182, 183, 185, 203, 228, 253, 257–58, 279, 304, 306, 311, 313; Panagia, Cava S., 183, 195, 196, 215, 233; Plemmyrium, 224–25, 226, 228, 234, 239, 253, 256, 257–58, 259, 260, 261, 266, 268, 270, 275, 280, 299, 304, 306, 311, 318, 339; Polichna, 226, 270, 281, 299–300; Portella del Fusco, 183, 192, 196, 197, 199, 283, 289, 305, 307; Quarries (Latomie), 347–48 and n.11; Radical Party, 70, 135–38, 164, 194, 206, 214, 218–20, 354 (*see also* s.v. Athenagoras and Diocles); Round Fort, 191–92, 194, 196, 198–99, 202–3, 215, 217–18, 222–23, 226 n.7, 229, 237, 283, 286, 287, 288, 289, 305, 307; Salita Ombra, 183, 193, 202, 222, 233, 286, 287, 288; Scala Greca, 183, 184, 185, 189, 195, 215, 218, 222, 233, 288; Siege of, 163, 170, 177–78, 186 and *passim* thereafter; Temenites, 164–65, 192, 196, 206, 218, 307; Topography, xi, 182–86, 194–97, 322–24; Trogilus, 194–96, 197, 199,

203, 204, 205, 215, 217, 221, 222–23, 226, 227, 229; Tyche, 183, 195 n.2, 215, 235, 347

Taenarum, 245
Tanagra, 66, 130
Tarentum (Taranto), 29, 31, 132, 138 n.6, 209, 210, 211, 273, 274; Gulf of, 38
Telecleides, 116, 125
Tell-el-Amarna, 12
Terias River, 143, 180
Teucrus, 119–20, 121, 122, 124, 126
Thapsus, 188, 189, 191, 192, 193, 199, 203, 215, 221, 234, 293
Thasos, 19
Theano, 149
Thebes, Thebans, 66, 245, 262
Themistocles, 30–31, 71 n.1, 87, 150, 152, 156
Theodorus, 119
Thespiae, Thespians, 245–46, 261, 288
Thessalus, 122
Thessaly, Thessalians, 14, 15, 35, 58, 67, 78
Thirty Tyrants, 80, 120, 250 n.2, 353–54
Thrace, Thracians, 19, 29, 30, 32, 34, 35, 41, 46, 48, 67, 74, 77–78, 82, 84, 89, 91, 106, 181, 262
Thucydides (Historian), xii, xiii, xiv, 13, 15, 24, 25, 26, 33, 37, 45, 49, 51, 52, 53, 62, 63–64, 65, 69, 70, 74, 79, 85, 86, 90, 91, 92, 96, 102, 105, 110, 117, 123, 127, 129, 132, 133, 134, 135, 139, 144, 156, 157, 158 n.4, 159 n.6, 160, 161 n.7, 162 n.8, 169, 174, 176, 178, 184, 185, 187,

191, 192, 194, 195 and n.1, 201, 210, 216, 220, 222, 227, 229 n.10, 236, 237, 243, 244, 250, 260, 262–63, 267 n.1, 274, 277, 285 n.4, 286 n.5, 287, 291, 298, 299, 303, 307, 309, 311, 313, 315, 317 n.2, 319 n.3, 323 and n.7, 324, 325, 328, 329 n.13, 330, 332, 337, 344, 345–46, 354

Thurii, 38, 39, 40, 41, 42, 53, 122, 132, 148, 149, 209–10, 211, 274

Timaea, 167, 168

Timaeus (Historian), 220, 345 n.-10

Timber, 15, 18–19, 20, 21, 24, 26, 28, 46, 57, 89, 261

Tiryns, 11

Tyrrhenian Sea, 39, 54, 81

Via Egnatia, 20–21, 45

Westlake, H. D., xiv, 68 72

Wheat, 14–15, 16, 18, 19–20, 21, 22–23, 25, 28, 38, 42, 50, 58, 67, 78, 87 n.6, 95, 102, 110, 140, 162, 177, 180, 204, 273, 355

Wine, 21, 26

Xanthippus, 101

Xenon, 245

Xenophon, 18

Xerxes, 15, 31, 71 n.1, 156

Zacynthus (Zante), 129, 251

Zea (Pacha Limani) Harbour, 3, 249

Zeno, 60

Zeus, 22, 112 (Ammon), 144, 155 (Olympian)